Mastering Unity Game Development with C#

Harness the full potential of Unity 2022 game development using C#

Mohamed Essam

Mastering Unity Game Development with C#

Copyright © 2024 Packt Publishing

All rights reserved. No part of this book may be reproduced, stored in a retrieval system, or transmitted in any form or by any means, without the prior written permission of the publisher, except in the case of brief quotations embedded in critical articles or reviews.

Every effort has been made in the preparation of this book to ensure the accuracy of the information presented. However, the information contained in this book is sold without warranty, either express or implied. Neither the author, nor Packt Publishing or its dealers and distributors, will be held liable for any damages caused or alleged to have been caused directly or indirectly by this book.

Packt Publishing has endeavored to provide trademark information about all of the companies and products mentioned in this book by the appropriate use of capitals. However, Packt Publishing cannot guarantee the accuracy of this information.

Group Product Manager: Rohit Rajkumar

Publishing Product Manager: Urvi Shah

Book Project Manager: Arul Viveaun S

Senior Editor: Rakhi Patel

Technical Editor: K Bimala Singha

Copy Editor: Safis Editing

Indexer: Hemangini Bari

Production Designer: Joshua Misquitta

DevRel Marketing Coordinators: Anamika Singh and Nivedita Pandey

First published: July 2024

Production reference: 1070624

Published by Packt Publishing Ltd.
Grosvenor House
11 St Paul's Square
Birmingham
B3 1RB, UK

ISBN 978-1-83546-636-0

www.packtpub.com

To my dear family, who always have my back. To my fiancée (soon-to-be wife), thank you for being my loving partner and my inspiration.

– Mohamed Essam

Contributors

About the author

Mohamed Essam is a highly skilled Unity developer with expertise in creating captivating gameplay experiences across various platforms. With a solid background in game development spanning over four years, he has successfully designed and implemented engaging gameplay mechanics for mobile devices and other platforms. His current focus lies in the development of a highly popular multiplayer game, boasting an impressive 20 million downloads. Equipped with a deep understanding of cutting-edge technologies and a knack for creative problem solving, Mohamed Essam consistently delivers exceptional results in his projects.

I'm deeply thankful for my supportive family, their encouragement and belief in me have been instrumental in my accomplishments. I would like to acknowledge the unwavering support of my fiancée, whose love and understanding have been my constant source of inspiration.

About the reviewer

Vahe Petrosyan is a skilled game developer with extensive experience in C++ and C#, specializing in Unity and Unreal Engine. He has created immersive VR experiences focused on education in medical fields and mental well-being and led the development of popular mobile games that have attracted thousands of players. His projects, particularly in Unity VR, demonstrate a commitment to enhancing learning and health through innovative gaming solutions.

Table of Contents

Preface xiii

Part 1: Game Design and Project Structure

1

An Introduction to Game Design and Project Management 3

Technical requirements	3	What about the player's experience?	7
Introduction to GDD	4	Let's talk about the Project organization	9
What is GDD?	4		
GDD and Pitch: A Comparative Perspective	4	Mastering Project Structure for Efficient Development	9
The Pitch: Sparking Enthusiasm for Your Game Concept	4	Summary	21
Understanding GDD elements	5		

2

Writing Clean and Modular C# Code for Unity Game Development 23

Technical requirements	23	What is the difference between the LSP and OCP?	32
Introduction to writing clean code	24	Interface Segregation Principle (ISP)	33
		Dependency Inversion Principle (DIP)	34
Principles of writing clean code	25	Understanding design patterns in game development	37
Single Responsibility Principle (SRP)	25		
Open-Closed Principle (OCP)	28		
Liskov Substitution Principle (LSP)	31	Creational patterns	37

Structural patterns	37	Refactoring techniques	49
Behavioral patterns	38	Questions	53
Coding conventions and best practices	48	Summary	54

Part 2: Advanced C# Game Development Techniques in Unity

3

Extending Functionality with Unity Plugins 57

Technical requirements	57	Cinemachine	69
Understanding Unity plugins	58	Best practices for using Unity plugins	82
Integrating Unity plugins	59		
New Input System	59	Summary	83

4

Implementing Engaging Game Mechanics Using C# in Unity 85

Technical requirements	85	Delving into the AI logic	99
Introducing game mechanics	86	Implementing challenge and reward systems using C#	120
Essential principles of game mechanics	86		
The connection between code and game mechanics	87	Challenges versus missions/quests	120
		Balancing difficulty levels for broad appeal	121
Implementing player behavior and AI logic using C#	88	Exploring reward systems	121
Writing the IHealth and IDamage interfaces	89	C# implementation of challenges and rewards	121
Implementing a shoot system	94	Summary	132

5

Designing Optimized User Interfaces with C# for Unity Games   133

Technical requirements	133	Understanding MVC – a teamwork of three roles	140
Introducing UI design in gaming	134	Understanding MVVM – a mix of views and models	142
Best practices and optimization techniques for UIs	135	Choosing the right path for Unity UI	143
Splitting up Canvases	135	Practical suggestions for enhancing your UI development	144
Avoiding too many Graphic Raycasters and turning off Raycast Target	137	Creating a UI system using C#	145
Efficiently managing UI object pools	138	The UIManager class	146
Hiding a Canvas the right way	139	The BaseView class	149
Efficient implementation of animations for UI Elements	139	Implementing MVVM	153
Effective handling of fullscreen UIs	139	Summary	154
Introducing architecture patterns (MVC and MVVM)	140		

Part 3: Data Management and Code Collaboration with C# in Unity

6

Effective Game Data Handling and Management with C# in Unity   157

Technical requirements	157	PlayerPrefs	166
Data organization and serialization with C#	158	Custom Save System	170
Understanding data structures	158	Data-driven gameplay with C#	181
Enhancing game performance with proper data structure selection	159	Creating data for stats	181
Serialization in Unity	160	Challenge system	183
Creating save and load systems using C#	166	Summary	185

7

Contributing to Existing Code Bases in Unity with C# — 187

Technical requirements	187	Mastering code conflict management	194
Introducing VCSs	187	**Understanding existing code bases**	**202**
Understanding VCSs	188	Practical exploration for the existing code base	202
Collaborating and resolving conflicts with C#	**192**	**Summary**	**205**
Best practices for collaborating	192		
Mastering branching and merging in collaboration	193		

Part 4: Advanced Integration and External Assets with C# in Unity

8

Implementing External Assets, APIs, and Pre-Built Components with C# in Unity — 209

Technical requirements	209	**Integrating analytics APIs with C#**	**231**
Leveraging pre-built assets with C#	**210**	Integrating GameAnalytics	232
Universal Render Pipeline (URP)	210	Example of GameAnalytics usage	237
Integrating backend services with C#	**222**	**Summary**	**239**
Backend services	222		

9

Optimizing the Game Using Unity's Profiler, Frame Debugger, and Memory Profiler — 241

Technical requirements	241	Exploring Unity's profiling tools in depth	242
Introducing Unity profiling tools	**242**	Understanding the profiling process	250

Performance optimization techniques	**258**
Physics and collisions	259
Audio	260
UI	261
Networking and multiplayer	262
AI and pathfinding	263
Build size	264
Rendering	267
Scripting	269
Memory management and optimization	**274**
The Memory Profiler	274
Summary	**292**

10

Tips and Tricks in Unity 293

Technical requirements	**293**
Productivity-boosting shortcuts with C#	**294**
Unity Editor shortcuts	294
Visual Studio shortcuts	298
Prefab workflow optimization	301
Advanced techniques and workflows with C#	**304**
ScriptableObjects	305
Custom editors	309
Troubleshooting and common challenges	**316**
Debugging techniques	316
Platform-specific challenges	322
Summary	**324**

Index 325

Other Books You May Enjoy 334

Preface

Welcome to the exciting world of game development and Unity mastery! In *Mastering Unity Game Development with C#*, we embark on a journey to unravel the secrets of creating captivating games and mastering the Unity game development platform.

Our focus is not just on creating games but on understanding the underlying principles that elevate your creations. Through practical examples and best practices, you'll delve into essential areas such as UI design, clean code architecture, optimization techniques, and game mechanics implementation. Each chapter is meticulously crafted to equip you with the skills needed to navigate the complexities of game development confidently.

What sets this book apart is its practical approach to game development. You'll not only learn the theory but also get hands-on experience with real-world examples, empowering you to apply your newfound knowledge immediately.

Drawing from my experience in the game development field and insights from industry experts, this book encapsulates years of knowledge and expertise. Whether you're a seasoned developer looking to enhance your skills or a novice venturing into game creation for the first time, this book provides a comprehensive guide to building immersive and successful games using Unity and C#.

Game development is not just a profession; it's a passion that fuels innovation and creativity. As you dive into this book, you'll not only learn to create games but also unlock the potential to carve your path in the thriving gaming industry.

Join me on this exhilarating journey as we delve into the art and science of creating engaging games, empowering you to make your mark in the ever-evolving landscape of game development. With this book, you'll gain practical skills, industry insights, and the confidence to excel in the competitive world of game development.

Who this book is for

This book caters primarily to developers and game designers who are eager to enhance their skills in Unity game development. While it covers foundational concepts, the focus is on mid-level to senior developers looking to delve deeper into advanced topics.

Background and experience:

- **Junior developers:** Individuals with some experience in Unity, such as creating scenes, scripting, and manipulating objects, will find this book valuable as it reinforces core concepts and provides step-by-step guidance

- **Mid-level to senior developers**: The book delves into advanced topics such as clean code architecture, optimization techniques, and integration of third-party assets and APIs, making it ideal for developers looking to elevate their game development skills
- **Game designers**: While the primary focus is on developers, game designers seeking a deeper understanding of Unity development and implementation of game mechanics will also find valuable insights and practical techniques in this book

Overall, whether you're a junior developer looking to solidify your knowledge or a seasoned developer aiming to refine your skills, this book offers a comprehensive guide to mastering Unity game development and creating immersive and polished games.

What this book covers

Chapter 1, An Introduction to Game Design and Project Management, provides an in-depth exploration of the key elements and principles of game design. It covers essential topics such as game mechanics, player experience, and storytelling techniques. Additionally, the chapter delves into effective project organization techniques aimed at streamlining game development processes.

Chapter 2, Writing Clean and Modular C# Code for Unity Game Development, delves into the art of writing clean and maintainable C# code following industry best practices. It covers the importance of documenting and structuring C# code for improved collaboration among team members. Furthermore, the chapter explores techniques for refactoring and optimizing existing C# code to enhance performance and scalability, ensuring a smooth and efficient game development process.

Chapter 3, Extending Functionality with Unity Plugins, delves into the exploration of different types of Unity plugins, helping readers identify and evaluate their functionalities. The chapter guides readers on integrating Unity plugins seamlessly into their projects to enhance overall functionality. Additionally, it provides insights into implementing functionality plugins using C# to introduce new features and enrich gameplay mechanics, thereby expanding the creative possibilities within Unity game development.

Chapter 4, Implementing Engaging Game Mechanics Using C# in Unity, delves into the analysis and application of the principles governing effective game mechanics using C#. The chapter guides readers through the implementation of challenge and reward systems using C# to elevate gameplay experiences. Additionally, it explores creating player behavior and AI logic, using C# to deliver interactive and responsive gameplay. Through these strategies, the chapter aims to enhance player engagement and immersion, fostering dynamic and captivating gaming experiences within Unity.

Chapter 5, Designing Optimized User Interfaces with C# for Unity Games, focuses on applying UI design principles using C# to craft visually appealing interfaces. Readers will learn to design effective visual hierarchies and layouts for UI elements, ensuring an optimal user experience. Additionally, the chapter covers the implementation of responsive and interactive UI elements using C#, enhancing overall user engagement and satisfaction within Unity game development.

Chapter 6, *Effective Game Data Handling and Management with C# in Unity*, delves into organizing and serializing game data using C# for efficient storage and retrieval. It covers the implementation of save and load systems using C# to effectively manage game progress. Additionally, the chapter explores creating data-driven gameplay elements using stored data with C#, enhancing the depth and interactivity of Unity game experiences.

Chapter 7, *Contributing to Existing Code Bases in Unity with C#*, focuses on utilizing version control systems to manage code repositories efficiently. It guides readers on collaborating effectively with shared code repositories and resolving code conflicts to maintain code quality during collaboration using C#. This chapter equips developers with essential skills and strategies for seamless teamwork and code management within Unity projects.

Chapter 8, *Implementing External Assets, APIs, and Pre-Built Components with C# in Unity*, dives into the integration of third-party assets, using C# to elevate game visuals and audio. It also covers the implementation of backend and analytics APIs, using C# to boost user engagement and enhance the overall gaming experience. This chapter equips developers with the skills needed to leverage external resources effectively within Unity projects, contributing to immersive and engaging gameplay.

Chapter 9, *Optimizing the Game Using Unity's Profiler, Frame Debugger, and Memory Profiler*, explores the utilization of Unity's profiling tools to pinpoint performance bottlenecks. Readers will learn to apply performance optimization techniques to enhance game performance effectively. Additionally, the chapter delves into managing memory usage and optimizing memory performance within the game, ensuring optimal performance and seamless gameplay experiences in Unity projects.

Chapter 10, *Tips and Tricks in Unity*, unveils a collection of productivity-boosting shortcuts for efficient Unity development with C#. Readers will explore advanced techniques and workflows using C# to elevate their game development processes. Moreover, the chapter equips readers with strategies to troubleshoot common challenges and discover effective solutions in Unity development, empowering them to overcome obstacles and achieve success in their projects.

To get the most out of this book

This book is designed for individuals who have some prior experience with Unity and are comfortable with C# programming. If you have a basic understanding of Unity's core functionalities, such as creating scenes, scripting, and manipulating objects, you are ready to dive into this book.

Software/hardware covered in the book	Operating system requirements
Unity3D 2022.3.13	Windows, macOS, or Linux
Visual Studio 2022	
GitHub Desktop	

If you are using the digital version of this book, we advise you to type the code yourself or access the code from the book's GitHub repository (a link is available in the next section). Doing so will help you avoid any potential errors related to the copying and pasting of code.

Download the example code files

You can download the example code files for this book from GitHub at `https://github.com/PacktPublishing/Mastering-Unity-Game-Development-with-C-Sharp`. If there's an update to the code, it will be updated in the GitHub repository.

We also have other code bundles from our rich catalog of books and videos available at `https://github.com/PacktPublishing/`. Check them out!

Conventions used

There are a number of text conventions used throughout this book.

`Code in text`: Indicates code words in text, database table names, folder names, filenames, file extensions, pathnames, dummy URLs, user input, and Twitter handles. Here is an example: "The `commit -a` command, or its equivalents, should only be employed during the initial commit of a project, typically when the project consists solely of `README.md` files."

A block of code is set as follows:

```
// Define WaitForSeconds as a variable
    private WaitForSeconds waitShort = new WaitForSeconds(2f);
```

Bold: Indicates a new term, an important word, or words that you see onscreen. For instance, words in menus or dialog boxes appear in **bold**. Here is an example: "Then, you can click on **Commit Staged** in the side panel to push the changes after the merge."

> Tips or important notes
> Appear like this.

Get in touch

Feedback from our readers is always welcome.

General feedback: If you have questions about any aspect of this book, email us at `customercare@packtpub.com` and mention the book title in the subject of your message.

Errata: Although we have taken every care to ensure the accuracy of our content, mistakes do happen. If you have found a mistake in this book, we would be grateful if you would report this to us. Please visit `www.packtpub.com/support/errata` and fill in the form.

Piracy: If you come across any illegal copies of our works in any form on the internet, we would be grateful if you would provide us with the location address or website name. Please contact us at `copyright@packt.com` with a link to the material.

If you are interested in becoming an author: If there is a topic that you have expertise in and you are interested in either writing or contributing to a book, please visit `authors.packtpub.com`.

Share your thoughts

Once you've read *Mastering Unity Game Development with C#*, we'd love to hear your thoughts! Scan the QR code below to go straight to the Amazon review page for this book and share your feedback.

`https://packt.link/r/1835466362`

Your review is important to us and the tech community and will help us make sure we're delivering excellent quality content.

Download a free PDF copy of this book

Thanks for purchasing this book!

Do you like to read on the go but are unable to carry your print books everywhere?

Is your eBook purchase not compatible with the device of your choice?

Don't worry, now with every Packt book you get a DRM-free PDF version of that book at no cost.

Read anywhere, any place, on any device. Search, copy, and paste code from your favorite technical books directly into your application.

The perks don't stop there, you can get exclusive access to discounts, newsletters, and great free content in your inbox daily

Follow these simple steps to get the benefits:

1. Scan the QR code or visit the link below

https://packt.link/free-ebook/9781835466360

2. Submit your proof of purchase
3. That's it! We'll send your free PDF and other benefits to your email directly

Part 1: Game Design and Project Structure

In this part, you'll immerse yourself in the intricate world of game design, exploring fundamental elements such as game mechanics, player experience, and storytelling techniques. Discover effective project management strategies tailored for game development, aimed at optimizing workflows and streamlining processes. Additionally, delve into the art of writing clean and maintainable C# code while following industry best practices, covering the importance of documenting and structuring code for improved collaboration. By combining these creative and technical aspects, you'll acquire the tools and knowledge necessary to bring your game ideas to life with efficiency, innovation, and code quality.

This part includes the following chapters:

- *Chapter 1, An Introduction to Game Design and Project Management*
- *Chapter 2, Writing Clean and Modular C# Code for Unity Game Development*

1

An Introduction to Game Design and Project Management

Step into the realm where creativity meets structure – the Introduction to Game Design and Project Organization. This chapter serves as your gateway to understanding the core principles that breathe life into games. In this chapter, we'll navigate through the essential elements of game design, exploring the art of crafting engaging mechanics and compelling narratives. Additionally, we'll unravel the secrets of effective project organization, providing you with the tools to streamline your development process. Whether you're dreaming of your first game or seeking to enhance your skills, this introduction lays the groundwork for an exciting adventure.

In this chapter, we're going to cover the following main topics:

- Introduction to GDD
- What about the player's experience
- Let's talk about the project organization

Technical requirements

Ready to dive into Unity development? Make sure your system is ready:

- **Unity Version 2022.3.13**: Download and install Unity, choosing version 2022.3.13 for optimal compatibility with the provided content.
- **Primary IDE - Visual Studio 2022**: The tutorials and code samples are crafted using Visual Studio 2022. Ensure it's installed to follow along seamlessly. Feel free to explore Rider or other IDEs if you prefer, though instructions are tailored for Visual Studio.
- **Sufficient System Resources**: Ensure your system meets Unity's minimum requirements for a smooth development experience.

- **GitHub Repository for Code Samples**: Access the code samples and project files on our dedicated GitHub repository: `https://github.com/PacktPublishing/Mastering-Unity-Game-Development-with-C-Sharp`. Clone or download the repository to have easy access to the code demonstrated in this chapter.

Introduction to GDD

Let's get into game design! We're diving into the world of Game Design Document (GDD). Making games isn't just about code; it's about creating experiences. These basics help turn ideas into exciting games. We'll explore what GDD is all about and how it helps make games that players love.

What is GDD?

A **Game Design Document**, or **GDD**, serves as a comprehensive guide that outlines the core themes, styles, features, mechanics, and ideas for your game project. Its main role is to effectively communicate the details of your project, whether to yourself as you progress in game development or to other stakeholders like team members, publishers, or potential players. Essentially, it's the tool that helps manage and develop the concept of your game, providing a crucial roadmap for its creation. While there's no strict standard for its format, a well-crafted GDD becomes an integral part of your game's development, ensuring clarity and alignment among the development team.

GDD and Pitch: A Comparative Perspective

When it comes to the GDD and the pitch, they serve distinct purposes in the game development process. The GDD is an in-depth document, capturing core elements and intricacies, offering a detailed guide for the development team. On the other hand, a pitch is a concise and impactful presentation crafted to generate interest and support. While the GDD provides comprehensive information throughout the game creation journey, the pitch acts as a teaser – a compelling snapshot to excite potential stakeholders.

The Pitch: Sparking Enthusiasm for Your Game Concept

A **pitch** is a powerful tool designed to ignite interest and support for your game concept. It's a brief, attention-grabbing presentation that swiftly communicates the essence of your game. Unlike the detailed nature of the GDD, the pitch is all about creating immediate excitement. It plays a vital role in capturing attention, generating curiosity, and laying the groundwork for potential collaboration with stakeholders.

The following image serves as a pitch for our game, providing a visual representation to illustrate the concept:

Fusion Fury Pitch:

Begin on an adrenaline-fueled journey in Fusion Fury, a top-down shooter for PC. Navigate procedurally generated levels, combine weapons, bend time, and battle evolving foes to restore order to shattered dimensions

Player Experience:

- Engage in dynamic weapon fusion, discovering synergies for varied playstyles.
- Master temporal distortion for precise combat decisions and survival against evolving enemies.
- ....

Game Mechanics:

- Combine weapons for unique hybrid aresenals.
- Utilize temporal distortion for strategic advantages.
- ......

Weapons and Items:

- Fusion Blaster: Fires energy projectiles; secondary fire initiates a fusion overload.
- Temporal Shifter: Shoots time-distorted projectiles; secondary fire releases a burst of temporal energy.
- ....

Level Design:

- Procedurally generated levels with diverse environments.
- Dynamic level structure with interconnected rooms and hazards.
- ....

Audio and Visuals:

- Energetic soundtrack adapting to combat intensity.
- ....

Conclusion:

Fusion Fury offers an immersive journey through fractured realities. Get ready for the Fusion Fury experience!

Figure 1.1 – Fusion Fury's Pitch

You will find a full GDD on `https://github.com/PacktPublishing/Mastering-Unity-Game-Development-with-C-Sharp`.

Understanding GDD elements

If you've ever wondered about the magic behind video games, you're in the right place. Join us on a beginner-friendly exploration of the GDD elements, demystifying the language of game development. The following list shows some of the GDD elements:

- **Game Concept**:
  - Description of the game's core idea and overall concept.
  - Defines the setting, theme, and main objectives of the game.

- **Core Game Mechanics**:
  - Detailed explanation of the fundamental rules and interactions governing the game.
  - Describes how the player will engage with and navigate the game world.

- **Gameplay Features**:
  - Identification and elaboration of key features that enhance the gameplay experience.
  - Includes unique selling points, special abilities, and innovative aspects.

- **Gameplay Breakdown**:
  - In-depth breakdown of different phases or levels within the game.
  - Outlines the progression and challenges players will encounter.

- **Project Scope Breakdown**:
  - Clear delineation of the scope of the project, including its limitations.
  - Defines what is included and, equally important, what is not included in the project.

- **Technical Requirements**:
  - Specifications related to the technology and tools needed for game development.
  - Includes information on platforms, programming languages, and software requirements.

- **Art and Sound Assets**:
  - Overview of the visual and auditory elements required for the game.
  - Describes character designs, environment art, sound effects, and music.

- **User Interface (UI) Design**:
  - Design of the user interface, including menus, HUD elements, and navigation.
  - Ensures a user-friendly and visually appealing experience.

- **Monetization Strategy**:
  - Discussion of how the game will generate revenue, if applicable.
  - Includes pricing models, in-app purchases, or other revenue streams.

- **Testing and Quality Assurance**:
  - Strategy for testing the game to identify and resolve bugs.
  - Ensures the game meets quality standards before release.

- **Marketing and Promotion**:
  - Outlines plans for promoting and marketing the game.
  - Identifies the target audience and strategies for building awareness.

These aren't the only elements you'd find in a GDD, but that's not our focus in this book. We also offer advice, especially for mid-development or indie game developers. It's often recommended not to create an overly detailed GDD at the start because you might need to make changes as your development journey progresses.

We'll use this GDD as we create the game in the next chapters. We'll learn how to understand the GDD, break it into tasks, and organize them to complete our game.

Let's discuss a crucial aspect related to the player's experience and why it's vital for the success of our game.

What about the player's experience?

Welcome to the heart of game development, where the magic happens—shaping the player's experience. In this Section, as this section serves as an introduction to help you understand player experience, we delve into the art of crafting immersive worlds that captivate players and leave a lasting impression. Player experience isn't just a feature; it's the soul of your game, and we're here to guide you through the elements that will elevate your players' journey.

Player experience, commonly referred to as **PX** or **User Experience** (**UX**), stands as a vital aspect outlined in the GDD. It embodies the overall impression and emotions players undergo while immersed in a video game. Here are key components related to player experience in a GDD:

- **Emotional Engagement**:
  - Describes intended emotional responses the game aims to evoke.
  - Identifies emotional journeys throughout different gameplay stages.

- **Immersion**:
  - Details how the game intends to engage players in its virtual world.
  - Discusses features like realistic graphics, sound design, and narrative depth.

- **Challenge and Difficulty**:
  - Outlines the balance between challenging gameplay and player engagement.
  - Defines the difficulty curve and its evolution throughout the game.

- **Reward System**:
  - Describes how the game rewards players for achievements.
  - Includes points, power-ups, achievements, or other incentives.

- **Player Progression**:
  - Explains how players advance, gain new abilities, or unlock content.
  - Outlines the sense of progression and achievement.

- **Narrative Impact**:
  - Discusses how the game's story contributes to the overall player experience.
  - Addresses the integration of narrative with gameplay mechanics.

- **User Interface (UI) Feedback**:
  - Defines how the UI communicates essential information to players.
  - Ensures clear, intuitive feedback for an enhanced overall experience.

- **Interactivity**:
  - Describes the level of player interaction with the game world.
  - Includes the responsiveness of controls, decision-making impact, and player agency.

- **Pacing**:
  - Outlines the rhythm and flow of the game, balancing tension, relaxation, and climax.
  - Ensures engaging pacing throughout the player's journey.

- **Accessibility**:
  - Addresses how the game accommodates players of various skill levels and preferences.
  - Ensures inclusivity and a positive experience for a diverse audience.

As you dive into crafting player experiences, remember that every part of your game, be it the gameplay mechanics or the storytelling, plays a role in engaging players. It's more than just creating a game; it's about connecting emotionally with your audience. Through a well-designed player experience, your game evolves from simple entertainment to a memorable journey for those who step into your virtual realms.

In the next section, we'll explore the process of structuring our Unity project, task organization, and the significance of incorporating version control.

Let's talk about the Project organization

Let's jump into project organization—an essential skill for solo developers and team players alike. This section reveals the keys to using Git for version control and Hack N Plan for project coordination. Mastering project organization boosts efficiency, whether you're working alone or with a team. Starting here sets the stage for a smoother game development journey. So, grab your toolkit, let's dive in, and make organization your superpower!

Whether working solo or in a team, organizing your game project saves time and adds flexibility. A structured approach in game development keeps you on track and streamlines workflows. It's like having a map for your journey—easing navigation through challenges and ensuring a smoother development path. Together, we'll embark on this journey, keeping chaos at bay and paving the way for efficient game creation.

Mastering Project Structure for Efficient Development

Let's delve into the ways we'll structure our project. We'll cover three main aspects:

- Discover the importance of using a version control system for seamless collaboration.
- Structuring and organizing the project within Unity, with helpful tips and best practices.
- Leveraging Hack N Plan to efficiently organize and manage tasks.

In the next few sections, we will explore each point to gain valuable insights and skills for effective project organization.

Version Control System

Using a version control system in game development is crucial for both solo developers and teams. It acts like a safety net for your project, allowing you to track changes, revert to previous versions if something goes wrong, and collaborate seamlessly with others.

Even when working alone, it safeguards against accidental errors and provides a structured way to manage your project's evolution. For teams, it ensures everyone stays on the same page, reduces conflicts, and simplifies collaboration, making the entire development process smoother and more organized. In essence, it's a tool that keeps your game development journey hassle-free and efficient.

In the vast world of version control systems, such as Git, Perforce, and Unity's official version control, Plastic, we'll simplify things in this book by focusing on Git and GitHub. While you're free to choose your preferred tools, we recommend using GitHub for better alignment with the provided code and seamless workflow tracking.

How version control works

Version control is like a safety net for your game project. Imagine you're trying out a new feature, but it doesn't quite work as expected. With version control, you can easily revert to a clean, functional version, undoing any experimental changes. It's like having a time machine for your project, letting you iterate on ideas without fear.

Moreover, if you need to switch gears and help out with a major issue in the main project, version control lets you save your changes for later. Once the urgent task is handled, you can seamlessly restore your experimental work. This system also prevents accidental overwrites when collaborating with a team. Every time you commit your work, you'll check for the latest updates, ensuring you don't clash with your teammates. While dealing with merge conflicts might sound daunting at first, it's a manageable process once you get the hang of it.

Best practices for Version Control

No matter the version control system you choose, various best practices can enhance your team's efficiency. Since each team has unique requirements, not every practice will suit all teams. The following are some of the best practices for version control:

- Commit frequently, but in small increments.

    Ensure that each commit corresponds to a specific task or ticket, keeping the changes focused and manageable. This practice makes it easier to identify and revert any negative changes without affecting positive ones in case of an issue.

- Stay up to date with the latest changes.

    Regularly pull the latest updates from the repository into your working copy to avoid working in isolation and minimize the chances of encountering merge conflicts. Incorporate this practice into your daily workflow for smoother collaboration and effective version control management.

- Maintain clean and descriptive commit messages.

    Clearly convey the purpose of each commit, making it easier to understand the project's history. If using a task ticketing system, consider including a ticket number in your commit for better traceability and collaboration.

In the next section, we will learn how to organize our Unity project and the importance of organizing the project properly.

Organizing a Unity project

Efficiently organizing your Unity project not only simplifies version control but also improves overall team collaboration, leading to a smoother workflow.

In this section, we will see how to structure our project and organize our folders. We will also learn about the various naming conventions and how to use them.

Folder Structure

Here are some best practices for organizing the folders inside Unity:

- Document naming conventions and folder structure for easy file organization; consider a style guide or project template.
- Maintain consistency in naming conventions; avoid deviations. Amend rules universally, and automate changes using scripts for large-scale updates.
- Avoid spaces in file and folder names to prevent issues with Unity's command line tools. Use CamelCase as an alternative.
- Create separate folders for testing or experimentation to keep non-production scenes organized. Subfolders with usernames can help divide work areas by team member.
- Keep internal assets separate from third-party ones, especially if obtained from the Asset Store or other plug-ins, as they may have their own project structure.

While there's no fixed rule for organizing your folders, the following *Figure 1.2* shows examples of how you might structure your Unity project:

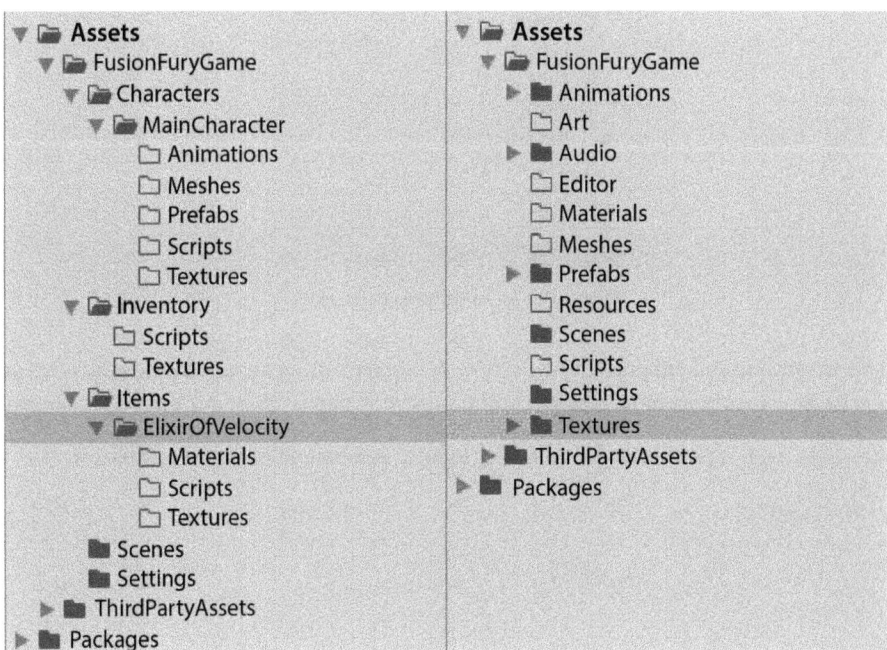

Figure 1.2 – Feature structure (left) and vertical structure (right)

These setups revolve around categorizing your project by asset type, features, or systems. While you're not obliged to use these specific folder names, they provide a helpful starting point.

For a more effective and streamlined organizational approach, it is advisable to utilize both methods simultaneously.

In the following figure, we can use combined structures for better approach:

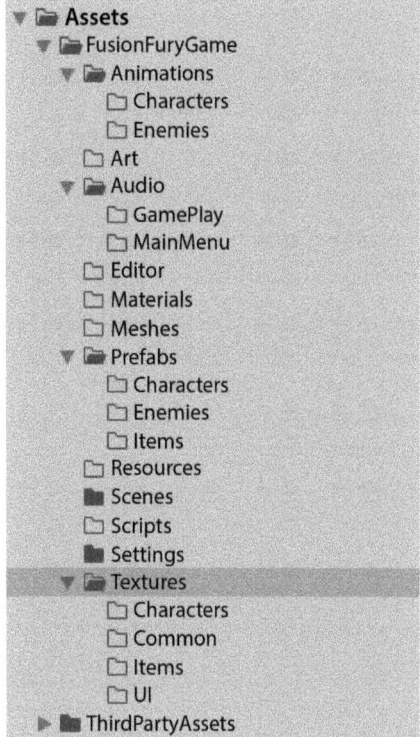

Figure 1.3 – Combined structure

Alright, let's streamline and enhance our workflow by implementing an automated system to create folders effortlessly, ensuring a more efficient and time-saving approach in our project management.

In the following script, we'll employ Unity Editor logic to generate folders and subfolders.

```
using UnityEditor;
using UnityEngine;
using System.Collections.Generic;
using System.IO;

public class CreateFolders : EditorWindow
{
    private static string projectName = "PROJECT_NAME";
```

```csharp
    [MenuItem("Assets/Create Default Folders")]
    private static void SetUpFolders()
    {
        CreateFolders window = ScriptableObject.
CreateInstance<CreateFolders>();
        window.position = new Rect(Screen.width / 2, Screen.height /
2, 400, 150);
        window.ShowPopup();
    }

    private static void CreateAllFolders()
    {
        List<string> folders = new List<string>
        {
            "Animations",
            "Audio",
            "Editor",
            "Materials",
            "Meshes",
            "Prefabs",
            "Scripts",
            "Scenes",
            "Shaders",
            "Textures",
            "UI"
        };

        foreach (string folder in folders)
        {
            if (!Directory.Exists("Assets/" + folder))
            {
                Directory.CreateDirectory("Assets/" + projectName +
"/" + folder);
            }
        }

        List<string> uiFolders = new List<string>
        {
            "Assets",
            "Fonts",
            "Icon"
        };
```

```
        foreach (string subfolder in uiFolders)
        {
            if (!Directory.Exists("Assets/" + projectName + "/UI/" +
subfolder))
            {
                Directory.CreateDirectory("Assets/" + projectName + "/
UI/" + subfolder);
            }
        }
        AssetDatabase.Refresh();
    }

    void OnGUI()
    {
        EditorGUILayout.LabelField("Insert the Project name used as
the root folder");
        projectName = EditorGUILayout.TextField("Project Name: ",
projectName);
        this.Repaint();
        GUILayout.Space(70);
        if (GUILayout.Button("Generate!")) {
            CreateAllFolders();
            this.Close();
        }
    }
}
```

The preceding code block shows static functions that you can use in the editor once you create the project to setup the folder structure you want.

You'll also have the flexibility to modify names, paths, and the entire structure. We'll make use of a dropdown menu when you click right click on mouse in the project tab within the editor to facilitate the creation of this folder structure.

In *Figure 1.4*, we can see the drop-down menu from which we can choose the **Create Default Folders** option to create our own default folders:

Let's talk about the Project organization   15

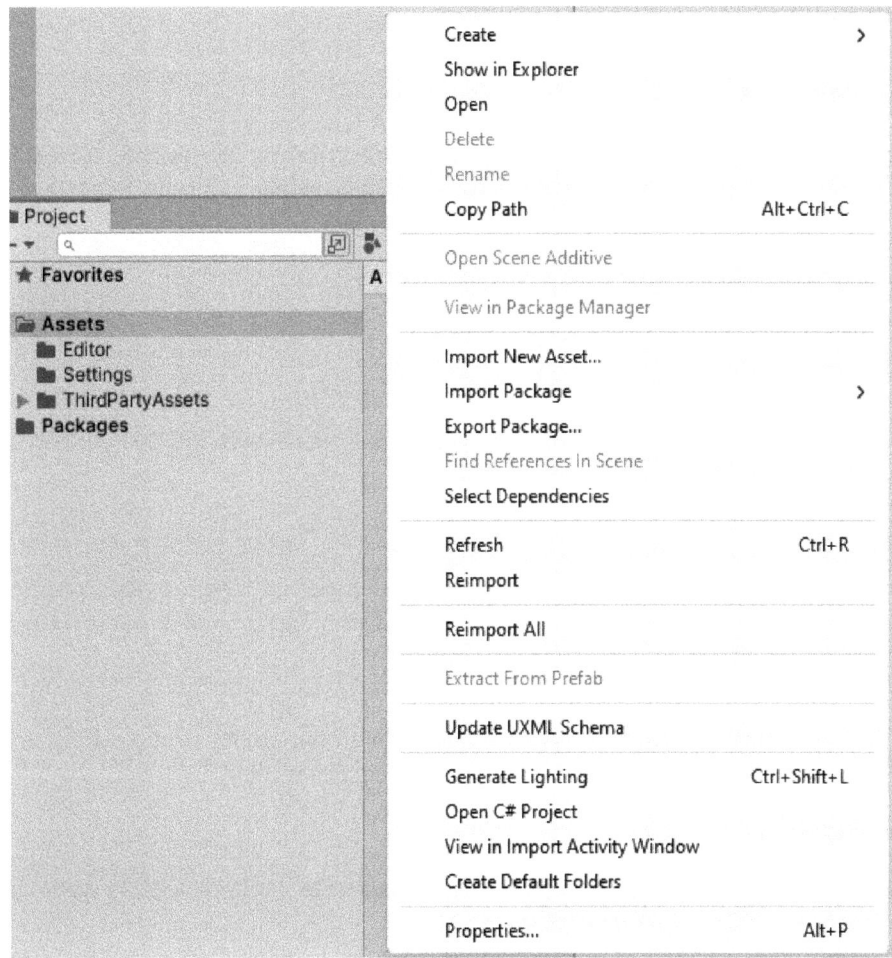

Figure 1.4 – Create default folders from menu

Once we click on the **Create Default Folders** option, you will see the following panel from where you can name the project:

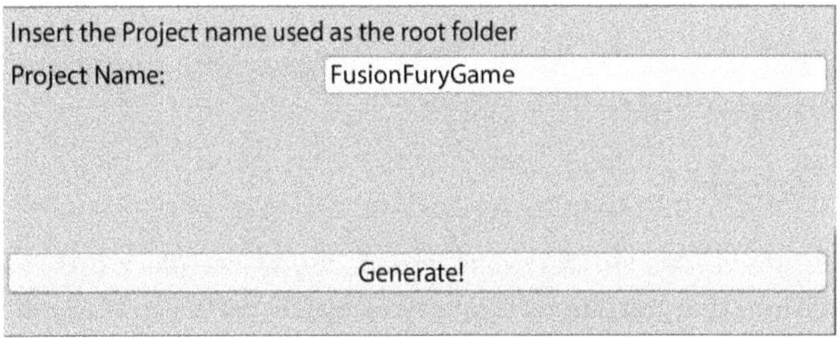

Figure 1.5 – Type project name

Once you name the project, click on **Generate!**.

Naming Standards

Setting standards isn't just about project folders. Having a consistent naming convention for GameObjects in scenes or Prefabs in project folders can simplify collaboration within your team. While there's no one-size-fits-all naming standard for GameObjects, here are some considerations:

- Use descriptive names:
    - Choose names you'll remember months from now.
    - Ensure others can understand and pronounce the names.
    - Avoid confusing abbreviations and spelling mistakes, for example, instead of `numBtn` use `numberButton` or `numericButton`.
- Use Camel case/Pascal case:
    - Enhance readability and typing accuracy, for examples, use `OutOfMemoryException` and `dateTimeFormat` and avoid using `Outofmemoryexception` and `datetimeformat`.
- Follow the design document naming:
    - Use exact spellings from the design document for locations, for example, if the design document mentions `HighSpellTower`, maintain that spelling.
- Use underscores sparingly:
    - Generally, avoid using underscores, but they are useful in specific cases. Like name clarity in long identifiers or avoiding name conflicts.
    - Prefixing with an underscore place it alphabetically first.
    - Denote variants of a specific object with underscores, for examples:
        - Active States: `EnterButton_Active`
        - Texture Maps: `Foliage_Diffuse`

In the next section, we'll explore techniques to streamline the workflow by utilizing presets, making the importing process more efficient:

Workflow Optimization

Other than deciding how and where to store your assets in the **Assets** folder, there are various design and development decisions that can enhance your work speed, particularly when utilizing version control. We will take a look at these in the following subsections.

Use Presets

Presets are predefined settings or configurations that you can save and apply to assets or components. Presets help you quickly apply consistent settings across different elements in your project, saving time and ensuring uniformity. They are commonly used for materials, lights, and other Unity components to streamline the development process. when you apply settings in one of the components you can select the preset window from the inspector and create a new preset to apply it later.

In *Figure 1.6*, you can see where to select the preset window in the inspector:

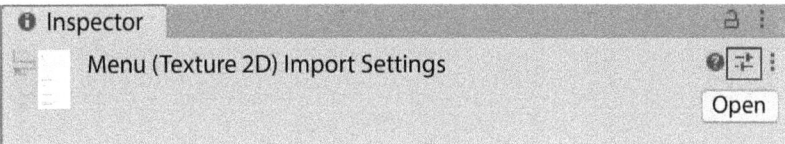

Figure 1.6 – Preset button

Applying settings from a preset

Using a Preset is straightforward—go to the **Select Preset** window — this window will appear once you click on the preset selector icon (*Figure 1.6*) — or drag the preset from the **Project** window to your GameObject with the component.

Figure 1.7 – Preset Menu

> **Important Note**
> When you apply a Preset, it's like making a copy of the settings from the Preset to your item. The Preset and the item aren't linked, so any changes to the Preset won't affect items you applied it to previously.

To apply a Preset using the **Select Preset** window, follow these steps:

1. Select the GameObjects or assets where you want to apply the Preset. Click the Preset selector (the slider icon) in the **Inspector**.

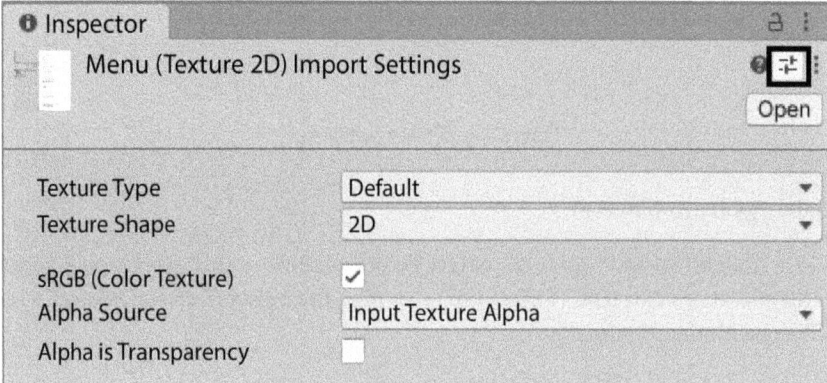

Figure 1.8 – Press on this button to choose preset

2. In the **Select Preset** window, find and select the Preset of your choice. By doing this, Unity will apply the selected Preset to your component, asset, or Project Settings.
3. Close the **Select Preset** window.

If you drag a component Preset onto your GameObject, you can do any one of the following things:

- Drop it on an existing GameObject in the **Hierarchy** window, and Unity will add a new component while copying properties from the Preset.
- Drop it on an empty area in the **Hierarchy** window to create a new, empty GameObject with properties from the Preset.
- Drop it on the **Inspector** window onto the title of an existing component, and Unity copies properties from the Preset.
- Drop it on an empty area in the **Inspector** window, and Unity will add a new component while copying properties from the Preset.

Separating your assets

The following are some general tips for your project:

- **Break Down Unity Scenes**: Divide levels into smaller scenes for efficient teamwork.
- **Use SceneManager for Additive Loading**: At runtime, employ SceneManager LoadSceneAsync with **Additive** mode.
- **Utilize Prefabs for Modularity**: Break work into Prefabs for easier management.

Here, we've shared just a handful of insightful tips to kickstart your project on the right foot, ensuring a clean and efficient foundation.

The HacknPlan Management tool

Now, let's talk about the Hack N Plan management tool. It's a crucial tool that will make organizing and managing your game development easier. Stay tuned as we explore its features, making your project management more straightforward and successful.

While numerous management tools exist, for the purposes of this book, we'll focus on demonstrating HacknPlan—a dedicated project management solution designed specifically for game development teams. Serving as a centralized hub, it caters to developers, designers, and team members, offering a suite of tools to effectively plan, monitor, and oversee the intricate process of creating video games. Key highlights of HacknPlan include:

- **Task Management**: Users leverage HacknPlan to organize and oversee tasks systematically, categorizing them effectively. This tool is well-suited for the dynamic and ever-evolving nature of game development projects.
- **Kanban Boards**: Utilizing a Kanban-style system, It's like sticky notes. HacknPlan provides a visually intuitive representation of tasks as they move through different project stages like **To Do**, **In Progress**, and **Done**.
- **Integration with Version Control Systems**: HacknPlan seamlessly integrates with version control systems like Git, fostering collaboration and ensuring meticulous tracking of changes contributed by diverse team members.
- **Time Tracking**: HacknPlan enables users to track time spent on various tasks, offering insights into project timelines and resource allocation.
- **Team Collaboration**: HacknPlan facilitates collaboration among team members by enabling task-related discussions, file sharing, and fostering overall communication within the platform.
- **Agile Methodology Support**: Aligned with agile development principles, HacknPlan empowers teams to adapt to changes effectively and implement gradual improvements through an iterative development process.

20   An Introduction to Game Design and Project Management

- **Roadmap Planning**: Teams can create and visualize project roadmaps on HacknPlan, outlining essential milestones and objectives for different development phases.
- **Game Design Documentation**: HacknPlan often includes tools for creating and managing game design documentation, ensuring a centralized repository for project-related information that's easily accessible to the team.

The following image shows the default screen inside HacknPlan which we can start adding cards for tasks check *Figure 1.9*:

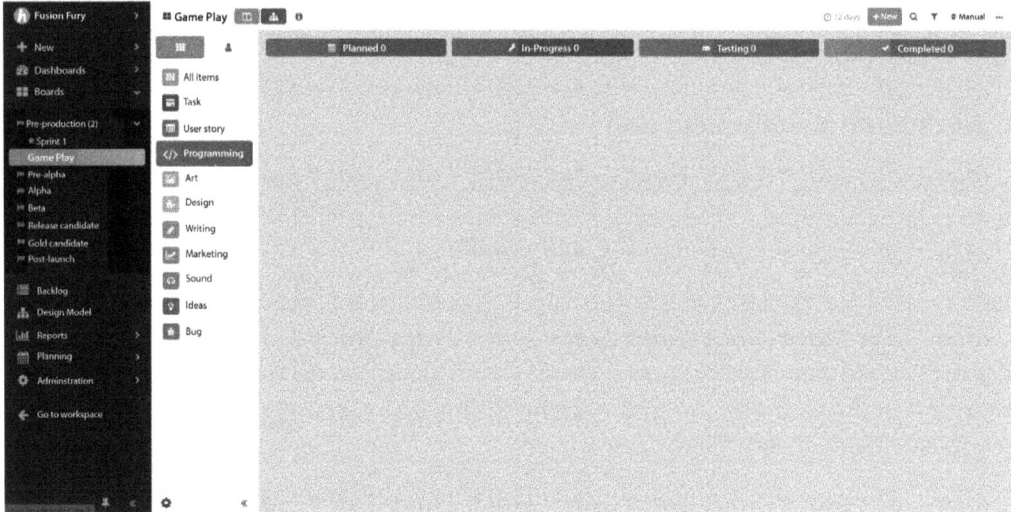

Figure 1.9 – Empty project at HacknPlan

The following image shows the example of organizing tasks, check *Figure 1.10*:

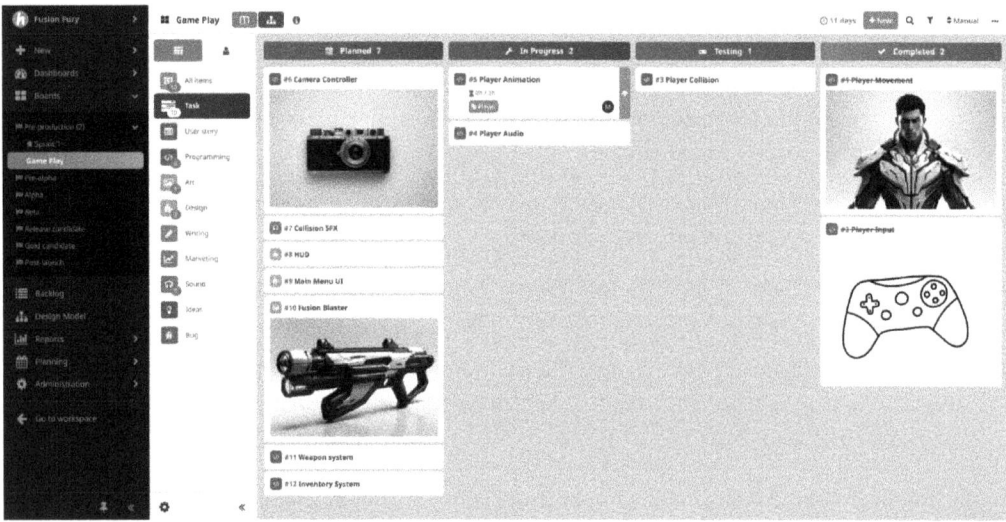

Figure 1.10 – Example of organizing cards

As we wrap up our exploration of organizing projects in game development, it's time to sum up what we've learned. We've dug into the essentials of working together seamlessly with version control, arranging our game elements efficiently within Unity, and mastering task management using Hack N Plan.

Now that we've covered these key aspects, you're standing at the end of this chapter with a toolbox of valuable skills. Whether you're a lone wolf or part of a team, these insights will be your companions in the world of game development.

So, as you close this chapter, remember that effective organization is not just a skill; it's the backbone of a successful game development adventure. May your future projects be smooth, your collaborations thrive, and your games leave a lasting impact. Best of luck as you apply these lessons to your game-making endeavours!

Summary

In this chapter, we looked into the basics of game design, introducing the GDD and how it shapes the gaming experience. Moving to project organization in Unity 2024, we explored the details of a version control system, understanding how it works and sharing best practices for working together. Then, we talked about organizing Unity projects, focusing on having a well-arranged folder system, using consistent names, and making work smoother. We also learned about presets and why it's important to keep assets separate.

The chapter ended with a closer look at "Hack N Plan," a helpful tool for team collaboration, organizing tasks well, and making communication effective. Now, with insights into game design basics, project organization tips, and powerful tools, we're ready for the hands-on part of game development. Join us in the next chapters for practical applications of these principles!

In the next chapter, *Writing Clean and Modular C# Code*, we'll delve deeper into project organization, focusing on clean and modular code structures. Building on this chapter's foundation, we'll explore game design principles through practical examples from our own game development.

A key highlight will be an exploration of SOLID principles and other software fundamentals, helping us write efficient code that follows best practices. This chapter aims to demystify the principles behind robust and flexible code, providing the tools to create captivating and enduring games.

Get ready to apply these principles hands-on, forging a path towards mastery in the art and science of game development.

2
Writing Clean and Modular C# Code for Unity Game Development

Welcome to *Chapter 2*, where we focus on the importance of clean and modular C# code for Unity game development. In the next pages, you'll learn practical skills to write clear and efficient code. We'll cover clean code principles, stress the significance of readability, and introduce industry best practices. You'll also explore conventions and code structuring for smoother collaboration. Additionally, we'll delve into refactoring and optimization techniques to enhance your C# code's performance and scalability. By the end of this chapter, you'll have the expertise to write, document, refactor, and optimize C# code effectively, laying a solid foundation for successful Unity game development.

In this chapter, we're going to cover the following main topics:

- Introduction to writing clean code
- C# code conventions and readability
- C# code refactoring and optimization techniques

Technical requirements

You will need the following to follow along with me in this chapter:

- **Unity version 2022.3.13**: Download and install Unity version 2022.3.13 or any other version. It is recommended to install the 2022 version.
- **Primary IDE – Visual Studio 2022**: Ensure Visual Studio 2022 is installed for optimal learning.
- **GitHub repository for code samples**: Access the code samples and project files of this chapter from our GitHub repository: `https://github.com/PacktPublishing/Mastering-Unity-Game-Development-with-C-Sharp/tree/main/Assets/Chapter%2002`. Clone or download the repository to have easy access to the code demonstrated in this chapter.

Introduction to writing clean code

Clean code refers to well-organized, readable, and easy-to-understand code. It's like writing a clear story that anyone can follow without getting lost in confusing jargon or messy paragraphs.

In software development, clean code matters a lot. First, it makes the code easier for everyone in the team to grasp, helping them work together smoothly. Second, it saves time because clean code is simpler to fix when something goes wrong. Lastly, it's like having a clean room – it just feels better and is easier to manage in the long run. In this list, we highlight the significance of employing clean code:

- **Building AAA games**: Have you come across "the power of clean code" on your coding journey? Well, it's like the secret sauce for cooking up high-quality code, especially when you're aiming to create top-notch AAA games. Clean code is the key ingredient for building games that stand out in the industry.

- **Working with others**: In the world of coding, we're never alone. Whether you're part of a company with high standards or collaborating on a project, the clean code mentality is your silent companion. You might not realize you're using it, but with a bit of knowledge, you can rock the industry by making your code clear and understandable for everyone on the team.

- **Flexibility in applying clean code**: The goal of this chapter isn't to force you to use all these clean code principles every single time. Sometimes you need to dive into coding first and then tidy up later. These aren't strict rules; they're more like tools you can pull out when needed. If a feature is familiar, and you know how to implement it with principles such as SOLID, go for it. But if you're unsure, start with the basics and refine your code so you gain a clearer picture of what's needed.

- **Every coder's struggle**: Picture this: you're tired of the endless coding and updates, facing issues as you go. Changing a feature becomes a headache, especially when the code turns into a messy puzzle. Dealing with testers feels like a never-ending loop of modifications. If this sounds familiar, you're not alone. This chapter is your guide to overcoming the struggles of code maintenance and updates.

- **Code that tells a story**: Ever written a piece of code and then completely forgotten what it was for? It happens to the best of us. This chapter is here to teach you how to write code that tells a story – a story that's clear and easy to follow and won't leave you scratching your head later.

- **Modularity and efficiency tips**: Get ready for some tips and tricks on how to make your code modular and efficient. I'll walk you through general principles and show you how to apply them in real-world scenarios. Plus, we'll dive into examples – messy code versus clean code – for each clean code principle, giving you a practical understanding of how to implement these ideas in your own projects.

Clean code is essential for building better software. By understanding its importance, you'll be better equipped to write code that's clear, understandable, and effective. In the next section, we will understand the principles of writing clean code.

Principles of writing clean code

In the world of **object-oriented programming** (**OOP**), clean code thrives on a foundation of five key principles known as **SOLID**. These principles act as guiding lights, helping us write code that's not just functional but also the following:

- **Easy to read and understand**: Anyone who picks up your code should be able to grasp its purpose and logic without too much effort
- **Maintainable**: Modifications and updates should be a breeze, even for someone unfamiliar with the code's history
- **Extendable and reusable**: Building on existing code should be straightforward, promoting code reuse and reducing redundancy

Let me tell you a story. Before I discovered SOLID principles, I often found myself struggling to figure out how to build features. Reaching the finish line felt like a messy, chaotic journey. Then, SOLID came along and changed everything. It was like a map, helping me organize my thoughts and code into a clear, structured path.

But SOLID wasn't just a clean code tool; it empowered me to become a better problem solver. It shifted my mindset from a "try hard" approach to a "create solutions" approach. I went from someone who wrestled with code to someone who crafted elegant solutions.

As software developers, our job is to solve problems. SOLID becomes your secret weapon in this battle. It provides the framework to tackle most challenges you'll encounter.

However, simply reading about SOLID isn't enough. True learning comes from applying it yourself. Grab your existing code and dive in! Experiment with incorporating SOLID principles and see how they transform your work. Trust me, the hands-on experience will solidify your understanding and unlock a whole new level of development mastery.

Single Responsibility Principle (SRP)

Let's discuss the **Single Responsibility Principle** (**SRP**) in the context of game development. The SRP suggests that a class should have only one reason to change, meaning it should only have one responsibility. In the gaming world, this translates to ensuring that each component or class is responsible for a single aspect of the game, making the code base more modular and maintainable.

When we begin coding, it's common to stuff all the logic into one massive class that takes on many jobs. It gets tricky trying to fix one issue without messing up other things in that class or introducing new logic that ends up making other sections act strangely.

Let's start with an example of a player controller script that combines various responsibilities and then refactor it to adhere to the SRP.

In the following code block, we can see the old `PlayerController` class, which has many responsibilities:

```
public class PlayerController : MonoBehaviour
{
    private Animator playerAnimator;
    private RigidBody rigidBody;

    private void Start()
    {
        playerAnimator = GetComponent<Animator>();
        rigidBody = GetComponent<RigidBody>();
    }

    private void Update()
    {
        // Logic for handling animations
        playerAnimator.SetBool("IsRunning",playerInput.IsRunning());

        // Logic for handling player input
        if (Input.GetKeyDown(KeyCode.Space))
        {
            rigidBody.AddForce(Vector3.up * jumpForce, ForceMode.Impulse);
        }

        // Logic for handling player movement

    }
}
```

Let's break down the big class into smaller classes, each with its own set of actions.

In the following code block, we can see the `PlayerAnimation` class, which is responsible for handling player animations:

```
public class PlayerAnimation : MonoBehaviour
{
    private Animator animator;

    private void Start()
    {
        animator = GetComponent<Animator>();
    }
```

```
        public void UpdateAnimation(bool isRunning)
        {
            animator.SetBool("IsRunning", isRunning);
        }
}
```

In the following code block, we can see the `PlayerMovement` class, which is responsible for handling player movement, and the `PlayerInput` class, which is responsible for handling player input:

```
public class PlayerMovement : MonoBehaviour
{
    public void Move(float horizontalInput)
    {
        // Logic for moving the player based on input
    }
     public void Jump()
    {
        // Logic for jumping the player based on input
    }

}
public class PlayerInput : MonoBehaviour
{
    public float HorizontalInput()
    {
        return Input.GetAxisRaw("Horizontal");
    }
    public bool IsJumping()
    {
        // Logic for determining if the player is jumping
        return Input.GetKeyDown(KeyCode.Space);
    }

    public bool IsRunning()
    {
        // Logic for determining if the player is running
        return Input.GetKey(KeyCode.LeftShift);
    }
}
```

In the following code block, we can see the `PlayerController` class acting as the orchestrator, delegating responsibilities:

```
public class PlayerController : MonoBehaviour
{
```

```
    private PlayerAnimation playerAnimation;
    private PlayerInput playerInput;
    private PlayerMovement playerMovement;

    private void Start()
    {
        playerAnimation = GetComponent<PlayerAnimation>();
        playerInput = GetComponent<PlayerInput>();
        playerMovement = GetComponent<PlayerMovement>();
    }

    private void Update()
    {
        playerMovement.Move(playerInput.HorizontalInput());

        if (playerAnimation != null)
        {
            playerAnimation.UpdateAnimation(playerInput.IsRunning());
        }

        if (playerInput.IsJumping())
        {
            playerMovement.Jump();
        }
    }
}
```

In this simplified version of the `PlayerController` class, we have separate classes for movement, input handling, and animations, making `PlayerController` more focused and adhering to the SRP. Each class handles its specific responsibility, enhancing code organization and clarity.

Open-Closed Principle (OCP)

Let's explore the **Open-Closed Principle (OCP)** in the context of game development. The OCP promotes the idea that a class should be open for extension while remaining closed for modification. In the context of game development, this implies the ability to introduce new features or functionalities without making changes to the existing code. This principle plays a crucial role in enhancing code flexibility and maintainability, allowing for the seamless addition of new elements to the game without disrupting the established framework.

An example of the *power-up dilemma* is as follows.

Imagine you have a basic power-up system in your game that grants bonus points. Using the OCP, you can create a base `PowerUp` class with common functionalities such as activation and duration. Then, you can create subclasses for different specific power-ups, such as double jump or temporary invincibility.

This way, adding a new power-up involves creating a new subclass without modifying the existing code. You're not stuck with a rigid system – the possibilities are endless!

OCP allows you to build games that are flexible, adaptable, and maintainable. It's like having a well-designed construction set, letting you create and expand your game world without limits.

In the following code block, we can see the base `PowerUp` class with common functionalities:

```
public abstract class PowerUp
{
    public abstract void Activate(); // Common activation logic
    public abstract void Deactivate(); // Common deactivation logic
}
```

In the following code block, we can see the subclass for `DoubleJumpPowerUp`:

```
public class DoubleJumpPowerUp : PowerUp
{
    public override void Activate()
    {
        // Specific activation logic for double jump
    }

    public override void Deactivate()
    {
        // Specific deactivation logic for double jump
    }
}
```

In the following code block, we can see the subclass for `TemporaryInvincibilityPowerUp`:

```
public class TemporaryInvincibilityPowerUp : PowerUp
{
    public override void Activate()
    {
        // Specific activation logic for temporary invincibility
    }

    public override void Deactivate()
    {
        // Specific deactivation logic for temporary invincibility
```

        }
    }

In the following code block, we can see the `PowerUpManager` class utilizing the power-ups:

```
public class PowerUpManager : MonoBehaviour
{
    private void Start()
    {
        // Example of using the power-up system
        PowerUp doubleJump = new DoubleJumpPowerUp();
        AddPowerUp(doubleJump);

        PowerUp invincibility = new TemporaryInvincibilityPowerUp();
        AddPowerUp(invincibility);
    }

    private void AddPowerUp(PowerUp powerUp)
    {
        powerUp.Activate();
        // Logic for adding power-up to the game
    }

    private void RemovePowerUp(PowerUp powerUp)
    {
        powerUp.Deactivate();
        // Logic for removing power-up from the game
    }
}
```

In this Unity example, the `PowerUp` class is extended with specific power-ups, such as `DoubleJumpPowerUp` and `TemporaryInvincibilityPowerUp`. The `PowerUp Manager` class demonstrates how to add and remove power-ups, and each power-up logs a message upon activation and deactivation. This structure allows for the addition of new power-ups without modifying the existing code, following the OCP.

Now, the fun part begins! We can use this system to connect each power-up subclass to its own prefab. When the player grabs a power-up, only the specific power-up associated with that prefab activates. This means adding new power-ups is a breeze – just create a new subclass and its prefab and voilà! You've expanded your game's possibilities without touching the core logic. This principle isn't just for power-ups, though. You can use it for enemies, items, abilities – the sky's the limit! So, go forth and build your awesome game with the power of the OCP!

Liskov Substitution Principle (LSP)

Let's explore the **Liskov Substitution Principle** (**LSP**) within the realm of game development. The LSP maintains that substituting objects of a superclass with objects of a subclass should not disrupt the program's correctness. In the context of game development, this implies that using derived classes (subclasses) should seamlessly integrate without compromising the expected functionality of the base class. This principle ensures the smooth interchangeability of classes, allowing for flexibility and ease of use in game development scenarios.

An example of the *sneaky enemy dilemma* is as follows.

Imagine you have a base class called `Enemy` with basic movement and attack behaviors. You then create two subclasses: `GroundEnemy` and `FlyingEnemy`. The LSP ensures that both subclasses behave as expected enemies, moving and attacking in ways that comply with the `Enemy` base class's definition. This means that any code designed to work with enemies, such as collision detection or damage calculation, will work seamlessly with both `GroundEnemy` and `FlyingEnemy` instances. This consistency simplifies development and allows you to focus on creating unique behaviors for each subclass without worrying about breaking core functionalities.

In the following code block, we can see the base class for `Enemy`:

```
public class Enemy : MonoBehaviour
{
    public virtual void Move()
    {// Basic movement logic for all enemies
    }
    public virtual void Attack()
    {// Basic attack logic for all enemies
    }
}
```

In the following code block, we can see the subclass for `GroundEnemy`:

```
public class GroundEnemy : Enemy
{
    public override void Move()
    {// Specific movement logic for ground enemies
    }

    public override void Attack()
    {// Specific attack logic for ground enemies
    }
}
```

In the following code block, we can see the subclass for `FlyingEnemy`:

```csharp
public class FlyingEnemy : Enemy
{
    public override void Move()
    {// Specific movement logic for flying enemies
    }

    public override void Attack()
    {// Specific attack logic for flying enemies
    }
}
```

In the following code block, we can see the `EnemyManager` class demonstrating the LSP:

```csharp
public class EnemyManager : MonoBehaviour
{
    void Start()
    {
        // Creating instances of GroundEnemy and FlyingEnemy
        Enemy groundEnemy = new GroundEnemy();
        Enemy flyingEnemy = new FlyingEnemy();

        // Using LSP, treating both enemies as base class
        groundEnemy.Move();
        groundEnemy.Attack();

        flyingEnemy.Move();
        flyingEnemy.Attack();
    }
}
```

In this Unity example, the `Enemy` class acts as the base class with basic movement and attack methods. The `GroundEnemy` and `FlyingEnemy` subclasses extend the base class and provide specific implementations for movement and attack. The EnemyManager class demonstrates the LSP by treating instances of both subclasses as instances of the base class, ensuring that code written to work with enemies functions seamlessly with both `GroundEnemy` and `FlyingEnemy` instances.

What is the difference between the LSP and OCP?

In game development, the key difference between the LSP and OCP lies in their focus and application.

The LSP ensures that derived classes can be seamlessly substituted for their base class without affecting program behavior. In a game, this means different types of enemies (e.g., ground and flying enemies) should be interchangeable without breaking the expected functionality.

The OCP encourages designing classes that are open for extension but closed for modification. In game development, this allows adding new features (e.g., new types of weapons) without altering existing code, promoting flexibility and maintainability.

To better illustrate their difference, here's an example. In a game system, consider a base class for weapons. Adhering to the LSP allows substituting specific weapon types without disrupting expected behaviors, while following the OCP enables extending the system to add new weapons without modifying existing code.

Interface Segregation Principle (ISP)

Now, let's talk about the **Interface Segregation Principle** (ISP) in the gaming world. The ISP suggests that a class shouldn't be required to do things it doesn't need to. Simply put, it encourages creating small, task-specific interfaces instead of big, general ones. In the context of game development, this means designing interfaces that suit each class's specific needs. This helps keep things clear, makes the code more focused, and allows for easier upkeep and changes in game development.

Let's see an example of the NPC interfaces dilemma.

Imagine you have NPCs in your game, each with various functionalities, such as wandering, talking, and trading. Applying the ISP ensures that each NPC only needs to implement interfaces relevant to its specific behaviors, avoiding unnecessary methods.

Without the ISP, in the following code block, we can see the INPC interface, which has general methods for all NPCs, with the FriendlyNPC and AggressiveNPC classes, which implement INPC:

```
public interface INPC
{
    void Wander();
    void Talk();
    void Trade();
}
public class FriendlyNPC : INPC
{
    public void Wander() { /* Implementation */ }
    public void Talk() { /* Implementation */ }
    public void Trade() { /* Implementation */ }
}

public class AggressiveNPC : INPC
{
    // Unnecessary implementations for Wander and Trade
    public void Wander() { /* Unnecessary Implementation */ }
    public void Talk() { /* Implementation */ }
    public void Trade() { /* Unnecessary Implementation */ }
}
```

With the ISP, in the following code block, we will separate interfaces based on functionality, with the `FriendlyNPC` and `AggressiveNPC` classes, which implement relevant interfaces:

```
public interface IWanderable
{
    void Wander();
}

public interface ITalkable
{
    void Talk();
}

public interface ITradable
{
    void Trade();
}

public class FriendlyNPC : IWanderable, ITalkable, ITradable
{
    public void Wander() { /* Implementation */ }
    public void Talk() { /* Implementation */ }
    public void Trade() { /* Implementation */ }
}

public class AggressiveNPC : ITalkable
{
    public void Talk() { /* Implementation */ }
}
```

In this adapted example, applying the ISP leads to separate interfaces for distinct NPC functionalities. Each NPC type (friendly or aggressive) can now implement only the interfaces relevant to its behavior, avoiding the implementation of unnecessary methods. This makes the system more modular and adaptable as different NPC types can adhere to their specific interfaces without being burdened by irrelevant methods.

Dependency Inversion Principle (DIP)

Let's discuss the **Dependency Inversion Principle (DIP)** in the context of game development. The DIP suggests that high-level modules (e.g., game logic) should not depend on low-level modules (e.g., specific implementations), but both should depend on abstractions (e.g., interfaces or abstract classes). Additionally, it promotes that details should depend on abstractions, not the other way around.

Let us see an example of the weapon manager dilemma.

Consider a game where the `WeaponManager` is responsible for handling different types of weapons wielded by the player. Without adhering to the DIP, the `WeaponManager` might directly instantiate and manage specific weapon classes, such as pistols and rifles. However, applying the DIP transforms the scenario. Now, the `WeaponManager` relies on an abstraction, say `IWeapon`, representing the common functionalities of all weapons.

In the following code block, we can see the high-level module and also the low-level modules *without the DIP*:

```
public class WeaponManager
{
    private Pistol pistol;
    private Rifle rifle;

    public WeaponManager()
    {
        pistol = new Pistol();
        rifle = new Rifle();
    }

    public void UseWeapons()
    {
        pistol.Fire();
        rifle.Fire();
    }
}

public class Pistol
{
    public void Fire() { /* Implementation */ }
}

public class Rifle
{
    public void Fire() { /* Implementation */ }
}
```

With the DIP, in the following code block, we can see the high-level module and low-level modules implementing the abstraction:

```
public interface IWeapon
{
    void Fire();
}
```

```csharp
public class WeaponManager
{
    private readonly List<IWeapon> weapons;

    public WeaponManager(List<IWeapon> weapons)
    {
        this.weapons = weapons;
    }

    public void UseWeapons()
    {
        foreach (var weapon in weapons)
        {
            weapon.Fire();
        }
    }
}


public class Pistol : IWeapon
{
    public void Fire() { /* Implementation */ }
}

public class Rifle : IWeapon
{
    public void Fire() { /* Implementation */ }
}
```

In this example, applying the DIP allows `WeaponManager` to depend on the abstraction (`IWeapon`), enabling easy extension with new weapon types without modifying the high-level module. This flexibility is crucial in game development, where new features and components may be added over time without disrupting existing code.

Implementing the SOLID principles in Unity is instrumental in achieving modular C# code, a crucial aspect of effective software design. Modularity, which involves breaking down a system into self-contained components, is facilitated by the SOLID principles, making the code not only easy to understand, maintain, and test but also adherent to the LSP.

Modularity's significance lies in its ability to enhance code organization. Applying the SRP ensures that each module has a single responsibility, fostering a focused and modular code base. The OCP supports extending code without changing existing modules, allowing the seamless addition of new features. The LSP ensures that derived classes can substitute their base classes without affecting program behavior, promoting consistency and predictability in Unity code.

In Unity development, effective code organization involves using namespaces and classes thoughtfully. The ISP tailors interfaces to specific functionalities, promoting a concise and modular design. **Dependency Injection** (**DI**), advocated by the DIP, creates loosely coupled modules, enhancing adaptability. In summary, the SOLID principles, including the LSP, guide the creation of modular and flexible C# code in Unity, ensuring a robust, maintainable, and consistent code base. In the following section, we'll explore design patterns in game development and learn how to implement them effectively in our code base.

Understanding design patterns in game development

Design patterns are proven solutions to common problems encountered in software development. In game development, they provide valuable tools for building robust, maintainable, and efficient games. The following section has an overview of design patterns and their types.

There are many design patterns, each applicable to specific situations. Here are some common types encountered in game development.

Creational patterns

Creational patterns are design patterns that provide structured approaches to object creation, ensuring flexibility and reusability while maintaining a clear separation between object creation and usage code. Here are some of these patterns:

- **Singleton**: Ensures only one instance of a class exists throughout the game. Useful for global objects such as game managers or audio players.
- **Factory Method**: Creates objects without specifying the exact class, promoting flexibility and code reuse.
- **Object Pool**: Pre-allocates and reuses objects to improve performance, especially for frequently created objects such as projectiles or enemies.

Structural patterns

Structural patterns focus on organizing classes and objects to form larger structures, enabling better composition and flexibility in managing complex relationships between entities within a system. Here are some of these patterns:

- **Flyweight**: Makes incompatible interfaces work together by translating calls between them. Useful for integrating external libraries or custom code.
- **Decorator**: Adds functionality to an object dynamically without subclassing it, promoting flexible object behavior.

Behavioral patterns

Behavioral patterns address communication and interaction between objects in a system, focusing on how objects collaborate and distribute responsibilities to achieve desired behaviors and functionalities. These patterns help manage algorithms, relationships, and responsibilities among objects to promote flexibility and extensibility in software design. Here are some of these patterns:

- **Observer**: Allows objects to subscribe to and be notified about changes in other objects, facilitating communication and event handling.
- **Strategy**: Defines a family of algorithms and encapsulates them to allow switching between them at runtime. Useful for handling different player actions or enemy behaviors.
- **State**: Encapsulates the behavior of an object based on its internal state, allowing for state-dependent behavior changes. Useful for handling character states such as walking, jumping, or attacking.

In the next few sections, we are going to talk about one design pattern from each type.

Singleton design pattern

The Singleton pattern ensures that a class has only one instance and provides a global point of access to that instance throughout the application. *Figure 2.1* illustrates the Singleton structure:

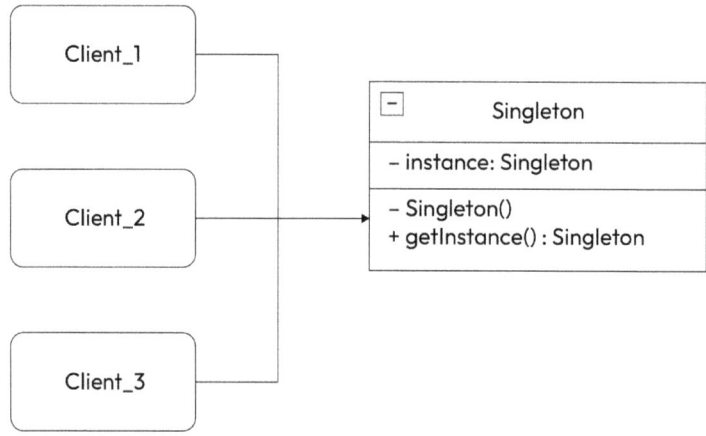

Figure 2.1 – Singleton design pattern structure

In the following code block, you can see an implementation example of Singleton in Unity:

```
public class GameManager : MonoBehaviour
{
```

```
    // Static reference to the instance
    private static GameManager _instance;

    // Public property to access the instance
    public static GameManager Instance
    {
        get
        {
            if (_instance == null)
            {
                // If the instance is null, create a new instance
                _instance = new GameObject("GameManager").
AddComponent<GameManager>();
            }
            return _instance;
        }
    }

    // Other GameManager properties and methods
    public void StartGame()
    {
        Debug.Log("Game Started!");
    }
}
```

In the following code block, we can see a usage example for the Singleton pattern:

```
public class PlayerController : MonoBehaviour
{
    private void Start()
    {
        // Accessing the GameManager instance
        GameManager.Instance.StartGame();
    }
}
```

In this example, `GameManager` is a Singleton responsible for managing the game state. The `PlayerController` class accesses the single instance to start the game. While Singletons offers global access and lazy initialization benefits, developers should carefully consider the potential drawbacks, especially in larger projects.

The following are some of the pros of using the Singleton pattern:

- **Global access**: Provides a single, globally accessible point to manage and control a specific aspect of the game, such as game state or settings
- **Lazy initialization**: The instance is created only when it is first needed, saving resources until it's required
- **Easy to implement**: The Singleton pattern is straightforward to implement and widely recognized, making it easy for developers to understand and use

The following are some of the cons of using the Singleton pattern:

- **Global state**: Singletons introduce a global state, and excessive use can lead to tight coupling and a global state that is challenging to manage
- **Potential for misuse**: Developers might overuse Singletons, leading to a proliferation of global instances, diminishing the benefits of encapsulation
- **Difficult to test**: Testing code that depends on Singletons can be challenging, as the global state may impact the results of unit tests

There is a principle, though, that exists to solve the singleton problem, and it's called dependency injection.

DI is a design pattern that addresses the concerns associated with tight coupling and global state by providing objects with their dependencies rather than letting them create those dependencies. In Unity, this is often achieved through constructor injection or property injection.

The following are the benefits of DI:

- **Reduced coupling**: By injecting dependencies, classes become less dependent on specific implementations, reducing tight coupling
- **Testability**: Classes with injected dependencies are often easier to test because you can provide mock or test implementations for those dependencies
- **Flexibility**: Different implementations of a dependency can be injected, enabling easy swapping of components without modifying existing code

DI can help mitigate some of the issues associated with the Singleton pattern in the following ways:

- **Reduced global state**: By injecting dependencies, you can avoid creating global singletons, reducing the overall global state in your application
- **Easier testing**: Code relying on injected dependencies is generally easier to test because you can replace real implementations with mock objects or test-specific instances
- **Improved modularity**: DI encourages a modular design where components are loosely coupled, making it easier to understand and maintain the code base

The Singleton design pattern provides a single, globally accessible instance of a class, offering convenience but potentially leading to issues such as tight coupling and difficulty in testing. DI addresses these concerns by allowing objects to be provided with their dependencies externally, reducing reliance on a global state. This promotes loose coupling, enhances testability, and improves code maintainability by decoupling components and facilitating the easier management of object life cycles.

Flyweight design pattern

The Flyweight pattern in Unity offers a solution for optimizing memory usage by sharing common data across multiple objects. It allows you to efficiently manage resources by storing shared data externally and referencing it when needed. *Figure 2.2* illustrates Flyweight's structure:

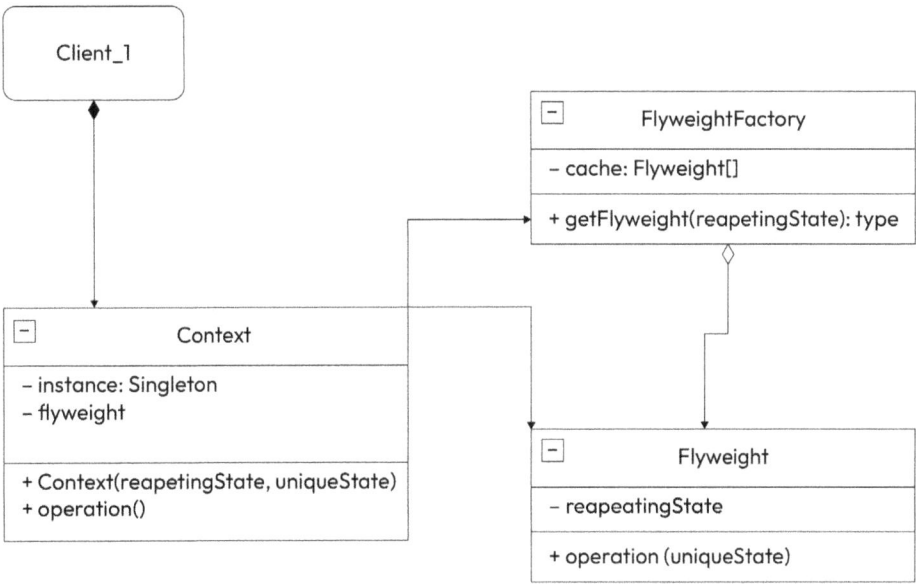

Figure 2.2 – Flyweight design pattern structure

In the following code blocks, you'll see an example scenario where the Flyweight pattern can be applied.

The `IWeapon` interface represents the shared properties and behaviors of weapons:

```
// Flyweight interface for weapons
public interface IWeapon
{
    void Fire();
}
```

The `Weapon` class implements the `IWeapon` interface and acts as a concrete Flyweight class representing individual weapons:

```
// Concrete flyweight class for shared weapon properties
public class Weapon : IWeapon
{
    private string name;
    private int damage;
    private string sound;

    public Weapon(string name, int damage, string sound)
    {
        this.name = name;
        this.damage = damage;
        this.sound = sound;
    }

    public void Fire()
    {
        Debug.Log($"{name} fired - Damage: {damage} - Sound: {sound}");
    }
}
```

The `WeaponFactory` class acts as a Flyweight factory, managing and reusing flyweight objects based on specific keys (e.g., weapon types):

```
// Flyweight factory class to manage and reuse flyweight objects
public class WeaponFactory
{
    private Dictionary<string, IWeapon> weapons;

    public WeaponFactory()
    {
        weapons = new Dictionary<string, IWeapon>();
    }

    public IWeapon GetWeapon(string key)
    {
        if (!weapons.ContainsKey(key))
        {
            switch (key)
            {
                case "pistol":
```

```
                    weapons[key] = new Weapon("Pistol", 30, "Bang!");
                    break;
                case "shotgun":
                    weapons[key] = new Weapon("Shotgun", 50, "Boom!");
                    break;
                case "rifle":
                    weapons[key] = new Weapon("Rifle", 40, "Pew
 Pew!");
                    break;
                default:
                    throw new ArgumentException("Invalid weapon key");
            }
        }
        return weapons[key];
    }
}
```

The `GameClient` class demonstrates how to use the flyweight objects retrieved from the factory, showcasing the reusability and memory efficiency of the Flyweight pattern:

```
public class GameClient : MonoBehaviour
{
    void Start()
    {
        WeaponFactory weaponFactory = new WeaponFactory();

        // Using flyweight objects
        IWeapon pistol = weaponFactory.GetWeapon("pistol");
        pistol.Fire();

        IWeapon shotgun = weaponFactory.GetWeapon("shotgun");
        shotgun.Fire();

        IWeapon rifle = weaponFactory.GetWeapon("rifle");
        rifle.Fire();

        // Reusing flyweight objects
        IWeapon anotherPistol = weaponFactory.GetWeapon("pistol");
        anotherPistol.Fire();
    }
}
```

This example simulates a game scenario where different types of weapons are represented as flyweight objects, and the factory efficiently manages these shared objects to optimize memory usage and improve performance.

The following are the pros of using the Flyweight pattern:

- **Memory optimization**: By sharing common data, the pattern reduces memory consumption, especially for large numbers of similar objects
- **Improved performance**: Sharing reduces the overhead of creating and managing redundant data, leading to better performance
- **Simplified code**: Separating shared and unique data promotes cleaner and more maintainable code

The following are the cons of using the Flyweight pattern:

- **Complexity**: Implementing the Flyweight pattern introduces additional complexity, especially when managing shared and unique states
- **Potential overhead**: While the pattern improves memory and performance, it may introduce overhead due to managing shared resources

Despite these considerations, the Flyweight pattern remains a valuable tool for efficient resource management in Unity projects, particularly in scenarios with many similar objects requiring memory optimization.

Observer design pattern

The Observer pattern in Unity promotes loose coupling between objects by allowing them to subscribe to events and receive notifications when those events occur. This way, objects can react to changes without needing to know the specific details of the object raising the event.

Figure 2.3 illustrates Observer's structure.

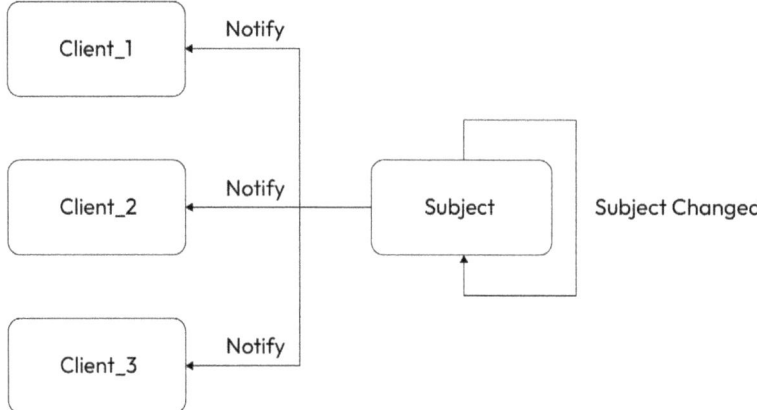

Figure 2.3 – Observer design pattern structure

Let's create a simple example in Unity to demonstrate the implementation of a health system using the Observer pattern.

In the following code block, we can see the `IHealthObserver` Observer interface and the `IHealthSubject` subject interface:

```
// Observer interface
public interface IHealthObserver
{
    void OnHealthChanged(int health);
}

// Subject interface
public interface IHealthSubject
{
    event Action<int> OnHealthChanged;
}
```

In the following code block, we can see the `HealthManager` class implementing `IHealthSubject`:

```
public class HealthManager : MonoBehaviour, IHealthSubject
{
    private int currentHealth;
    public int MaxHealth { get; private set; } = 100;

    // Event to notify observers when health changes
    public event Action<int> OnHealthChanged;

    private void Start()
    {
        currentHealth = MaxHealth;
    }

    // Method to damage the character
    public void TakeDamage(int damage)
    {
        currentHealth -= damage;
        currentHealth = Mathf.Clamp(currentHealth, 0, MaxHealth);

        // Notify observers about the health change
        OnHealthChanged?.Invoke(currentHealth);

        // Check for death condition
        if (currentHealth == 0)
```

```
        {
            Debug.Log("Character has died!");
            // Additional logic for character death...
        }
    }
}
```

In the following code block, we can see the `UIObserver` class implementing `IHealthObserver`:

```
public class UIObserver : MonoBehaviour, IHealthObserver
{
    public void OnHealthChanged(int health)
    {
        // Update UI elements based on the received health value
        Debug.Log($"Health UI Updated: {health}");
        // Additional UI update logic...
    }
}
```

In the following code block, we can see the `GameplayObserver` class implementing `IHealthObserver`:

```
public class GameplayObserver : MonoBehaviour, IHealthObserver
{
    public void OnHealthChanged(int health)
    {
        // Update gameplay mechanics based on the received health value
        Debug.Log($"Gameplay Updated: {health}");
        // Additional gameplay update logic...
    }
}
```

In the following code block, we can see a usage example for the Observer pattern in Unity:

```
public class GameExample : MonoBehaviour
{
    private void Start()
    {
        HealthManager healthManager = new HealthManager();
        UIObserver uiObserver = new UIObserver();
        GameplayObserver gameplayObserver = new GameplayObserver();

        // Register observers with the HealthManager
```

```
        healthManager.OnHealthChanged += uiObserver.OnHealthChanged;
        healthManager.OnHealthChanged += gameplayObserver.
OnHealthChanged;

        // Simulate damage to the character
        healthManager.TakeDamage(20);
    }
}
```

In this example, the `HealthManager` class represents the subject, and the `UIObserver` and `GameplayObserver` classes represent observers. When the character takes damage, `HealthManager` triggers the `OnHealthChanged` event, notifying all registered observers. Each observer then updates its state based on the received health value, demonstrating the Observer pattern in action.

The following are the pros of using the Observer pattern:

- **Improved decoupling**: Objects are not dependent on each other's implementation details, promoting loose coupling and modularity
- **Enhanced maintainability**: Code becomes easier to understand and modify because event handling is centralized and observers are decoupled
- **Increased flexibility**: Allows for the dynamic addition and removal of observers, making the system more adaptable to changing requirements

The following are the cons of using the Observer pattern:

- **Increased complexity**: Introduces additional abstraction layers compared to direct communication, which can slightly increase code complexity
- **Performance overhead**: Event handling involves method calls and potentially data transfer, which can lead to some performance overhead

Overall, the Observer pattern is a powerful tool for facilitating communication between objects and managing dynamic changes in Unity. The benefits of loose coupling and flexibility outweigh the drawbacks in most situations involving event-driven behavior.

Additionally, here are some other applications of the Observer pattern in Unity:

- Implementing state machines for characters and enemies
- Updating UI elements based on changes in game state (e.g., score, level, and inventory)
- Triggering animations or sound effects based on specific events in the game

Remember, you can find all the examples on GitHub for reference.

It's not mandatory to use these patterns in all your code. They serve as solutions to common problems, but sometimes, implementing patterns might complicate things unnecessarily. The key is to focus on solving the problem at hand first and then look for the best solution. In the following section, we will delve into coding conventions and explore best practices for writing clear code.

Coding conventions and best practices

Maintaining consistent and clear code is essential for effective development and collaboration. Adhering to recognized conventions and best practices enhances code clarity, maintainability, and readability. Here's a breakdown of key aspects of C# coding:

C# naming conventions: Understanding and implementing C# naming conventions is pivotal for maintaining code consistency and clarity. Let's delve into best practices for naming variables, methods, classes, and namespaces to ensure our code is both readable and expressive:

- **Variables**: Adopt **camelCase** (e.g., `playerScore`, `enemyHealth`) and opt for descriptive names conveying the variable's purpose (e.g., `currentLevel`, `isGameOver`). Avoid abbreviations unless widely understood (e.g., fps for frames per second).
- **Methods**: Utilize **PascalCase** (e.g., `StartGame`, `MovePlayer`) and ensure the method name precisely reflects its functionality. Use verbs for action-oriented methods (e.g., `CalculateDamage`, `LoadLevel`).
- **Classes**: Employ PascalCase for class names (e.g., `Player`, `EnemyController`) and avoid generic names such as `MyClass` or `NewClass`. Choose descriptive names representing the class's purpose.
- **Namespaces**: Apply PascalCase for namespaces (e.g., `MyGame.Characters`, `Utility.Math`) and organize code into meaningful hierarchical namespaces.
- **Meaningful and descriptive names**: Crafting meaningful and descriptive names is fundamental to writing clear and understandable code. Let's explore guidelines for selecting names that accurately convey the purpose and type of variables, avoiding ambiguity and enhancing code readability:
  - Choose names that accurately reflect the represented entity.
  - Avoid ambiguous names such as `temp` or `data`.
  - Use prefixes and suffixes to clarify variable types (e.g., `isJumping`, `playerPosition`).
- **Code formatting**: Mastering code formatting is a fundamental aspect of writing clean and organized code. Let's explore key elements such as indentation, spacing, and comments to enhance readability and structure in your programming endeavors:
  - **Indentation**: Employ consistent indentation for enhanced readability and structure
  - **Spacing**: Introduce appropriate spacing around operators, keywords, and parentheses

- **Comments**: Include comments to elucidate complex logic, clarify algorithms, and document code functionality

• **Error handling and exception management**: Error handling and exception management are critical aspects of software development, ensuring robustness and reliability in handling unexpected scenarios. Let's delve into effective strategies, such as using `try-catch` blocks and providing meaningful feedback, to manage errors gracefully and enhance user experience:

  - Implement robust error handling for graceful management of unexpected situations
  - Use `try-catch` blocks to capture exceptions and provide meaningful user feedback
  - Avoid ignoring errors to prevent unpredictable behavior

• **Method and class length**: When it comes to method and class length, maintaining a balance between conciseness and clarity is paramount to fostering maintainable code bases. Let's explore strategies for keeping methods and classes concise while ensuring they remain focused and easy to understand, promoting code readability and maintainability:

  - Strive for concise and focused methods and classes
  - Steer clear of "monolithic classes" handling everything, making them challenging to understand and maintain
  - Extract complex functionality into separate methods for clarity and reusability

• **Additional best practices**: In pursuit of robust and maintainable code, embracing additional best practices beyond the fundamentals is essential. Let's delve into strategies:

  - Employ meaningful constants instead of magic numbers
  - Minimize the use of global variables
  - Avoid deeply nested code and excessive indentation

Embarking on a journey through essential coding conventions and best practices, we explored fundamental aspects such as C# naming conventions, where clarity and consistency reign supreme. We discussed the nuances of meaningful and descriptive names, mastering the art of code formatting, navigating error handling and exception management, and optimizing method and class length, as well as discovered additional best practices to refine your code base for robustness and clarity.

Let's explore some refactoring techniques with examples.

Refactoring techniques

Refactoring techniques involve breaking down long and complex methods into smaller, focused functions and eliminating duplicated code to adhere to principles such as **Don't Repeat Yourself** (**DRY**) and **Keep It Simple, Stupid** (**KISS**), ultimately resulting in cleaner and more maintainable Unity projects.

Let's look at a couple of examples of code smells in Unity projects that may indicate a need for refactoring.

Example 1: Long and complex method

In the following code block, we can see that the `PlayerController` class has a long method:

```
public class PlayerController : MonoBehaviour
{
    public void HandlePlayerInput()
    {
        // ... (code for handling input)

        if (isMoving)
        {
            // ... (code for player movement)
        }

        if (isShooting)
        {
            // ... (code for shooting logic)
        }

        // ... (more complex logic)

        if (isJumping)
        {
            // ... (code for jumping)
        }

        // ... (more code)

        if (isDucking)
        {
            // ... (code for ducking)
        }

        // ... (more code)

        if (isInteracting)
        {
            // ... (code for interacting with objects)
        }

        // ... (even more code)
```

        }
}

The code smell here is the `HandlePlayerInput` method is lengthy and handles multiple tasks, making it hard to maintain. Refactor it into smaller, dedicated functions for specific player actions, such as movement, shooting, and jumping.

After refactoring, in the following code block, we can see the `PlayerController` class has methods for each piece of logic instead of a large method:

```
public class PlayerController : MonoBehaviour
{
    public void HandlePlayerInput()
    {
        HandleMovement();
        HandleShooting();
        HandleJumping();
        HandleDucking();
        HandleInteracting();
    }

    private void HandleMovement()
    {
        // ... (code for player movement)
    }

    private void HandleShooting()
    {
        // ... (code for shooting logic)
    }

    private void HandleJumping()
    {
        // ... (code for jumping)
    }

    private void HandleDucking()
    {
        // ... (code for ducking)
    }

    private void HandleInteracting()
    {
        // ... (code for interacting with objects)
```

        }
}

Example 2: Duplicated code

In the following code block, we can see the `EnemyAI` class has duplicated logic:

```
public class EnemyAI : MonoBehaviour
{
    public void AttackPlayer()
    {
        // ... (code for attacking player)
    }

    public void AttackAlly()
    {
        // ... (same code for attacking ally)
    }

    public void AttackBoss()
    {
        // ... (same code for attacking boss)
    }
}
```

The code smell here is that duplicated code for attacking the player, ally, and boss poses maintenance hurdles. Refactor by crafting a single method for attacking and invoking it with distinct parameters to eliminate redundancy.

After refactoring, in the following code block, we can see `EnemyAI` has common code for attacking:

```
public class EnemyAI : MonoBehaviour
{
    public void Attack(Entity target)
    {
        // ... (common code for attacking)
    }

    // Usage examples:
    // enemyAI.Attack(player);
    // enemyAI.Attack(ally);
    // enemyAI.Attack(boss);
}
```

These refactoring examples adhere to the DRY and KISS principles, resulting in cleaner and more maintainable Unity code. In the next couple of bullet points, we will take a look at the definitions of DRY and KISS:

- **DRY principle**: The DRY principle is a software development concept advocating for the avoidance of code duplication. It emphasizes that each piece of knowledge or logic within a system should have a single, unambiguous representation to reduce redundancy. By following DRY, developers aim to enhance maintainability, reduce the chance of errors, and improve code readability.
- **KISS principle**: The KISS principle suggests that simplicity should be a key goal in design and decision-making. It encourages developers to favor straightforward, uncomplicated solutions over complex ones. KISS asserts that simplicity often leads to better understandability, maintainability, and reduced chances of errors. The principle is a reminder to avoid unnecessary complexity when solving problems.

By identifying and addressing code smells in Unity projects, we ensure cleaner, more maintainable code. Through examples such as breaking down long methods and eliminating duplicated code, we adhere to principles such as DRY and KISS, resulting in improved code quality and readability.

Time to demonstrate your knowledge! Give these questions and challenges a try.

Questions

- What is the primary goal of writing clean code?
- Implement a singleton pattern for managing game settings such as sound volume, music volume, and screen resolution. Ensure that there is only one instance of the settings manager throughout the game.
- Create a singleton score manager that tracks the player's score across multiple game levels or scenes. Ensure that the score manager instance persists between scene changes.
- Implement a flyweight pattern using object pooling for bullets in a shooting game. The flyweight should efficiently manage the creation and reuse of bullet objects to minimize memory overhead during gameplay.
- Design a flyweight pattern for rendering a tile-based map in a 2D game. Optimize the rendering process by reusing flyweight tile objects for similar tile types, such as grass, water, and rocks.
- Develop an observer pattern-based event system for handling in-game events such as player deaths, power-up pickups, and level completions. Implement observers for different event types and ensure efficient event broadcasting.
- Create an observer pattern implementation to update UI elements dynamically based on game events. For example, update health bars, score displays, and inventory icons using observers for player health changes, score increments, and item pickups.

- Combine singleton, flyweight, and observer patterns to design a player character system. Use the singleton pattern for player input handling, flyweight for managing player animations efficiently, and observers for handling player state changes (e.g., health, inventory).
- Design a game system (e.g., inventory management, quest tracking) and choose the most suitable design patterns (singleton, flyweight, observer, etc.) to implement various aspects of the system. Justify your design decisions based on SOLID principles and scalability.

Summary

To wrap up this chapter, remember that writing neat and well-organized C# code is key for successful Unity game development. The skills you've gained, such as naming things sensibly and arranging code logically, will make your game creation journey smoother. Keeping things simple and avoiding repeated code make your work easier to grasp and maintain. Applying these ideas will lead to games with code that just makes sense, making you a more efficient and effective game developer. It's important to note that the journey toward clean code and best practices is ongoing. You don't have to apply all the principles in every project, but consistently incorporating them into your coding mindset will enhance your skills over time.

Now, gear up for the next chapter, where you'll explore Unity plugins. You will discover how to identify and evaluate various types of plugins, seamlessly integrating them into your projects. This knowledge will empower you to enhance game features, save development time, and implement new mechanics using C#. So, get ready for *Chapter 3*, where you'll broaden your Unity toolkit and elevate your game development skills.

Part 2: Advanced C# Game Development Techniques in Unity

In this part, you will explore various Unity plugins to enhance game functionality, integrate plugins seamlessly using C#, and enrich gameplay mechanics. You will analyze game mechanics, implement challenge systems, and create AI logic using C# for engaging gameplay experiences. You will also apply UI design principles using C# to craft visually appealing interfaces, ensuring optimal user experience and interaction within Unity games.

This part includes the following chapters:

- *Chapter 3, Extending Functionality with Unity Plugins*
- *Chapter 4, Implementing Engaging Game Mechanics Using C# in Unity*
- *Chapter 5, Designing Optimized User Interfaces with C# for Unity Games*

3
Extending Functionality with Unity Plugins

Welcome to *Chapter 3*, where we'll delve into the world of Unity plugins. We'll explore how to effectively integrate these plugins into your projects. This chapter aims to familiarize you with the different types of plugins available in the Unity ecosystem and guide you through the process of seamlessly incorporating them. By grasping the fundamentals of plugin integration, you'll be able to make the most of existing solutions, enhance your game features, and save valuable development time. Let's jump in and discover how Unity plugins can significantly boost your game development capabilities.

In this chapter, we're going to cover the following main topics:

- Understanding Unity plugins
- Integrating Unity plugins
- Best practices for using Unity plugins

Technical requirements

You will need the following to follow this chapter:

- **Unity version 2022.3.13**: Download and install Unity version 2022.3.13 or any other version. It is recommended to install the 2022 version.
- **Primary IDE – Visual Studio 2022**: Ensure Visual Studio 2022 is installed for optimal learning.
- **GitHub repository for code samples**: Access code samples and project files on our GitHub repository: `https://github.com/PacktPublishing/Mastering-Unity-Game-Development-with-C-Sharp/tree/main/Assets/Chapter%2003`. Clone or download the repository to have easy access to the code demonstrated in this chapter.

Understanding Unity plugins

In the world of game development, Unity plugins are like handy tools that developers can add to their toolkit. Think of them as special add-ons or extra features that make building games easier and more exciting.

Let's explore here how these optional upgrades can elevate your game development endeavors:

- **Boost to game development**: Unity plugins are essential tools in the world of game development. These compact bundles of code serve as valuable additions to Unity, acting much like specialized ingredients seamlessly integrated into your game. Crafted by fellow developers, these plugins are generously shared within the Unity community, offering benefits to all.

- **The significance of Unity plugins in game development**: The appeal of Unity plugins lies in their ability to enhance game development effortlessly. Picture this: you're constructing a game, and you envision characters with incredibly smooth movements or breathtaking special effects such as dazzling explosions. Instead of grappling with complex code to achieve these elements, Unity plugins provide a solution. They save time and effort by leveraging the expertise of skilled developers, allowing you to relish the outcomes.

- **Extending functionality – elevating games to new heights**: Extending functionality with plugins is akin to granting your game superpowers. It goes beyond the basics, allowing you to incorporate various features without delving into the complexities of starting from square one. It's like an upgrade for your game, making it more enjoyable and engaging.

Unity plugins play a vital role in the realm of game development, equipping developers with a toolbox to amplify the capabilities of Unity. It's crucial to discern between two main categories of plugins: core plugins and extra plugins. Core plugins, inherent to Unity, provide foundational functionalities right out of the box. On the flip side, extra plugins act as optional upgrades, allowing you to tailor your toolkit to suit the specific needs of your project. To better understand these distinctions, let's consider a comparison:

Plugin Type	Description
Core plugins	Pre-packaged with Unity, offering foundational functionalities
Extra plugins	Optional upgrades that can be chosen based on specific project requirements

In this chapter, we will prioritize additional plugins as they play a crucial role in enhancing the project, delving into how to seamlessly extend and integrate them into your projects. Our spotlight on the extra plugins falls on the **new Input System** and **Cinemachine** – as essential extra plugins, prominent choices for enhancing your game without delving into the core functionalities.

In the next section, we will start talking about installing the plugins and how to extend them using C# scripts.

Integrating Unity plugins

Let's delve into the seamless process of integrating external plugins into your Unity projects. Discover how this skill unlocks a world of possibilities, enhancing your game development experience with refined character movements, cinematic visual effects, and more. Dive in and elevate your projects.

We will start with the new Input System and how to use it for handling input for our character.

New Input System

Unity handles input through two systems: the older Input Manager, which is integrated into the editor, and the more recent Input System package. The aged Input Manager is an integral part of Unity's core, readily available if you choose not to install the Input System package. Offering a fresher perspective, the Input System package enables you to employ any input device to govern your Unity content, taking the place of Unity's traditional Input Manager. Installation of the new Input System package is a breeze – simply use the Package Manager. We will install it and use it in this section.

In the following table, we'll compare the old Input System with the new one, highlighting their key differences:

Feature	Old Input Manager	New Input System
Device support	Limited to keyboards, mice, and gamepads	Unified API for all devices
Input actions	Basic button and axis mappings	Complex actions with triggers and combinations
Architecture	Polling-based continuously checks input states at regular intervals, such as every frame, to detect changes and respond to user actions in real-time	Event-driven relies on triggering callbacks or events based on user actions, promoting modularity and efficient handling of input events without continuous polling
Performance	Can be sluggish	Efficient and responsive
Extensibility	Closed system	Open-source and extensible

Excited for more exploration? Look forward to the following section, where we'll delve into configuring the system, crafting personalized actions, and unlocking its full potential.

> **Note**
> Please be aware that the new Input System is compatible with Unity versions 2019.4 and above, and it necessitates the .NET 4 runtime. Projects utilizing the old .NET 3.5 runtime are not supported.

60 | Extending Functionality with Unity Plugins

In the following figure, you can choose **Input System** inside the **Package Manager** and install it:

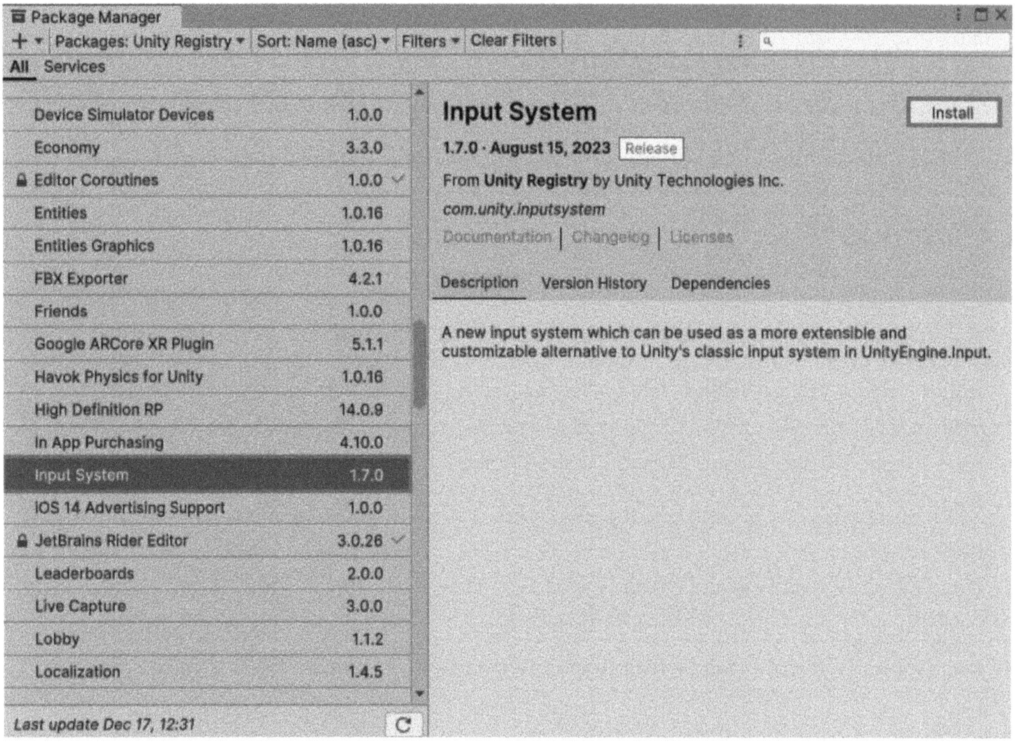

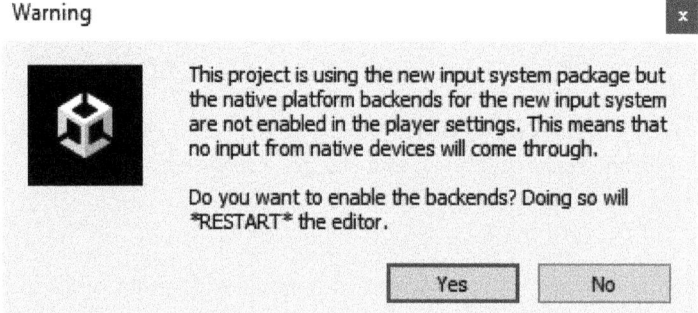

Figure 3.1 – Input System package inside Package Manager panel

After finishing the installation process, Unity will ask you if you want to enable the new backends. By choosing **Yes**, Unity will enable the new backends and disable the old backends, and the Unity Editor will restart. You can see a **Warning** message in the following figure:

Figure 3.2 – Warning message after installing the new Input System

Please take note that you have the option to simultaneously enable both the old and new systems. To accomplish this, set **Active Input Handling** to **Both**.

Locate the relevant setting in the **Player** settings (navigate to **Edit | Project Settings | Player**), specifically under **Active Input Handling**. Feel free to adjust this setting at your convenience; however, please note that making changes will necessitate restarting the Editor.

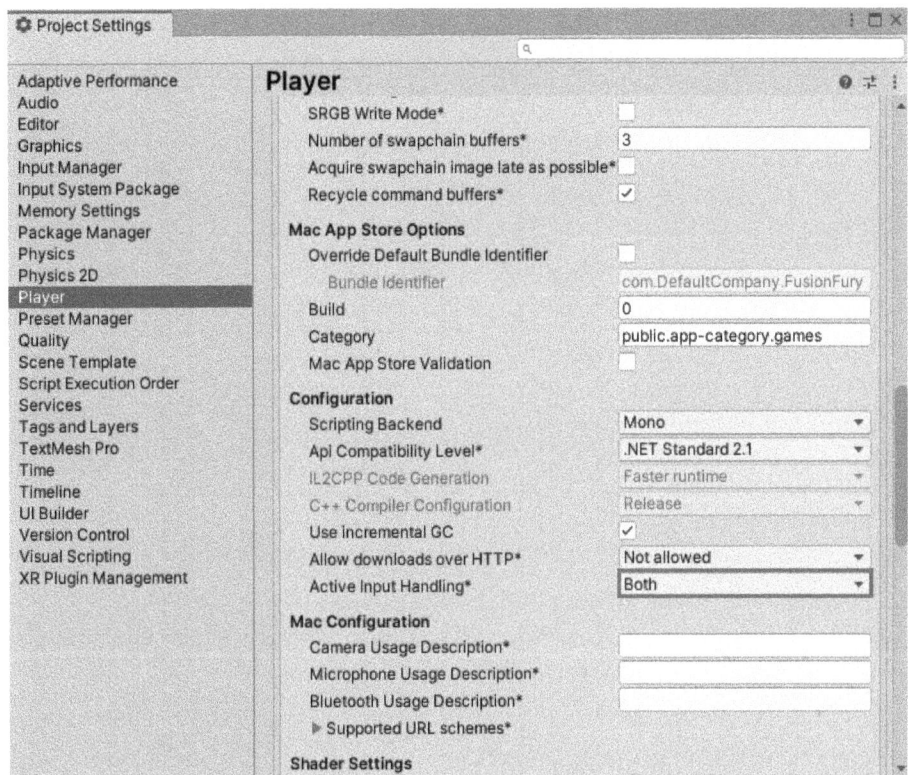

Figure 3.3 – Input settings inside the Project Settings

Now that we've been introduced to the new Input System, let's explore its implementation.

Implementing Unity's new Input System

In this subsection, our focus shifts to the practical application of Unity's new Input System. Get ready to dive into hands-on learning as we guide you through the step-by-step process of implementation. By the end of this section, you'll have the skills and knowledge needed to seamlessly integrate the new Input System into your Unity projects, enhancing control and responsiveness. Let's get hands-on and delve into the practical steps of implementing this powerful tool together.

In Unity's new Input System, `InputActions` are pivotal for defining and structuring input controls such as keyboard keys, mouse buttons, and controller inputs within an InputActionAsset. These actions are bound to specific input bindings and organized into logical groupings called **Action Maps**, facilitating modular and customizable input handling. The `PlayerInput` component integrates

InputActions into GameObjects, allowing for efficient input event handling through callbacks and events. InputActions support rebinding and overrides, empowering players to customize input bindings while maintaining a cohesive Input System architecture that enhances modularity and reusability compared to Unity's legacy Input System. Let's use the new Input System.

1. Create a new input action (**Create | Input Actions**) in the folder inside your project, as you can see in the next figure:

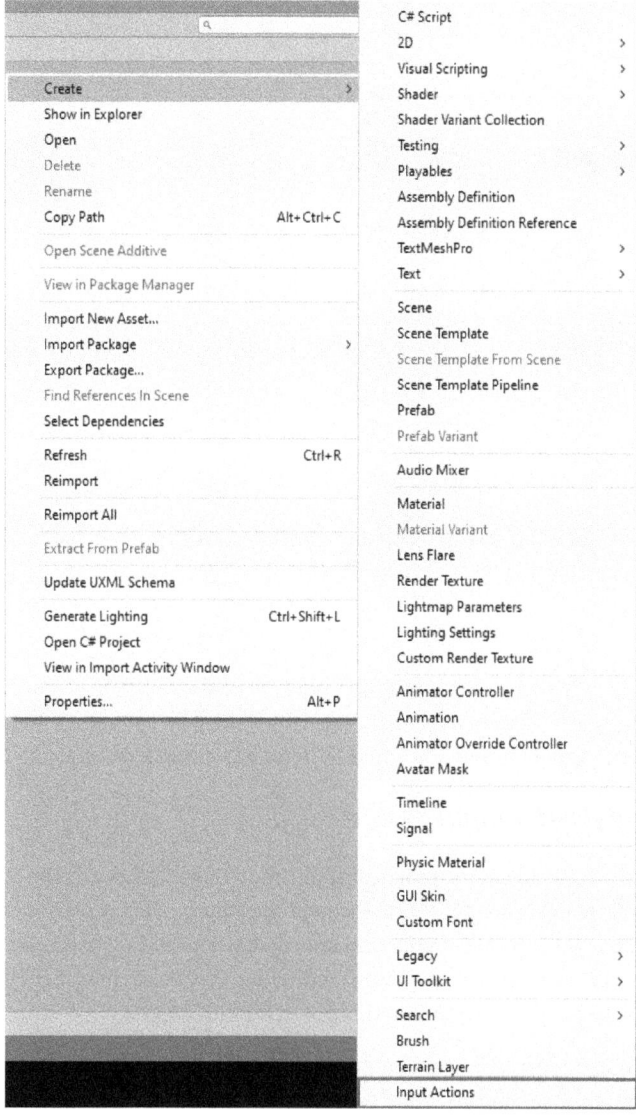

Figure 3.4 – Choosing Input Actions from the Create panel

Integrating Unity plugins   63

2. Then, you can open this input action, and a new panel will appear, as shown in the following figure:

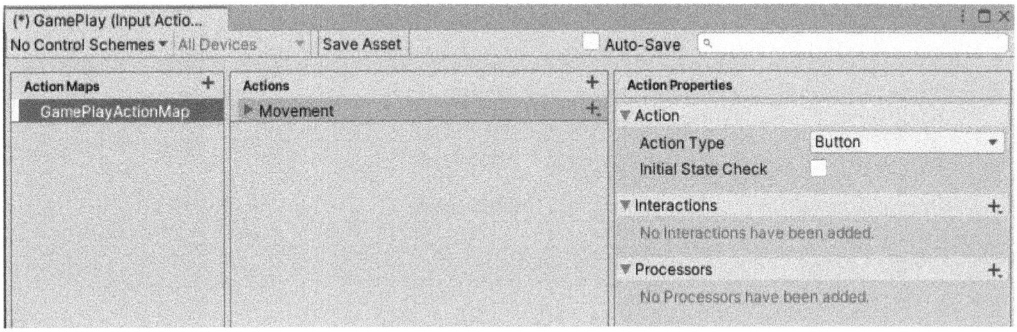

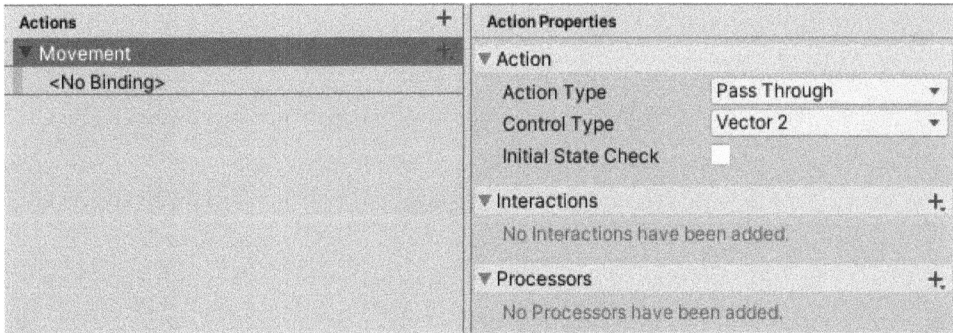

Figure 3.5 – Input Action panel

3. Change the **Action Type** value to **Pass Through** and **Control Type** to **Vector 2**, as you can see in the following figure:

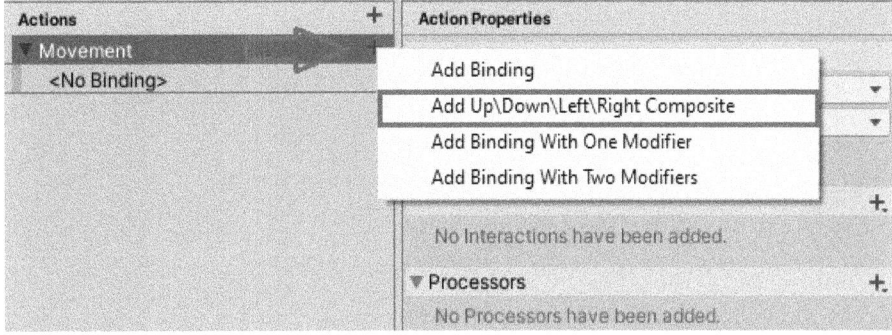

Figure 3.6 – Action Properties

4. Then, choose to add bindings for movement, as you can see in the next figure:

Figure 3.7 – Choosing bindings for movement

64   Extending Functionality with Unity Plugins

5. Here, you can rename the name of the movement binding. Also, you can start to set the input keys for each process in the **Path** dropdown, as you can see in the following figure:

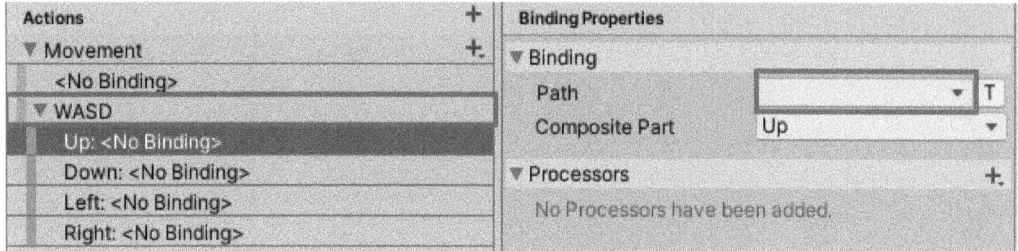

Figure 3.8 – Movement binding

6. The magic of the new Input System shines as you can assign multiple bindings for the same action across different devices, as demonstrated in the following figure:

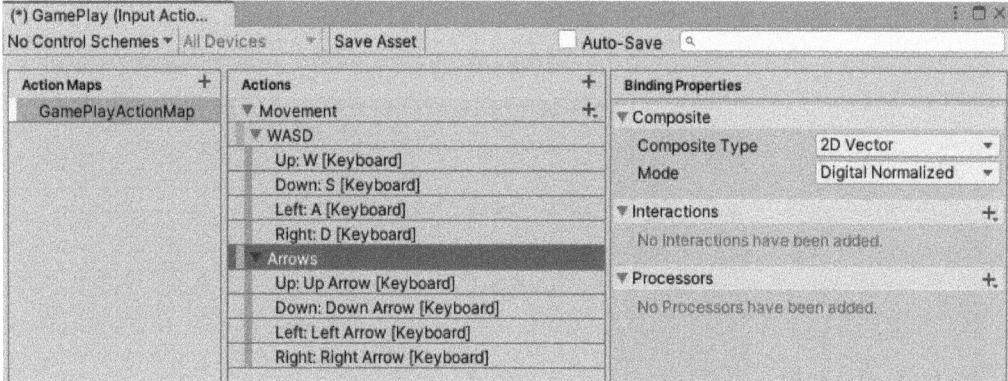

Figure 3.9 – Arrows bindings

7. You can also add new actions for **Jump** and **Dash**, but for them, you need to change the **Action Type** value to **Button**. Your final settings should look something like this:

Integrating Unity plugins 65

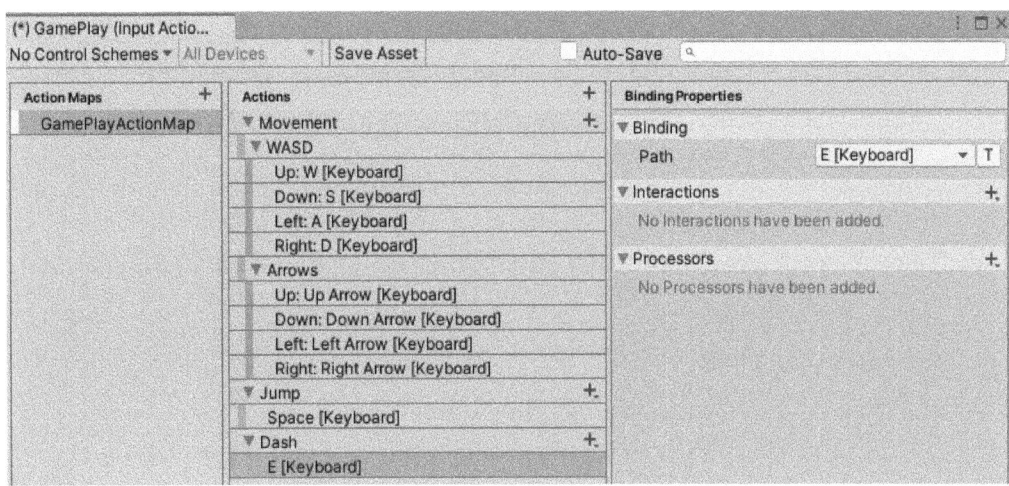

Figure 3.10 – Adding Jump and Dash

8. As the final step for this input action asset, you need to return to the input action in **Inspector** and choose **Generate C# Class** for it:

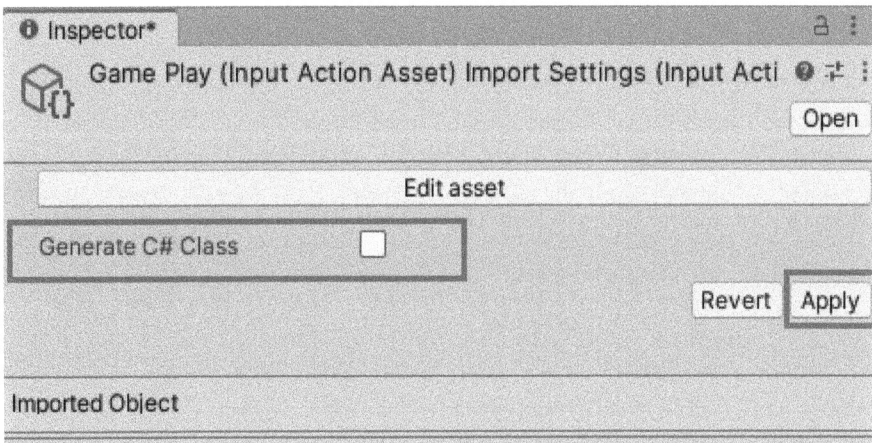

Figure 3.11 – Generating an input class

9. Then, we will create a wrapper script to take callbacks from the inputs and invoke new actions to perform movement:

We are going to create a wrapper for using the new Input System, starting with implementing gameplay map actions in our `PlayerInput` script as follows:

```
public class PlayerInput : MonoBehaviour , GamePlay.
IGamePlayMapActions
```

10. Also, we will register callbacks for this action and create events so that we can use them later in our `PlayerMovement` script, as you can see in the following code block:

```
private GamePlay gameplayControls;
public static UnityAction onJump = delegate { };
public static UnityAction onDash = delegate { };
public static UnityAction<Vector2> onMovement = delegate { };

    private void OnEnable()
    {
        if (gameplayControls == null)
        {
            gameplayControls = new GamePlay();
            gameplayControls.GamePlayMap.SetCallbacks(this);
        }
        gameplayControls.GamePlayMap.Enable();
    }


    private void OnDisable()
    {
        gameplayControls.GamePlayMap.Disable();
    }
```

11. Now, magic happens here. When we get the action callback and then invoke our events, we will subscribe to these events in the `PlayerMovement` script, as you can see in the following code block:

```
public class PlayerMovement : MonoBehaviour
    {
        private void OnEnable()
        {
            PlayerInput.onJump += Jump;
            PlayerInput.onDash += Dash;
            PlayerInput.onMovement += MovementInput;
        }

        private void OnDisable()
        {
            PlayerInput.onJump -= Jump;
            PlayerInput.onDash -= Dash;
            PlayerInput.onMovement -= MovementInput;
        }
```

Here are the functions for movement in the `PlayerMovement` script:

```
private void MovementInput(Vector2 input)
    {
        movementVector = input;
    }

    private void MovePlayer()
    {
        Vector3 movement = new Vector3(movementVector.x , 0f
, movementVector.y) * moveSpeed * Time.deltaTime;
        transform.Translate(movement);
    }

    private void Jump()
    {
        if (isGrounded)
        {
            playerRigidbody.AddForce(Vector3.up * jumpForce,
ForceMode.Impulse);
            isGrounded = false;
        }
    }

    private void Dash()
    {
        if (canDash)
        {
            Vector3 dashVector = new
Vector3(movementVector.x, 0f, movementVector.y).normalized;
            playerRigidbody.AddForce(dashVector * dashForce,
ForceMode.Impulse);

            canDash = false;
            Invoke(nameof(ResetDash), dashCooldown);
        }
    }


    private void FixedUpdate()
    {
        MovePlayer();
        CheckGrounded();
    }
```

```
            private void CheckGrounded()
            {
                isGrounded = Physics.Raycast(groundChecker.position,
    Vector3.down, groundDistance, groundLayer);
            }

            private void ResetDash()
            {
                canDash = true;
            }
```

Voilà! The new Input System is now employed for player movement.

Discussing advanced techniques

In the upcoming section, we are going to talk about more advanced techniques for the new Input System. Let's explore Unity's Input System features by looking at Interactions and Processors, which help adjust input signals before they activate actions:

- **Interactions**: Interactions modify or filter the raw input signal before reaching the action. Unity's Input System provides a variety of built-in Interactions, such as **Tap**, **Slow Tap**, and **Press**, each serving specific use cases. For example, we can utilize **Multi Tap** for double jumps or activating special powers, while **Press** can help solve parts of puzzles in the game.

  In the following figure, you can find a list of Interactions to be applied:

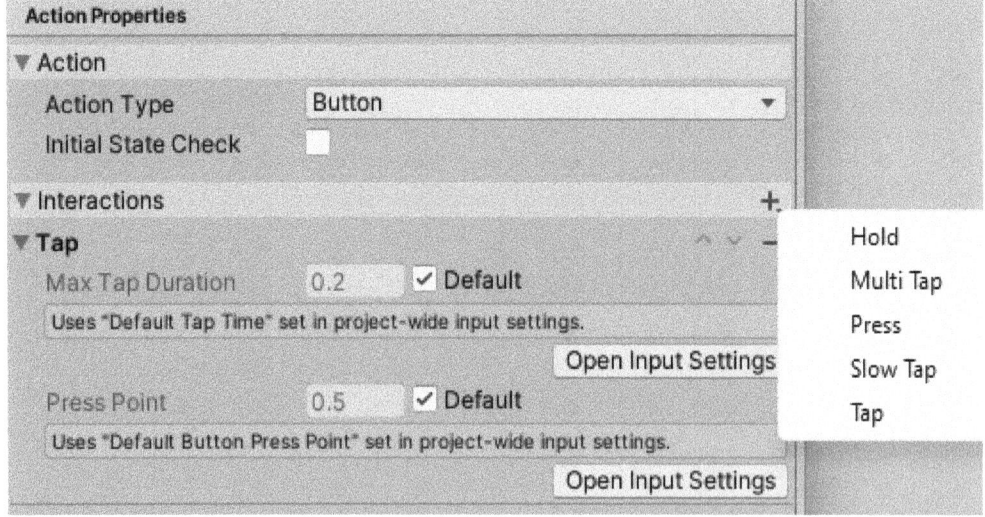

Figure 3.12 – Interactions

- **Processors**: Processors are applied to the input data after the Interaction but before the action triggers. They allow you to manipulate the input data, such as scaling, inverting, or smoothing analog values. Processors contribute to the fine-tuning of input behavior; you can apply them on controls, bindings, and actions.

In the following figure, you will find a list of Processors to be applied:

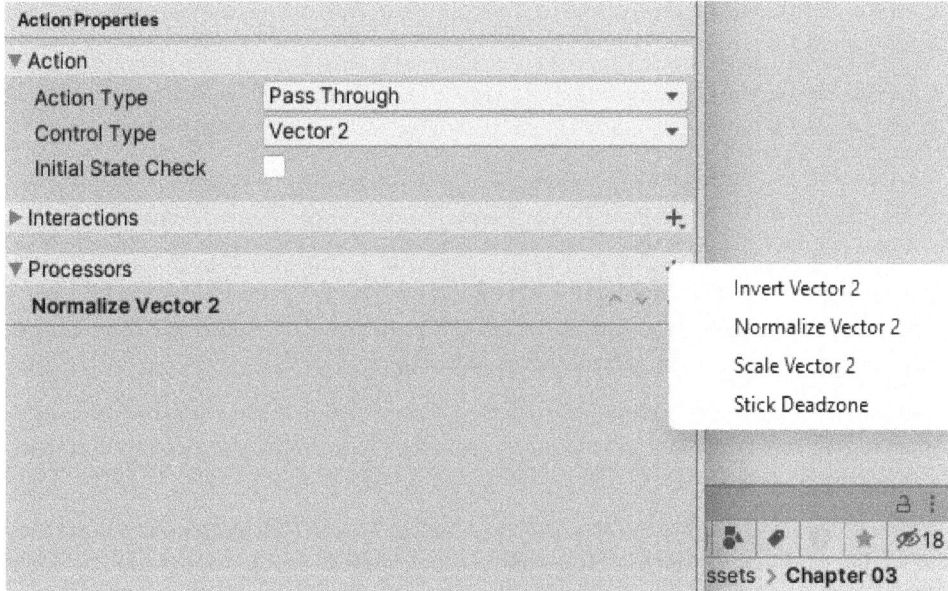

Figure 3.13 – Processors

Having gained insights into Unity's Input System, we now understand how Interactions and Processors refine input signals, enhancing control mechanisms within our game development endeavors. In the next section, let's delve into Cinemachine, an essential tool in Unity that revolutionizes game development with cinematic flair.

Cinemachine

Let's talk about Cinemachine, a game-changer in Unity that takes your game development to cinematic levels. If you're a Unity developer, Cinemachine is your go-to tool for effortlessly managing dynamic camera moves, crafting cinematic scenes, and enhancing the way players navigate virtual worlds.

At its core, Cinemachine introduces virtual cameras, which are like your personal camera crew for the digital stage. No need for complex camera scripts – Cinemachine simplifies the process, making it easy to guide player perspectives. Whether you want action-packed shots, serene landscapes, or immersive story moments, Cinemachine lets you play director without the headaches.

Benefits of Cinemachine

Explore the array of features Cinemachine offers for seamless and captivating camera control and storytelling in Unity game development as follows:

- **Intuitive controls**: Cinemachine provides a user-friendly interface and intuitive controls, eliminating the need for complex camera scripting and making it accessible to developers of all skill levels
- **Effortless perspective guidance**: With Cinemachine, you can effortlessly guide player perspectives, from dynamic action sequences to serene landscapes, without delving into intricate code
- **Realism with procedural noise**: Cinemachine introduces realism into scenes through procedural noise, offering subtle yet impactful effects such as camera shakes during key moments, enhancing the overall gaming experience
- **Composer for automatic framing**: The **Composer** component automates the camera's position and **field-of-view** (**FOV**) adjustments, ensuring focus on essential elements, streamlining the framing process, and saving valuable development time
- **Seamless Timeline integration**: Cinemachine seamlessly integrates with Unity's Timeline, enabling the easy creation of cinematic sequences for a more immersive and narrative-driven gaming experience
- **Enhanced storytelling capabilities**: Beyond a camera system, Cinemachine acts as a creative ally, enhancing storytelling capabilities and making games more captivating and memorable for players

In summary, Cinemachine presents an array of features designed to streamline camera control and enhance storytelling in Unity game development, offering intuitive controls, effortless perspective guidance, realism with procedural noise, automated framing with the **Composer** component, seamless Timeline integration, and enhanced storytelling capabilities.

Using Cinemachine in our game

Let's kick off our journey with Cinemachine by exploring how to integrate it into our game seamlessly. In this subsection, we will learn how to install Cinemachine and set up your virtual camera for enhanced scene management and dynamic camera movements.

In the following figure, you can see the **Package Manager** panel, from which you can choose and install packages and wait till the editor finishes compiling scripts:

Integrating Unity plugins 71

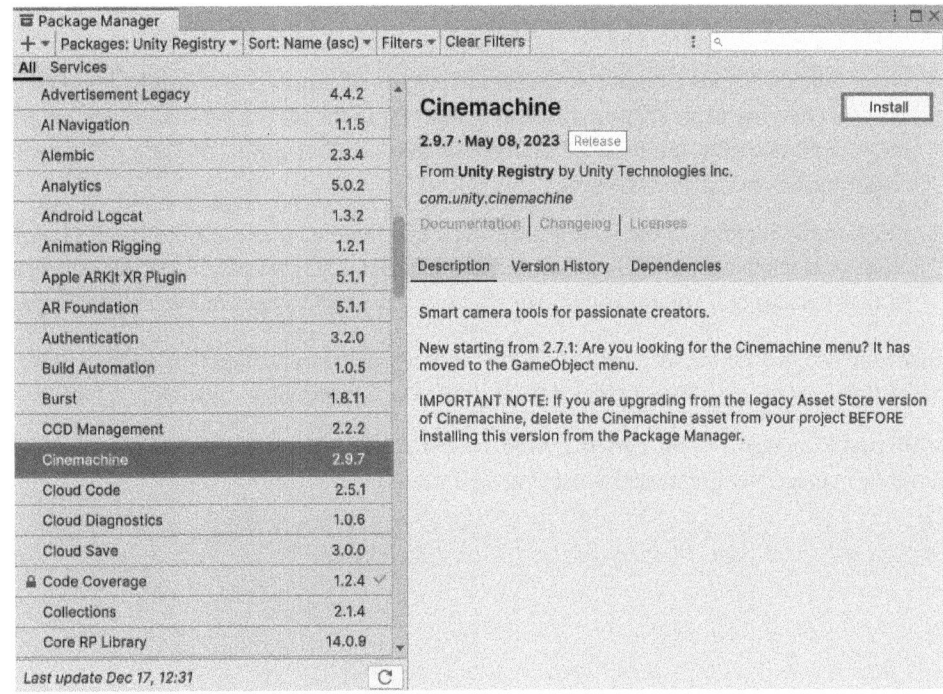

Figure 3.14 – Installing Cinemachine from the Package Manager

Unity provides a variety of cameras within the Cinemachine package. Let's discuss some of these cameras and their respective uses:

- **Freelook Camera (CinemachineFreeLook)**:

    - *Usage*: The Freelook Camera provides versatile control for creating dynamic and cinematic camera movements in 3D environments. It is often used for character exploration, action sequences, and immersive gameplay experiences where fluid camera motion adds depth and engagement.

    - *Key features*: Allows for multi-axis rotation, adjustable follow and look-at targets, customizable damping for smooth transitions, and the ability to define multiple rig configurations for different camera behaviors.

- **Virtual Camera (CinemachineVirtualCamera)**:

    - *Usage*: The Virtual Camera serves as a foundational camera tool in Cinemachine, offering precise control over framing, composition, and behavior. It is suitable for a wide range of scenarios, including character tracking, scene framing, cutscenes, and scripted camera sequences.

    - *Key features*: Provides options for target tracking, damping settings for smooth transitions, customizable FOV, **depth of field** (**DOF**), and various blending modes for seamless camera transitions and effects.

- **2D Camera (CinemachineVirtualCamera)**:

  - *Usage*: The 2D Camera variant of CinemachineVirtualCamera is specifically designed for 2D game development, offering similar functionality to the 3D Virtual Camera but tailored for 2D environments. It is ideal for platformers, side-scrolling games, and other 2D projects requiring dynamic camera control.

  - *Key features*: Supports 2D-specific settings such as orthographic mode, pixel-perfect camera setup, pixel snapping, and follow and dead zones tailored for 2D gameplay mechanics. Allows for smooth tracking of 2D characters, parallax effects, and cinematic camera movements in 2D space.

In the following demonstration, we'll implement the Virtual Camera to highlight the specific changes that occur when transitioning from Unity's default camera to Cinemachine cameras.

Choose **Virtual Camera** from the **Cinemachine** list. When you try to add components, the main camera will be managed by Cinemachine moving forward:

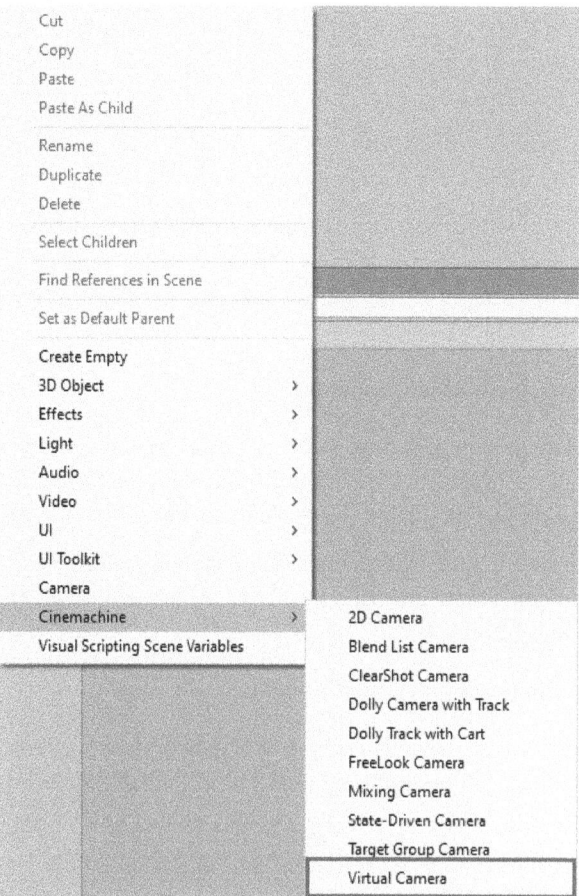

Figure 3.15 – Virtual Camera option

After choosing **Virtual Camera**, the **CinemachineBrain** component will be added to the **MainCamera** GameObject, as seen in *Figure 3.16*. The **CinemachineBrain** component orchestrates multiple virtual cameras, managing their activation, blending, and behavior for smooth transitions and dynamic camera control, crucial for creating immersive and visually engaging scenes in Unity projects using Cinemachine:

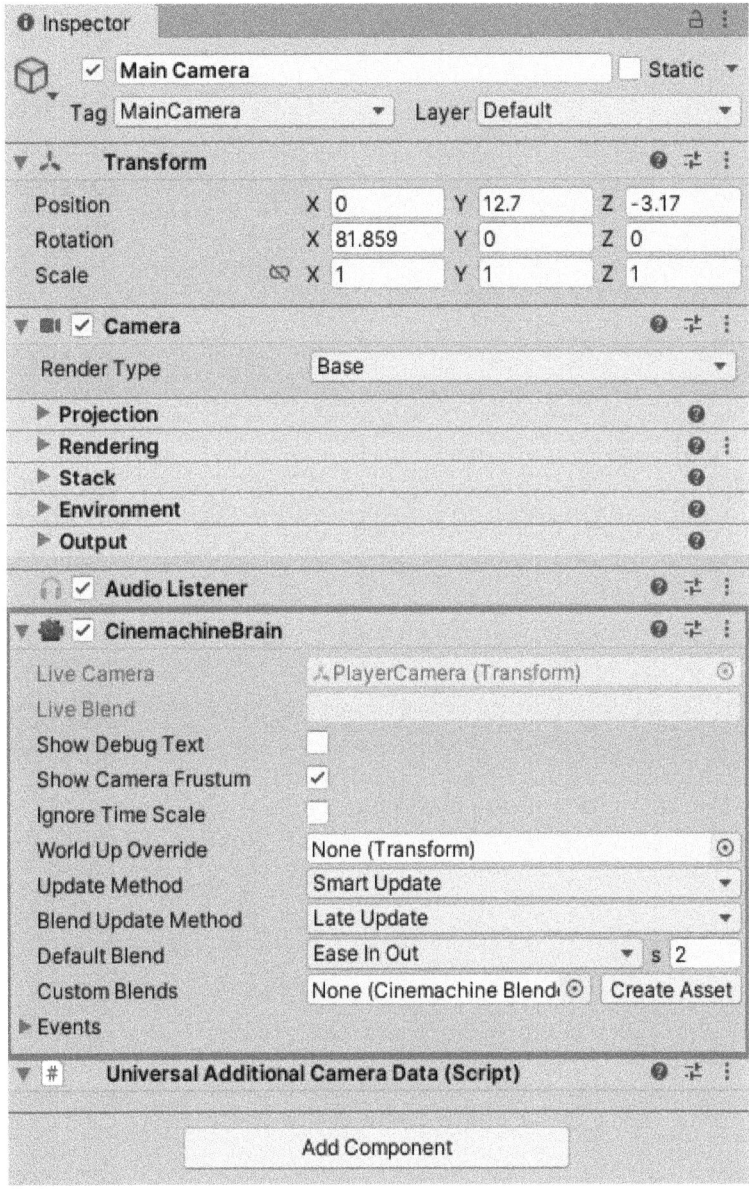

Figure 3.16 – CinemachineBrain component

Also, it will create a new game object for this virtual camera inside the scene that has the **CinemachineVirtualCamera** component, as seen in the following figure:

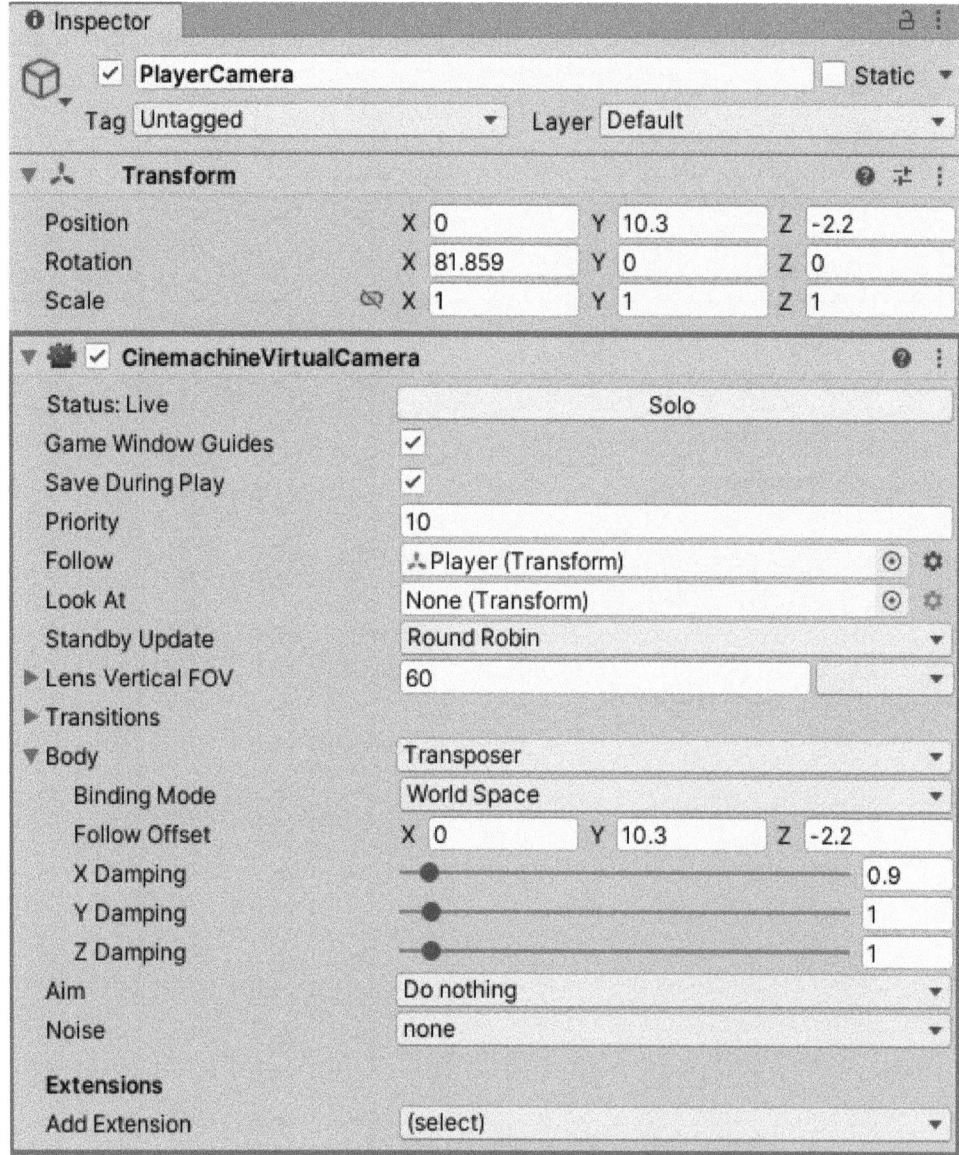

Figure 3.17 – CinemachineVirtualCamera component

In summary, you successfully integrated Cinemachine into your game, allowing for streamlined camera management and dynamic virtual camera movements to enhance your game's visual experience.

Enhancing gameplay dynamics – adding shake effects with Cinemachine

Utilizing Cinemachine to elevate our game experience, we'll now explore the integration of effects, specifically focusing on incorporating a shake effect using the **CinemachineImpulseListener** component. This essential component in Unity's Cinemachine package acts as a crucial receiver of impulse signals from other Cinemachine modules, translating them into impactful visual and auditory effects within the game. Its primary function involves listening for impulse signals triggered by events such as collisions or explosions, enabling developers to apply customizable parameters such as intensity and duration for immersive feedback experiences. Seamlessly integrated with Cinemachine modules, the **CinemachineImpulseListener** component enhances gameplay and cinematic effects by delivering synchronized and dynamic responses to in-game events, thus significantly enhancing the overall immersive and engaging player experience.

The shake effect stands out as a highly impactful element in game design, contributing significantly to the overall player experience. Whether applied to simulate fire, collisions, or other gameplay elements, this effect adds a layer of dynamism and engagement. Integrating a shake effect effectively enhances the player's immersion during gameplay, creating a more compelling and enjoyable experience.

We will begin implementing this feature in the following steps:

1. We will start by clicking on **Add Extension**. It will show us a menu like this:

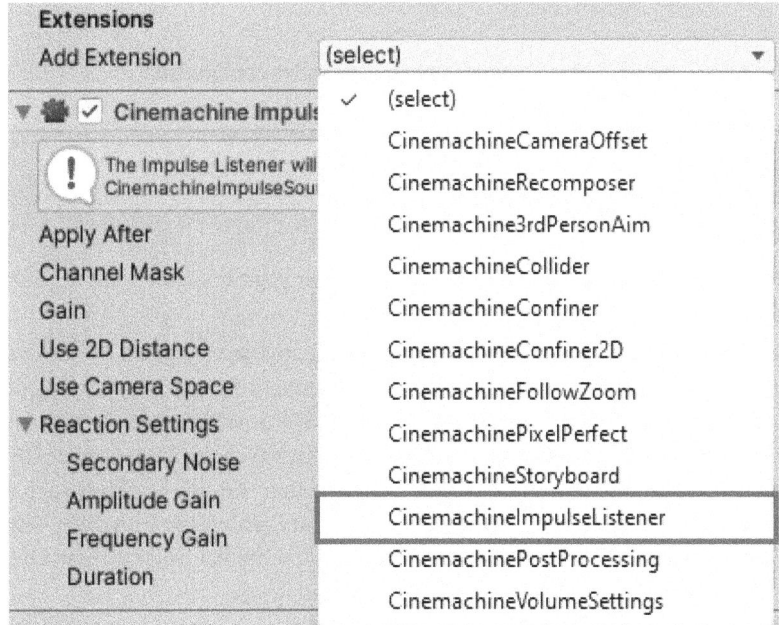

Figure 3.18 – Extensions menu

2. Then, we click on the **CinemachineImpulseListener** component to add to our camera.

   We can tweak the values inside this component to achieve a better effect for our game, as you can see in the following figure:

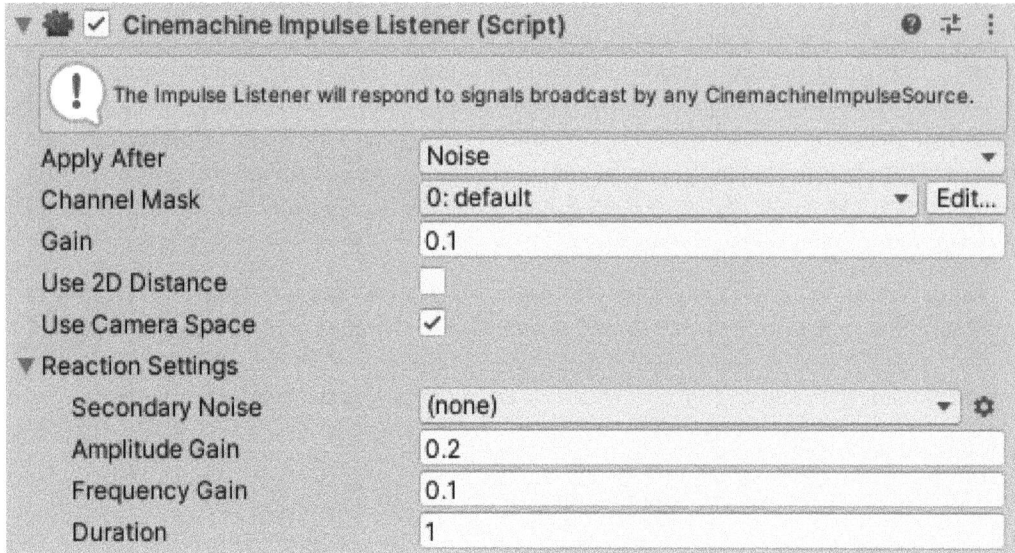

Figure 3.19 – CinemachineImpulseListener component

You can learn more about values in Unity's official documentation: `https://docs.unity3d.com/Packages/com.unity.cinemachine@2.3/manual/`.

> **Tip**
> For most Unity components, tooltips appear when you hover your mouse over the variable name.

Then, we need to add **CinemachineImpulseSource** to a game object. In our case, we can easily add it to the player game object, as most Interactions will be from this player. The **CinemachineImpulseSource** component in Unity's Cinemachine package is a versatile tool for generating impulse signals that simulate impactful events within a game. By defining parameters such as intensity and duration, we can create a range of effects such as camera shakes, controller vibrations, or screen flashes. Integrated seamlessly with other Cinemachine components, **CinemachineImpulseSource** enhances gameplay and cinematic experiences by allowing dynamic responses to events and fine-tuning effects for immersive and engaging player experiences. Its customization options and scripting capabilities enable us to tailor effects to match the game's aesthetics and mechanics, adding depth and interactivity to the overall game world.

Integrating Unity plugins 77

We will need a reference to **CinemachineImpulseSource** in our scripts to start using it:

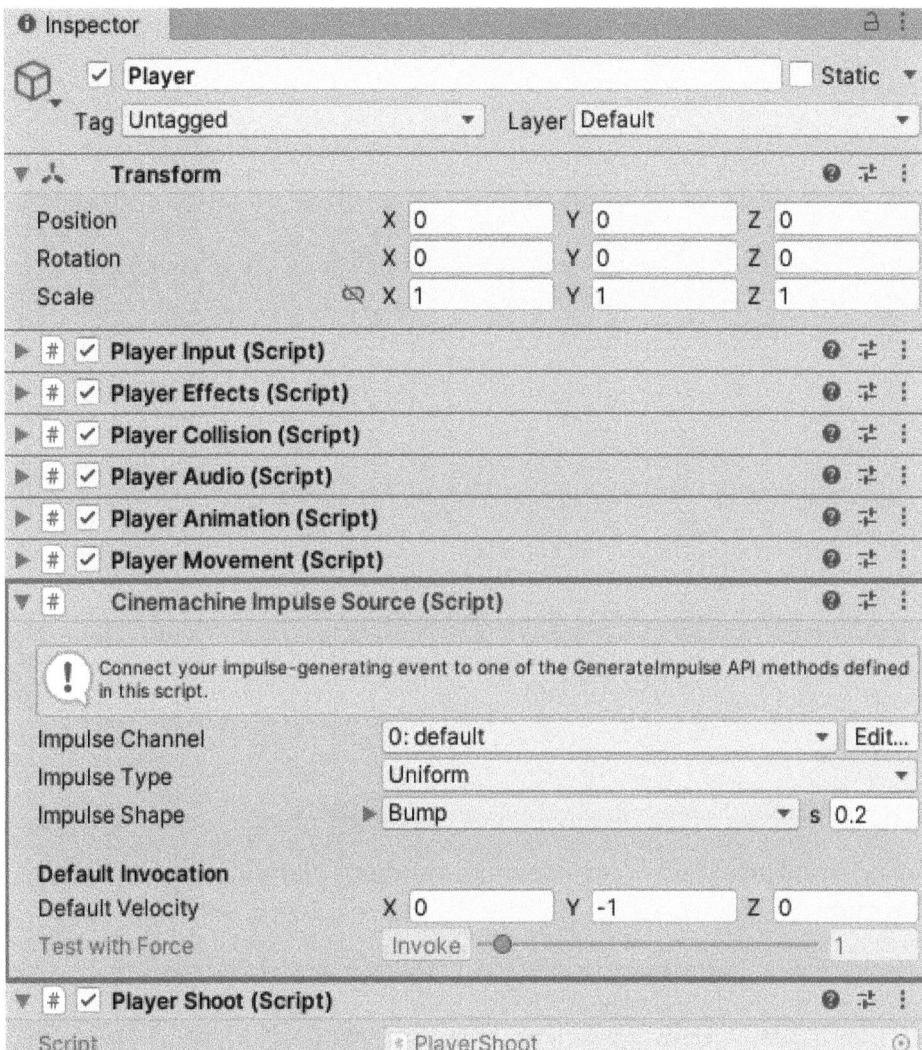

Figure 3.20 – CinemachineImpulseSource component

3. Now, we will use the `PlayerEffects` script, which will subscribe to the `PlayerShoot` fire event to generate an impulse.

   In the following code, we will generate an impulse when the player shoots fire:

   ```
   [RequireComponent(typeof(CinemachineImpulseSource))]
       public class PlayerEffects : MonoBehaviour
       {
   ```

```
                private CinemachineImpulseSource cinemachineImpulse;

                private void OnEnable()
                {
                    PlayerShoot.onFire += ApplyShootFireEffect;
                }

                private void OnDisable()
                {
                    PlayerShoot.onFire -= ApplyShootFireEffect;
                }


                private void Start()
                {
                    cinemachineImpulse =
    GetComponent<CinemachineImpulseSource>();
                }


                private void ApplyShootFireEffect()
                {
                    cinemachineImpulse.GenerateImpulse();
                }
            }
```

That's it! Now, whenever the player shoots, the effect will be applied.

Dynamic cinematic experiences – seamless camera blending with Cinemachine

Another application of **Cinemachine** lies in its ability to manage multiple cameras concurrently and seamlessly blend between them at runtime. This functionality proves valuable in scenarios where you want to create a dedicated camera for specific in-game events. For instance, you can design a special camera that triggers when the player encounters a boss, automatically activating when the player enters a boss room.

In the following figure, you can find the option to add custom blends in the Cinemachine component. Click **Create Asset** to generate a new scriptable object, which will be responsible for managing the transition between cameras, as well as orchestrating the tween action during the transition:

Integrating Unity plugins   79

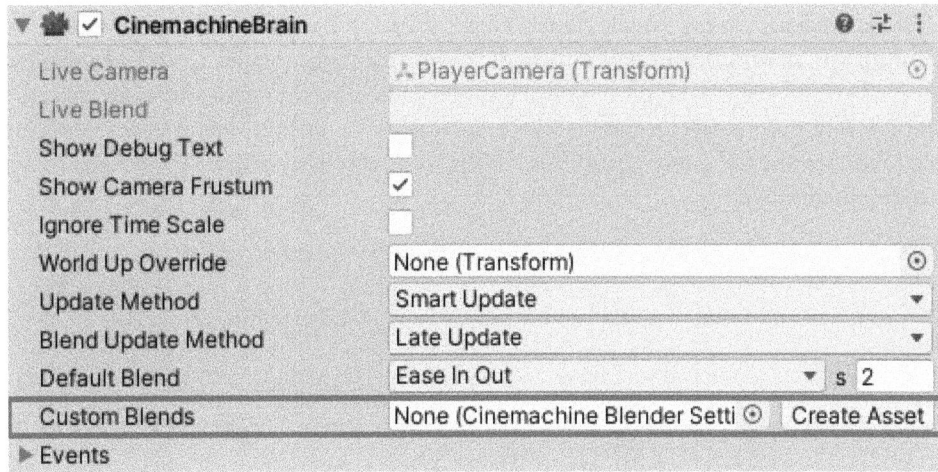

Figure 3.21 – Custom Blends section in Cinemachine component

As seen in the following figure, using a scriptable object for **CinemachineBlenderSettings**, you can add transitions between cameras. The **CinemachineBlenderSettings** component in Unity's Cinemachine package is instrumental in orchestrating smooth transitions between virtual cameras within a scene. By defining blend curves, weighting parameters, and blend techniques, we can control the rate, style, and visual dominance of camera blending, resulting in seamless and visually engaging camera movements during gameplay or cinematic sequences. With support for prioritization, triggering mechanisms, and extensive customization options, **CinemachineBlenderSettings** empowers us to create dynamic and immersive camera transitions tailored to the game's aesthetics and narrative, enhancing overall player experience and immersion:

Figure 3.22 – CinemachineBlenderSettings scriptable object

To utilize this functionality, you can enable or disable the game objects of the cameras or adjust the priority of the current camera by increasing it and decreasing the priority of the previous camera.

I have created a manager to oversee the control of all cameras in the game. At present, we have two cameras: the player camera and the boss camera. In the provided code snippet, you'll find a singleton manager for cameras, tasked with the responsibility of coordinating the operations of all cameras in the game. Notably, this manager features a `SwitchCamera()` function, which accepts an `Enum` parameter representing the camera type. This enables us to selectively activate the desired camera based on the specified type:

```
public class CameraManager : Singlton<CameraManager>
   {
       // Dictionary to map enum values to Cinemachine virtual cameras
       public GenericDictionary<CameraType, CinemachineVirtualCamera> cameraDictionary = new GenericDictionary<CameraType, CinemachineVirtualCamera>();

       // Reference to the currently active virtual camera
       private CinemachineVirtualCamera currentCamera;

       void Start()
       {
          SwitchCamera(CameraType.PlayerCamera);
       }


       // Function to switch between virtual cameras using the enum
       public void SwitchCamera(CameraType newCameraType)
       {
          // Disable the current camera
          if (currentCamera != null)
          {
              currentCamera.gameObject.SetActive(false);
          }

          // Enable the new camera based on the enum
          if (cameraDictionary.ContainsKey(newCameraType))
          {
              currentCamera = cameraDictionary[newCameraType];
              currentCamera.gameObject.SetActive(true);
          }
          else
          {
              Debug.LogWarning("Camera of type " + newCameraType + " not found in the dictionary.");
          }
```

```
        }
    }

    // Enum to represent different cameras
    public enum CameraType
    {
        PlayerCamera,
        BossCamera,
        // Add more camera types as needed
    }
```

You can find all the code in our GitHub repo, the link to which is mentioned in the *Technical requirements* section.

> **Note**
> I have chosen to use enums instead of strings for better performance efficiency.

The following code outlines the enum for various camera types:

```
public enum CameraType
    {
        PlayerCamera,
        BossCamera,
        // Add more camera types as needed
    }
```

The following code snippet provides an illustrative example of usage within the `PlayerCollision` class:

```
namespace FusionFuryGame
{
    public class PlayerCollision : MonoBehaviour
    {
        private void OnTriggerEnter(Collider other)
        {
            if (other.CompareTag("BossArea"))
            {
                CameraManager.Instance.SwitchCamera(CameraType.BossCamera);
            }
        }

        private void OnTriggerExit(Collider other)
```

```
            {
                if (other.CompareTag("BossArea"))
                {
                    CameraManager.Instance.SwitchCamera(CameraType.
        PlayerCamera);
                }
            }
        }
    }
```

> **Tip**
> Given the abundance of Unity plugins, it's essential to pick the right one for your project.

In conclusion, Cinemachine offers Unity developers intuitive camera controls, effortless perspective guidance, realism with procedural noise, automatic framing, seamless Timeline integration, and enhanced storytelling capabilities. As we conclude this section, we have explored its features and benefits, preparing to leverage its power in our game development endeavors.

Best practices for using Unity plugins

Before integrating plugins into your project, it's essential to thoroughly explore their functionality, understand their documentation, assess compatibility and potential impact, evaluate specific features, stay updated with releases, check version compatibility, maintain project integrity, set up a testing environment, document integrations for future reference, and track and resolve issues encountered during integration:

- **Exploring plugin functionality**: Before adding a plugin, thoroughly explore its features and functionalities
- **Understanding documentation**: Dive into the plugin's documentation for a clear understanding of its capabilities
- **Compatibility and impact assessment**: Evaluate how the plugin aligns with your project, considering aspects such as performance and potential conflicts
- **Feature assessment**: Assess specific features to ensure they meet your project's requirements
- **Keeping plugins updated**: Stay informed about updates, bug fixes, and new features for your integrated plugins
- **Version compatibility checks**: Verify that the plugin aligns with the current Unity version, exercising caution during Unity updates
- **Maintaining project integrity**: Back up your entire project before making significant changes to avoid data loss

- **Testing environment**: Create a dedicated testing environment to evaluate plugin updates or modifications
- **Documentation for future reference**: Create detailed integration documentation and include configurations, settings, and troubleshooting steps
- **Issue tracking and resolution**: Maintain a record of encountered issues and their resolutions for future reference

In summary, exploring, understanding, assessing, updating, checking compatibility, maintaining integrity, testing, documenting, and tracking issues are crucial steps in effectively integrating and managing plugins within your Unity project.

Summary

In wrapping up this chapter, we've covered the ins and outs of Unity plugins, understanding the basic and extended features they offer. You've also learned how to integrate the new Input System and Cinemachine using C#, gaining practical skills to enhance your game development projects. We've emphasized the importance of adopting best practices when working with plugins, setting the stage for more efficient integration into your projects. As you reflect on keeping your code organized and neat, these skills will be valuable as you continue your journey toward becoming a skilled Unity developer.

Looking ahead to the next chapter, *Creating Fun Game Mechanics with C# in Unity*, get ready to expand your game development toolkit. Building on what you've learned about clean coding practices, you'll explore how to bring excitement to your games through the expressive C# programming language. Imagine seamlessly incorporating your knowledge of plugins and organized code into the creation of engaging game mechanics. The upcoming chapter promises exciting challenges and discoveries that will further enhance your Unity development skills. Get ready to dive into the world of crafting immersive and enjoyable game mechanics in *Chapter 4*. Happy coding on this ongoing journey of skill-building!

4
Implementing Engaging Game Mechanics Using C# in Unity

Welcome to *Chapter 4*, where we invite you into the dynamic world of game development. As you delve into this chapter, your journey will begin by exploring the foundational principles that drive successful game mechanics. This initial step involves an introduction to game mechanics, allowing you to grasp the essential concepts that form the backbone of captivating gameplay.

Following this, you'll seamlessly transition into the realm of player behavior and AI before delving into the topics of challenge and reward systems. This journey unravels the art of crafting interactive and responsive gaming experiences.

By the end of this chapter, you'll be equipped with not only theoretical insights but also practical skills to shape immersive gaming adventures in Unity using the power of C#.

In this chapter, we're going to cover the following main topics:

- Introducing game mechanics
- Implementing player behavior and AI logic using C#
- Implementing challenge and reward systems using C#

Technical requirements

You can access the code samples and project files on our dedicated GitHub repository: `https://github.com/PacktPublishing/Mastering-Unity-Game-Development-with-C-Sharp/tree/main/Assets/Chapter%2004`.

Clone or download the repository so that you have easy access to the code demonstrated in this chapter.

Introducing game mechanics

Game mechanics are the rules and systems that shape how a game is played. Think of them as the behind-the-scenes mechanisms that define the player's experience. They are vital for crafting engaging gameplay, influencing everything from movement and combat to how a story unfolds. Successful games, such as *Mario* with its jumping mechanics, or *Tetris* with its block arrangement challenges, showcase how well-crafted mechanics can create memorable and enjoyable experiences for players.

Game mechanics go beyond just making a game work; they subtly tell stories by how players interact. Whether it's in fighting games with complex combat or in platformers with puzzle-solving, these mechanics add to the overall story. When players follow the game's rules, they're not just watching; they become part of the story.

So, understanding and creating game mechanics is like becoming skilled at interactive storytelling. Each button that's pressed or moved in the game helps the story move along, making every playthrough a unique and personal journey.

In the following section, we will talk about the essential principles you need to know about game mechanics.

Essential principles of game mechanics

Now, let's get into the important stuff that makes games enjoyable. We're talking about the basic rules that shape how players have fun. It's all about finding the right balance, giving feedback, and making sure players feel in control. These simple things turn games into exciting adventures where every move adds to the fun.

Balance

Balance in games is like ensuring everyone gets a fair shot at having fun. Picture a game where one character is super strong, making it impossible for others to enjoy. That wouldn't be fair, right? Game developers work hard to create a balanced experience where each player or character has a chance to shine. Take *Overwatch*, for example. In this game, each hero boasts unique abilities, and no one is overwhelmingly powerful or weak. It's this careful balance that ensures a level playing field, allowing everyone to have a good time and contribute to the game's excitement.

Furthermore, balance goes beyond characters; it extends to the overall gameplay. Imagine a game with levels that are either too easy or impossibly hard – players would quickly lose interest. Achieving balance in challenges, difficulty, and rewards keeps players engaged. Games that strike this delicate balance provide a satisfying and enjoyable experience for players of all skill levels, making them want to keep playing and exploring what the game has to offer.

Feedback

In the world of gaming, **feedback** is the game's way of talking to you, letting you know how you're doing. It's like a pat on the back when you do something right or a gentle nudge when you could improve.

In *Minecraft*, for instance, when you successfully mine resources, a satisfying sound accompanies the action. That sound is feedback, a small celebration telling you that you've accomplished a task.

Think about playing a racing game without any feedback – no cheering crowd, no speedometer ticking up – it would be a bit strange, right? Good feedback, whether it's visual, auditory, or haptic, is essential for making players feel accomplished and guiding them through the game's challenges.

Moreover, feedback extends to storytelling in games. Choices you make should have consequences, and the game should let you know how your decisions impact the story. Effective feedback creates a dynamic connection between the player and the game world, making every action feel meaningful. Whether it's triumphant music after a successful quest or a subtle change in the environment based on your decisions, feedback adds depth to the gaming experience, ensuring players stay engaged and invested in the virtual world they're exploring.

Player agency

Player agency is like having a steering wheel in a game – you get to make choices and have control over your virtual adventure. In *The Elder Scrolls V: Skyrim*, this principal shines brightly. Right from the start, you decide who your character is going to be. Do you want to be a brave warrior, a sneaky thief, or a powerful wizard? The game doesn't force you down a specific path; instead, it lets you carve out your own story.

This freedom to make choices extends beyond character creation. As you progress through the game, you encounter various quests and challenges, and here, again, player agency takes center stage. You can decide how to approach a situation – do you want to negotiate, fight, or sneak past enemies? Your choices influence not just the immediate outcome but also the overall story. Your version of *Skyrim* might be entirely different from someone else's because player agency allows for diverse experiences.

Having player agency transforms a game into more than just a set path with predetermined outcomes. It transforms it into your story, where your decisions matter, and the game adapts to your choices. This sense of control and the ability to shape your unique adventure is what makes player agency a key principle in creating immersive and personally meaningful gaming experiences.

In the following section, we are going to understand the relationship between code and game mechanics.

The connection between code and game mechanics

Now, here's the cool part – the code is what turns ideas into action in the game. It's like a rulebook that tells the game what to do. If you want to create a game where players can shoot lasers, you'd write code to make it happen. So, the relationship between code and game mechanics is like a chef's recipe for a delicious meal – the code guides the game to do exactly what we want.

Understanding these coding basics is like having the keys to the game-making kingdom. It allows you to bring your game ideas to life and create all sorts of cool stuff. Plus, the more you understand C#, the more you can make your games do awesome things. So, get ready to dive into the world of coding in this chapter – it's not as tricky as it sounds, and it's the secret sauce that makes games so much fun to play!

Implementing player behavior and AI logic using C#

In this section, we'll be getting into how games are made, looking at how players act and how computer-controlled characters (we call it AI) think in games. Figuring out how players act and how game characters react is a big deal in making games fun. It's like giving players a script to follow, just like actors in a play. Players bring the game to life, a bit like how actors make a story interesting. We'll look at different types of games, checking out how players act in all sorts of situations, from big adventures to tactical fights.

Then, we'll check out AI, the smart computer stuff that makes game enemies, friends, and other characters feel real. AI isn't just code; it's like magic that makes challenges exciting, enemies tricky, and friends helpful. We'll explain the basic ideas behind this digital magic, kind of like understanding the cues a conductor gives to an orchestra, guiding all the actions and reactions in a game.

So, we're on a journey to make player behavior and AI logic less mysterious using C# – a fancy way to talk to computers. You'll be all set to make games that feel real, keeping players interested and making your game super exciting!

- **Understanding player behavior design**: In the realm of player behavior design, crafting a responsive game involves the fundamental aspect of **health management**. **Health**, being a universal concept for both players and enemies, is a core behavior that greatly influences the overall gaming experience. To achieve a modular and extensible system, we must introduce an IHealth interface that encapsulates essential functions, such as tracking maximum health, current health, taking damage, and healing. By adopting this interface, we can establish a unified approach to health management that applies to both players and enemies. This not only streamlines the code base but also allows for easy expansion and modification as the game evolves.

- **Shooting mechanics**: In addition to health, we'll delve into shooting mechanics, a pivotal player behavior in a shooting game. Rather than a simplistic shooting script, we'll opt for a modular approach, creating separate components for bullets, projectiles, and weapons. This modular design enables flexibility and scalability, making it easier to introduce new weapons, tweak projectile behaviors, and enhance overall gameplay dynamics.

- **Introduction to AI logic**: Transitioning to AI logic, we'll explore fundamental concepts that breathe life into in-game adversaries. Basic AI principles encompass understanding the role of AI in creating dynamic and challenging gameplay. The AI system becomes a crucial component in determining enemy behaviors, ranging from simple wandering to complex attack patterns. By delving into these concepts, we'll gain insights into the decision-making processes that drive AI-controlled entities, contributing to the overall richness of the gaming experience.

- **Coding player behavior and AI**: Moving from theory to practice, we'll embark on the practical implementation of player behavior and AI logic using C# scripts. The IHealth and IDamage interfaces become the cornerstone for implementing health-related functionalities, ensuring a consistent and manageable approach across diverse game elements. The modular shooting system will take shape as we learn to handle bullets, projectiles, and weapons separately, promoting code reusability and maintainability.

To reinforce learning, we'll engage in hands-on demonstrations, showcasing the step-by-step creation of C# scripts for player behavior and AI logic in the subsequent sections. We'll gain proficiency in designing and implementing responsive player behaviors, fostering an understanding of how to bring dynamic AI characters to life within the Unity game development environment.

Let's start by writing the IHealth interface and establishing the fundamental logic for it.

Writing the IHealth and IDamage interfaces

In the following code block, we've introduced the IHealth interface, which incorporates properties for maximum and current health, along with essential functions for setting maximum health, inflicting damage, and facilitating healing. Here, we'll create an interface to manage the health logic throughout the entire game. I've designed it so that it oversees the health of each entity once they implement this interface. This approach will simplify communication between entities and prove beneficial when we also create the IDamage interface. Implementing IDamage in components responsible for dealing damage will allow us to affect the health component seamlessly:

```
namespace FusionFuryGame
{
    public interface IHealth
    {
        float MaxHealth { get; set; }   // Property for maximum health
        float CurrentHealth { get; set; }   // Property for current health

        void TakeDamage(float damage);  // Method to apply damage
        void SetMaxHealth();  // Method to set current health to max health

        void Heal();             // Method to apply healing
    }
}
```

Next, we will create the `IDamage` interface, which will feature a central function for dealing damage. Subsequent classes will implement this interface, handling damage calculations internally and conveying the resulting damage value to other classes, as demonstrated in the following code block:

```
namespace FusionFuryGame
{
    public interface IDamage
    {
        float GetDamageValue();   // Method to retrieve the damage value
    }
}
```

Now, we must integrate the `IHealth` interface into the player. Therefore, we will generate the `PlayerHealth` component and affix it to the player's `GameObject`. The `PlayerHealth` class will manage all functions related to the player's health, including setting the maximum health and processing damage. When the player's health falls to zero or below, the player dies. It's designed as a separate class that you attach to the player's GameObject, facilitating communication with enemies, as illustrated in the following code block:

```
namespace FusionFuryGame
{
    public class PlayerHealth : MonoBehaviour, IHealth
    {
        public static UnityAction onPlayerDied = delegate { };
        public float startingMaxHealth = 100;  // Set a default starting maximum health for the player


        public float healInterval = 2f;   // Time interval for healing
        public float healAmount = 5f;     // Amount of healing per interval

        private WaitForSeconds healIntervalWait;  // Reusable WaitForSeconds instance
        private Coroutine healOverTimeCoroutine;
        public float MaxHealth { get; set; }
        public float CurrentHealth { get; set; }
```

In the preceding code, I've included the required variables related to the player's health and healing. Additionally, a coroutine will ensure the player heals gradually within the `PlayerHealth` class:

```
        void OnDestroy()
        {
            // Ensure to stop the healing coroutine when the object is destroyed
```

```
        if (healOverTimeCoroutine != null)
            StopCoroutine(healOverTimeCoroutine);
    }

    void Start()
    {
        SetMaxHealth();  // Set initial max health
        healIntervalWait = new WaitForSeconds(healInterval);
        StartHealingOverTime();
    }
```

Let's take a look at the preceding code:

- `OnDestroy`: This method ensures that the healing coroutine is stopped when the player object is destroyed to prevent memory leaks
- `Start`: This method initializes the player's health parameters, sets their maximum health, creates a `WaitForSeconds` instance for healing intervals, and starts the healing coroutine:

```
    public void TakeDamage(float damage)
    {
        // Implement logic to handle taking damage
        CurrentHealth -= damage;

        // Check for death or other actions based on health status
        if (CurrentHealth <= 0) onPlayerDied.Invoke();
    }

    public void SetMaxHealth()
    {
        MaxHealth = startingMaxHealth;


    }

    public void Heal()
    {
        CurrentHealth += healAmount;
        CurrentHealth = Mathf.Min(CurrentHealth, MaxHealth);
    }

    private void StartHealingOverTime()
```

```
        {
            healOverTimeCoroutine = StartCoroutine(HealOverTime());
        }

        private IEnumerator HealOverTime()
        {
            while (true)
            {
                yield return healIntervalWait;
                Heal();
            }
        }
    }
}
```

Let's break down the preceding code:

- `TakeDamage`: This method handles the logic for deducting health from the player when they take damage. It also checks if the player's health has reached zero, triggering the `onPlayerDied` event if necessary.
- `SetMaxHealth`: This method sets the maximum health of the player to the specified starting maximum health value.
- `Heal`: This method restores the player's health. It increments the current health by the specified healing amount and ensures that the player's current health does not exceed the maximum health.
- `StartHealingOverTime`: This method initiates the healing coroutine that's responsible for gradually restoring the player's health over time.
- `HealOverTime`: This coroutine runs indefinitely, waiting for the specified healing interval and then invoking the `Heal` method to restore the player's health.

Now, let's examine the `PlayerCollision` component and understand how the player incurs damage. The following code block demonstrates the process of the player taking damage either directly from the enemy or from their projectiles. This class acts as a bridge between the player's health component and the `IDamage` interface of the colliding object. We can utilize `PlayerHealth` and obtain damage through the `IDamage` interface by using the `OnCollisionEnter` method:

```
namespace FusionFuryGame
{
    public class PlayerCollision : MonoBehaviour
    {
        private PlayerHealth playerHealth;
        private IDamage enemyDamage;
```

```csharp
        private void Start()
        {
            playerHealth = GetComponent<PlayerHealth>();
        }

        private void OnCollisionEnter(Collision collision)
        {
            if (collision.gameObject.CompareTag("Enemy") || collision.gameObject.CompareTag("EnemyProjectile"))
            {
                if (collision.gameObject.TryGetComponent(out enemyDamage))
                {
                    playerHealth.TakeDamage(enemyDamage.GetDamageValue());
                }
            }

        }
    }
}
```

Now, let's look at the different variables we used here:

- `private PlayerHealth playerHealth;`: This is a reference to the `PlayerHealth` component that's attached to the same GameObject. This component manages the health of the player.
- `private IDamage enemyDamage;`: This is an interface reference for handling damage inflicted by enemies or enemy projectiles.
- `Start`: This method retrieves the `PlayerHealth` component that's attached to the same GameObject during initialization.
- `OnCollisionEnter`: This method is invoked automatically when a collision occurs that involves the GameObject. It checks if the collision involves an enemy or an enemy projectile by comparing tags. If the collision involves an enemy or an enemy projectile, it attempts to retrieve the `IDamage` component from the colliding object using `TryGetComponent`. If successful, it invokes the `TakeDamage` method of the `PlayerHealth` component to apply damage to the player's health.

Overall, this script handles collisions between the player character and enemy entities or enemy projectiles. Upon collision, it retrieves the damage value from the colliding object and applies it to the player's health, ensuring proper damage management in the game.

In the next section, we will explore how the player engages in shooting enemies. However, before delving into that, we'll implement a shoot system to ensure both the player and the enemy can make use of it.

Implementing a shoot system

In this section, we'll create classes for shooting. Here, we'll incorporate the `IDamage` interface into the `BaseProjectile` class, which serves as the foundation for all ammunition types. This allows us to compute the damage that will be applied to the health component.

In the following code block, we're configuring the damage value, which will be calculated for the player or enemies. This is a general system that can be applied to all objects:

```
namespace FusionFuryGame
{
    public abstract class BaseProjectile : MonoBehaviour, IDamage
    {
        private float damage;

        public virtual void SetDamageValue(float value)
        {
            damage = value;
        }

        public float GetDamageValue()
        {
            return damage;
        }

    }
}
```

Let's look at the variables that were used here:

- `private float damage;`: This variable stores the damage value associated with the projectile.
- `public virtual void SetDamageValue(float value)`: This method allows subclasses to set the damage value for the projectile. It takes a float parameter value representing the damage to be set. When called, it assigns the provided value to the damage variable. The `virtual` keyword indicates that this method can be overridden by subclasses to provide specialized behavior if needed.
- `GetDamageValue Method`: This method retrieves the damage value of the projectile. It simply returns the value stored in the damage variable.

Overall, this abstract class provides a blueprint for projectile objects in the game. Subclasses can inherit from this class and customize the behavior of projectiles by overriding the `SetDamageValue` method or adding additional functionality as needed. The `GetDamageValue` method allows other game components to access the damage value of projectiles when needed, enabling consistent damage handling throughout the game.

Next, we can create the `BaseWeapon` script, which is versatile enough to be utilized by both players and enemies, considering that enemies will also possess weapons. Each weapon will be associated with an attached projectile, allowing for the creation of various projectile types.

Additionally, there is the concept of `weaponPower`, a variable that varies from one weapon to another, influencing the applied damage. `muzzleTransform` serves as the point for shooting projectiles, and `projectileForce` dictates the movement of the projectile.

Lastly, we must define the `Shoot` function, as illustrated in the following code block:

```
namespace FusionFuryGame
{
    public abstract class BaseWeapon : MonoBehaviour
    {
        [SerializeField] protected BaseProjectile attachedProjectile;
        [SerializeField] protected float weaponPower;
        [SerializeField] protected Transform muzzleTransform;
        [SerializeField] protected float projectileForce;
        public virtual void Shoot( float fireDamage)
        {
           // Instantiate the projectile from the object pool
            GameObject projectileObject = ObjectPoolManager.Instance.GetPooledObject(attachedProjectile.tag);

            if (projectileObject != null)
            {
               // Set the position of the projectile to the gun's muzzle position
                projectileObject.transform.position = muzzleTransform.position;

               // Get the rigid body component from the projectile
                Rigidbody projectileRb = projectileObject.GetComponent<Rigidbody>();

                if (projectileRb != null)
                {
                   // Apply force to the projectile in the forward vector of the weapon
```

```
                projectileRb.AddForce(muzzleTransform.forward * 
projectileForce, ForceMode.Impulse);

                // Modify the fire damage by adding the current 
weapon's power
                float modifiedDamage = fireDamage + weaponPower;

                // Apply damage and other logic to the projectile 
(consider implementing IDamage interface)
                attachedProjectile.SetDamageValue(modifiedDamage);
            }
            else
            {
                // Handle if the projectile doesn't have a rigid body
                Debug.LogWarning("Projectile prefab is missing 
Rigidbody component.");
            }
          }
       }
    }
}
```

Let's look at the serialized fields:

- `protected BaseProjectile attachedProjectile`: This refers to the type of projectile attached to the weapon. It is serialized to allow assignment in Unity's **Inspector** view.
- `protected float weaponPower`: This refers to the power of the weapon. It is serialized to allow for adjustments in the **Inspector** view.
- `protected Transform muzzleTransform`: This refers to the position where projectiles spawn, typically the muzzle of the weapon.
- `protected float projectileForce`: This refers to the force that's applied to the projectile when it's shot from the weapon.
- `Shoot`: This method is responsible for shooting the weapon. First, it attempts to get a pooled projectile object from Object Pool Manager. If a projectile object is retrieved, it sets its position to the muzzle of the weapon and adds force to propel it forward. This method also modifies the fire damage by adding the weapon's power to it. Finally, it applies the modified damage and any other logic to the projectile, potentially by implementing an `IDamage` interface.

Overall, this abstract class provides a foundation for implementing different types of weapons in the game. Subclasses can inherit from this class to create specific weapon types and customize their behavior as needed. The `Shoot` method handles the spawning and firing of projectiles, allowing for flexible and dynamic weapon functionality.

The following code block provides an example of utilizing `BaseWeapon` with the `SimpleGun` class. We're going to use it with the player for shooting enemies, so it will be used as the player's weapon:

```
namespace FusionFuryGame
{
    public class SimpleGun : BaseWeapon
    {
        public override void Shoot( float fireDamage)
        {
            base.Shoot( fireDamage );
            //Add here special logic for the gun if needed
        }
    }
}
```

Let's break down the code:

- `SimpleGun`: This class represents a specific type of gun in the game. It inherits from the `BaseWeapon` class, indicating that it shares characteristics and functionality with other weapons but may have specialized behavior.

- Override Shoot:

  - `public override void Shoot(float fireDamage)`: This method overrides the Shoot method defined in the `BaseWeapon` class

  - The `base.Shoot(fireDamage)` statement calls the Shoot method from the base class (`BaseWeapon`), allowing the gun to perform the standard shooting behavior defined in the base class

In summary, the `SimpleGun` class extends the functionality of the `BaseWeapon` class by providing its own implementation of the Shoot method. This allows for specialized behavior while leveraging the common functionality provided by the base class.

Now, let's present the `PlayerShoot` component, which encompasses the shooting logic. In this context, the player awaits input actions and possesses the current weapon. In *Chapter 6*, which focuses on data handling, we'll create scriptable objects for weapon statistics. This way, we can substitute the weapon's power with the weapon's stats, utilizing the power derived from it. We can also make different stats for the same weapon, as illustrated in the following code block:

```
namespace FusionFuryGame {
    public class PlayerShoot : MonoBehaviour
    {
        public static UnityAction onFire = delegate { };
        [SerializeField] BaseWeapon currentWeapon;
        [SerializeField] private float fireDamage;
        [SerializeField] private float shootingInterval = 0.5f;   //
Set the shooting interval in seconds
```

```csharp
        private float timeSinceLastShot = 0f;

        private void Update()
        {
            timeSinceLastShot += Time.deltaTime;
        }

        private void OnEnable()
        {
            PlayerInput.onShoot += OnShootFire;
        }

        private void OnDisable()
        {
            PlayerInput.onShoot -= OnShootFire;
        }

        private void OnShootFire()
        {
            // Check if enough time has passed since the last shot
            if (timeSinceLastShot >= shootingInterval)
            {
                // Shoot in the forward vector of the weapon and pass player power stat
                currentWeapon.Shoot(fireDamage);

                // Reset the timer
                timeSinceLastShot = 0f;

                // Invoke the onFire event
                onFire.Invoke();
            }
        }
    }
}
```

Let's break down the preceding code:

- `onFire` Event:

  - `public static UnityAction onFire = delegate { };`: This static event is triggered whenever the player fires a shot. Other scripts can subscribe to this event to perform actions when the player shoots.

- **Serialized fields**:

    - `currentWeapon`: This field holds a reference to the current weapon the player is using
    - `fireDamage`: This field represents the damage value of the player's shots
    - `shootingInterval`: This field specifies the time interval between consecutive shots

- **Event subscriptions**:

    - `OnEnable()`: Subscribes the `OnShootFire` method to the `onShoot` event when the object is enabled
    - `OnDisable()`: Unsubscribes the `OnShootFire` method from the `onShoot` event when the object is disabled

- `OnShootFire`: This method is invoked when the player performs a shoot action (`onShoot` event). It checks if enough time has passed since the last shot. If so, it triggers the `Shoot` method of the current weapon, resets the shot timer, and invokes the `onFire` event.

Overall, the `PlayerShoot` class facilitates player shooting mechanics by controlling the shooting interval, managing events for shooting actions, and delegating the shooting logic to the current weapon.

> **Note**
> Make sure that you assign distinct tags to projectiles associated with both the player and the enemies. This prevents conflicts when they collide with each other.

Currently, the player possesses the capability to both shoot and endure damage. In the following subsection, we will delve into the AI logic for our game.

Delving into the AI logic

Welcome to the world of **AI logic**! In this section, we'll explore the algorithms and decision-making processes that bring intelligence to our game characters. We'll discover how AI logic enhances navigation, strategy, and dynamic interactions, elevating the overall gaming experience. Join us as we unravel the secrets behind crafting smart behaviors for a more immersive virtual world. Plus, we'll delve into the implementation of a finite state machine to create distinct states for all enemies, allowing seamless transitions between behaviors.

In the upcoming steps, we'll integrate the `NavMesh` package into our project. However, before delving into AI logic, it's essential to include the navigation package in the project. Follow these steps to do so:

> **Note**
> Before Unity 2022, navigation was pre-implemented; however, starting from Unity 2022, it must be added via Package Manager.

1. Access **Package Manager** to install the **AI Navigation** package, as shown in *Figure 4.1*:

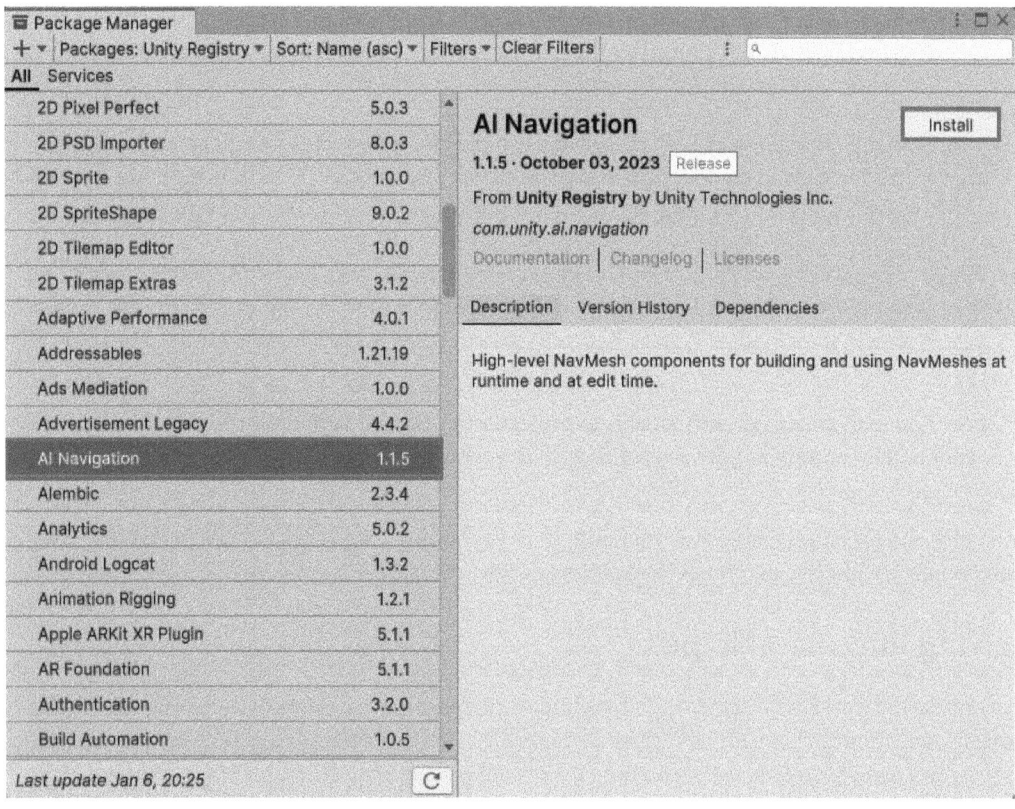

Figure 4.1 – Installing AI Navigation via Package Manager

2. Following the installation, you'll notice a new menu that allows you to toggle the visibility of **NavMesh** surfaces and access other options concerning **AI Navigation**. This menu is integrated into the *scene toolbar*, as illustrated in *Figure 4.2*:

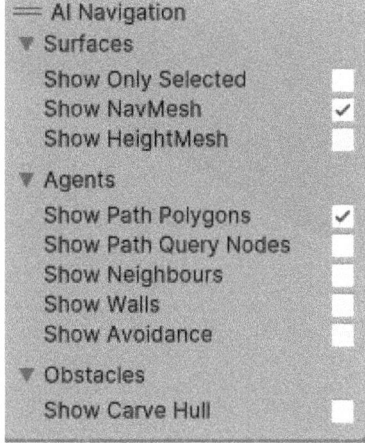

Figure 4.2 – The AI Navigation menu in the Scene view

Additional reading

You can explore the **AI Navigation** settings or find more information in the official Unity documentation: https://docs.unity3d.com/Packages/com.unity.ai.navigation@1.1/manual/index.html.

3. To begin utilizing this feature, we'll need to incorporate a **NavMesh Surface** property into the scene. You can choose this from the **Create** menu, as shown in *Figure 4.3*:

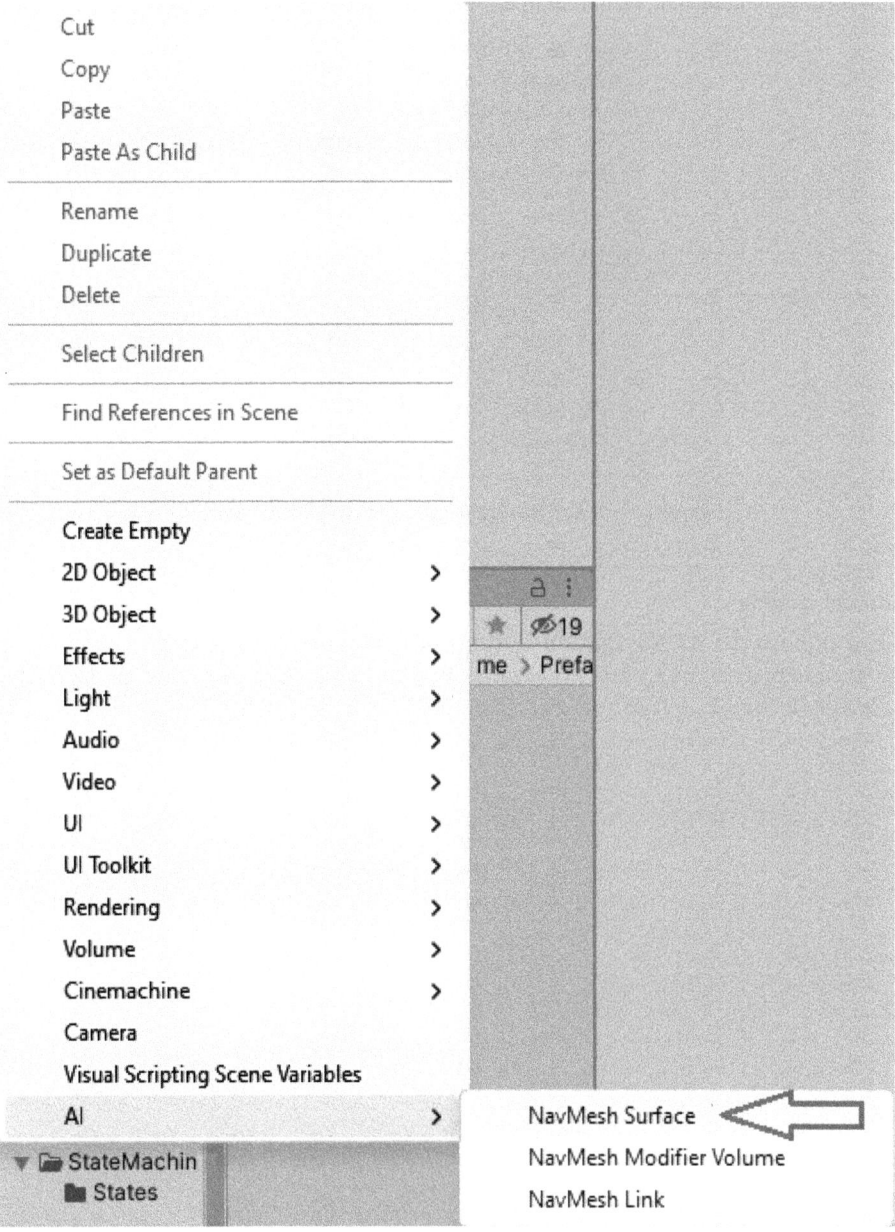

Figure 4.3 – Choosing NavMesh Surface from the Create menu

4. Subsequently, **NavMesh Surface** will be included, at which point you can proceed to **Bake** the surface. This refers to the process of precomputing and storing navigation data for AI pathfinding, as demonstrated in *Figure 4.4*:

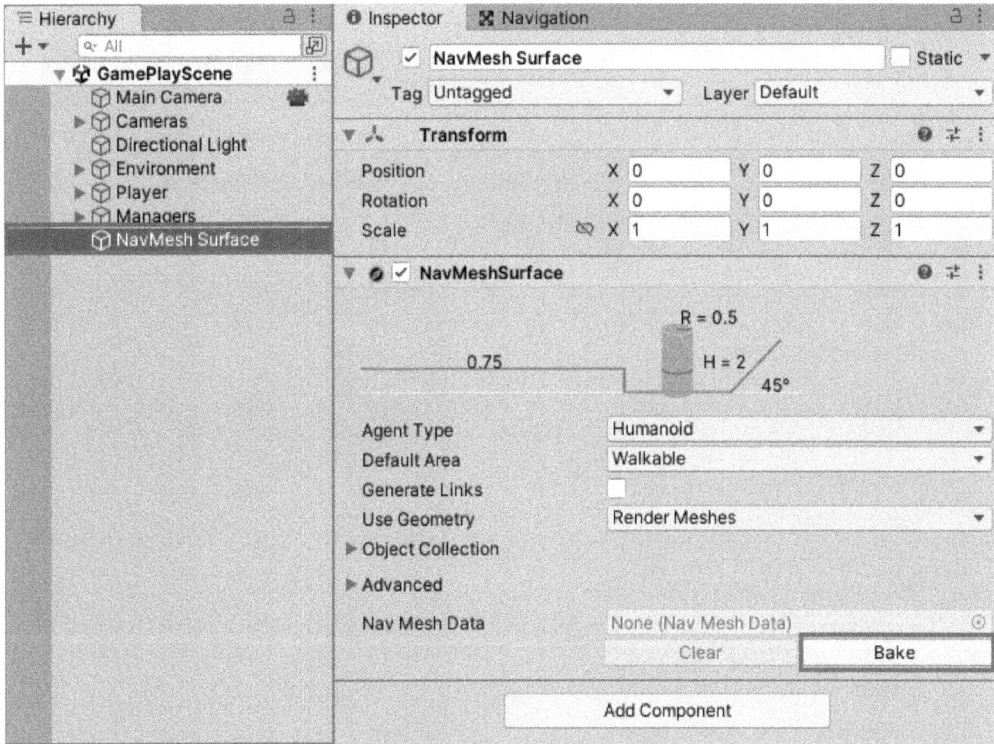

Figure 4.4 – The Bake action in the NavMeshSurface component

> **Note**
> Before initiating the baking process, it's crucial to remove the player and dynamic objects to prevent the creation of empty spaces in the resulting baking.

5. You can also include additional AI agents by navigating to the **Navigation** tab under **Window** in the top bar. Choose **AI** and then **Navigation**, avoiding the **Navigation (Obsolete)** option, as illustrated in *Figure 4.5*:

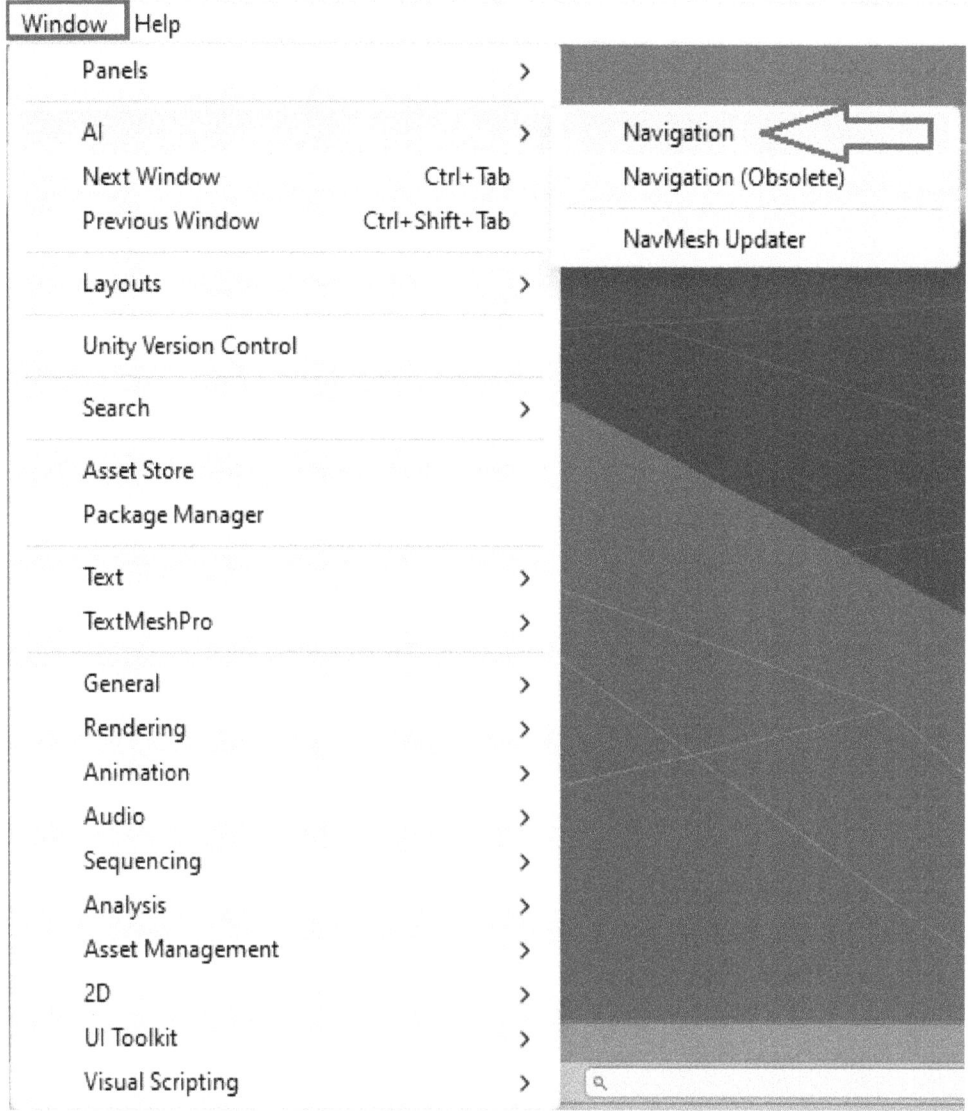

Figure 4.5 – Selecting Navigation

6. In the **Navigation** tab, you have the option to include more **Agents** with various settings, allowing for increased diversity in enemy behavior, as depicted in *Figure 4.6*:

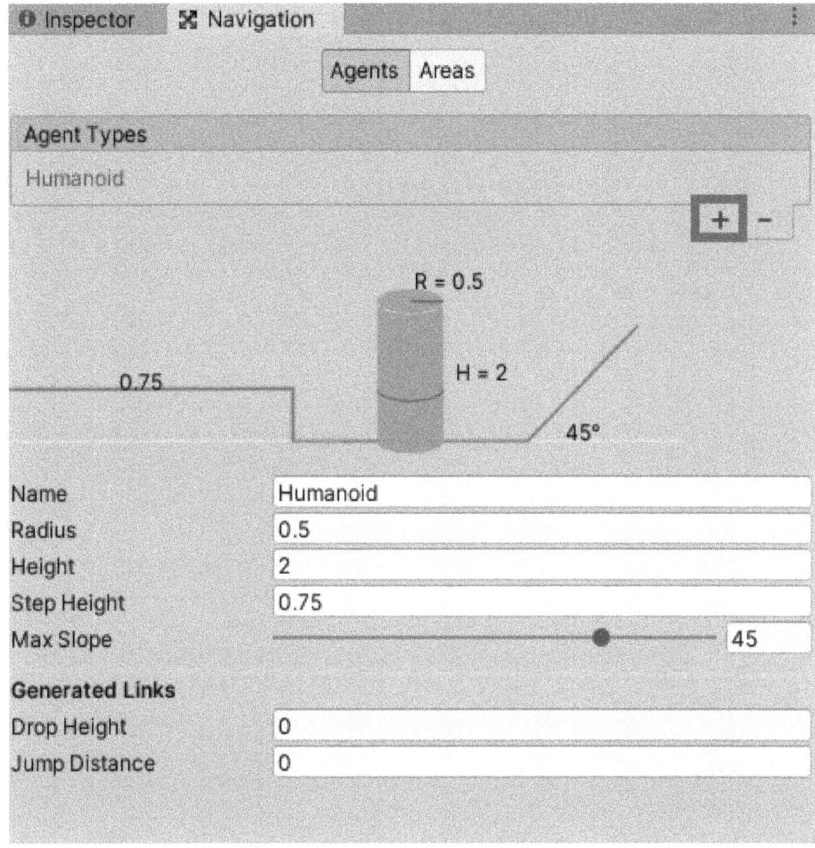

Figure 4.6 – Adding more agents via the Navigation tab

7. Additionally, you have the flexibility to introduce more **Areas**, providing variations in your gameplay. As shown in the following screenshot, you can designate areas as **Walkable**, **Not Walkable**, or even as **Jump** areas, tailoring them to the specific requirements of your game:

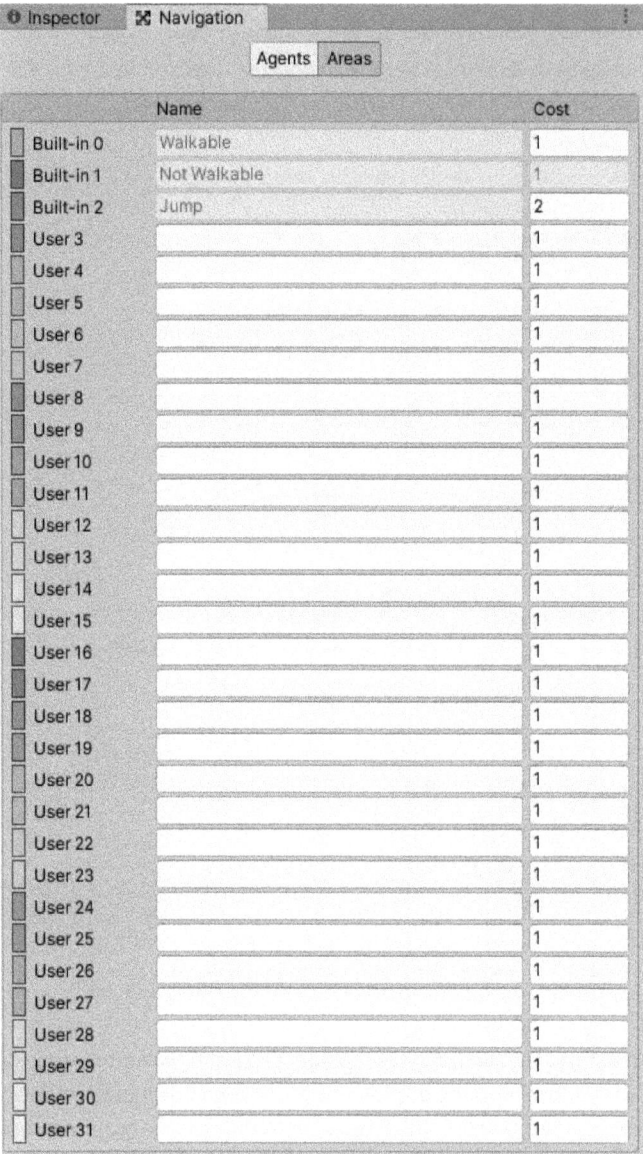

Figure 4.7 – Areas in the Navigation tab

8. Now that we've familiarized ourselves with adding additional areas or agents, we won't be making further modifications to them. I've mentioned them for informational purposes only. Now, let's proceed with integrating AI into our game. To do so, we must attach the **Nav Mesh Agent** component to the enemies to enable navigation, as illustrated in *Figure 4.8*. We have the flexibility to adjust values tailored to our game, such as changing the speed and when the AI will stop when the AI has reached its goal. For further details, please refer to the official *Unity documentation*:

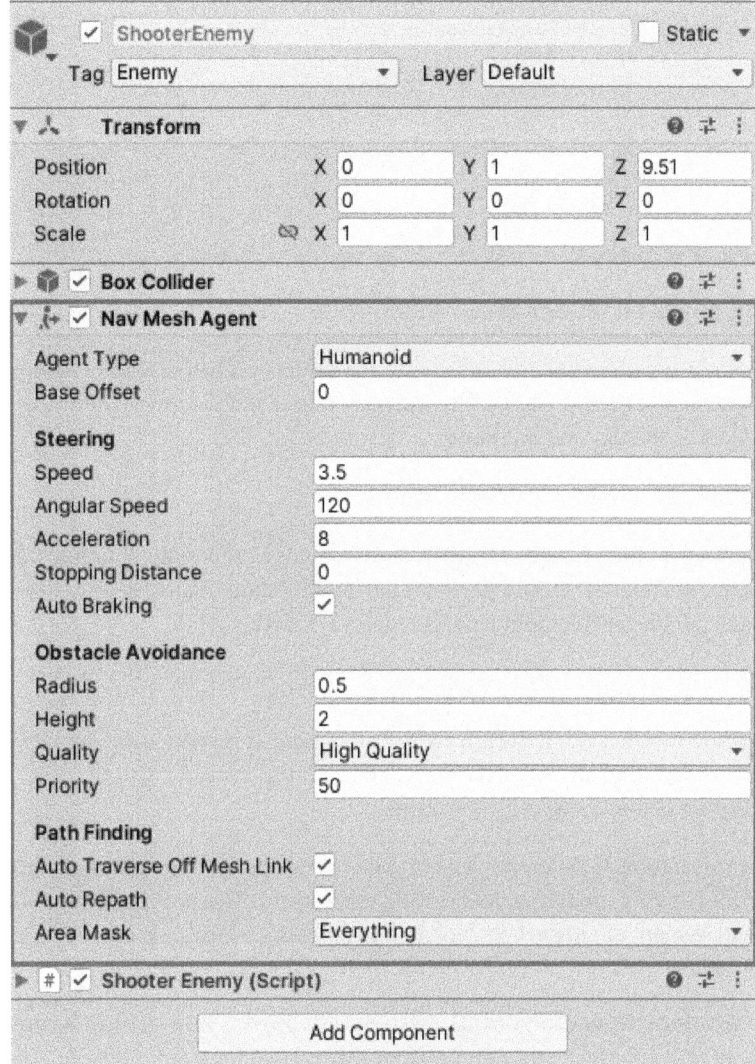

Figure 4.8 – The Nav Mesh Agent component for one of the enemies

After installing the package, we'll kick off the AI logic. We'll begin by establishing the `BaseEnemy` class and laying down the foundation for the state system since we intend to construct a finite state machine.

Let's start with the interface for states. The foundational structure is provided in the following code block:

```
namespace FusionFuryGame
{
    public interface IEnemyState
    {
```

```
        void EnterState(BaseEnemy enemy);
        void UpdateState(BaseEnemy enemy);
        void ExitState(BaseEnemy enemy);
    }
}
```

Let's take a closer look at this code:

- `void EnterState(BaseEnemy enemy)`:
  - This method is responsible for setting up the initial conditions and behaviors when the enemy enters this state. It takes a `BaseEnemy` object as a parameter, allowing us to access the enemy's properties and methods.

- `void UpdateState(BaseEnemy enemy)`:
  - This method is called repeatedly while the enemy is in this state. It defines the logic and actions that the enemy should perform during this state. Again, it takes a `BaseEnemy` object as a parameter to manipulate the enemy's behavior.

- `void ExitState(BaseEnemy enemy)`:
  - This method is called when the enemy exits this state. It is responsible for cleaning up any resources or resetting any variables associated with this state. As with the other methods, it also accepts a `BaseEnemy` object parameter.

By implementing this interface, different classes representing specific enemy states can define their unique behavior for entering, updating, and exiting those states. This approach allows for modular and organized management of enemy behavior, making it easier to add, remove, or modify states as needed within the game.

Let's move on to creating enemy components, starting with: `EnemyHealth`. This component will integrate the `IHealth` interface and handle all health-related logic for enemies. Check out the following code block:

```
    public class EnemyHealth : MonoBehaviour, IHealth
    {
        [SerializeField] float startingMaxHealth = 100;   // Set a
 default starting maximum health for the Enemy
        private float maxHealth;
        private float currentHealth;

        [SerializeField] float healAmount = 5f;     // Amount of
 healing per interval
```

```csharp
        [SerializeField] float healInterval = 2f;  // Time interval for healing

        private WaitForSeconds healIntervalWait;  // Reusable WaitForSeconds instance
        private Coroutine healOverTimeCoroutine;

        public UnityAction onEnemyDied = delegate { };
        public float MaxHealth
        {
            get { return maxHealth; }
            set { maxHealth = value; }
        }

        public float CurrentHealth
        {
            get { return currentHealth; }
            set
            {
                currentHealth = Mathf.Clamp(value, 0, MaxHealth);
                if (currentHealth <= 0)
                {
                    onEnemyDied.Invoke();
                }
            }
        }
        private void Start()
        {
            SetMaxHealth();  // Set initial max health
            healIntervalWait = new WaitForSeconds(healInterval);
            StartHealingOverTime();
        }

        public void SetMaxHealth()
        {
            MaxHealth = startingMaxHealth;
        }

        public void TakeDamage(float damage)
        {
            // Implement logic to handle taking damage
            CurrentHealth -= damage;
        }
```

```csharp
        //we can also just heal in some states only
        public void Heal()
        {
            CurrentHealth += healAmount;
            CurrentHealth = Mathf.Min(CurrentHealth, MaxHealth);
        }
        private void StartHealingOverTime()
        {
            healOverTimeCoroutine = StartCoroutine(HealOverTime());
        }

        private IEnumerator HealOverTime()
        {
            while (true)
            {
                yield return healIntervalWait;
                Heal();
            }
        }
    }
```

Let's understand the `EnemyHealth` component:

- `startingMaxHealth`: Default starting maximum health for the enemy.
- `healAmount`: Amount of healing per interval
- `healInterval`: Time interval for healing
- `healIntervalWait`: Reusable `WaitForSeconds` instance for healing
- `healOverTimeCoroutine`: Coroutine for healing over time
- `maxHealth`: Maximum health of the enemy
- `currentHealth`: Current health of the enemy
- `TakeDamage(float damage)`: Handles damage taken by the enemy
- `SetMaxHealth()`: Sets the maximum health of the enemy
- `Heal()`: Heals the enemy over time
- `StartHealingOverTime()`: Starts the coroutine for healing over time
- `HealOverTime()`: The coroutine method for healing over time

Next up is the `EnemyAnimations` component, which is responsible for managing the animations of the enemy. Let's delve into its code block:

```
public class EnemyAnimations : MonoBehaviour
{
    private Animator animator;

    private void Start()
    {
        animator = GetComponent<Animator>();
    }

    public void StartAttackAnimations()
    {
        animator.SetBool("IsAttacking", true);
    }

    public void StopAttackAnimations()
    {
        animator.SetBool("IsAttacking", false);
    }

}
```

Here, `StartAttackAnimations()` and `StopAttackAnimations()` manage attack animations.

Next, we'll implement the collision logic for the enemy in the `EnemyCollision` class. This class will handle collisions with the player, allowing the enemy to take damage. Look at the following code block for details:

```
public class EnemyCollision : MonoBehaviour
{
    private IDamage playerDamage;
    private EnemyHealth healthComponent;

    private void Start()
    {
        healthComponent = GetComponent<EnemyHealth>();
    }
    //we can also make layers for them and reduce calculations of collision in layer matrix in project settings
    private void OnCollisionEnter(Collision collision)
    {
```

```
            if (collision.gameObject.CompareTag("PlayerProjectile"))
            {
                if (collision.gameObject.TryGetComponent(out playerDamage))
                {
                    healthComponent.TakeDamage(playerDamage.GetDamageValue());
                }
            }
        }
    }
```

Let's look at what the `EnemyCollision` class does:

- `playerDamage`: Represents the damage that's inflicted by the player
- `damage`: Damage inflicted when the enemy collides with the player
- `OnCollisionEnter(Collision collision)`: Handles collisions with player projectiles

The final component in the enemy's logic is EnemyShoot. It's responsible for firing projectiles using the attached weapon. Implement the `IDamage` interface here so that it will pass the damage value to the player. Refer to the following code block for details:

```
    public class EnemyShoot : MonoBehaviour , IDamage
    {
        [SerializeField] float damage; //when the enemy collide with the player

        public BaseWeapon attachedWeapon;   // Reference to the attached Weapon
        [SerializeField] float fireDamage; //when the enemy shoot the player
        public void FireProjectile()
        {
            attachedWeapon.Shoot(fireDamage);
        }

        public float GetDamageValue()
        {
            // You can implement more sophisticated logic here based on enemy stats
            return damage;
        }
    }
```

Let's look at what `EnemyShoot` does:

- `fireDamage`: Damage inflicted when the enemy shoots the player
- `attachedWeapon`: Reference to the attached weapon of the enemy
- `FireProjectile()`: Initiates the firing of the attached weapon
- `GetDamageValue()`: Retrieves the damage value

Now, let's create the `BaseEnemy` class is an abstract class that defines the basic functionality and attributes of an enemy in a game. It will utilize state machine logic and contain references for the shooting and animation components of the enemies. This class facilitates communication between different states of the enemy, making it suitable for use with all enemies:

```
[RequireComponent(typeof(EnemyHealth) , typeof(EnemyAnimations) ,
typeof(EnemyShoot)) ]
    [RequireComponent(typeof(EnemyCollision))]
    public abstract class BaseEnemy : MonoBehaviour
    {
        public Transform player;
        [HideInInspector] public NavMeshAgent navMeshAgent;

        // Reference to the current state
        protected IEnemyState currentState;

        // Define the different states
        public IEnemyState wanderState;
        public IEnemyState idleState;
        public IEnemyState attackState;
        public IEnemyState deathState;
        public IEnemyState chaseState;

        public float attackRange = 5f;

        [SerializeField] internal float chaseSpeed;
        [SerializeField] internal float rotationSpeed;

        internal EnemyAnimations animationComponent;
        internal EnemyShoot shootComponent;
        internal EnemyHealth healthComponent;
        protected virtual void Start()
        {
            // Initialize states
            wanderState = new WanderState();
            idleState = new IdleState();
```

```csharp
            attackState = new AttackState();
            chaseState = new ChaseState();
            deathState = new DeathState();

            // Set initial state
            currentState = wanderState;

            // Get references
            player = GameObject.FindGameObjectWithTag("Player").transform;
            navMeshAgent = GetComponent<NavMeshAgent>();
            animationComponent = GetComponent<EnemyAnimations>();
            shootComponent = GetComponent<EnemyShoot>();
            healthComponent = GetComponent<EnemyHealth>();
            healthComponent.onEnemyDied += OnDied;
        }

        protected virtual void Update()
        {
            // Update the current state
            currentState.UpdateState(this);
        }
```

Let's take a closer look at this code so that we understand it:

- `player`: Reference to the player's `Transform` value
- `navMeshAgent`: Reference to the `NavMeshAgent` component for navigation
- `currentState`: Reference to the current state of the enemy
- `wanderState`, `idleState`, `attackState`, `deathState`, `chaseState`: Different states of the enemy (wandering, idle, attacking, dead, and chasing, respectively)
- `attackRange`: The range within which the enemy can attack
- `chaseSpeed`: The speed at which the enemy chases the player
- `rotationSpeed`: The speed of rotation for the enemy
- `Start()` Method: Initializes states, sets the initial state, and gets references
- `Update()` Method: Updates the current state of the enemy

Now, let's delve into the state machine logic that's responsible for transitioning between states:

```csharp
        public bool PlayerInSight()
        {
```

```csharp
            Vector3 directionToPlayer = player.position - transform.position;
            float distanceToPlayer = directionToPlayer.magnitude;

            // Create a ray from the enemy's position towards the player
            Ray ray = new Ray(transform.position, directionToPlayer.normalized);
            RaycastHit hit;

            // Check if the ray hits something
            if (Physics.Raycast(ray, out hit, distanceToPlayer))
            {
                // Check if the hit object is the player
                if (hit.collider.CompareTag("Player"))
                {
                    // The player is in sight
                    return true;
                }
            }

            // No direct line of sight to the player
            return false;
        }

        public bool PlayerInRange()
        {
            Vector3 directionToPlayer = player.position - transform.position;
            float distanceToPlayer = directionToPlayer.magnitude;

            // Check if the player is within the attack range
            if (distanceToPlayer <= attackRange)
            {
                // Calculate the angle between the enemy's forward direction and the direction to the player
                float angleToPlayer = Vector3.Angle(transform.forward, directionToPlayer.normalized);

                // Set a cone angle to define the attack range
                float attackConeAngle = 45f; // Adjust this value based on your game's requirements

                // Check if the player is within the cone angle
                if (angleToPlayer <= attackConeAngle * 0.5f)
```

```
                {
                    // The player is in range and within the attack
cone
                    return true;
                }
            }

            // Player is not within attack range or cone angle
            return false;
        }

        public bool IsIdleConditionMet()
        {
            return !PlayerInSight() && !PlayerInRange();
        }


        public void TransitionToState(IEnemyState newState)
        {
            currentState?.ExitState(this);
            currentState = newState;
            currentState?.EnterState(this);
        }
          private void OnDied()
        {
            healthComponent.onEnemyDied -= OnDied;
            // Trigger death logic if health reaches zero
            TransitionToState(deathState);
        }
    }
```

To understand this code, let's examine its functions:

- `PlayerInSight()` and `PlayerInRange()`: These functions check if the player is in sight or range, respectively
- `IsIdleConditionMet()`: Checks if the conditions for idling have been met
- `TransitionToState()`: Transitions to a new state
- `OnDied()` Method: Transitions to the death state

Now, let's move on to the states. First, we'll implement `IEnemyStates` so that we can include the base methods. Then, in the subsequent code block, we'll develop the logic for `IdleState`, detailing the actions the enemy will take in this state. `IdleState` is the default state for all enemies. Here, we simply check for the conditions of other states so that we can transition to them when their respective logic is met:

```
public class IdleState : IEnemyState
   {
        private float idleTime = 3f; // Set the duration for which the enemy stays idle
        private float timer; // Timer to track the idle time
        public void EnterState(BaseEnemy enemy)
        {
            timer = 0f;
        }

        public void ExitState(BaseEnemy enemy)
        {
            //Logic for Exit
        }

        public void UpdateState(BaseEnemy enemy)
        {
            // Logic to be executed while in the idle state
            timer += Time.deltaTime;

            if (timer >= idleTime)
            {
                enemy.TransitionToState(enemy.wanderState);
            }
            else if (enemy.PlayerInSight())
            {
                enemy.TransitionToState(enemy.chaseState);
            }
            else if (enemy.PlayerInRange())
            {
                enemy.TransitionToState(enemy.attackState);
            }
        }
    }
```

Let's take a closer look at the preceding code:

- **Variables**:
  - `idleTime`: This variable determines the duration for which the enemy remains idle
  - `timer`: This variable tracks the elapsed time while the enemy is in the idle state

- **Methods**:
  - `EnterState(BaseEnemy enemy)`: This method is called when the enemy enters the idle state. Here, it initializes the timer.
  - `ExitState(BaseEnemy enemy)`: This method is called when the enemy exits the idle state. Currently, it's empty, but you can add logic here if needed.
  - `UpdateState(BaseEnemy enemy)`: This method is called every frame to update the state of the enemy. Here's what happens:
  - The timer is incremented by the time elapsed since the last frame
  - If the idle time exceeds the specified duration (`idleTime`), the enemy transitions to the wander state, indicating it's ready to move around
  - If the enemy detects the player within its line of sight (`PlayerInSight()`), it transitions to the chase state to pursue the player
  - If the player is within the attack range (`PlayerInRange()`), the enemy transitions to the attack state to engage the player

This code ensures that the enemy behaves as expected while in the idle state, transitioning to other states based on specific conditions, such as time elapsed and player proximity.

In the following class, `AttackState`, we also implement `IEnemyState` so that we can modify the base methods so that they fit the attack state. The attack state is the state that all enemies will enter when they are attacking the player. It includes logic for tracking the player's position and firing projectiles toward the player, along with handling associated animations:

```
public class AttackState : IEnemyState
{
    private float attackTimer;  // Timer to control the attack rate
    private float timeBetweenAttacks = 1.5f;  // Adjust as needed based on your game's requirements

    public void EnterState(BaseEnemy enemy)
    {
        enemy.animationsComponent.StartAttackAnimations();
        attackTimer = 0f;
    }
```

```csharp
    public void UpdateState(BaseEnemy enemy)
    {

        LookAtPlayer(enemy);

        attackTimer += Time.deltaTime;

        if (attackTimer >= timeBetweenAttacks)
        {
            AttackPlayer(enemy);
            attackTimer = 0f;  // Reset the timer after attacking
        }
    }

    public void ExitState(BaseEnemy enemy)
    {
        enemy.animationsComponent.StopAttackAnimations();
    }

    private void LookAtPlayer(BaseEnemy enemy)
    {

        Vector3 lookDirection = enemy.player.position - enemy.transform.position;
        lookDirection.y = 0;  // Keep the enemy's rotation in the horizontal plane
        Quaternion rotation = Quaternion.LookRotation(lookDirection);
        enemy.transform.rotation = Quaternion.Slerp(enemy.transform.rotation, rotation, Time.deltaTime * enemy.rotationSpeed);
    }

    private void AttackPlayer(BaseEnemy enemy)
    {
        enemy.shootComponent.FireProjectile();
    }
}
```

Here's an explanation for this code:

- **Methods**:

    - `EnterState`: Initializes the attack state, starts attack animations, and resets the attack timer.
    - `UpdateState`: Checks if it's time to attack based on the time between attacks. It ensures that the enemy is facing the player and initiates the attack if conditions are met.

- `ExitState`: Stops attack animations when exiting the state.
- `LookAtPlayer`: Calculates the direction to look at the player and smoothly rotates the enemy toward the player.
- `AttackPlayer`: Causes the enemy to perform an attack action, such as firing a projectile.

With that, you've learned how to create states, enabling you to effortlessly add more states so that you can tailor your game.

Now that we've established the interaction loop between the enemy and the player, allowing them to shoot at each other, the next step involves creating a prefab for each enemy – for instance, implementing the `ShooterEnemy` base class and adding this component to the respective `GameObject`, turning it into a prefab. Similarly, for projectiles, remember that it's essential to modify tags based on whether they're for the player or the enemy.

Implementing challenge and reward systems using C#

Challenges breathe life into the gaming experience, pulsating with excitement and unpredictability, guiding players through pivotal moments that require skill, strategy, and determination. These obstacles ensure players stay fully immersed in the gaming world, crafting a dynamic landscape that turns each gaming session into an adventure, complete with unexpected twists and turns.

In games such as *Dark Souls*, challenges manifest in the form of formidable enemies and intricate level designs. Players are tested on their combat skills and adaptability, creating an intense and rewarding experience. *Super Mario Bros.* introduces challenges through precise platforming, timing, and defeating enemies. Each level presents a new set of challenges, gradually increasing in complexity.

Challenges versus missions/quests

While challenges, missions, and quests share common ground in engaging players, they differ in their nature. **Challenges** often refer to specific obstacles or tasks that test a player's abilities, such as completing a level within a time limit or defeating a powerful adversary. **Missions and quests**, on the other hand, are broader objectives that contribute to the game's narrative and involve a series of tasks that may include challenges. The distinction lies in the focused, skill-testing nature of challenges, making them pivotal components of dynamic gameplay.

In *The Legend of Zelda: Breath of the Wild*, a challenge might involve solving a complex puzzle shrine and testing the player's problem-solving skills. In contrast, a mission could be part of the game's overarching narrative, such as rescuing a character or retrieving a special item. Challenges offer immediate, skill-based hurdles, while missions contribute to the overall progression and storytelling.

Balancing difficulty levels for broad appeal

Achieving a harmonious difficulty curve is essential to cater to players of varying skill levels. Balancing challenges ensures that both novice and experienced players find engagement without encountering excessive frustration. Games such as *Celeste* masterfully balance difficulty, starting with simple challenges and gradually introducing more complex ones, allowing players to grow alongside the game's intricacies.

Successful games often employ techniques such as **adaptive difficulty scaling** or optional challenges to accommodate diverse player skill levels. This careful balance prevents discouragement for newcomers while providing a satisfying experience for seasoned players seeking greater challenges.

Exploring reward systems

Reward systems in gaming are like treasured prizes waiting for triumphant players after they've overcome tough challenges. These systems are closely linked to the challenge dynamics, acting as the driving force that propels players forward. Rewards come in various forms – power-ups, upgrades, or in-game currency, along with narrative progress and cosmetic items, each with its unique appeal.

In games such as *The Legend of Zelda*, conquering tricky dungeons or defeating tough bosses often rewards players with new tools or abilities to progress in the story. In RPGs such as *The Witcher 3*, completing side quests not only gives experience points and in-game money but also unlocks new storylines or equipment. The connection between challenges and rewards ensures that overcoming obstacles not only tests the player's skills but also promises valuable incentives, boosting player engagement and satisfaction.

Successfully blending rewards into the gameplay loop ensures that challenges aren't just hurdles but opportunities for growth. This fosters a sense of accomplishment and progression. Players are motivated to take on tougher challenges for the promise of more significant rewards, creating a satisfying gaming experience. The seamless integration of rewards makes the gaming journey fulfilling and enjoyable.

C# implementation of challenges and rewards

Moving from theory to practice, our C# implementation of challenges and rewards brings coding insights to life. With illustrative code snippets, you'll gain hands-on experience, bringing challenges to life and rewarding players meaningfully. We'll discuss the delicate balance that's needed to keep players engaged and motivated, understanding how challenge difficulty correlates with the magnitude of rewards.

Introducing the challenge logic

Let's begin by establishing the foundational data structure for challenges. This can be seen in the following class. Every challenge will share this common set of data, simplifying runtime tracking and allowing prizes to be assigned:

```
[Serializable]
public class CommonChallengeData
{
    public bool isCompleted;
    public RewardType rewardType;   // Type of reward
    public int rewardAmount;         // Amount or value of the reward
    … other challenge Data
}
```

Let's proceed to the `BaseChallenge` class, which features the logic for starting and completing challenges. Refer to the following code block for details. All challenges will derive from this script, customizing their logic within its methods:

```
public abstract class BaseChallenge : MonoBehaviour
{
    public CommonChallengeData commonData;

    public abstract void StartChallenge();
    public abstract void CompleteChallenge();
}
```

Let's take a closer look:

- `public CommonChallengeData commonData`: This is a public variable of the `CommonChallengeData` type. It holds data that might be common across various types of challenges. It allows derived classes to access and modify shared challenge data.

- `public abstract void StartChallenge()`: This is an abstract method declaration without any implementation. It specifies that any class inheriting from `BaseChallenge` must provide its own implementation for the `StartChallenge` method. This method likely contains logic to initialize or begin the challenge.

- `public abstract void CompleteChallenge()`: Similar to `StartChallenge()`, this is another abstract method that any derived class must implement. It is responsible for handling the completion of the challenge, which may involve updating the UI, awarding rewards, or triggering other game events.

In summary, `BaseChallenge` serves as a template for creating different types of challenges in a game. It defines common functionality that all challenges should have, such as starting and completing the challenge, while allowing specific implementations to vary based on the type of challenge.

Let's transition to `ChallengeManager`, a central entity that houses all challenges and takes on the responsibility of initiating challenges. Currently, it includes a dictionary for storing all challenge components by their respective types, encompassing all challenge types. It also features a method to commence challenges, which will be invoked by `LevelManager`.

Consequently, each level can have a designated challenge, and the manager maintains a reference to the current challenge. All of these functionalities are detailed in the following code script:

```
public class ChallengeManager : Singleton<ChallengeManager>
{
    // Define different types of challenges
    public enum ChallengeType
    {
        EnemyWaves,
        TimeTrials,
        LimitedResources,
        NoDamageRun,
        AccuracyChallenge
    }


    public GenericDictionary<ChallengeType, BaseChallenge> challengeDictionary = new GenericDictionary<ChallengeType, BaseChallenge>();


    public void StartChallenge(ChallengeType challengeType)
    {
        if (challengeDictionary.TryGetValue(challengeType, out BaseChallenge challengeScript))
        {
            if (!challengeScript.commonData.isCompleted)
            {
                SetCurrentChallenge(challengeScript);
                currentChallenge.StartChallenge();
            }
            else
            {
                Debug.Log("Challenge already completed!");
            }
        }
```

```
            else
            {
                Debug.LogError($"No challenge script found for
ChallengeType {challengeType}");
            }
        }


        private BaseChallenge currentChallenge;

        private void SetCurrentChallenge(BaseChallenge
challengeScript)
        {
            if (currentChallenge != null)
            {
                currentChallenge.CompleteChallenge();
            }

            currentChallenge = challengeScript;
        }
    }
```

Here's an explanation of the `ChallengeManager` class:

- `public enum ChallengeType`: This is an enumeration that defines different types of challenges available in the game. Each challenge type represents a specific kind of gameplay challenge, such as `EnemyWaves`, `TimeTrials`, `LimitedResources`, `NoDamageRun`, and `AccuracyChallenge`.

- `public GenericDictionary<ChallengeType, BaseChallenge> challengeDictionary`: This is a generic dictionary that maps `ChallengeType` enum values to corresponding `BaseChallenge` objects. It stores instances of different challenge scripts associated with their respective challenge types.

- `public void StartChallenge(ChallengeType challengeType)`: This method is responsible for starting a challenge of the specified type. It retrieves the corresponding challenge script from the dictionary based on the provided challenge type and then calls the `StartChallenge()` method of the retrieved script.

- `private BaseChallenge currentChallenge`: This private field holds a reference to the currently active challenge. It is used to track and manage the state of the current challenge being played.

- `private void SetCurrentChallenge(BaseChallenge challengeScript)`: This method sets the current challenge to the one provided as an argument. Before setting the new challenge, it ensures that any existing challenge is completed by calling its `CompleteChallenge()` method.

In summary, the `ChallengeManager` class facilitates the management and execution of different types of challenges in the game. It provides methods to start challenges, handle the completion of challenges, and track the current active challenge. The use of a singleton pattern ensures centralized control over challenge management operations.

Now, let's shift our focus to the individual challenges. The following code block contains an example that implements the `BaseChallenge` class, integrating custom logic specific to the `Enemy Waves` challenge. When the challenge starts, enemies are spawned near the player. Additionally, it includes logic to reward the player upon completing the challenge. This is facilitated by the `RewardManager` class:

```
public class EnemyWavesChallenge : BaseChallenge
{
    public int totalWaves = 5;  // Adjust as needed
    private int currentWave = 0;

    public override void StartChallenge()
    {
        if (!commonData.isCompleted)
        {
            StartCoroutine(StartEnemyWavesChallenge());
        }
        else
        {
            Debug.Log("Challenge already completed!");
        }
    }

    IEnumerator StartEnemyWavesChallenge()
    {
        while (currentWave < totalWaves)
        {
            yield return StartCoroutine(SpawnEnemyWave());
            currentWave++;
        }
        CompleteChallenge();
    }

    public override void CompleteChallenge()
    {
        if (!commonData.isCompleted)
        {
            RewardManager.Instance.GrantReward(commonData);
            commonData.isCompleted = true;
        }
```

```
            else
            {
                Debug.Log("Challenge already completed!");
            }
        }

        IEnumerator SpawnEnemyWave()
        {
            // Adjust spawn positions, enemy types, and other
parameters based on your game
            Debug.Log($"Spawning Wave {currentWave + 1}");

            yield return new WaitForSeconds(2f);
        }
    }
```

Here's an explanation of the `EnemyWavesChallenge` class:

- `public int totalWaves = 5`: This variable determines the total number of waves for the enemy challenge. Game designers can adjust this value to set the desired number of waves.

- `private int currentWave = 0`: This variable keeps track of the current wave during the challenge. It starts at 0 and increments as waves are spawned.

- `public override void StartChallenge()`: This method overrides the `StartChallenge()` method that's inherited from the `BaseChallenge` class. It initiates the enemy waves challenge if it's not already completed. Inside this method, a coroutine named `StartEnemyWavesChallenge()` is started to handle the wave spawning process.

- `IEnumerator StartEnemyWavesChallenge()`: This coroutine function manages the spawning of enemy waves. It runs until the current wave count reaches the total number of waves specified. Inside the loop, it waits for a wave to be spawned using the `SpawnEnemyWave()` coroutine.

- `public override void CompleteChallenge()`: This method overrides the `CompleteChallenge()` method from the base class. It grants rewards for completing the challenge using `RewardManager` and marks the challenge as completed.

- `IEnumerator SpawnEnemyWave()`: This coroutine function represents the logic for spawning an enemy wave. Game designers can adjust spawn positions, enemy types, and other parameters to customize the wave spawning process. In this example, it logs a message indicating the wave being spawned and waits for a set duration before spawning the next wave.

In summary, the `EnemyWavesChallenge` class defines a challenge where waves of enemies are spawned sequentially. It provides methods to start the challenge, spawn enemy waves, and handle the completion of the challenge by granting rewards. Game designers can customize the wave spawning process and adjust parameters according to the game's requirements.

The previous example is just one of the challenges provided. You can find all the challenges in this book's GitHub repository (see the *Technical requirements* section). Lastly, here's `LevelManager`, which is tasked with assigning a suitable challenge for the current level:

```
public class LevelManager : Singleton<LevelManager>
{
    public GenericDictionary<int, ChallengeType> levelChallengeMapping = new GenericDictionary<int, ChallengeType>();
    public int currentLevel;
    private void Start()
    {
        StartChallengeForCurrentLevel(currentLevel);
    }
    public void StartChallengeForCurrentLevel(int currentLevel)
    {
        if (levelChallengeMapping.TryGetValue(currentLevel, out ChallengeType challengeType))
        {
            // Start the challenge associated with the current level
            ChallengeManager.Instance.StartChallenge(challengeType);
        }
        else
        {
            Debug.LogError($"No challenge mapped for Level {currentLevel}");
        }
    }
}
```

Here's an explanation of the `LevelManager` class:

- `public GenericDictionary<int, ChallengeType> levelChallengeMapping`: This dictionary stores mappings between levels and their corresponding challenge types. The key represents the level number, and the value represents the type of challenge associated with that level.
- `public int currentLevel`: This variable stores the current level of the game.
- `private void Start()`: This method is called when the `LevelManager` object is initialized. It automatically starts the challenge associated with the current level.
- `public void StartChallengeForCurrentLevel(int currentLevel)`: This method starts the challenge for the specified current level. It checks if a challenge has been

mapped for the current level in the `levelChallengeMapping` dictionary. If a mapping is found, it retrieves the associated challenge type and starts the corresponding challenge using `ChallengeManager`.

- `ChallengeManager.Instance.StartChallenge(challengeType)`: This line of code invokes the `StartChallenge` method of the `ChallengeManager` singleton instance, passing the challenge type associated with the current level as an argument.

In summary, the `LevelManager` class facilitates the initiation of challenges based on the current level of the game. It ensures that the correct challenge is started for each level by looking up the challenge type associated with the current level in the `levelChallengeMapping` dictionary and then invoking the `StartChallenge` method of the `ChallengeManager` singleton instance.

Implementing the reward system

Now, let's delve into the reward system, a crucial element in the gameplay flow that allows users to receive rewards. This feature is essential for user motivation and engagement

Here's `RewardManager`, which is tasked with providing the user with rewards based on the challenge data. As we can see, it communicates with other managers to enable the user to receive specific rewards:

```csharp
public class RewardManager : Singlton<RewardManager>
{

    // Define different types of rewards
    public enum RewardType
    {
        PowerUp,
        UnlockableWeapon,
        ScoreMultiplier,
        SecretArea,
        Coins
    }


    public void GrantReward(CommonChallengeData commonData)
    {
        // Add code here to handle the specific reward type
        switch (commonData.rewardType)
        {
            case RewardType.PowerUp:
                // Grant temporary power-up
                break;
            case RewardType.UnlockableWeapon:
                // Unlock a new weapon
```

```
                    break;
                case RewardType.ScoreMultiplier:
                    ApplyScoreMultiplier(commonData.rewardAmount);
                    break;
                case RewardType.SecretArea:
                    // Grant items found in a secret area
                    break;
                case RewardType.Coins:
                    GrantCoins(commonData.rewardAmount);
                    break;
            }
        }

        private void ApplyScoreMultiplier(int multiplier)
        {
            ScoreManager.Instance.ApplyMultiplier(multiplier);
            Debug.Log($"Score Multiplier Applied: {multiplier}x");
        }

        private void GrantCoins(int coinAmount)
        {
            CurrencyManager.Instance.AddCoins(coinAmount);
            Debug.Log($"Coins Granted: {coinAmount}");
        }
    }
```

Here's an explanation of the `RewardManager` class:

- `public enum RewardType`: This enumeration defines different types of rewards that can be granted to the player, such as power-ups, unlockable weapons, score multipliers, items found in secret areas, and coins.

- `public void GrantReward(CommonChallengeData commonData)`: This method is responsible for granting rewards to the player. It takes a `CommonChallengeData` object as a parameter, which contains information about the type and amount of reward to be granted.

- `switch (commonData.rewardType)`: This switch statement checks the type of reward specified in the `CommonChallengeData` object and executes the corresponding reward logic based on `RewardType`.

- `case RewardType.PowerUp`: This case allows temporary power-ups to be granted to the player.

- `case RewardType.UnlockableWeapon`: This case allows new weapons to be unlocked for the player.

- `case RewardType.ScoreMultiplier`: This case applies a score multiplier to the player's score by invoking the `ApplyScoreMultiplier` method with the specified multiplier value.
- `case RewardType.SecretArea`: This case allows items to be found in secret areas.
- `case RewardType.Coins`: This case grants coins to the player by invoking the `GrantCoins` method with the specified coin amount.
- `private void ApplyScoreMultiplier(int multiplier)`: This method applies a score multiplier to the player's score by invoking the `ApplyMultiplier` method of the `ScoreManager` singleton instance.
- `private void GrantCoins(int coinAmount)`: This method adds coins to the player's currency balance by invoking the `AddCoins` method of the `CurrencyManager` singleton instance.

Overall, the `RewardManager` class provides a centralized mechanism for managing and granting various types of rewards to the player upon completing challenges.

The following code block contains `CurrencyManager`, which is responsible for overseeing in-game currency. However, the focus here is on a segment dedicated to adding coins to the player:

```
Public class CurrencyManager : Singlton<CurrencyManager>
{
    private int currentCoins;
    public void AddCoins(int amount)
    {
        currentCoins += amount;
        Debug.Log($"Coins: {currentCoins}");
    }
}
```

Here's an explanation of the `CurrencyManager` class:

- `private int currentCoins`: This variable stores the current number of coins the player has.
- `public void AddCoins(int amount)`: This method allows you to add coins to the player's currency balance. It takes an integer parameter amount, representing the number of coins to add to the current balance.
- `currentCoins += amount`: This line increments the `currentCoins` variable by the specified amount, effectively adding coins to the player's balance.

Overall, the `CurrencyManager` class provides a simple yet essential functionality for managing the player's currency balance, specifically adding coins to their total balance.

The following code block contains `ScoreManager`, which is tasked with managing the player's score and implementing a scoring multiplier:

```
public class ScoreManager : Singlton<ScoreManager>
{
    private float currentScore;
    private int scoreMultiplier = 1;

    public void ApplyMultiplier(int multiplier)
    {
        scoreMultiplier *= multiplier;
    }
    private void ResetMultiplier()
    {
        scoreMultiplier = 1;
    }
    public void AddScore(int scoreValue)
    {
        // Adjust score based on the current multiplier
        currentScore += scoreValue * scoreMultiplier;

        Debug.Log($"Score: {currentScore}");
    }
}
```

Here's an explanation of the `ScoreManager` class:

- `private float currentScore`: This variable stores the current score of the player.
- `private int scoreMultiplier = 1`: This variable represents the score multiplier, which starts at 1 by default.
- `public void ApplyMultiplier(int multiplier)`: This method allows you to apply a score multiplier to the current score. It takes an integer parameter multiplier, which adjusts the score multiplier accordingly.
- `*scoreMultiplier = multiplier`: This line multiplies the existing score multiplier by the specified multiplier, effectively adjusting the score multiplier.
- `private void ResetMultiplier()`: This method resets the score multiplier to its default value of 1.
- `public void AddScore(int scoreValue)`: This method adds a specified score value to the player's current score. It takes an integer parameter called `scoreValue`, representing the score to add to the current score.

- `currentScore += scoreValue * scoreMultiplier`: This line adjusts the current score based on the score value and the current score multiplier. It multiplies the score value by the score multiplier and adds it to the current score.

Overall, the `ScoreManager` class handles score calculations and updates, including applying multipliers and adding score values to the player's total score.

This example highlights the vital relationship between challenges and the reward system in game development. Challenges provide engaging obstacles and objectives, fostering player interaction and progression. Integrated with the reward system, completing challenges becomes not just an accomplishment but a satisfying experience, offering incentives that motivate players. This dynamic interplay enhances the overall gaming experience, ensuring players remain engaged, motivated, and fulfilled throughout their journey in the game world.

In *Chapter 6*, which focuses on data handling, I intend to introduce a save system that will store all pertinent data, encompassing the elements we've discussed so far. This chapter will delve into the specifics of implementing this system.

The provided scripts serve as demonstrations, and you can find the complete logic in this book's GitHub repository.

Summary

In this chapter, we delved into essential Unity game development principles, specifically addressing game mechanics with a focus on C#. We underscored their significance in shaping engaging gameplay, encompassing aspects such as balance, feedback, and player agency. This provided you with practical skills in C# coding for implementing effective game mechanics. Transitioning to the next section, *Implementing player behavior and AI logic using C#*, we explored player behavior design and foundational AI concepts. Additionally, we emphasized the crucial role of challenges and reward systems in elevating the player experience and fostering engagement.

In *Chapter 5, Designing Optimized User Interfaces with C# for Unity Games*, you will delve into the domain of UI design principles and responsive UI elements. By mastering UI design techniques using C#, you'll be able to craft visually appealing and immersive interfaces. This chapter aims to augment your skills in designing effective visual hierarchies, layouts, and responsive UI elements, ultimately contributing to an enhanced user experience, including optimized UI elements.

As you embark on this ongoing journey of skill-building, the upcoming chapter holds exciting challenges and discoveries. Happy coding!

5
Designing Optimized User Interfaces with C# for Unity Games

Welcome to *Chapter 5*, where we will learn how to optimize **user interfaces** (**UIs**) for our Unity games using the versatile capabilities of C#. This chapter equips you with practical skills to enhance the performance of your UI and ensure a smooth user experience. The first skill focuses on utilizing C# for efficient UI optimization, maximizing the performance of your UI elements. Following this, we delve into strategies for creating an optimized UI system in C#, providing insights into structuring and managing views effectively. Throughout this chapter, the presented system acts as a flexible framework, allowing you to customize and optimize UI elements based on your game's unique requirements. Let's dive into the world of optimized UIs, leveraging the power of C# to refine the performance and functionality of your Unity game interfaces.

In this chapter, we're going to cover the following main topics:

- Introducing UI design in gaming
- Best practices and optimizing techniques for UI
- UI system using C#

Technical requirements

All the code files of this chapter can be found at: https://github.com/PacktPublishing/Mastering-Unity-Game-Development-with-C-Sharp/tree/main/Assets/Chapter%2005.

Introducing UI design in gaming

In the exciting world of making games, the UI is like the link between the player and the cool virtual world made by game creators. UI design isn't just about making things look good; it's super important in shaping how players experience the game. This section talks about why UI design is a big deal in games and how it really affects how much players get into the game and how much they like it:

- **The first impression**:

  Think of the UI as the first hello between the game and the player. A well-made UI grabs attention, sets the vibe, and makes the game look and feel unique. Whether you're on the main menu or playing the game, every part adds up to the first feeling you get when you start playing.

- **Enhancing player immersion:**

  Playing a game should feel like you're right there in the action. A well-thought-out UI blends smoothly with the game, so you stay focused on playing without getting distracted. Whether it's cool movements, matching themes, or easy controls, the UI becomes a big part of the game's story.

- **Guiding user interaction:**

  The UI is like a helpful guide showing players what to do in the game. From health bars to markers for quests, each thing gives important information without confusing players. Making the UI clear and simple is super important so that players can think about their moves and the tricky parts of the game, not figuring out the buttons.

- **Impact on player engagement:**

  A UI that's easy to understand and looks good really keeps players interested. If moving around menus is smooth and the game responds well, players want to spend more time playing. On the flip side, a badly made UI can make players frustrated, not want to play, and ruin the fun.

- **Adapting to diverse platforms:**

  Since we play games on all kinds of devices now, the UI has to work well on everything. It's like speaking different languages for each device, making sure the game feels right no matter whether you're using a computer, console, or phone.

Making the UI in games is like finding the right mix of making things look good and work well. It's about picking colors and fonts, how things are spaced out, and also making sure everything runs smoothly. Using C# in Unity lets game makers use these cool design ideas and make interfaces that not only look awesome but also do their job well.

As we go through this chapter, we'll check out the basic ideas behind UI design and see how C# can help make really great UIs that make playing games even more awesome.

Transitioning to best practices and optimization techniques for UIs, we'll explore strategies to enhance UI performance and responsiveness next.

Best practices and optimization techniques for UIs

In this section, we are going to talk about some optimization techniques for UIs along with some best practices to have a better performance. Let's get started.

Splitting up Canvases

Issue: *Modifying a single element on the UI Canvas triggers a complete Canvas refresh, impacting performance.*

The Unity UI relies on the Canvas as its fundamental component. It creates meshes representing UI elements, refreshes these meshes when there are changes, and sends draw calls to the GPU for actual UI display.

Mesh generation is resource-intensive, requiring UI Elements to be grouped into batches for efficiency in draw calls. Due to the cost of batch regeneration, it's essential to minimize unnecessary refreshes. The challenge arises when even a single element changes on a Canvas, prompting a full Canvas re-evaluation to determine the optimal way to redraw its elements.

Many users construct their entire game's UI on a single Canvas with numerous elements. Altering just one element can lead to a significant CPU spike, consuming multiple milliseconds.

Solution: Divide your Canvases.

Each Canvas functions as an independent entity, segregating its elements from those on other Canvases. Leverage the Unity GUI's support for multiple Canvases by segmenting your Canvases, addressing the batching challenges within Unity UI.

Nested Canvases offer another solution, enabling the creation of complex hierarchical UIs without the need to consider the spatial arrangement of elements across Canvases. Child Canvases additionally insulate content from both their parent and sibling Canvases. They maintain individual geometry and conduct independent batching. An effective strategy for segmentation is based on the refresh frequency of elements. Place static UI Elements on a distinct Canvas, reserving smaller sub-Canvases for dynamic elements that update simultaneously. Additionally, ensure uniformity in Z values, materials, and textures for all UI Elements on each Canvas.

In our game, let me illustrate with an example. We'll set up a Canvas for the overall scene and, within this main canvas, each panel will function as an individual Canvas. This means that when we make updates, such as to the HUD canvas during gameplay, we won't be affecting the **Pause** panel or any other panels. It's crucial to ensure that every panel or view has its dedicated canvas component, preventing performance issues when updates are applied.

136   Designing Optimized User Interfaces with C# for Unity Games

The following figure shows the division of the gameplay scene canvases into smaller sub-canvases.

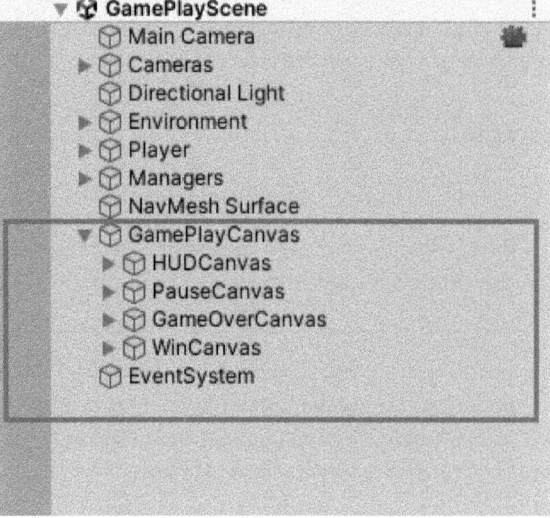

Figure 5.1 – GamePlayCanvas hierarchy

The following figure shows the **GamePlayCanvas** which contains all canvases:

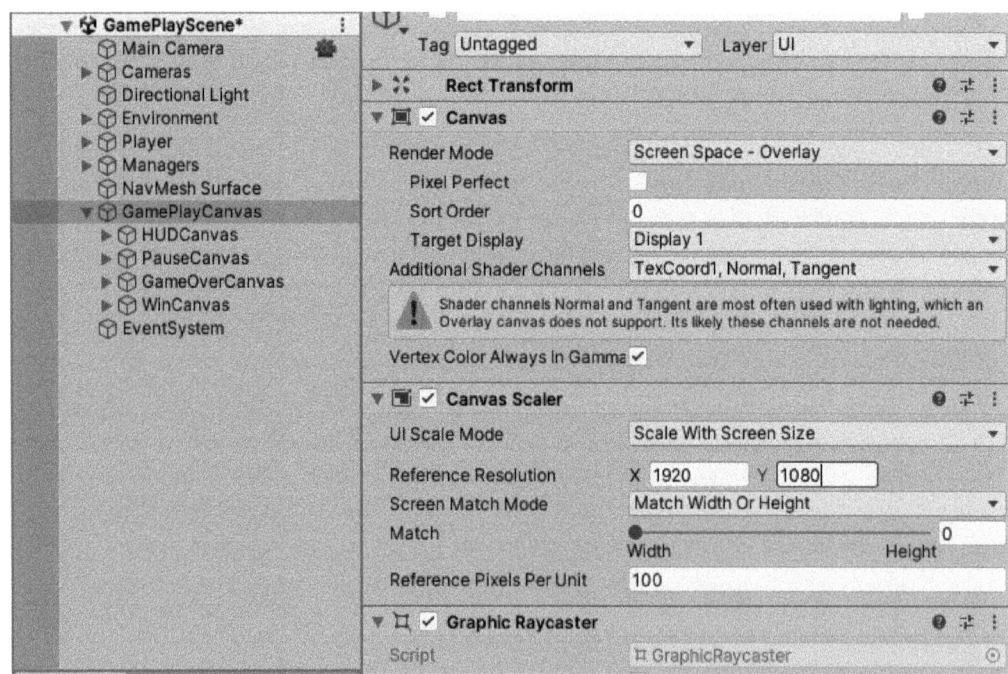

Figure 5.2 – GamePlayCanvas GameObject

The following figure shows the **PauseCanvas** which is a child of **GamePlayCanvas**:

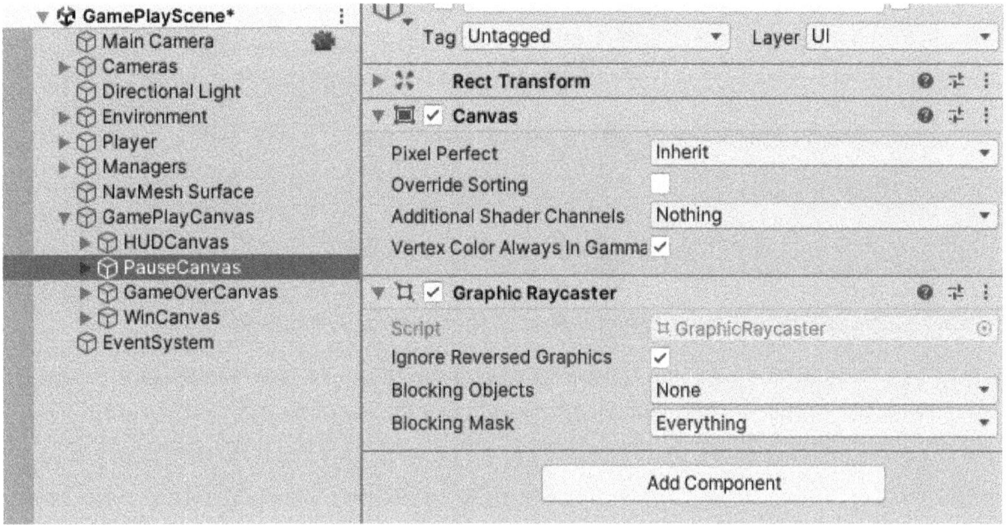

Figure 5.3 – PauseCanvas GameObject

Avoiding too many Graphic Raycasters and turning off Raycast Target

Issue #1: *Not using Graphic Raycaster well*

The **Graphic Raycaster** helps with turning your clicks or taps on the screen into things the game understands. It's like a translator between your actions and the game's UI, figuring out what you're touching and sending that information to the right parts of the game. You need this thing on every screen that needs your touch, even on smaller screens inside the big one. But it goes through all the places you touch on the screen and checks whether they're inside a UI's area, which can be a bit much.

Even though it's called a Graphic Raycaster, it doesn't exactly cast rays. By default, it only cares about UI graphics. It looks at all the UI parts that want to know when you touch them and checks whether the spot where you touch matches up with the UI parts that are set up to respond.

The problem is that not all UI parts want to be bothered when you touch them.

Solution: Get rid of Graphic Raycasters from screens or UI elements where you don't need them, especially if there are things that don't really care if you touch them. Also, switch off the part that checks whether some things on the screen can be touched for elements that don't change or don't need your touch. In the following figure, notice the **Raycast Target** setting in the `Image` component – we only turn it off for images that you can't interact with:

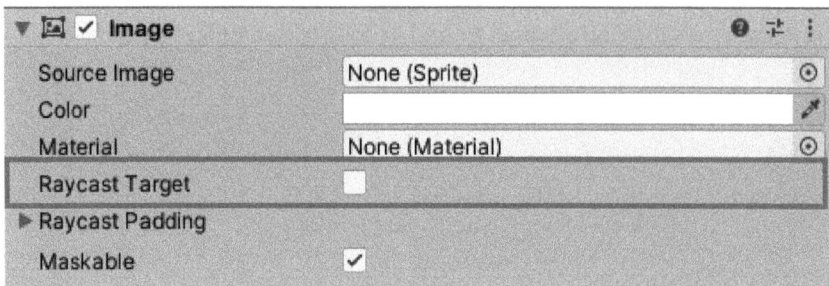

Figure 5.4 – RayCast Target variable

Issue #2: *Sometimes the Graphic Raycaster does more than just translate touches.*

When you set **Render Mode** on your Canvas to **Worldspace Camera** or **Screen Space Camera**, a blocking mask can be added. This mask determines whether the Raycaster will cast rays using 2D or 3D physics, determining whether any physics object obstructs the user's ability to interact with the UI.

Solution: Casting rays via 2D or 3D physics can be resource-intensive, so use this feature judiciously. To minimize the number of Graphic Raycasters, exclude them from non-interactive UI Canvases since, in such cases, there is no need to check for interaction events.

In the following figure, you can see the **Graphic Raycaster** component:

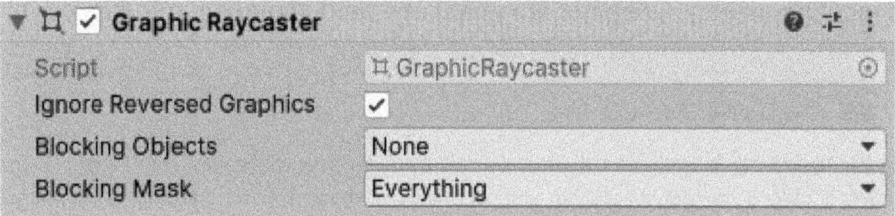

Figure 5.5 – Graphic Raycaster component

Efficiently managing UI object pools

Issue: *Inefficient practices in UI object pooling*

Frequently, individuals engage in pooling UI objects by first changing their parent and then disabling them, resulting in unnecessary complications.

Solution: Optimize for deactivating the object first before reassigning its parent within the pool.

This strategy ensures that the original hierarchy is dirtied only once. Once the object is reparented, there's no need for an additional round of hierarchy changes, and the new hierarchy remains unaffected. When extracting an object from the pool, follow the sequence of reparenting it first, updating your data, and then activating it to maintain efficiency.

Hiding a Canvas the right way

Issue: *Uncertain about efficiently hiding a Canvas*

There are times when you want to keep UI Elements and Canvases out of sight. But how can you achieve this in an effective manner?

Solution: Deactivate the `Canvas` component itself.

By disabling the `Canvas` component, you stop the generation of draw calls to the GPU, rendering the Canvas invisible. Importantly, the Canvas retains its vertex buffer, preserving all meshes and vertices. Consequently, re-enabling it doesn't trigger a rebuild; it simply resumes drawing.

Furthermore, deactivating the `Canvas` component avoids initiating the resource-intensive `OnDisable/OnEnable` callbacks within the Canvas hierarchy. Just exercise caution when disabling child components that execute computationally demanding per-frame code.

Efficient implementation of animations for UI Elements

Issue: *Implementing animators on the UI*

When animators are applied to the UI, they consistently affect UI Elements in every frame, even when the animation value remains constant.

Solution: Employ code for UI animation.

Restrict the use of animators to dynamic UI Elements that undergo constant changes. For elements that infrequently change or experience temporary alterations triggered by events, opt for coding your animations or utilizing a tweening system, a system you can make through code or you can use third-party assets for that. Various effective solutions for this purpose can be found on the Unity Asset Store. For our game, we will use the free `DoTween` package for this.

Effective handling of fullscreen UIs

Issue: *Performance issues with fullscreen UIs*

When a pause or start screen occupies the entire display, the remaining elements of the game continue rendering in the background, potentially leading to performance problems.

Solution: Hide everything else.

If you present a screen that overlays the entire scene, deactivate the camera responsible for rendering the 3D scene. Likewise, disable Canvas elements positioned beneath the top Canvas.

Contemplate reducing `Application.targetFrameRate` when engaging a fullscreen UI, as there is no necessity for updates at a **60 fps** rate.

Now that we have understood the best practices and optimization techniques for the UI, let's move on to the next section where we will explore some architectural patterns.

Introducing architecture patterns (MVC and MVVM)

In the world of game development, organizing and managing the UI is crucial for creating engaging and efficient experiences. Two widely used architectural patterns – namely, **Model-View-Controller** (**MVC**) and **Model-View-ViewModel** (**MVVM**) – provide frameworks for structuring UI elements in a way that enhances clarity and maintainability. MVC separates the application into three interconnected components — the **model** for data and logic, the **view** for the user interface, and the **controller** for managing user input. On the other hand, MVVM introduces **ViewModel** as a mediator between the model and the view, simplifying presentation logic and data binding, which is the automatic synchronization of data between the UI and the underlying data model in software applications. In this section, we will explore the practical application of these patterns in Unity game development, offering insights and guidance to help you make informed decisions about structuring your game's UI.

Understanding MVC – a teamwork of three roles

In the following figure, you can see the arrangement of the MVC pattern and how its components interact.

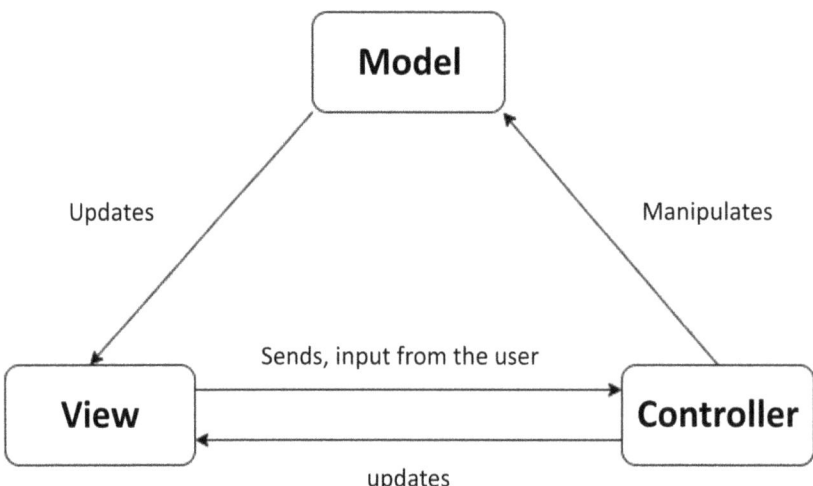

Figure 5.6 – MVC structure

Let's understand a little bit more about the MVC structure:

- **Model**:

  - *Essence*: Represents the data and business logic of the application
  - *Unity implementation*: Often implemented as `ScriptableObject` or regular C# class instances
  - *Role*: Manages data, enforces business rules, and communicates changes to the view

- **View**:

  - *Essence*: Represents the UI elements, responsible for displaying data to the user
  - *Unity implementation*: Comprises Unity UI components, such as `Canvas`, `Text`, `Image`, and so on
  - *Role*: Renders the data from the model and handles user input interactions, forwarding them to the controller

- **Controller**:

  - *Essence*: Acts as an intermediary between the model and the view, handling user input and updating the model and view accordingly
  - *Unity implementation*: A `MonoBehaviour` script attached to Unity UI elements or game objects.
  - *Role*: Listens for user input, updates the model, and instructs the view to reflect changes

- **Interaction flow**:

  - *User input*: Captured by the controller
  - *Model update*: The controller updates the model based on user input
  - *View update*: The view receives notifications from the model and updates the UI accordingly

- **Pros in Unity**:

  - *Simplicity*: Well suited for smaller projects and straightforward UI structures
  - *Unity compatibility*: Aligns seamlessly with Unity's built-in UI system

- **Cons in Unity**:

  - *Potential complexity*: May lead to increased complexity as the project grows
  - *Data binding challenges*: Achieving efficient data binding might require additional effort

Let's move on to understanding the next architectural pattern, MVVM.

Understanding MVVM – a mix of views and models

In the following figure, you can see the arrangement of the MVVM pattern and how its components interact:

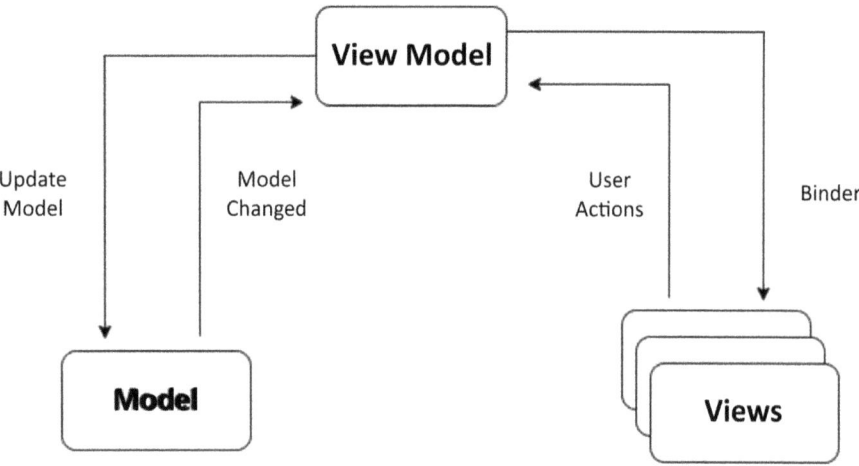

Figure 5.7 – MVVM structure

Let's understand a little bit more about the MVVM structure:

- **Model**:
  - *Essence*: Represents the data and business logic, similar to MVC
  - *Unity implementation*: `ScriptableObject` or regular C# class instances, much like in MVC
  - *Role*: Manages data, enforces business rules, and communicates changes to the view

- **View**:
  - *Essence*: Represents the UI, responsible for displaying data
  - *Unity implementation*: Unity UI components, same as in MVC
  - *Role*: Renders the data from the model and handles user input interactions, forwarding them to the controller

- **ViewModel**:
  - *Essence*: Acts as an intermediary between the model and the view, exposing properties and commands

- *Unity implementation*: A `MonoBehaviour` script that facilitates data binding
- *Role*: Simplifies data binding by exposing data and logic for the view to bind to directly

- **Interaction flow**:
  - *User input*: Captured by the view or directly by the ViewModel
  - *Model update*: The ViewModel updates the model based on user input
  - *View update*: When data changes occur in the model, they automatically update the view through data binding

- **Pros in Unity**:
  - *Enhanced data binding*: Streamlines the process of updating the UI in response to changes in the underlying data
  - *Testability*: ViewModel components can be tested independently, fostering maintainability

- **Cons in Unity**:
  - *Learning curve*: May pose a learning curve for developers unfamiliar with the pattern
  - *Overhead of abstraction*: Introducing an additional layer with the ViewModel might be considered over-engineering for smaller projects

Now that we understand what MVC and MVVM are, let's explore how to decide between them for our project based on certain factors.

Choosing the right path for Unity UI

The following points explain why we would choose MVC in Unity:

- **Well-established compatibility**: Unity's built-in UI system aligns naturally with the principles of MVC
- **Simplicity for smaller projects**: For smaller projects or when simplicity is crucial, MVC can be a pragmatic choice

The following points explain why we would choose MVVM in Unity:

- **Data-driven complexity**: MVVM shines in scenarios demanding efficient data binding and complex UI structures
- **Scaling for larger projects**: MVVM facilitates scalability and maintainability, making it a robust choice for larger endeavors

The following points will help you select your approach:

- **Consider project size**: MVC's simplicity may be advantageous for smaller projects, while MVVM's enhanced data binding and testability are beneficial for larger endeavors
- **Evaluate data binding needs**: If efficient data binding is crucial, MVVM might be the preferred choice

The journey through Unity UI development is a dynamic exploration, guided by the architectural choices of MVC and MVVM. While MVC offers simplicity and familiarity, MVVM introduces a layer of abstraction, elevating data binding and testability. As you navigate the Unity UI architecture, consider the specific needs of your project, the complexity of your UI, and the familiarity of your development team. Whether adhering to the clarity of MVC or embracing the sophistication of MVVM, the path you choose defines not only the structure of your UI but also the foundation of an immersive player experience. For our game, we will go with the MVC structure.

Practical suggestions for enhancing your UI development

Here are some tips that can be beneficial for you while working on UI.

- Create Prefabs for the most frequently used elements:
  - For this, consider using the title text as an example and attaching components to it. This makes it easier to implement changes later, as any modifications will impact all the elements in the game. Additionally, you can create images and any other UI elements.

- Use Sprite Atlases:
  - A Sprite Atlas is a feature in Unity that allows you to pack multiple Sprite textures into a single texture asset. This is particularly useful for optimizing and improving the performance of your game, as it reduces the number of draw calls by combining multiple Sprites into one texture.

  Here are some key points about Sprite Atlas in Unity:
  - **Draw call optimization**: By using Sprite Atlases, Unity can efficiently render multiple Sprites with a single draw call, which can significantly improve performance, especially on mobile devices.
  - **Grouping textures**: Sprite Atlases enable you to group multiple Sprites or textures together, making it easier to manage and organize your game assets.
  - **Texture packing**: Unity's Sprite Atlas system performs automatic texture packing, arranging individual Sprites within the Atlas to minimize wasted space and optimize texture usage.
  - **Mipmapping**: Sprite Atlases support mipmapping, which helps improve the rendering quality of textures when they are viewed from a distance.

- **Atlas variants**: Unity allows you to create different variants of Sprite Atlases for different platforms or screen resolutions, ensuring optimal performance across various devices.
- **Integration with Unity Editor**: You can create and manage Sprite Atlases directly within the Unity Editor, making it convenient for game developers to visualize and adjust their assets.

• Design alignment using a transparent image overlay:

- When provided with a designer's view sample, you can overlay an image representing the final result with slight transparency. This allows you to align and organize the view according to the design.

• Using the UI Extensions package:

- Discover the UI Extensions package, a valuable toolkit that significantly amplifies the capabilities of Unity's native UI system. Here's an overview of its key features:

  - **Extensive controls**: With over 70 additional UI controls, it offers advanced text fields (auto-complete, password masking, multi-line), sliders, progress bars, checkboxes, toggles, color pickers, dropdowns, list views, tree views, grids, tooltips, modal windows, context menus, toolbars, docking panels, and more.
  - **Customization flexibility**: Enjoy extensive customization options for existing UI elements, including the addition of shadows, outlines, and other visual effects, animation of properties (position, color, size), and the creation of custom layouts and interactions.
  - **Utility functions**: Benefit from various helpful utility functions for easy alignment and positioning of elements. Moreover, discover a shortcut for anchoring elements to corners, particularly useful for managing multiple resolutions, especially in mobile games.

  This package provides a robust set of tools and features, making UI development in Unity more flexible and efficient.

Now that we understand practical tips and architectural pattern (MVC and MVVM) structures, let's dive into creating a UI system using C# to efficiently handle UI behavior in our Unity project.

Creating a UI system using C#

In this section, we will create a C# system for handling UI behavior, leveraging optimization tips and the MVC structure to achieve our objectives. This involves creating a `UIManager` class to oversee views, a `BaseView` class containing core view logic, and a practical example demonstrating the implementation of the UI system.

The UIManager class

To kick off this system, we'll establish a base class called `UIManager`. This class will handle the invocation of `show` and `hide` functions for views and will act as a container for all the views. For each scene, we'll create a child of `UIManager`, responsible for controlling the views within that specific scene. This scene-specific manager will hold all the views, providing us with better control over them. This setup allows us to hide all views, ensuring that only one view is active at a time, which is advantageous for performance.

The following code block provides a sample of the `UIManager` base class, which includes generic functions for showing and hiding views:

```
public class UIManager : Singleton<UIManager>
{
    public GenericDictionary<Type, BaseView> views = new 
GenericDictionary<Type, BaseView>();

    private BaseView lastActiveView;




    protected override void Awake()
    {
        base.Awake();
    }

    // Register a view with the UIManager
    public void RegisterView<T>(T view) where T : BaseView
    {
        if (view != null && !views.ContainsKey(typeof(T)))
        {
            views.Add(typeof(T), view);
        }
    }

    // Show a view
    public void ShowView<T>() where T : BaseView
    {
        if (views.ContainsKey(typeof(T)))
        {
            var view = views[typeof(T)];
            // Show the new view
            view.Show();
            lastActiveView = view;
        }
        else
```

```csharp
        {
            Debug.LogError("The View Of Type is Not Exist " +
typeof(T).ToString());
        }

    }

    public void HideView<T>()
    {
        if (views.ContainsKey(typeof(T)))
        {
            var view = views[typeof(T)];

            if (view.IsVisible())
                view.Hide();
        }
    }




    // Hide the currently active view
    public void HideActiveView()
    {
        if (lastActiveView != null)
        {
            lastActiveView.Hide();
            lastActiveView = null;
        }
    }



    public BaseView GetView(Type viewType)
    {
        if (views.ContainsKey(viewType)) return views[viewType];
        else return null;
    }

    public T GetView<T>()
    {
        if (views.ContainsKey(typeof(T))) return (T)Convert.
ChangeType(views[typeof(T)], typeof(T));
        else return (T)Convert.ChangeType(null, typeof(T));
    }
}
```

In the preceding code block, we employed generic functions to handle the showing and hiding of views based on their type directly, avoiding the use of strings for improved performance.

We begin by registering the view and adding it to the dictionary, enabling us to hide or show it throughout the gameplay session. Additionally, we have functions to retrieve the view when needed, allowing access or performing specific actions on that view.

Utilizing UIManager

To utilize this class, we can create child classes for each scene and either attach this component to a GameObject or simply place it on the main canvas of the scene.

As evident in the upcoming code block, we have `HUDManager`, which inherits from `UIManager`. We will attach it to the main canvas of the gameplay scene to manage and control all views associated with this scene:

```
public class HUDManager : UIManager
{
    //Override Methods or Add new Logic here
}
```

In the following figure, you'll notice the `HUDManager` component connected to the main canvas:

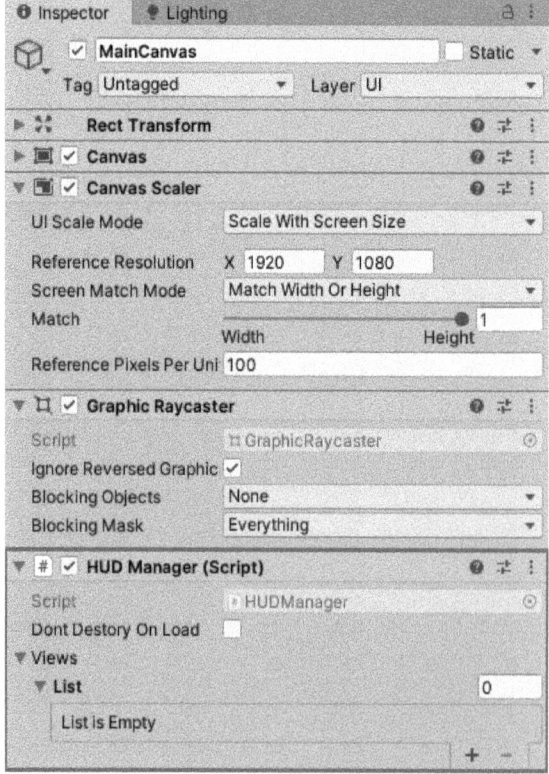

Figure 5.8 – The HUDManager component

Now, we can proceed to the other key component of the UI system, which is the `BaseView` class.

The BaseView class

In the UI system, we require a foundational class for all views, encompassing core functions that define the view's behavior, actions, or logic during `hide` and `show` operations. While the UI manager is responsible for invoking these functions, the underlying logic resides in the base class. We predominantly utilize `hide` and `show` canvas processes for efficiency, and for animations during these operations, we leverage the DoTween package.

In the following code block, you'll find the `BaseView` class along with its core functions:

```csharp
public abstract class BaseView : MonoBehaviour
{
    private Canvas canvas;
    public bool isActiveView;
    public GameData gameData;

    public UITween tweenComponent;


    protected virtual void Start()
    {
        canvas = GetComponent<Canvas>();

    }
    // Show this view
    public virtual void Show()
    {
        isActiveView = true;
        canvas.enabled = true;
        gameObject.SetActive(true);
        PlayTweens(true);
        ShowView();
    }
    public virtual void ShowView()
    {

    }
    // Hide this view
    public virtual void Hide()
    {
        PlayTweens(false);
    }

    private void OnOutTweenComplete()
    {
```

```
            isActiveView = false;
            canvas.enabled = false;
        }

        public virtual void HideCanvas()
        {
            canvas.enabled = false;
        }

        // Return true if this view is currently visible
        public bool IsVisible()
        {
            return canvas.enabled;
        }

        private void PlayTweens(bool state)
        {
            if (state)
            {
                tweenComponent?.PlayInTween();
            }
            else
            {
                if (tweenComponent == null)
                {
                    OnOutTweenComplete();
                }
                else
                {
                    tweenComponent.PlayOutTween(OnOutTweenComplete);
                }
            }
        }
    }
}
```

The `BaseView` class serves as a foundational element within our UI system, facilitating essential functionalities crucial for managing views in Unity projects. At its core, this class offers methods to both show and hide views seamlessly. Moreover, it seamlessly integrates with `tween` components, enabling the application of animations during view transitions. Beyond its fundamental functions, the `BaseView` class provides a suite of auxiliary methods, offering invaluable support for implementing the intricate logic of our game.

Now that we understand the functionality of the `BaseView` class, let's proceed to grasp the functionality of the `UITween` component, which is utilized for animating the views.

The UITween component

The `UITween` component serves as a wrapper that I've created for utilizing `DoTween`, simplifying the process of adding and removing animations in the Inspector for showing or hiding views.

You can locate all of these classes and additional resources in the GitHub repository, the link to which is mentioned in the Technical requirements section.

In the following figure, you'll observe the `UITween` component. This serves as a sample class, and we can adjust it to suit our game.

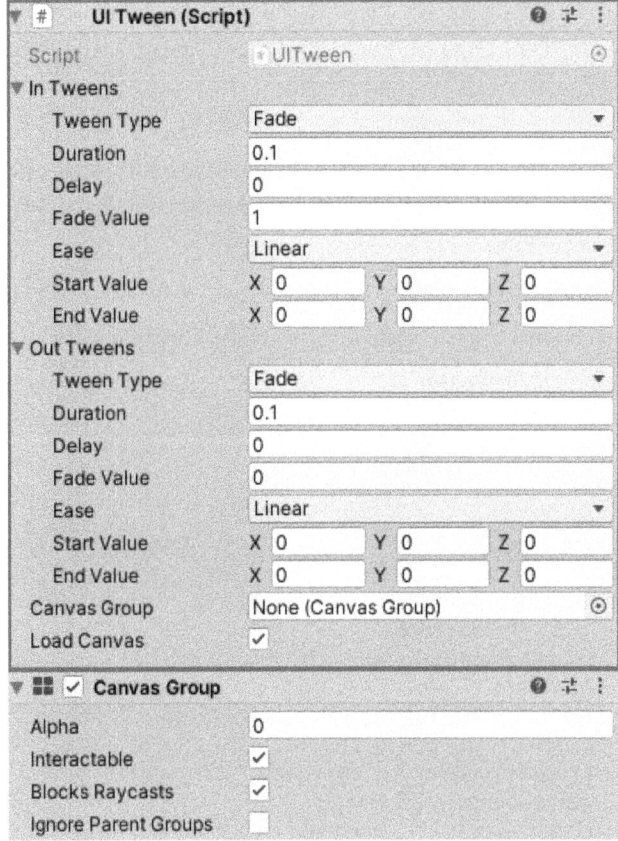

Figure 5.9 – The UITween component

Utilizing BaseView

To utilize the `BaseView` class, all you need to do is create a child class for each view in the game, enabling the use of core functions. Afterward, you can incorporate specific logic for each view.

In the following code block, you'll see an example of the `BaseView` class usage:

```
public class TopBarView : BaseView
{
    protected override void Start()
    {
        base.Start();

        StartUIManager.Instance.RegisterView<TopBarView>(this);
        Show();
    }

    //Add here logic for displaying the currencies for the player
}
```

The `TopBar` class, functioning as a view class, will be responsible for displaying elements such as the player's currency in the game. Simply attach the `TopBar` class to a `TopBar` Canvas GameObject in your game scene, and you're done.

In the following figure, you'll observe the `TopBarView` component attached to its canvas:

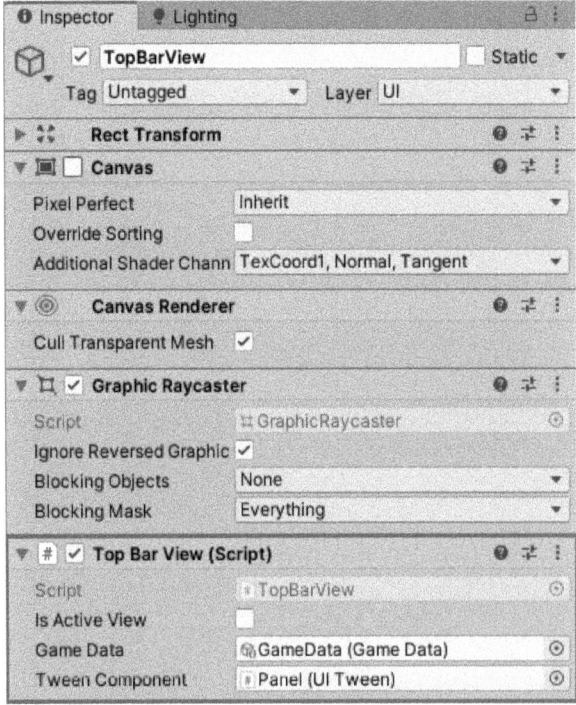

Figure 5.10 – The TopBarView component

This system serves as an abstract framework for the UI system, providing a foundation that can be customized or extended with additional logic as needed for the game. Feel free to tailor and expand upon this structure according to the specific requirements of your game.

Next, let's take an example to see how MVVM would be implemented.

Implementing MVVM

Implementing the MVVM structure in Unity involves separating the logic and data management from the UI elements. Let's look at an example implementation of MVVM in Unity.

In the following code block, `PlayerData` represents the data structure, such as player level and score:

```
// Model
public class PlayerData
{
    public int playerLevel;
    public int playerScore;
}
```

In the following code block, `PlayerViewModel` acts as an intermediary between the model and the view. It holds the logic for data manipulation and exposes properties that the view can bind to:

```
// ViewModel
public class PlayerViewModel : MonoBehaviour
{
    private PlayerData playerData;

    // Properties for data binding
    public int PlayerLevel => playerData.playerLevel;
    public int PlayerScore => playerData.playerScore;

    private void Start()
    {
        playerData = new PlayerData();
    }

    public void UpdatePlayerData(int level, int score)
    {
        playerData.playerLevel = level;
        playerData.playerScore = score;
    }
}
```

In the following code block, `PlayerView` represents the UI elements and is responsible for displaying data from `ViewModel`. It subscribes to `ViewModel` events and updates UI elements based on changes in `ViewModel`:

```
// View
public class PlayerView : MonoBehaviour
{
    [SerializeField] private PlayerViewModel playerViewModel;

    private void Start()
    {
        // Subscribe to ViewModel events
        playerViewModel.UpdatePlayerData(1, 100); // Example initialization
    }

    private void Update()
    {
        // Example of data binding
        Debug.Log("Player Level: " + playerViewModel.PlayerLevel);
        Debug.Log("Player Score: " + playerViewModel.PlayerScore);
    }
}
```

This structure allows for a clear separation of concerns, with `ViewModel` handling the logic and data manipulation while the view focuses solely on UI representation. Data binding ensures that changes in `ViewModel` automatically reflect in the view, promoting a more organized and maintainable code base.

Summary

In this chapter, we learned how to improve our game interfaces using C#. We started by getting better at making the parts of the UI work faster. Then, we figured out ways to organize and control the different views in our game. The skills you picked up here gave you the tools to make your UI look good and run smoothly based on what your game needs.

In the upcoming *Chapter 6*, we'll dive into handling game data using C#. We'll learn how to organize and save game information in Unity. These skills will help us manage game progress, save and load game states, and create features that use stored data. As you continue on this coding adventure, you'll discover new ways to handle game data effectively with C#. Get ready for more coding challenges in the upcoming chapter. Happy coding!

Part 3: Data Management and Code Collaboration with C# in Unity

In this part, you'll delve into the efficient handling and management of game data using C# in Unity, organizing and serializing data for streamlined storage and retrieval. You will explore the implementation of save and load systems to manage game progress effectively. Additionally, you will enhance gameplay depth and interactivity by creating data-driven elements using stored data with C#. Transitioning to code management, you will learn to utilize version control systems for efficient code repository management in Unity projects. You will also learn how to collaborate effectively with shared code repositories, resolve conflicts, and maintain code quality during teamwork using C#.

This part includes the following chapters:

- *Chapter 6, Effective Game Data Handling and Management with C# in Unity*
- *Chapter 7, Contributing to Existing Code Bases in Unity with C#*

6
Effective Game Data Handling and Management with C# in Unity

Welcome to *Chapter 6*, where we'll delve into effective game data handling and management using C# in Unity. Through practical exploration, you'll learn how to organize, store, and retrieve game data seamlessly. From understanding data organization and serialization to implementing save and load systems, you'll be able to empower players to preserve their progress and craft dynamic, data-driven gameplay experiences. By the end of this chapter, you'll have mastered the art of wielding C# for efficient game data management, unlocking endless possibilities for immersive gameplay. Let's embark on this journey together, where mastery of game data opens doors to boundless creativity in game development.

In this chapter, we're going to cover the following main topics:

- Data organization and serialization with C#
- Creating save and load systems using C#
- Data-driven gameplay with C#

Technical requirements

To complete this chapter, you must have the following:

- **Unity version 2022.3.13**: Download and install Unity, choosing version `2022.3.13` for optimal compatibility with the provided content.

- **Primary IDE – Visual Studio 2022**: The tutorials and code samples in this chapter have been crafted using Visual Studio 2022. Ensure it's installed so that you can follow along seamlessly. Feel free to explore Rider or other IDEs if you prefer, though note that the instructions that have been provided are tailored for Visual Studio.
- **GitHub repository for code samples**: You can access the code samples and project files for this chapter via this book's dedicated GitHub repository: `https://github.com/PacktPublishing/Mastering-Unity-Game-Development-with-C-Sharp/tree/main/Assets/Chapter%2006`. Clone or download the repository so that you have easy access to the code provided in this chapter.

Data organization and serialization with C#

In this section, we'll dive into data organization and serialization with C# in Unity. Here, we'll learn how to manage game data efficiently. First, we'll talk about picking the right data structures, such as arrays and lists, and how to make your own. Then, we'll cover serialization, which helps save and load game data. Then, we'll explore Unity's options, such as **JavaScript Object Notation** (**JSON**) and **eXtensible Markup Language** (**XML**). By covering some simple examples, we'll show you how to organize and save game data neatly using C#. Let's start learning how to master game data management!

Understanding data structures

Selecting the appropriate data structure for storing information in your game involves considering factors such as the type of data, how frequently it will be accessed, and the operations you need to perform on that data. Here are some examples to illustrate how you can choose the right method:

- **Arrays**: Use arrays when you have a fixed-size collection of elements of the same type.

    For instance, if you have a game with a set number of levels, as shown in the following code, you might use an array to store level data, such as scores or the completion status for each level:

    ```
    int[] levelScores = new int[10]; // An array to store scores for 10 levels
    ```

- **Lists**: Lists are dynamic arrays that can grow or shrink in size at runtime. They are suitable when you need to add or remove elements frequently.

    For example, if you have a game with an inventory system where items can be added or removed dynamically, a list would be more appropriate. Take a look at the following code for an example:

    ```
    List<string> inventoryItems = new List<string>(); // A list to store inventory items
    inventoryItems.Add("Sword");
    inventoryItems.Add("Potion");
    ```

- **Dictionaries**: Dictionaries are useful when you need to associate keys with values. They are ideal for situations where you need to quickly look up values based on specific keys.

    - For instance, if you have a game with a leaderboard, you might use a dictionary to map player names to their scores, as shown here:

        ```
        Dictionary<string, int> leaderboard = new Dictionary<string,
        int>(); leaderboard.Add("Player1", 1000);
        leaderboard.Add("Player2", 1500);
        ```

- **Custom data structures**: Sometimes, none of the built-in data structures are the perfect fit for your needs. In such cases, you can create custom data structures tailored to your specific requirements.

    - For example, if you're developing a complex RPG game, you might create a custom data structure to represent character attributes and abilities. The `Character` class is one such custom data structure:

        ```
        public class Character {
          public string Name;
          public int Health;
          public int AttackDamage;
        }
        ```

By carefully considering the nature of your data and the operations you need to perform, you can choose the most appropriate data structure for your game, ensuring optimal performance and efficient data management.

Enhancing game performance with proper data structure selection

In the world of game creation, where speed and efficiency matter most, picking the right data structures is crucial. It helps game makers achieve smoother and faster gameplay, making their games more enjoyable for players.

Choosing the appropriate data structure can significantly benefit game performance in several ways:

- **Optimized memory usage**: Using the right data structure helps minimize memory usage, which is crucial for performance, especially in resource-intensive games.

    - For example, if your game only needs to store a fixed number of elements of the same type, using an array instead of a list can save memory because arrays have a fixed size.

- **Faster access and retrieval**: Certain data structures offer faster access and retrieval times, which can improve overall game responsiveness.

  - For instance, dictionaries provide constant-time lookups, making them ideal for scenarios where you need to quickly retrieve values based on keys, such as accessing player data in a leaderboard.

- **Efficient data manipulation**: Choosing the appropriate data structure can streamline data manipulation operations, leading to smoother gameplay experiences.

  - Lists, for example, allow for efficient insertion and removal of elements, making them suitable for dynamic scenarios such as managing an inventory where items are frequently added or removed.

- **Enhanced code readability and maintainability**: Using the right data structure can make your code more readable and maintainable, leading to easier debugging and future updates. Custom data structures tailored to your game's specific needs can improve code organization and clarity, making it easier for you and other developers to understand and modify the code base.

  - For instance, if your game includes challenges, you can design a custom class specifically for managing these challenges. Within this class, you can incorporate attributes such as a list of rewards and a unique identifier for each challenge. This approach enhances the readability of your code base.

- **Reduced processing overhead**: Optimal data structures help reduce processing overhead, contributing to smoother gameplay and better overall performance.

  - For example, if your game needs to iterate through a collection of elements in a specific order, using a list instead of a dictionary can eliminate unnecessary key-value pair lookups, resulting in faster iteration times.

In summary, selecting the appropriate data structure is critical for optimizing game performance as it helps minimize memory usage, improve access times, streamline data manipulation, enhance code readability, and reduce processing overhead. By understanding the characteristics and advantages of different data structures, game developers can design more efficient and responsive gameplay experiences for players.

In the upcoming subsection, we'll delve deeper into Unity's serialization, exploring its role in efficiently saving and loading data.

Serialization in Unity

Serialization is the process of converting complex objects or data structures into a format that can be easily stored or transmitted and then reconstructed later. In the context of Unity game development, serialization plays a crucial role in saving and loading game data. By serializing game objects and their properties, Unity can store them in a format that can be saved to disk or transferred over the network, allowing for persistence between sessions and enabling features such as saving games and networked multiplayer.

Serialization is a fundamental aspect of game development for several reasons:

- **Persistence between sessions**: Serialization allows game state and player progress to be saved and loaded between gameplay sessions. This enables features such as saving and loading game progress, maintaining player inventories, and preserving game settings.

- **Network communication**: Serialization facilitates transmitting game data over the network, which is essential for multiplayer games, client-server architectures, and online features. By serializing game objects and messages, Unity can send data between clients and servers efficiently.

- **Data interchange**: Serialization allows data to be exchanged between different systems and platforms. For example, game data can be serialized into a standardized format such as JSON or XML, allowing it to be shared with other applications or integrated with web services.

- **Data persistence**: Serialization allows data to be stored in a structured format, such as files or databases, ensuring that it persists even when the game isn't running. This is crucial for features such as saving and loading user preferences, high scores, and game configurations.

By understanding the principles of serialization and mastering Unity's serialization options, we can implement robust and flexible data management systems, enabling features such as save games, networked multiplayer, and data-driven gameplay mechanics. Serialization is a fundamental tool in our toolkit, empowering us to create immersive and dynamic gaming experiences across platforms and genres.

In Unity, serialization is seamlessly integrated into the engine's workflow, allowing us to easily save and load game data using built-in APIs and utilities. Unity provides various serialization options, including JSON, XML, and binary serialization, each suited to different use cases and requirements. As we can see in this section.

Let's explore the options that are available in Unity so that we can integrate them into our game. We'll begin by defining each option and providing an example for better understanding. We'll delve into each one and illustrate their usage.

JSON serialization and deserialization

JSON is a lightweight data-interchange format that is commonly used for transmitting data between a server and a web application. In Unity, JSON serialization and deserialization are useful for scenarios where you need to exchange data with external systems or web services.

Example: In the following code block, we're utilizing Unity's built-in system to serialize and deserialize data:

```
// Serialize object to JSON string
string jsonString = JsonUtility.ToJson(myObject);
```

```
// Deserialize JSON string back to object
MyClass deserializedObject = JsonUtility.
FromJson<MyClass>(jsonString);
```

XML serialization and deserialization

XML is a versatile format that is used for data exchange and configuration settings. Unity supports XML serialization and deserialization, making it suitable for scenarios where you need to work with legacy systems or integrate with platforms that use XML as the data interchange format.

Example: The following code block demonstrates how to serialize and deserialize data to and from XML.

To utilize this type of serialization, you must include the using System.IO; and using System.Xml.Serialization; namespaces, like so:

```
// Serialize object to XML string
XmlSerializer serializer = new XmlSerializer(typeof(MyClass));
StringWriter writer = new StringWriter();
serializer.Serialize(writer, myObject);
string xmlString = writer.ToString();

// Deserialize XML string back to object
StringReader reader = new StringReader(xmlString);
MyClass deserializedObject = (MyClass)serializer.Deserialize(reader);
```

Let's take a closer look at the XML serialization and deserialization provided here:

- **Serialization process**:

    - Serialization is the process of converting an object into a format that can be easily stored or transmitted and reconstructed later

    - `XmlSerializer` is a class provided by the .NET framework for serializing and deserializing objects to and from XML format

    - `XmlSerializer serializer = new XmlSerializer(typeof(MyClass));`: This line creates an instance of the `XmlSerializer` class that specifies the type of object (`MyClass`) to be serialized

    - `StringWriter writer = new StringWriter();`: This line creates a `StringWriter` object, which is used to write XML content as a string

    - `serializer.Serialize(writer, myObject);`: This line serializes the `myObject` instance of `MyClass` into XML format and writes it to `StringWriter`

    - `string xmlString = writer.ToString();`: This line converts the XML content written to `StringWriter` into a string representation and stores it in the `xmlString` variable

- **Deserialization process**:

    - Deserialization is the process of reconstructing an object from its serialized XML representation.
    - `StringReader reader = new StringReader(xmlString);`: This line creates a `StringReader` object, which is used to read XML content from a string.
    - `(MyClass)serializer.Deserialize(reader);`: This line deserializes the XML content from `StringReader` back into an object of the `MyClass` type. The `Deserialize` method of the `XmlSerializer` class is used for this purpose.
    - The deserialized object is then assigned to the `deserializedObject` variable, ready for use in the program.

In summary, the provided code block demonstrates how to serialize an object of the `MyClass` type as an XML string and then deserialize the XML string back into an object of the same type using the `XmlSerializer` class in C#. This process allows objects to be easily persisted to storage or transmitted over a network in XML format and reconstructed later for use in the application.

Binary serialization and deserialization

Binary serialization and deserialization are ideal for scenarios where you need to save and load game data efficiently, such as implementing save games or storing configuration settings locally on the user's device. Binary serialization provides a compact representation of data and faster read/write times compared to text-based formats such as JSON or XML.

Example: The following code block shows how to serialize and deserialize data to and from binary format.

To utilize this type of serialization, you must include the `using System.IO;` and `using System.Runtime.Serialization.Formatters.Binary;` namespaces, as follows:

```
// Serialize object to binary format
BinaryFormatter formatter = new BinaryFormatter();
MemoryStream stream = new MemoryStream();
formatter.Serialize(stream, myObject);
byte[] binaryData = stream.ToArray();

// Deserialize binary data back to object
stream = new MemoryStream(binaryData);
MyClass deserializedObject = (MyClass)formatter.Deserialize(stream);
```

Let's take a closer look at this code block:

- **Serialization process**:

    - Serialization is the process of converting an object into a format that can be easily stored or transmitted and reconstructed later

- `BinaryFormatter` is a class provided by the .NET framework for serializing and deserializing objects to and from binary format
  - `BinaryFormatter formatter = new BinaryFormatter();`: This line creates an instance of the `BinaryFormatter` class, which is used for binary serialization
  - `MemoryStream stream = new MemoryStream();`: This line creates a `MemoryStream` object, which is used to store binary data in memory
  - `formatter.Serialize(stream, myObject);`: This line serializes the `myObject` instance into binary format and writes it to `MemoryStream`
  - `byte[] binaryData = stream.ToArray();`: This line converts the binary data written to `MemoryStream` into a byte array, which can be easily stored or transmitted
- **Deserialization process**:
  - Deserialization is the process of reconstructing an object from its serialized binary representation.
  - `stream = new MemoryStream(binaryData);`: This line creates a new `MemoryStream` object, initialized with the binary data stored in the `binaryData` byte array.
  - `(MyClass)formatter.Deserialize(stream);`: This line deserializes the binary data from the `MemoryStream` back into an object of the `MyClass` type. The `Deserialize` method of the `BinaryFormatter` class is used for this purpose.
  - The deserialized object is then assigned to the `deserializedObject` variable, ready for use in the program.

In summary, the preceding code block demonstrates how to serialize an object of the `MyClass` type to binary format and then deserialize the binary data back into an object of the same type using the `BinaryFormatter` class in C#. This process allows objects to be easily persisted to storage or transmitted over a network in binary format and reconstructed later for use in the application.

ScriptableObject serialization

ScriptableObjects are Unity assets that allow you to store data in a serialized format and create custom editor interfaces for modifying that data in Unity Editor. They are useful for managing configuration settings, defining game parameters, and creating reusable components that can be shared across multiple game objects.

Example: In the following code blocks, we will explore an example of scriptable object data. Then, we'll demonstrate how to utilize serialization and deserialization with scriptable objects.

The first code block contains a ScriptableObject that's designed for game settings, encapsulating essential data relevant to the game's operation:

```
[CreateAssetMenu(fileName = "NewSettings", menuName = "Game
Settings")]
```

```
public class GameSettings : ScriptableObject {
    public int playerHealth;
    public int enemyCount;
    public float playerSpeed;
}
```

For the second code block, the SettingsManager class contains a reference to the GameSettings data and includes functions for saving and loading settings:

```
public class SettingsManager : MonoBehaviour {
    public GameSettings gameSettings;

    // Serialize the GameSettings ScriptableObject to a file
    public void SaveSettings() {
        string jsonSettings = JsonUtility.ToJson(gameSettings);
        System.IO.File.WriteAllText(Application.persistentDataPath + "/settings.json", jsonSettings);
    }

    // Deserialize the GameSettings ScriptableObject from a file
    public void LoadSettings() {
        if (System.IO.File.Exists(Application.persistentDataPath + "/settings.json")) {
            string jsonSettings = System.IO.File.ReadAllText(Application.persistentDataPath + "/settings.json");
            gameSettings = JsonUtility.FromJson<GameSettings>(jsonSettings);
        }
    }
}
```

Let's take a closer look at the SettingsManager class:

- The SaveSettings() method:
  - public void SaveSettings() { ... }: This method is responsible for saving the game settings to a file
  - JsonUtility.ToJson(gameSettings): This method serializes the gameSettings object to JSON format
  - System.IO.File.WriteAllText(...): This method writes the serialized JSON data to a file named settings.json in the persistent data path of the application

- The `LoadSettings()` method:
  - `public void LoadSettings() { ... }`: This method is responsible for loading the game settings from a file
  - `System.IO.File.Exists(...)`: This method checks if the `settings.json` file exists in the persistent data path
  - `System.IO.File.ReadAllText(...)`: This method reads the JSON data from the `settings.json` file
  - `JsonUtility.FromJson<GameSettings>(jsonSettings)`: This method deserializes the JSON data back into a `GameSettings` object and assigns it to the `gameSettings` variable

Overall, the `SettingsManager` class provides functionality to save and load game settings using JSON serialization and deserialization. It demonstrates basic file I/O operations in Unity for handling persistent data.

Regarding ScriptableObjects, we have the flexibility to save them using XML or binary formats, and we can treat them as custom classes that encapsulate specific data.

To summarize, choosing the appropriate serialization and deserialization options in Unity depends on factors such as data interchange requirements, performance considerations, and integration with external systems. Understanding the strengths and limitations of each option allows developers to make informed decisions and implement efficient data management solutions in their Unity projects.

Having understood the importance of data organization, let's consider the role save and load systems can play in a game's management.

Creating save and load systems using C#

Save and load systems play a pivotal role in managing game progress and ensuring seamless player experiences. In this section, we'll delve into various methods, from basic **PlayerPrefs** to more robust file-based save systems, enabling us, as developers, to preserve and retrieve player data within Unity efficiently.

PlayerPrefs

PlayerPrefs in Unity serve as a straightforward solution for storing key-value pairs, which is crucial for preserving simple game data. Understanding PlayerPrefs is fundamental for efficiently managing basic player preferences and progress within Unity projects. Operating as a key-value store, PlayerPrefs is specifically designed for storing player preferences and small data amounts between game sessions. Its simple interface facilitates setting and retrieving data, making it ideal for managing settings, user preferences, and basic game progress.

Usage tips

Let's explore essential usage tips for maximizing the benefits of PlayerPrefs in Unity game development, including insights into data serialization, encryption, and security measures, as well as performance optimization techniques:

- **Data serialization**: While PlayerPrefs natively supports storing basic data types, such as integers, floats, and strings, more complex data structures require serialization. We can serialize custom data structures into a format that's compatible with PlayerPrefs, enabling us to store and retrieve complex game data.
- **Encryption and security**: You can protect sensitive player data by implementing encryption mechanisms before storing them in PlayerPrefs. By encrypting PlayerPrefs data, we can safeguard against unauthorized access and protect player privacy.
- **Optimizing performance**: PlayerPrefs access involves disk I/O operations, which can impact performance, especially in resource-intensive games. To mitigate performance overhead, batch PlayerPrefs operations where possible and minimize frequent read/write operations during gameplay.

Incorporating these usage tips will help us optimize PlayerPrefs usage, ensuring data security, performance efficiency, and effective handling of complex game data in Unity projects.

Now, let's look at an example demonstrating how to utilize PlayerPrefs for saving and loading data.

In this first code block, the `GameData` class is a custom class containing game data fields that must be saved and loaded:

```
// Define a class for game data serialization
[System.Serializable]
public class GameData {
    public int playerLevel;
    public int playerExperience;
    // Additional game data fields...
}
```

The second code block contains the save and load functions, which use PlayerPrefs with the `GameData` class:

```
// Save game data to PlayerPrefs
public void SaveGame() {
    GameData gameData = new GameData();
    // Populate game data with current game state
    gameData.playerLevel = PlayerController.instance.level;
    gameData.playerExperience = PlayerController.instance.experience;
```

```csharp
    // Serialize game data to JSON
    string jsonData = JsonUtility.ToJson(gameData);

    // Save serialized data to PlayerPrefs
    PlayerPrefs.SetString("GameData", jsonData);
    PlayerPrefs.Save();
}

// Load game data from PlayerPrefs
public void LoadGame() {
    if (PlayerPrefs.HasKey("GameData")) {
        // Retrieve serialized data from PlayerPrefs
        string jsonData = PlayerPrefs.GetString("GameData");

        // Deserialize JSON data to game data object
        GameData gameData = JsonUtility.FromJson<GameData>(jsonData);

        // Apply loaded game data to game state
        PlayerController.instance.level = gameData.playerLevel;
        PlayerController.instance.experience = gameData.playerExperience;
    }
}
```

Let's take a closer look at the saving and loading functions:

- SaveGame():

  - This function is responsible for saving the game data.

  - It initializes a new instance of the GameData class, which likely contains fields representing various aspects of the game state.

  - The current game state is then captured and stored in the GameData instance. In this example, it appears to be capturing the player's level and experience from a PlayerController singleton instance.

  - Next, the game data is serialized to JSON format using JsonUtility.ToJson().

  - Finally, the serialized JSON data is stored in PlayerPrefs using PlayerPrefs.SetString() with the GameData key, and PlayerPrefs.Save() is called to persist the changes.

- `LoadGame()`:

  - This function loads the saved game data.

  - First, it checks if existing game data is stored in `PlayerPrefs` by using the `GameData` key alongside `PlayerPrefs.HasKey()`.

  - If there is saved data, it retrieves the serialized JSON string from `PlayerPrefs` using `PlayerPrefs.GetString("GameData")`.

  - The JSON data is then deserialized back into a `GameData` object using `JsonUtility.FromJson<GameData>()`.

  - Finally, the loaded game data is applied to the game state. In this example, it seems to be setting the player's level and experience back to their saved values.

Overall, these functions provide a simple mechanism for saving and loading game data using PlayerPrefs, allowing for basic persistence of game state between sessions.

Now that we've discussed the significant benefits of PlayerPrefs, let's examine situations where it may not be the optimal choice.

Exploring the limitations and alternatives to PlayerPrefs

While PlayerPrefs offers convenience and simplicity for storing small amounts of data in Unity games, it also has several limitations and disadvantages that may prompt us to explore alternative solutions:

- **Limited storage capacity**: PlayerPrefs has a limited storage capacity, making it unsuitable for storing large amounts of data or complex data structures. Attempting to store excessive data in PlayerPrefs can lead to performance issues and memory constraints.

- **Security concerns**: PlayerPrefs data is stored in plain text in the player's registry (on Windows) or a **plist** file (on macOS and iOS), making it susceptible to tampering and unauthorized access. For applications that require enhanced security measures or compliance with data protection regulations, PlayerPrefs may not provide adequate protection for sensitive data.

- **Platform dependencies**: PlayerPrefs storage locations and behavior may vary across different platforms and devices. This platform dependency can introduce inconsistencies and compatibility issues when deploying games to multiple platforms, requiring developers to implement platform-specific handling or alternative storage solutions.

- **Limited data types**: PlayerPrefs supports a limited set of data types, including integers, floats, and strings. Complex data structures, arrays, or custom objects cannot be directly stored in PlayerPrefs without serialization and conversion, leading to additional complexity and potential performance overhead.

- **Persistence challenges**: PlayerPrefs data is persisted across game sessions, but it may not persist across different devices or installations. Uninstalling or reinstalling the game, clearing application data, or switching devices can result in the loss of PlayerPrefs data, affecting player progress and preferences.

- **Performance overhead**: Accessing PlayerPrefs involves disk I/O operations, which can introduce performance overhead, especially when reading or writing large amounts of data frequently. For applications that require high-performance data storage or real-time data access, PlayerPrefs may not meet performance requirements.

Due to these limitations and considerations, we may opt for alternative data storage solutions, such as binary serialization, JSON serialization, database systems, or cloud-based storage services. These solutions offer greater flexibility, scalability, security, and performance for managing game data, especially in scenarios involving large datasets, complex data structures, or stringent security requirements. While PlayerPrefs remains a convenient option for simple data storage needs, we should carefully evaluate our requirements and consider alternative solutions when designing data management systems for Unity games.

Custom Save System

In the constantly changing world of game creation, the need for strong and flexible save systems becomes more and more clear. Enter the Custom Save System – a smart solution that's designed to handle the complexities of data management with skill and effectiveness. Unlike usual methods, such as PlayerPrefs, the **Custom Save System** gives us a versatile set of tools, including encryption, options for saving to the cloud, and smooth integration with scriptable objects.

Custom Save System features

Let's explore what features we can use in our custom save system:

- **Generic functionality**: The custom save system boasts generic functions for saving and loading data, allowing for seamless integration with various scriptable objects. With dynamic parameters and return values tailored to the specific needs of each data type, it ensures adaptability and versatility in data management.

- **Encryption and decryption**: Security is paramount in the world of game development. Leveraging encryption and decryption mechanisms, the Custom Save System ensures the confidentiality and integrity of sensitive player data. Through robust cryptographic algorithms, it guards against unauthorized access and tampering, fostering player trust and confidence.

We'll kick things off by crafting ScriptableObjects to manage the system's data. I'll draft the `PlayerData` script, which will store essential player information, as demonstrated in the subsequent code block:

```
[CreateAssetMenu(fileName = "PlayerData", menuName = "Data/Player
Data")]
```

```
public class PlayerData : ScriptableObject
{
    public string playerName;
    public int playerLevel;
    public float playerExperience;
}
```

Additionally, I'll craft a script for GameSettings, which will store relevant game data, as exemplified in the subsequent code block:

```
[CreateAssetMenu(fileName = "GameSettings", menuName = "Data/Game Settings")]
public class GameSettings : ScriptableObject
{
    public int soundVolume;
    public bool isFullScreen;
    public int graphicsQuality;
}
```

After creating these scripts, you can right-click, select **Create**, and choose **Data** to generate instances for both game settings and player data in the project. Organize them by creating a folder named Data and placing the instances inside it. Once you've done this, they'll be structured similarly to the settings instance shown in *Figure 6.1*:

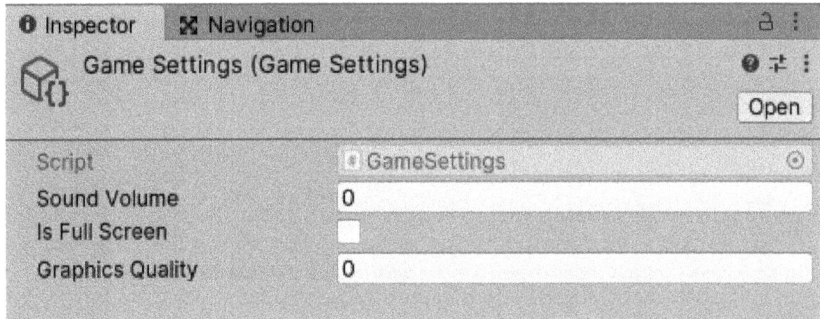

Figure 6.1 – Game Settings ScriptableObject instance

These data files have been provided for demonstration purposes only, allowing you to adjust them according to your project requirements.

Next, we'll proceed by creating a save manager script. However, before diving into that, we must integrate **NewtonSoft** into our project manually since it's not included in Unity Editor version 2022.3.13. Follow these steps:

1. Navigate to the top bar and open the **Window** menu, then select **Package Manager**. Click on the **Add** button located in the top-left corner. This action will prompt a menu to appear, as shown in *Figure 6.2*:

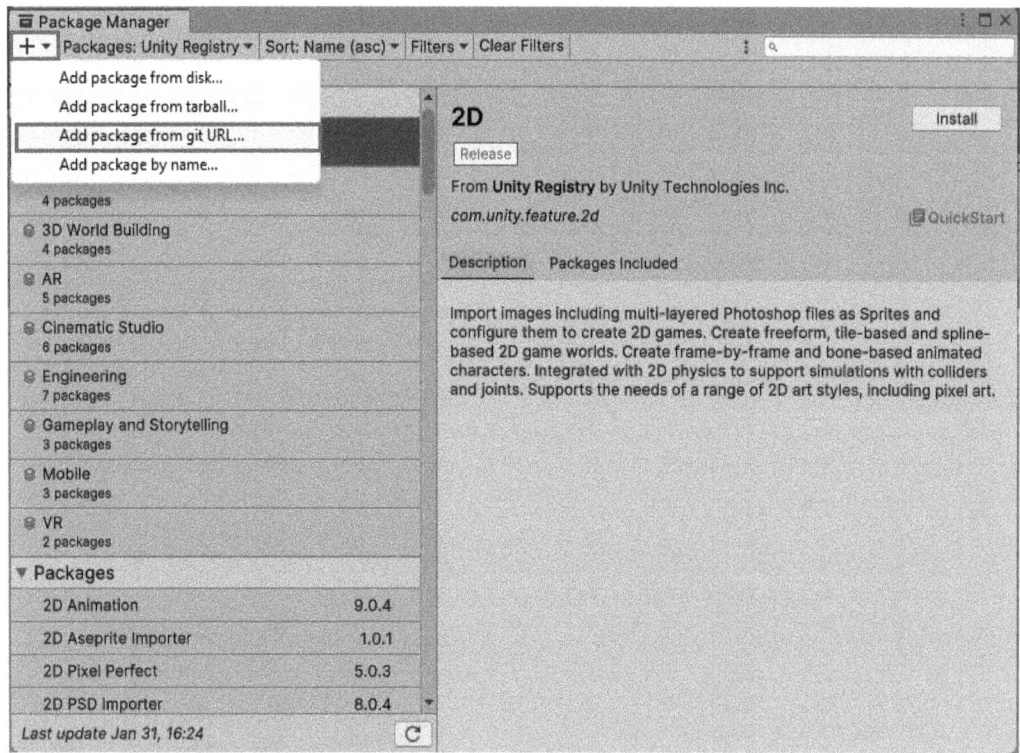

Figure 6.2 – Adding the package from the git URL in the Package Manager panel

2. Paste com.unity.nuget.newtonsoft-json into the provided panel, then click **Add**, as depicted in *Figure 6.3*:

Creating save and load systems using C#

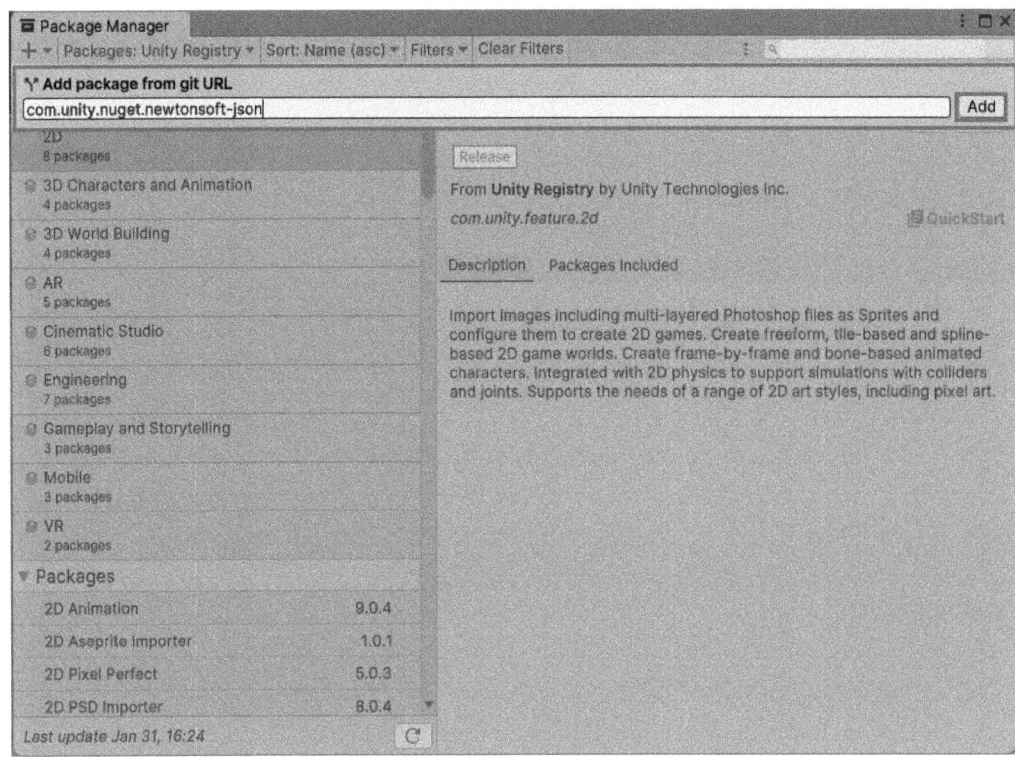

Figure 6.3 – Adding the link for the git URL in the Package Manager panel

Wait for the installation to finish and for Unity Editor to compile before creating the `SaveManager` script.

The SaveManager script

This script is the fundamental component that's responsible for saving and loading data in our game. As mentioned earlier, this approach is not standard, but rather one method we'll utilize for our game. Feel free to adopt this method or implement your own approach according to your needs. The following code block contains the `SaveManager` script:

```
public class SaveManager : MonoBehaviour
{
    private const string saveFileName = "saveData1.dat";
    private const string cloudSaveFileName = "cloudSaveData.dat";

    private static byte[] key = Convert.FromBase64String("kwAXmhR48HenPp04YXrKSNfRcFSiaQx35BlHnI7kzK0=");
    private static byte[] iv = Convert.FromBase64String("GcVb7iqWex9uza+Fcb3BCQ==");
    public static void SaveData(string key, string data)
    {
```

```csharp
            string filePath = Path.Combine(Application.persistentDataPath, saveFileName);

            // Load existing data
            Dictionary<string, string> savedData = LoadSavedData();

            // Add or update data based on its key
            savedData[key] = data;

            // Serialize the entire dictionary
            string jsonData = JsonConvert.SerializeObject(savedData);
            byte[] encryptedData = EncryptData(jsonData);

            // Write the serialized data to the file
            using (FileStream fileStream = new FileStream(filePath, FileMode.Create))
            {
                fileStream.Write(encryptedData, 0, encryptedData.Length);
            }


        }

        public static string LoadData(string key)
        {
            string filePath = Path.Combine(Application.persistentDataPath, saveFileName);

            // Load existing data
            Dictionary<string, string> savedData = LoadSavedData();

            // Extract data based on its key
            if (savedData.ContainsKey(key))
            {
                return savedData[key];
            }
            else
            {
                Debug.LogWarning("No save data found for key: " + key);
                return null;
            }
        }
```

Let's take a closer look at the save and load methods that will be used from other scripts:

- `SaveData`:
  - Saves a key-value pair to a file
  - Loads existing data, updates or adds new data based on the key, and serializes the dictionary to JSON
  - Encrypts the JSON data and writes it to the file

- `LoadData`:
  - Loads data from the save file based on the provided key
  - Checks if the key exists in the dictionary and returns the corresponding value
  - Logs a warning and returns `null` if the key doesn't exist

The following code block contains static methods that handle input/output operations to load and save game data:

```
        private static Dictionary<string, string> LoadSavedData()
        {
            string filePath = Path.Combine(Application.persistentDataPath, saveFileName);

            if (File.Exists(filePath))
            {
                byte[] encryptedData = File.ReadAllBytes(filePath);
                string jsonData = DecryptData(encryptedData);
                return JsonConvert.DeserializeObject<Dictionary<string, string>>(jsonData);
            }
            else
            {
                Debug.LogWarning("No save data found.");
                return new Dictionary<string, string>();
            }
        }

        public static void DeleteSaveData()
        {
            string filePath = Path.Combine(Application.persistentDataPath, saveFileName);

            if (File.Exists(filePath))
```

```
        {
            File.Delete(filePath);
            Debug.Log("Save data deleted.");
        }
        else
        {
            Debug.LogWarning("No save data found to delete.");
        }
    }
```

Let's take a closer look at the previous code block:

- `LoadSavedData`:

  - Loads saved data from the file and returns it as a dictionary

  - Reads encrypted data, decrypts it, deserializes JSON into a dictionary, and returns it

- `DeleteSaveData`: Deletes the save data file if it exists

In the following code block, we're dealing with encryption and decryption to secure the data:

```
        private static byte[] EncryptData(string data)
        {
            using (Aes aesAlg = Aes.Create())
            {
                aesAlg.Key = key;
                aesAlg.IV = iv;

                ICryptoTransform encryptor = aesAlg.
CreateEncryptor(aesAlg.Key, aesAlg.IV);

                using (MemoryStream msEncrypt = new MemoryStream())
                {
                    using (CryptoStream csEncrypt = new
CryptoStream(msEncrypt, encryptor, CryptoStreamMode.Write))
                    {
                        using (StreamWriter swEncrypt = new
StreamWriter(csEncrypt))
                        {
                            swEncrypt.Write(data);
                        }
                        return msEncrypt.ToArray();
                    }
                }
```

```
            }
        }

        private static string DecryptData(byte[] encryptedData)
        {
            using (Aes aesAlg = Aes.Create())
            {
                aesAlg.Key = key;
                aesAlg.IV = iv;

                ICryptoTransform decryptor = aesAlg.
CreateDecryptor(aesAlg.Key, aesAlg.IV);

                using (MemoryStream msDecrypt = new
MemoryStream(encryptedData))
                {
                    using (CryptoStream csDecrypt = new
CryptoStream(msDecrypt, decryptor, CryptoStreamMode.Read))
                    {
                        using (StreamReader srDecrypt = new
StreamReader(csDecrypt))
                        {
                            return srDecrypt.ReadToEnd();
                        }
                    }
                }
            }
        }
    }
```

Let's consider the encryption methods (`EncryptData` and `DecryptData`):

- Encrypts and decrypts data using the `AES` encryption algorithm
- Encrypts input data using the encryption key and `IV` (`EncryptData`)
- Decrypts encrypted data using the same key and `IV` (`DecryptData`)

In this script, there's a method called `SaveData` for saving data. It requires the data to be in string format, along with its corresponding key. We have opted to store the data in a dictionary of string and string, enabling us to easily manage loading and saving data for various files.

For loading, we're decrypting the string data and then loading it.

Additionally, I've implemented **AES encryption** methods to secure the data during encryption and decryption processes. While the details of AES encryption are beyond the scope of this book, you're encouraged to explore it further if you're interested in learning about encryption techniques.

To facilitate the generation of keys and IV, I've prepared a helper script. You can utilize this script by attaching it to a GameObject within your scene. This script will enable you to create the necessary key and IV for encryption purposes. You can find the generated keys in the `SaveManager` script; there's no need to repeat the creation process as it only occurs once.

You can obtain the `KeyAndIVGenerator` script from the following code block:

```
public class KeyAndIVGenerator : MonoBehaviour
{
    public static void GenerateKeyAndIV()
    {
        using (Aes aes = Aes.Create())
        {
            aes.GenerateKey();
            aes.GenerateIV();

            // Convert key and IV to base64 strings for easy storage and usage
            string base64Key = Convert.ToBase64String(aes.Key);
            string base64IV = Convert.ToBase64String(aes.IV);

            Debug.Log("Generated Key: " + base64Key);
            Debug.Log("Generated IV: " + base64IV);
        }
    }

    private void Start()
    {
        GenerateKeyAndIV();
    }
}
```

Here's an explanation of the `KeyAndIVGenerator` class:

- The `KeyAndIVGenerator` class contains a method named `GenerateKeyAndIV`, which is responsible for generating encryption keys and **initialization vectors** (**IVs**).

- Inside the `GenerateKeyAndIV` method, the `KeyAndIVGenerator` class creates an instance of the `Aes` class using the `Aes.Create()` method, which represents the AES algorithm.

- Then, it calls the `GenerateKey()` and `GenerateIV()` methods on the `Aes` instance to generate a random encryption key and `IV`.

- After generating the key and IV, it converts them into base64 strings using the `Convert.ToBase64String()` method. `Base64` encoding is used for easy storage and usage of the key and `IV`.

- Finally, it logs the generated key and IV to the console using Debug.Log() for debugging purposes.
- The Start method is called when the KeyAndIVGenerator object is initialized, and it invokes the GenerateKeyAndIV method to generate the key and IV when the object starts.

Overall, this code block demonstrates how to generate encryption keys and IV values using the AES algorithm and convert them into base64 strings for storage and usage. This is commonly used in cryptography for securing data.

The following code block provides an example of the GameManager script, which utilizes the save and load methods from SaveManager to manage the process of saving and loading PlayerData and GameSettings:

```csharp
public class GameManager : MonoBehaviour
{
    public PlayerData playerData;
    public GameSettings gameSettings;

    private void Start()
    {
        LoadGameData();
    }
    private void OnApplicationQuit()
    {
        SaveGameData();
    }
```

Let's consider the Unity callback functions:

- In the Start method, it calls the LoadGameData function to load the player data and game settings when the game starts
- The OnApplicationQuit method is invoked when the application is about to quit, and it calls the SaveGameData function to save the player data and game settings before exiting

The following code block contains the logic for loading and saving data:

```csharp
    private void LoadGameData()
    {
        if (playerData == null)
        {
        }
        else
        {
```

```
                    JsonUtility.FromJsonOverwrite(SaveManager.
LoadData("playerData"), playerData);
            }

            if (gameSettings == null)
            {
                gameSettings = ScriptableObject.
CreateInstance<GameSettings>();
            }
            else
            {   JsonUtility.FromJsonOverwrite(SaveManager.
LoadData("gameSettings"), gameSettings);
            }
        }

        private void SaveGameData()
        {
            SaveManager.SaveData("playerData", JsonUtility.
ToJson(playerData));
            SaveManager.SaveData("gameSettings", JsonUtility.
ToJson(gameSettings));
        }
    }
```

Let's take a closer look at the saving and loading functions:

- The `LoadGameData` function loads the player data and game settings from the save files using the `SaveManager.LoadData` method. If the data is not found, it creates new instances of `PlayerData` and `GameSettings`.

- The `SaveGameData` function saves the player data and game settings to the save files using the `SaveManager.SaveData` method. It converts the data objects into JSON format using `JsonUtility.ToJson` before saving.

Overall, this code block demonstrates a basic implementation of loading and saving game data using JSON serialization. It ensures that the player data and game settings are persisted across game sessions, allowing for a seamless gaming experience.

In this section, we learned how to save and load scriptable objects, the techniques of saving and loading to a file, encrypting using AES to protect the data, and how to generate encryption keys. Finally, we've practiced using these concepts practically.

Now, we need to understand the benefits of using a custom approach over PlayerPrefs.

Advantages over PlayerPrefs

While PlayerPrefs offers simplicity, the Custom Save System goes beyond its limitations, providing a variety of features and functionalities unmatched by traditional storage methods. By reducing performance overhead and improving data security, it marks a new era of data management in Unity game development.

To summarize, the Custom Save System represents innovation and creativity – a testament to the ongoing pursuit of excellence in game development. With its capacity to streamline data management, enhance security measures, and improve player experiences, it has become the cornerstone of modern game development practices, reshaping the landscape with each save.

In the next section, we are going to implement ScriptableObjects with the player progress part of our game while saving and loading data.

Data-driven gameplay with C#

Data-driven design is an approach to game development where game behavior, content, and configuration are defined and controlled by external data files rather than hardcoded into the game's source code. This approach offers several benefits, including increased flexibility, easier content iteration, and enhanced maintainability. By separating game data from code, we can modify game behavior, tweak parameters, and add new content without requiring code changes, thus accelerating iteration cycles and empowering designers to experiment with gameplay mechanics.

Let's begin with one of the uses of ScriptableObjects for managing data.

Creating data for stats

We have the `PlayerMovement` script in our project, as shown in the following code block, which handles the player's movement:

```
public class PlayerMovement : MonoBehaviour
{
    public float moveSpeed = 5f;
    public float jumpForce = 5f;
    public float dashForce = 10f;
    public float dashCooldown = 2f;

    public Transform groundChecker;
    public LayerMask groundLayer;
    public float groundDistance;

    public Rigidbody playerRigidbody;
    private bool isGrounded = true;
```

```
        private bool canDash = true;

        private Vector3 movementVector;

    private void MovePlayer()
    {
        Vector3 movement = new Vector3(movementVector.x , 0f ,
movementVector.y) * moveSpeed * Time.deltaTime;
        transform.Translate(movement);
    }

//rest of code
}
```

Here, we can create a ScriptableObject that will contain the parameters of player movement, such as speed and force. Then, we can obtain a reference to that ScriptableObject.

The following code block contains a ScriptableObject named `PlayerStats` that will store movement data:

```
[CreateAssetMenu(fileName = "PlayerStats", menuName = "Data/Player
Stats")]

 public class PlayerStats : ScriptableObject
 {
     [SerializeField] float moveSpeed = 5f;
     [SerializeField] float jumpForce = 5f;
     [SerializeField] float dashForce = 10f;
     [SerializeField] float dashCooldown = 2f;

     public float MoveSpeed { get => moveSpeed; set => moveSpeed =
value; }
     public float JumpForce { get => jumpForce; set => jumpForce =
value; }
     public float DashForce { get => dashForce; set => dashForce =
value; }
     public float DashCooldown { get => dashCooldown; set =>
dashCooldown = value; }
 }
```

Now, we can utilize the `PlayerStats` ScriptableObject as a variable within the player movement script and substitute any previous logic that used the movement variables with the player stats accordingly:

```
    public class PlayerMovement : MonoBehaviour
    {
        public PlayerStats playerStats;
```

```
        public Transform groundChecker;
        public LayerMask groundLayer;
        public float groundDistance;

        public Rigidbody playerRigidbody;
        private bool isGrounded = true;
        private bool canDash = true;

        private Vector3 movementVector;
        private void MovePlayer()
        {
           Vector3 movement = new Vector3(movementVector.x , 0f ,
    movementVector.y) * playerStats.MoveSpeed * Time.deltaTime;
           transform.Translate(movement);
        }
    //rest of code
    }
```

We did this because we require a single reference for all movement parameters, and it will be convenient later to apply or adjust the stats from other scripts, such as special power-ups, without altering the code within the player movement script. We can directly modify the ScriptableObject, and it will impact the player's movement.

Moreover, if we include items in our game, consolidating all data into individual ScriptableObjects for each type of item would streamline usage and modifications across all objects. Without directly referencing those objects, we can alter the data file, and it will impact all objects utilizing that data.

Let's consider another use for ScriptableObjects.

Challenge system

We can utilize ScriptableObjects for player progression within challenges, allowing us to effectively track challenges and save the progress made.

We will commence by migrating CommonChallengeData into a ScriptableObject, as demonstrated in the following code block:

```
    [CreateAssetMenu(fileName = "CommonChallengeData", menuName =
  "Data/Common Challenge Data")]

    [Serializable]
    public class CommonChallengeData : ScriptableObject
    {
        public bool isCompleted;
        public RewardType rewardType; // Type of reward
```

```
        public int rewardAmount;       // Amount or value of the reward
    }
```

Then, upon completion of the challenge, we can utilize the save manager we previously established to store the challenge statistics. This can be seen in the `CompleteChallenge` function within `EnemyWavesChallenge` in the following code block:

```
    public class EnemyWavesChallenge : BaseChallenge
    {
        //Rest of Code

        public override void CompleteChallenge()
        {
            if (!commonData.isCompleted)
            {
                RewardManager.Instance.GrantReward(commonData);
                commonData.isCompleted = true;

                SaveManager.SaveData(challengeSavedKey, JsonUtility.ToJson(commonData));
            }
            else
            {
                Debug.Log("Challenge already completed!");
            }
        }

        //Rest of code
    }
```

We included the last line in the `CompleteChallenge` method to save the challenge data within the completion function of the challenge. Thus, before commencing the challenge, we will verify its completion status in the challenge manager.

Additionally, we must utilize the data loading functionality from the `SaveManager` script within the `StartChallenge` function inside `ChallengeManager`, as illustrated in the following code block:

```
    public class ChallengeManager : Singlton<ChallengeManager>
    {
        //Rest of code

        public void StartChallenge(ChallengeType challengeType)
        {
```

```csharp
            if (challengeDictionary.TryGetValue(challengeType, out 
BaseChallenge challengeScript))
            {
                JsonUtility.FromJsonOverwrite(SaveManager.
LoadData(challengeScript.challengeSavedKey), challengeScript.
commonData);
                if (!challengeScript.commonData.isCompleted)
                {
                    SetCurrentChallenge(challengeScript);
                    currentChallenge.StartChallenge();
                }
                else
                {
                    Debug.Log("Challenge already completed!");
                }
            }
            else
            {
                Debug.LogError($"No challenge script found for 
ChallengeType {challengeType}");
            }
        }


//Rest of code
    }
```

This is a straightforward method to transition existing code for utilizing ScriptableObjects or an improved data management approach. Furthermore, it integrates saving and loading functionalities to monitor challenge progress. While designing the system from scratch would offer a better data handling strategy, this system was constructed differently. We had the opportunity to modify it in this chapter, emphasizing the importance of adapting existing code bases. We'll delve deeper into refining these skills in *Chapter 7*.

To summarize, data-driven gameplay with C# offers a powerful framework for creating dynamic, customizable, and immersive gaming experiences. By embracing data-driven design principles, and leveraging ScriptableObjects for modular gameplay elements, we can build flexible, extensible, and engaging games that captivate players and stand the test of time.

Summary

In this chapter, we delved into concepts and techniques that are vital for efficient game development. We began by exploring the importance of data structures and their impact on game performance, emphasizing the significance of choosing the appropriate data structure for optimal results. Serialization in Unity took center stage as we navigated Unity's serialization options, including XML, JSON, and binary serialization methods. We discussed the nuances of each serialization method and its suitability for different scenarios, laying the groundwork for robust data management in Unity projects.

We continued by doing a deep dive into PlayerPrefs and its limitations in Unity game development, paving the way for the Custom Save System. Through detailed discussions and practical examples, we unveiled the features and advantages of the Custom Save System over PlayerPrefs, highlighting its role in elevating data-driven gameplay experiences. The `SaveManager` Script emerged as a pivotal component, facilitating seamless data saving and loading operations with enhanced efficiency and flexibility. By leveraging C# and scriptableObjects, we are empowered to embrace data-driven gameplay mechanics and optimize the challenge system for enhanced user engagement and progression. Through meticulous exploration and hands-on learning, this chapter has equipped us with the knowledge and tools needed to master data organization and serialization in Unity with C#.

In *Chapter 7*, we'll dive into the realm of collaborative game development and version control systems. Building on our foundational knowledge, we'll explore how to effectively contribute to existing code bases and collaborate within development teams using C#. From understanding version control systems to mastering code merging and conflict resolution techniques, we'll equip ourselves with essential skills to navigate shared code repositories seamlessly. Through practical examples and step-by-step guidance, we'll learn about the intricacies of collaborating with shared code repositories and maintaining code quality in a team environment. Join us as we delve deeper into the collaborative aspects of game development, paving the way for enhanced teamwork and code management practices.

7
Contributing to Existing Code Bases in Unity with C#

Welcome to *Chapter 7*. This chapter will equip you with essential collaboration skills for working in development teams using C#. We will explore **version control systems** (**VCSs**), code merging, and conflict resolution for seamless teamwork. We will also cover mastering version control, collaborating with shared repositories, and resolving conflicts using C#. Finally, we will get an understanding of existing code bases to navigate structures, review documentation, and communicate effectively. Mastering all these skills will promote effective team contribution and maintain code quality in Unity projects.

In this chapter, we're going to cover the following main topics:

- Introducing VCSs
- Collaborating and resolving conflicts with C#
- Understanding existing code bases

Technical requirements

You will need the following to follow this chapter:

- **Primary IDE - Visual Studio 2022**: The tutorials and code samples are crafted using Visual Studio 2022. Ensure it's installed to follow along seamlessly. Feel free to explore Rider or other IDEs if you prefer, though instructions are tailored for Visual Studio.

- **GitHub Desktop**: Ensure it's installed to follow along seamlessly.

Introducing VCSs

A VCS is a tool used in software development to manage changes to files. It acts like a detailed record keeper, documenting every alteration made to project files.

Here's why it matters:

- **Tracking changes**: In a collaborative project, multiple people may work on the same files. A VCS records all modifications, ensuring transparency and accountability.
- **Facilitating collaboration**: With a VCS, team members can see who made specific changes and when. This transparency fosters smooth collaboration and prevents conflicts.
- **Reverting changes**: Mistakes happen, but a VCS allows us to revert to earlier versions of files if needed. It acts as a safety net, providing a way to undo errors.
- **Maintaining organization**: A VCS helps maintain orderliness by categorizing changes and providing a structured approach to managing project files. It enables teams to work efficiently and stay organized.

In conclusion, a VCS is a crucial tool for software development teams. It helps keep track of changes, encourages teamwork, allows for fixing mistakes, and ensures that projects stay organized.

In the upcoming section, we will delve into understanding VCSs, exploring the two main types: distributed and centralized systems.

Understanding VCSs

When you create a new repository in your VCS, you open up the main branch. This is also known as the trunk master. The trunk master serves as the starting point for the main code base, which then goes through compilation and deployment to reach the end user.

But what about branches? Branching occurs when code is extracted from the master branch to create separate paths. This allows us to modify the code without impacting the main version directly. By using branches, we avoid the need to consolidate all changes in one place; instead, we can track modifications to our code over time. The VCS can then integrate these separate branches back into the main one. If we're not prepared to merge other changes into the main branch, we can store them in a separate branch and merge them later.

Having a good branching strategy is important to prevent conflicts and errors in the code. Luckily, robust VCSs make it easy for teams to sync with the main branch and resolve any potential conflicts – even after changes have been made to the main branch.

Now that we've grasped the fundamental workings of VCSs, let's explore the two primary types that play a pivotal role in shaping collaborative development processes: distributed and centralized systems.

Distributed VCSs

A **distributed VCS**, or **DVCS**, is a type of VCS where every user has a complete copy of the project's repository on their local computer. This means that you can work on the project even when they're offline.

The following diagram shows the structure of a DVCS:

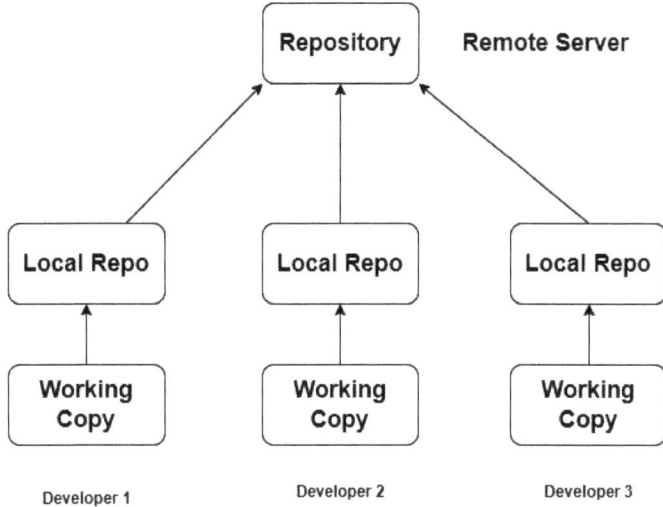

Figure 7.1 – DVCS structure

Here's how it works:

- **Local copies**: With a DVCS, each user has their own local copy of the entire project's history, including all files and changes made over time. This allows you to work independently and make changes without relying on a central server.

- **Flexible collaboration**: Since each user has their own copy of the repository, they can work on different features or fixes without interfering with each other's work. They can commit changes to their local repository and share them with others later.

- **Enhanced security**: Because the entire project history is stored locally, a DVCS provides redundancy and security. Even if the central server goes down, you can continue working on your local copies and later sync changes with the central repository once it's back online.

- **Efficient branching and merging**: DVCS systems such as **Git** offer powerful branching and merging capabilities. You can create branches to work on new features or experiment with changes without affecting the main project. You can later merge your changes back into the main branch when ready.

Git is an example of a DVCS. It allows users to maintain their own complete copy of the project's repository on their local computer. This means that you have access to the entire project history and can work on it even when you're offline.

With Git, you can create branches to work on new features or fixes without affecting the main code base. These branches can later be merged back into the main branch once your changes are complete.

Git also facilitates collaboration among team members by allowing you to share your changes with others through a shared remote repository. Other team members can then pull your changes from the remote repository to their local copies.

Overall, Git's distributed nature and powerful branching capabilities make it a preferred choice for many development teams. It provides flexibility, efficiency, and seamless collaboration for managing and tracking changes in software projects.

In summary, a DVCS allows us to work independently, collaborate effectively, and maintain project history and integrity, even in decentralized environments. It provides flexibility, security, and powerful features for managing and tracking changes in software projects.

Centralized VCSs

A **centralized VCS (CVCS)** is a type of VCS where there is a single central repository that stores all files and their respective versions.

The following diagram shows the structure of a CVCS:

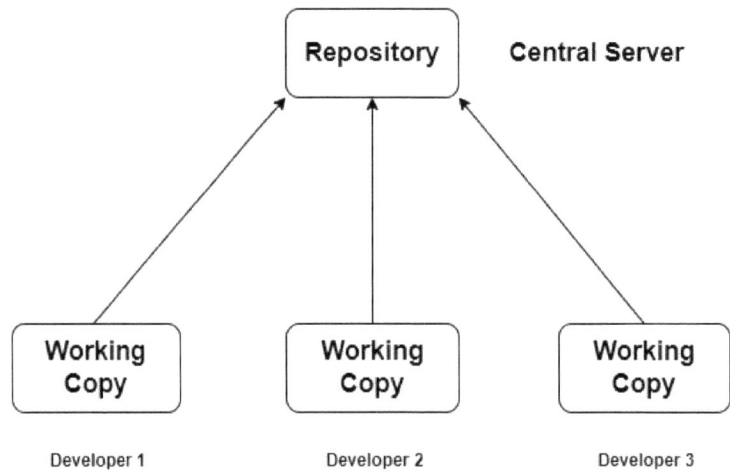

Figure 7.2 – CVCS structure

Here's how it works:

- **Single repository**: In a CVCS, all users access and work on the same central repository. This means that there is only one copy of the project's history, stored on a central server.

- **Limited offline access**: Since the repository is centralized, users typically need to be connected to the central server to access files and make changes. This can limit the ability to work offline or in environments with limited connectivity.

- **Collaborative workflow**: Users commit their changes directly to the central repository, where they are visible to all team members. This facilitates collaboration and ensures that everyone is working with the latest version of the code.
- **Potential bottlenecks**: In a CVCS, the central server can become a bottleneck, especially in large teams or projects with heavy usage. If the server goes down, developers may be unable to access or commit changes until it is restored.
- **Limited branching**: CVCS systems typically offer limited branching capabilities compared to distributed systems such as Git. Users may need to coordinate closely to avoid conflicts when working on different features or changes.

SVN, or **Subversion**, is an example of a CVCS. In SVN, there is a single central repository that stores all project files and their respective versions.

Unlike DVCSs such as Git, SVN does not provide users with their own local copies of the entire project's history. Instead, users interact directly with the central repository to access files and make changes.

SVN facilitates a collaborative workflow by allowing developers to commit their changes directly to the central repository. This ensures that everyone is working with the latest version of the code and helps maintain project integrity.

While SVN lacks some of the flexibility and offline capabilities of DVCSs, it remains a popular choice for many development teams, especially in centralized environments where strict control over the code base is desired.

In summary, a CVCS relies on a single central repository for storing and managing project files and versions. While it facilitates collaboration and provides a centralized **source of truth** (**SoT**), it may pose challenges in terms of offline access, potential bottlenecks, and limited branching capabilities.

Next, let's delve into essential Git commands.

In the following table, you'll find essential Git commands. Make sure you have Git installed on your system:

Command	Description
`git init`	Initializes a new Git repository in the current directory
`git clone [url]`	Clones an existing Git repository from a remote server to your local machine
`git add [file]`	Adds a file or changes to the staging area to be included in the next commit
`git commit -m "[message]"`	Commits changes to the local repository with a descriptive message
`git push`	Uploads local repository content to a remote repository

`git pull`	Downloads changes from a remote repository and merges them into the local repository
`git status`	Displays the status of the working directory and the staging area
`git log`	Shows a list of commits in the repository, along with details such as author, date, and commit message
`git branch`	Lists all branches in the local repository
`git checkout [branch]`	Switches to the specified branch
`git merge [branch]`	Merges changes from the specified branch into the current branch
`git remote -v`	Lists all remote repositories associated with the local repository

Many commands may be overwhelming, especially considering our book's context. Instead, we'll rely on **graphical user interface** (**GUI**) tools such as the GitHub Desktop app for version control, where most actions can be performed through the **user interface** (**UI**). Feel free to depend on the GUI for all processes.

In the next section, we will explore best practices for collaborating on code and resolving conflicts efficiently.

Collaborating and resolving conflicts with C#

Navigating collaborative environments and maintaining code quality are vital aspects of software development. Let's explore effective collaboration, conflict resolution, and code quality maintenance in the following sections.

Best practices for collaborating

Effective collaboration is essential for successful project development, and adopting best practices ensures smooth teamwork and code management throughout the process. The following are some best practices to follow when working with VCSs:

- **Frequent and incremental commits for a streamlined workflow**: Making small, frequent commits is an uncomplicated yet highly effective enhancement for your workflow, even though it poses a challenge for some developers. In the context of other project management tools, where tasks are typically broken down into manageable parts, the same approach should be applied to commits. Each commit should specifically correspond to one task or ticket unless a single line of code miraculously addresses multiple issues. For more extensive features, it's beneficial to break them down into smaller tasks and create commits for each one. The primary advantage of opting for smaller commits is the increased ease of detecting and reverting undesired changes in case something goes wrong.

- **Prioritize getting the latest changes**: Make it a habit to fetch the latest changes from the repository into your working copy whenever it's feasible. It's not advisable to work in isolation as this raises the risk of encountering merge conflicts.

- **Mindful committing for a smooth workflow**: Refrain from making hasty commits. The `commit -a` command, or its equivalents, should only be employed during the initial commit of a project, typically when the project consists solely of `README.md` files. A commit should exclusively encompass files pertinent to the specific change being committed to the repository. Exercise caution, especially when dealing with Unity projects, as certain modifications may inadvertently affect multiple files, such as scenes, Prefabs, or Sprite Atlases, even if not intended. Accidentally committing changes to a scene that another team member is concurrently editing can lead to complications for them during their own commit process, necessitating the merging of your changes beforehand.

- **Crafting clear commit messages**: Maintain clarity in your commit messages as they narrate the evolution of your project. It's more convenient to trace the addition of new gameplay mechanics in your game when the commit message explicitly states, "`implemented new enemy behavior for level 3`" rather than opting for a more casual expression such as, "`added some cool stuff to level 3`." When utilizing a task ticketing system such as Jira or GitLab, it's advantageous to include a ticket number in your commit message. Many systems can be configured to integrate with smart commits, enabling you to reference tickets and update their status directly from your commit message. For instance, a commit message such as "`JRA-123 #close #comment task completed`" would close the JRA-123 Jira ticket and append the comment "task completed" to the ticket.

In the realm of collaborative coding, mastering these best practices not only fosters seamless teamwork but also streamlines code management throughout project development.

Mastering branching and merging in collaboration

Understanding branching and merging strategies for collaborative development is crucial for effective teamwork in software projects. Next are some ideas and guidelines to assist you with this.

The following are some crafting branching and merging strategies:

- **Feature branches**: Work on new features or fixes in separate branches. This practice maintains the cleanliness of the main branch while enabling us to work independently.

- **Release branches**: Create branches specifically for release candidates to stabilize the code base before deployment.

- **Hotfix branches**: Establish branches to address critical issues or bugs in production without disrupting ongoing development.

- **Long-lived branches**: Some projects may require long-lived branches for ongoing development efforts or specific feature sets.

Exploring branches, forks, and pull requests offers valuable insights into the intricacies of collaborative coding and VCSs:

- **Branches**: Create feature branches for each new task or feature you work on. This keeps changes isolated and makes it easier to review and merge code.
- **Forks**: In open source projects, contributors often fork the main repository to work on changes independently. Forks allow for experimentation without affecting the original code base.
- **Pull requests**: Pull requests (or merge requests) are a key mechanism for proposing changes and initiating code review. They provide a structured way to discuss and approve modifications before merging them into the main branch.
- **Code reviews**: Emphasize the importance of thorough code reviews in the pull request process. Reviewing code helps maintain code quality, identify potential issues, and share knowledge among team members.

Encouraging a clear branching and merging strategy, along with effective use of branches, forks, and pull requests, promotes collaboration, code quality, and project stability in software development teams.

Mastering code conflict management

Understanding the nature of code conflicts and how to resolve them is essential for seamless collaboration and project success. Let's delve into common types of conflicts and learn practical techniques for resolving them in Unity projects.

Exploring code conflict origins and navigating conflict resolution in Unity projects

Understanding the origins of code conflicts is crucial for maintaining a harmonious development environment and ensuring smooth collaboration among team members, Let's delve into specific points that contribute to these conflicts:

- **Merge conflicts**: When multiple contributors modify the same file or code block, conflicting changes can arise during merging
- **Structural changes**: Renaming files, relocating directories, or altering project structures can introduce conflicts
- **Dependency dilemmas**: Incompatible dependencies or divergent library versions across project components can lead to conflicts
- **Branch divergence**: Significant deviations from the main branch make merging changes back into the main code base challenging

Next, we'll explore two methods to resolve conflicts:

- **Manual conflict resolution**: Learn to review conflicting changes in code files and decide which modifications to retain, modify, or discard
- **Version control integration**: Explore how Git and other VCSs integrate with Unity, offering built-in merge tools and third-party plugins for conflict resolution

Next, let's engage in practical conflict resolution.

Practical conflict solving

After understanding the causes of conflicts, it's essential to learn how to resolve them. I'll share an example of a conflict from one of my current projects and how I successfully resolved it. While the conflict wasn't significant, the approach used for resolving code conflicts applies universally. Let's proceed with resolving code conflicts using GitHub Desktop and Visual Studio.

When your local changes conflict with modifications made to the same file on the remote server, the following panel will be displayed:

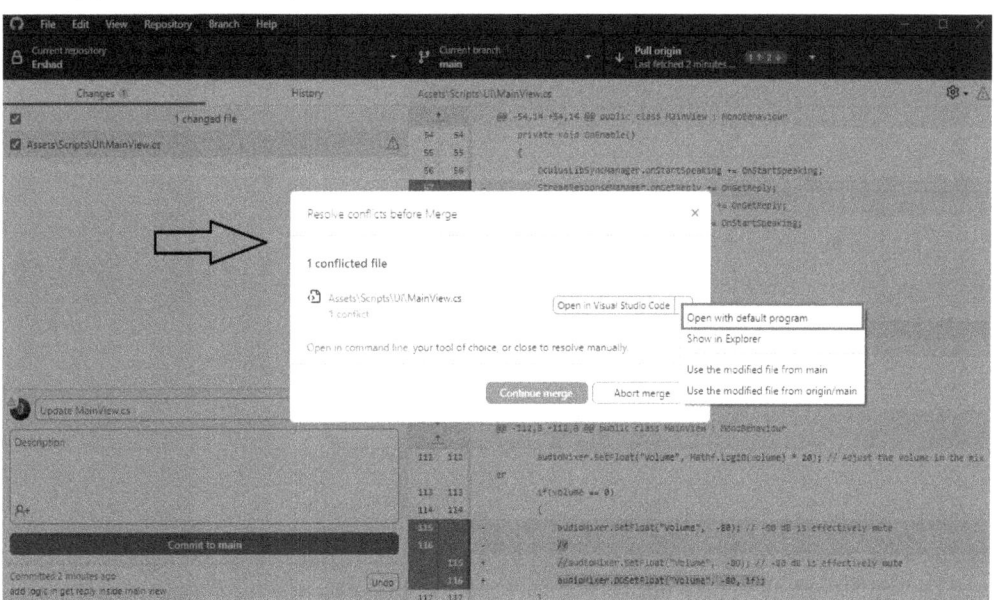

Figure 7.3 – Resolve conflict panel in GitHub Desktop

When this panel appears, it signals the need to compare and decide between conflicting versions of the same file from different sources. In GitHub Desktop, this panel represents the conflict resolution interface. By clicking the drop-down button, you can select your preferred editing program, such as Visual Studio or Visual Studio Code. For this example, when you select Visual Studio as the default program, the editor will open. You can choose to click on the **Open Merge Editor** option, as illustrated in the following figure:

Figure 7.4 – Conflict mode in Visual Studio

In the Merge Editor, you'll notice there are three sections: the incoming or remote version, the current or local version, and the resulting file after merging. Here, you need to review the changes and decide whether to combine them or keep one version based on the flow of the feature or task requirements. Once you or the responsible senior has finished editing, click on **Accept Merge**:

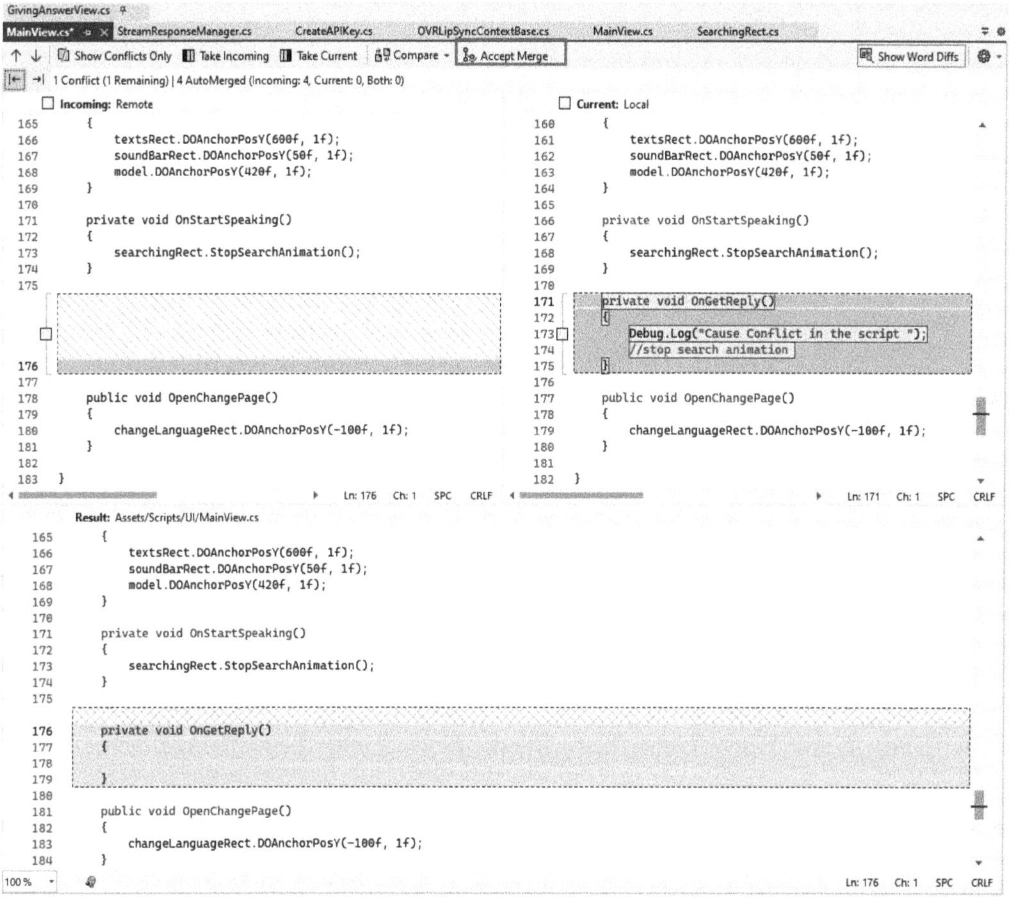

Figure 7.5 – Merge Editor in Visual Studio

After closing the Merge Editor, you'll notice that the sidebar now includes an option to commit the changes. Then, you can click on **Commit Staged** in the side panel to push the changes after the merge, as you can see in the following figure:

Figure 7.6 – File after editing the conflict

> **Remember**
> You'll need to focus, especially when the same file is involved in two different tasks, ensuring that the logic of both tasks continues to work properly.

Let's use the **command-line interface** (**CLI**) to resolve merge conflicts efficiently.

Exploring code conflict origins and navigating conflict resolution using the CLI

The CLI remains a fundamental and widely used method for resolving Git conflicts. While GUIs are available and can provide visual aids for conflict resolution, many developers, particularly those comfortable with terminal-based workflows, prefer the command line as their default approach. The CLI offers granular control, precise navigation through code changes, and efficient merging capabilities, making it a robust tool for managing Git conflicts effectively.

To test this, ensure you have another branch in your project. We will then modify the same file in the two branches to create a conflict and resolve it. Let's get started:

1. Navigate to your project directory and open the terminal there, or use the `cd` command in the terminal to navigate to your project directory.

2. Alternatively, ensure that you are currently in one of your other branches. In my case, I have a branch called `feature/branch-name`.

3. Use the `git checkout branch-name` command to switch to the desired branch, as demonstrated in the following figure:

```
PS D:\GameDevelopment\Projects\Freelancing\-Mastering-Unity-2024-Game-Development-with-C-> checkout feature/branch-name
Already on 'feature/branch-name'
Your branch is up to date with 'origin/feature/branch-name'.
PS D:\GameDevelopment\Projects\Freelancing\-Mastering-Unity-2024-Game-Development-with-C->
```

Figure 7.7 – Checkout feature branch

4. Now, let's make a modification to a file. In my case, I'll comment out a line in a script, as shown in the following figure:

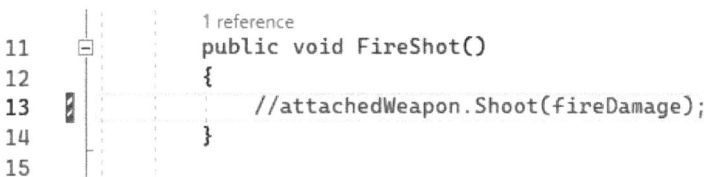

Figure 7.8 – Commenting out a line in a function

5. We need to add and commit that file using `git add filename` followed by `git commit -m "commit message"`, as you can see in the following figure:

```
PS D:\GameDevelopment\Projects\Freelancing\-Mastering-Unity-2024-Game-Development-with-C-> add Assets/FusionFuryGame
/Scripts/Enemy/EnemyShoot.cs
PS D:\GameDevelopment\Projects\Freelancing\-Mastering-Unity-2024-Game-Development-with-C-> commit -m "Make a change
in a file"
[feature/branch-name a959255] Make a change in a file
 1 file changed, 1 insertion(+), 1 deletion(-)
PS D:\GameDevelopment\Projects\Freelancing\-Mastering-Unity-2024-Game-Development-with-C->
```

Figure 7.9 – Committing changes

6. Push your changes:

```
PS D:\GameDevelopment\Projects\Freelancing\-Mastering-Unity-2024-Game-Development-with-C-> push
Enumerating objects: 26, done.
Counting objects: 100% (26/26), done.
Delta compression using up to 12 threads
Compressing objects: 100% (14/14), done.
Writing objects: 100% (14/14), 1.16 KiB | 1.16 MiB/s, done.
Total 14 (delta 12), reused 0 (delta 0), pack-reused 0
remote: Resolving deltas: 100% (12/12), completed with 7 local objects.
To https://github.com/PacktPublishing/-Mastering-Unity-2024-Game-Development-with-C-.git
   f21bd89..a880e09  feature/branch-name -> feature/branch-name
PS D:\GameDevelopment\Projects\Freelancing\-Mastering-Unity-2024-Game-Development-with-C->
```

Figure 7.10 – Pushing changes

7. Now, we can go to another branch; in my case, I will return to the main branch using the `git checkout` command:

```
PS D:\GameDevelopment\Projects\Freelancing\-Mastering-Unity-2024-Game-Development-with-C-> git checkout main
Switched to branch 'main'
Your branch is up to date with 'origin/main'.
PS D:\GameDevelopment\Projects\Freelancing\-Mastering-Unity-2024-Game-Development-with-C-> 
```

Figure 7.11 – Returning to the main branch

8. Modify the same file to make a conflict, then we need to add, commit, and push changes.
9. Then, return to the feature branch again.
10. Next, execute the `merge` command from the main branch, as illustrated in the following figure:

```
PS D:\GameDevelopment\Projects\Freelancing\-Mastering-Unity-2024-Game-Development-with-C-> git merge main
Auto-merging Assets/FusionFuryGame/Scripts/Enemy/EnemyShoot.cs
CONFLICT (content): Merge conflict in Assets/FusionFuryGame/Scripts/Enemy/EnemyShoot.cs
Automatic merge failed; fix conflicts and then commit the result.
PS D:\GameDevelopment\Projects\Freelancing\-Mastering-Unity-2024-Game-Development-with-C-> 
```

Figure 7.12 – Merging from the main branch

We can also use the `git status` command to identify the file or files that require conflict resolution:

```
PS D:\GameDevelopment\Projects\Freelancing\-Mastering-Unity-2024-Game-Development-with-C-> git status
On branch feature/branch-name
Your branch is up to date with 'origin/feature/branch-name'.

Changes not staged for commit:
  (use "git add <file>..." to update what will be committed)
  (use "git restore <file>..." to discard changes in working directory)
        modified:   Assets/FusionFuryGame/Scripts/Enemy/EnemyShoot.cs

no changes added to commit (use "git add" and/or "git commit -a")
PS D:\GameDevelopment\Projects\Freelancing\-Mastering-Unity-2024-Game-Development-with-C-> 
```

Figure 7.13 – Checking conflict files

11. Open the file in the editor to resolve the conflict, as illustrated in the following figure:

```
11          public void FireShot()
12          {
13  <<<<<<< HEAD
14              //attachedWeapon.Shoot(fireDamage);
15  =======
16              Debug.Log("SHot Start");
17              attachedWeapon.Shoot(fireDamage);
18  >>>>>>> main
19          }
20
```

Figure 7.14 – Conflict code

12. After making the necessary edits, add and commit the file:

```
PS D:\GameDevelopment\Projects\Freelancing\-Mastering-Unity-2024-Game-Development-with-C-> git add Assets/FusionFuryGame
/Scripts/Enemy/EnemyShoot.cs
PS D:\GameDevelopment\Projects\Freelancing\-Mastering-Unity-2024-Game-Development-with-C-> git commit -m "File after mer
ge"
[feature/branch-name 5d4f15d] File after merge
PS D:\GameDevelopment\Projects\Freelancing\-Mastering-Unity-2024-Game-Development-with-C-> |
```

Figure 7.15 – Commit after solving the conflict

13. Use `git status` to ensure everything is clear:

```
PS D:\GameDevelopment\Projects\Freelancing\-Mastering-Unity-2024-Game-Development-with-C-> git status
On branch feature/branch-name
Your branch is up to date with 'origin/feature/branch-name'.

nothing to commit, working tree clean
PS D:\GameDevelopment\Projects\Freelancing\-Mastering-Unity-2024-Game-Development-with-C-> |
```

Figure 7.16 – Checking status

14. Now, push the branch after resolving the conflict:

```
PS D:\GameDevelopment\Projects\Freelancing\-Mastering-Unity-2024-Game-Development-with-C-> git push origin feature/branc
h-name
Enumerating objects: 21, done.
Counting objects: 100% (21/21), done.
Delta compression using up to 12 threads
Compressing objects: 100% (9/9), done.
Writing objects: 100% (9/9), 922 bytes | 922.00 KiB/s, done.
Total 9 (delta 7), reused 0 (delta 0), pack-reused 0
remote: Resolving deltas: 100% (7/7), completed with 6 local objects.
To https://github.com/PacktPublishing/-Mastering-Unity-2024-Game-Development-with-C-.git
   a880e09..5d4f15d  feature/branch-name -> feature/branch-name
PS D:\GameDevelopment\Projects\Freelancing\-Mastering-Unity-2024-Game-Development-with-C-> |
```

Figure 7.17 – Pushing the feature branch

By using the CLI, we can efficiently resolve conflicts in Git repositories by navigating to the project directory, switching to the branch containing the conflict, modifying the conflicting file, adding and committing the changes, pushing the branch, and finally merging the changes with the main branch.

In summary, mastering code conflict management involves understanding conflict origins and resolution techniques. In this section, we explored common conflict types such as merge conflicts and structural changes, and we delved into practical conflict resolution methods using tools such as GitHub Desktop, Visual Studio, and the CLI. By learning to navigate conflicts effectively, we ensure smooth collaboration and project success in Unity projects.

In the upcoming section, we will explore how to effectively work with existing projects, providing instructions and a practical example for guidance.

Understanding existing code bases

When delving into an existing code base, there are key steps to take to familiarize yourself with its structure and functionality:

- **Project structure and organization**: Begin by exploring the project's directory structure and organization. Understand how files and folders are arranged and grouped according to functionality or modules.

- **Review documentation**: Look for any available documentation, including README files, wiki pages, or inline comments within the code. Documentation can provide valuable insights into the project's purpose, architecture, and design decisions.

- **Identify key components and relationships**: Identify key components, modules, and their relationships within the code base. Determine how different parts of the code interact with each other and understand the overall architecture.

- **Utilize code analysis tools and integrated development environment (IDE) features**: Make use of code analysis tools and features provided by your IDE to explore code dependencies, inheritance hierarchies, and function calls. Tools such as static code analyzers can help identify potential issues or areas for improvement.

- **Understand coding standards and conventions**: Familiarize yourself with coding standards and conventions used in the project. Pay attention to naming conventions, code formatting, and documentation practices to ensure consistency across the code base.

- **Communicate with team members**: Engage with team members or project leads to gain insights into the code base and its design decisions. Discuss any questions or uncertainties you have and leverage their expertise to deepen your understanding.

Beginning work on an existing project demands time and dedication to grasp its complexities. Yet, this initial exploration establishes a base for fruitful contributions, ensuring the project's durability and ease of maintenance. As you familiarize yourself with the code base, you'll gain the ability to suggest improvements, tackle problems, and engage in effective collaboration with the project team.

Practical exploration for the existing code base

We'll illustrate the code review process with an example, either after following the preceding steps or by considering these steps beforehand.

If you're assigned a task in a new project, you can either proceed independently following these steps, seek guidance from your senior or leader if needed, or check if there's a similar approach already implemented in the game.

My preferred method is to begin at the end and work backward to the source. For example, if you're dealing with UI logic, start by examining the button's onclick action to determine which function it calls. Then, navigate to that script to review the function.

Then, you can examine the logic and check for additional calls to other scripts. Continue this process until you reach the core of the logic. Sometimes, a function may involve numerous calls to other scripts, so review them one by one to comprehend how they interact. This process enhances your understanding of the project. If the logic involves managers, you'll grasp their responsibilities. Consequently, when you tackle tasks related to these managers in the future, you'll be better equipped to understand and connect the logic effectively.

If you're assigned a new task and realize the manager, such as one handling player or game data, lacks a necessary function, you can simply append a new function to that manager. This approach allows you to expand the manager's capabilities to accommodate your requirements seamlessly.

When collaborating with a third party, it's beneficial to examine example scenes or scripts to grasp their functionality. By experimenting with and modifying these examples, you can gain insights into their usage and adapt them for your own features, focusing only on the essential logic needed for your project.

Now, let's see an example we will follow to see how we can understand the existing code base.

Example:

I'm currently examining the sound toggle function in the `SettingsView` script, which handles muting or unmuting the sound effects in another project I'm involved in:

1. I begin by navigating to the `SettingsView` script in the hierarchy and locating the toggle button.
2. Then, I examine the action triggered when the value changes and identify the associated function or functions. Additionally, it's important to verify if the toggle is referenced in the view script and if the function is attached through code. As illustrated in the following figure, the function can be found in the **Inspector**:

204　Contributing to Existing Code Bases in Unity with C#

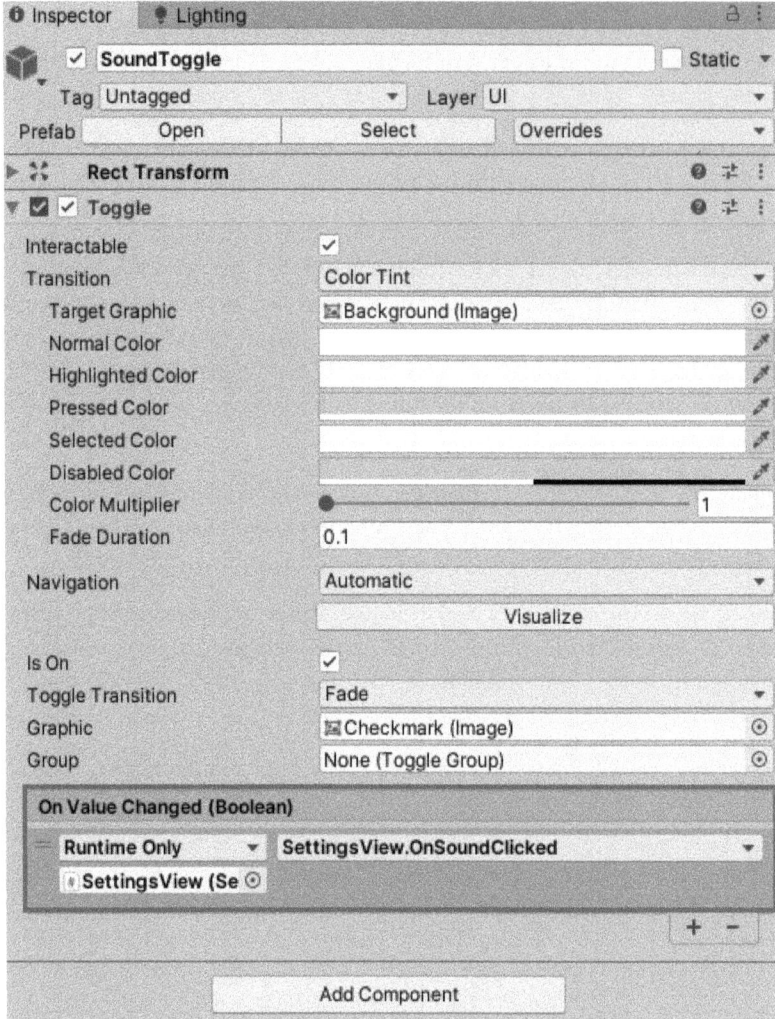

Figure 7.18 – SoundToggle component

3. Next, we should navigate to the `SettingsView` script to examine the logic of `OnSoundClicked`, as illustrated in the following figure:

```
0 references
public void OnSoundClicked(bool state)
{
    int volume = state == true ? 1 : 0;
    AudioManager.Instance.SetSFXVolume(volume);
}
```

Figure 7.19 – OnSoundClicked function in the SettingsView script

4. In the `OnSoundClicked` function, we adjust the volume state based on the input, and then we invoke the `AudioManager` script, which handles all audio-related logic in the game.

When we access the `SetSFXVolume` function, as shown in the next figure, you can observe its associated logic:

```
2 references
public void SetSFXVolume(float volume)
{
    audioMixer.SetFloat("SFXVolume", Mathf.Log10(volume) * 20);
    playerData.SetSoundState(volume == 1 ? true : false);
}
```

Figure 7.20 – SetSFXVolume function in the AudioManager script

5. In the `SetSFXVolume` function, we adjust the sound effects volume in the audio mixer, enabling us to control all audio sources linked to this mixer, muting or unmuting their sound. Additionally, the second line manages the sound state data, facilitating its persistence and storage locally or in the cloud.

6. We will now examine the function responsible for setting the sound state in the `GameData` script, which manages the game's data, as you can see in the following figure:

```
1 reference
public void SetSoundState(bool state)
{
    isSoundOn = state;
}
```

Figure 7.21 – SetSoundState function in the GameData script

In summary, the advantage we gain is the presence of a script dedicated to audio control within the game, equipped with functions that can be utilized in future tasks related to audio management. Additionally, there exists a script named `GameData`, tasked with managing the game's data. This allows us to reference it later for any data-related requirements, such as retrieving saved data or storing new data states.

This example is straightforward to follow, but the steps are comprehensive. Feel free to apply these steps to your projects or when you're dealing with new ones.

Summary

In this chapter, we learned about working with existing code in Unity using C#. We explored how to use VCSs, merge code, and fix conflicts when collaborating on projects. By understanding these concepts, we can work better with other developers and maintain code quality. The chapter also covered how to understand project structures, review documentation, and communicate effectively with team members. By taking the time to understand existing projects, we can contribute more effectively and make better decisions.

In *Chapter 8*, we'll look at adding outside assets and features to Unity games using C#. We'll learn how to use pre-made assets to improve game visuals and add new features such as analytics and monetization. Get ready for new ways to enhance your games in the upcoming chapter!

Part 4: Advanced Integration and External Assets with C# in Unity

In this part, you will delve into integrating third-party assets, pre-built components, and APIs, using C# to enhance game visuals and user engagement within Unity projects. You will learn how to leverage external resources effectively, contributing to immersive gameplay experiences. Explore Unity's profiling tools to identify performance bottlenecks and apply optimization techniques for enhanced game performance and memory management. Discover productivity-boosting shortcuts and advanced workflows using C# to streamline game development processes, troubleshoot challenges, and achieve success in Unity development.

This part includes the following chapters:

- *Chapter 8, Implementing External Assets, APIs, and Pre-built Components with C# in Unity*
- *Chapter 9, Optimizing the Game Using Unity's Profiler, Frame Debugger, and Memory Profiler*
- *Chapter 10, Tips and Tricks in Unity*

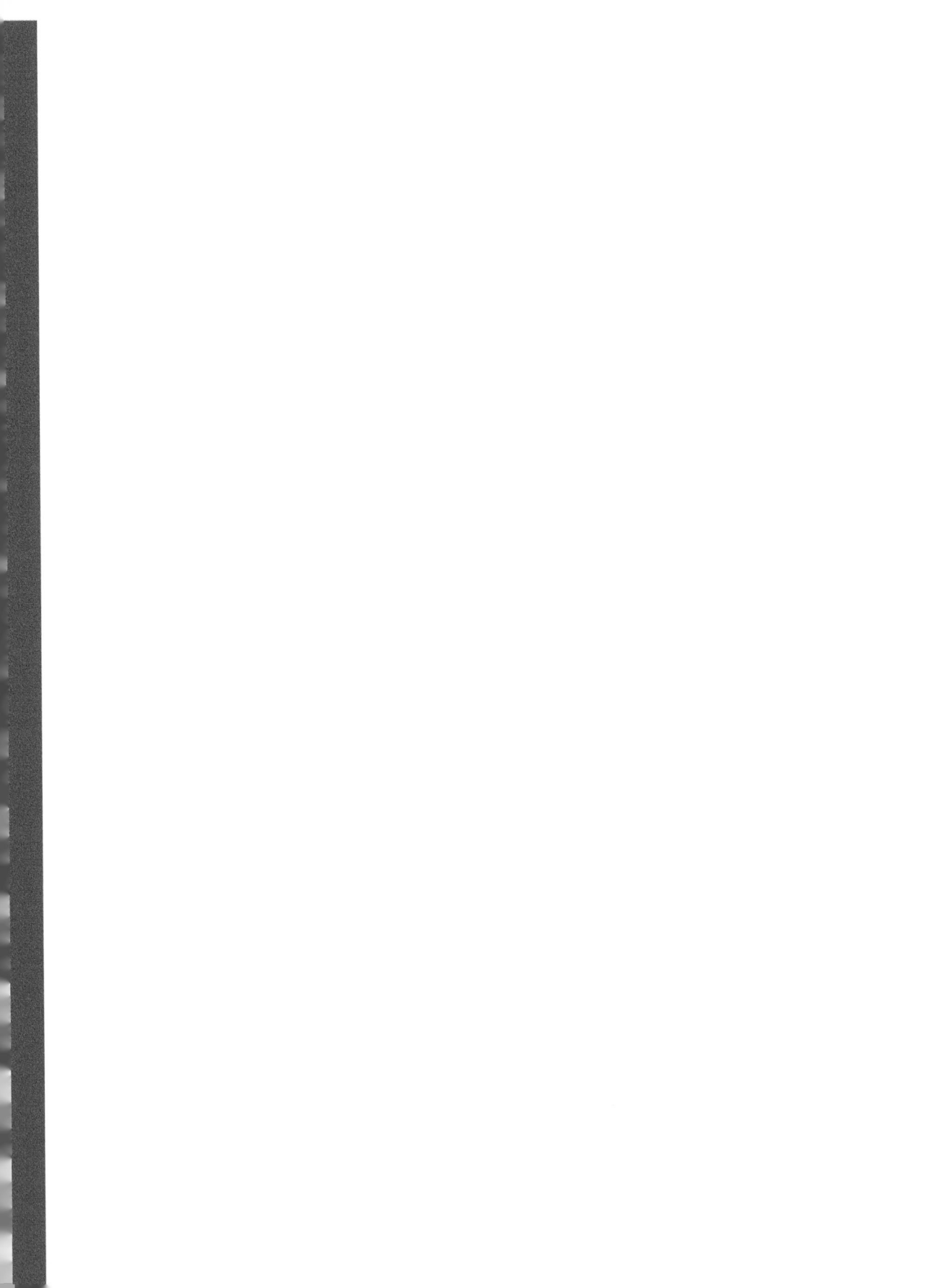

8

Implementing External Assets, APIs, and Pre-Built Components with C# in Unity

Welcome to *Chapter 8*, where we will delve into essential aspects of game development using C#. We will begin by exploring the integration of pre-built assets, a fundamental skill for enhancing game visuals and performance. Then, we will delve into the integration of rendering pipelines, which is crucial for optimizing game visuals and achieving better performance. After that, we will discuss the significance of backend services in game development, focusing on authentication logic as a prime example of their importance. Lastly, we will explore analytics APIs and their pivotal role in understanding player behavior and optimizing game performance. Throughout this chapter, I'll demonstrate how to implement these key components into our game, empowering you to create immersive and engaging gaming experiences.

In this chapter, we're going to cover the following main topics:

- Leveraging pre-built assets with C#
- Integrating backend services with C#
- Integrating analytics APIs with C#

Technical requirements

All the code files of this chapter can be found at: https://github.com/PacktPublishing/Mastering-Unity-Game-Development-with-C-Sharp/tree/main/Assets/Chapter%2008.

Leveraging pre-built assets with C#

In the vast world of game development, time is as valuable as the pixels on our screens. Every moment counts, and each bit of code shapes the worlds players will explore. This is where third-party assets come in handy—they are efficient tools that enhance creativity in the changing landscape of game design.

Imagine this: you're a new game developer with a bright vision. You dream of vast landscapes, detailed character animations, and sounds that take players to faraway lands. However, the journey from idea to reality is full of challenges, and time is hard to come by.

Third-party assets, often underappreciated in game development, play a crucial role. These readily available resources form the backbone of game creation, bringing virtual worlds to fruition. From grand landscapes to subtle environmental details, third-party assets simplify the complex task of asset creation, allowing us to focus on refining gameplay and improving player experiences.

But why are they so important? Firstly, third-party assets offer a wealth of resources created by experts. Whether you need stunning environments, realistic characters, or chilling sound effects, the vast array of third-party assets has it all. These assets fuel creativity, sparking imagination and helping us turn ideas into reality quickly.

Furthermore, the benefits go beyond convenience. By using pre-built assets, we can focus on the core of our games—the gameplay itself. Free from creating assets, they can craft immersive worlds, compelling stories, and unforgettable experiences that capture players' hearts and endure over time.

In this section, we'll explore the utilization of pre-built assets available in Unity's Package Manager, such as **URP**, which provides advanced rendering options. Let's begin our exploration.

Universal Render Pipeline (URP)

In this section, we'll explore the **Universal Render Pipeline** (**URP**), a powerful tool that helps create stunning visuals and optimize performance in our Unity projects.

URP is a rendering solution provided by Unity Technologies. It's designed to strike a balance between visual quality and performance, making it suitable for a wide range of platforms and devices, including mobile, consoles, and PCs.

URP offers a flexible and efficient rendering pipeline that allows for the creation of visually appealing games while ensuring smooth performance across different hardware configurations. Whether you're creating a stylized indie game or a realistic AAA title, URP provides the tools and features needed to bring your vision to life.

Choosing between Unity's render pipelines – URP versus HDRP

Unity offers two distinct rendering pipelines, URP and the **High-Definition Render Pipeline** (HDRP), each tailored to different needs and requirements in game development. Let's explore the key differences between the two and the reasons why you might choose one over the other for your game.

In the following table, I've outlined a comparison between Unity's render pipelines, highlighting key points to assist you in determining the most suitable pipeline for your project.

Aspect	URP	HDRP
Graphics Fidelity	URP is designed for optimized rendering performance while maintaining a balance between visual quality and efficiency. It supports features such as real-time lighting, shadows, and post-processing effects.	HDRP aims to deliver high-quality visuals and graphical fidelity, especially for high-end platforms such as PCs and consoles. It offers advanced rendering features such as physically based rendering and volumetric lighting.
Platform Compatibility	URP is optimized for cross-platform development, making it suitable for a diverse range of devices and platforms, including mobile devices, consoles, and PCs.	HDRP is tailored for high-end platforms and may require more powerful hardware to achieve optimal performance. It may not be as suitable for mobile devices or lower-end PCs due to its higher demands
Art Style and Visual Direction	URP is versatile and accommodates a wide range of art styles and visual directions, including stylized, cartoonish, or realistic art styles. It allows for visually appealing results across different genres and themes.	HDRP is well suited for projects aiming for photorealistic graphics and immersive visual experiences. It offers advanced rendering features and high-fidelity effects enhancing realism and immersion.
Development Time and Resources	URP provides a balance between visual quality and development efficiency with a streamlined workflow and easier setup. It is accessible to developers with limited resources or time constraints.	HDRP offers advanced features and graphical capabilities, but it may require additional development time and resources to fully leverage its potential. It needs careful optimization and tuning for desired performance.

In summary, the choice between URP and HDRP depends on various factors, including your project's target platforms, desired graphical fidelity, art style, and available development resources. If you prioritize performance, cross-platform compatibility, and a balance between visual quality and efficiency, URP may be the preferable option. On the other hand, if your project demands high-end visuals, photorealism, and advanced graphical effects, HDRP may be the better choice, provided you have the necessary resources and hardware to support it.

Now that we have understood the contrast between the two distinct rendering pipelines in Unity, let's proceed to install URP.

Installing URP into our project

> **Important note**
> Before upgrading to a custom render pipeline, it's essential to back up your project.

We've already chosen the URP package for our project. However, if it hasn't been configured in your project yet, you can simply access **Package Manager** and select the **Universal RP** option, as you can see in *Figure 8.1*:

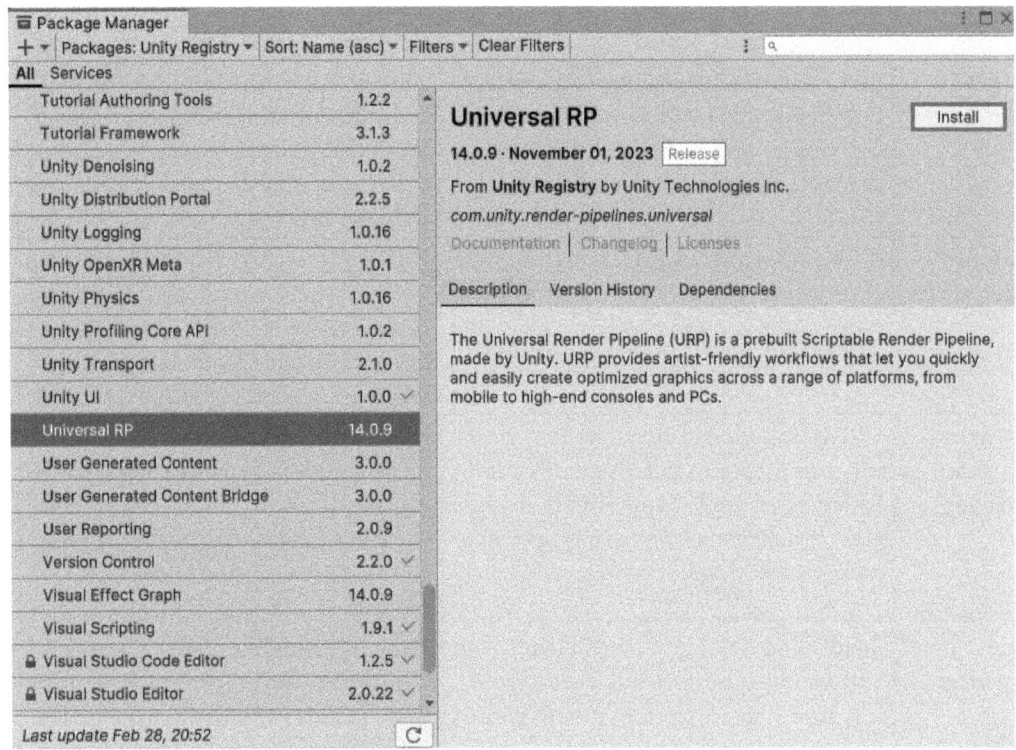

Figure 8.1 – Installing the URP package

When you click on **Install**, Unity will install the package and its dependencies.

> Note
> If you are migrating from the built-in pipeline to URP or High-Definition RP, there are specific instructions to adhere to. You'll need to adjust all materials to utilize the new shaders provided by these packages. However, given that our game has been utilizing these packages from the outset, imported files such as model materials will already be configured to use the shaders provided by those packages.

Since migrating from the built-in is not our primary objective, I won't delve into upgrading to URP. You can explore additional possibilities by referring to the official documentation:

- If you are using URP version 13.1 or newer, there is a built-in converter available. Please refer to this page for more information on how to utilize this converter: `https://docs.unity3d.com/Packages/com.unity.render-pipelines.universal@14.0/manual/features/rp-converter.html`.

- If you are using a URP version prior to 13.1, you need to refer to this link: `https://docs.unity3d.com/Packages/com.unity.render-pipelines.universal@13.0/manual/upgrading-your-shaders.html`.

In the next subsection, we will discover the power of Unity's URP, a versatile package offering optimized rendering, custom shaders, and enhanced lighting for creating visually stunning projects across multiple platforms.

Exploring URP in Unity – features and functionality

The URP package in Unity provides developers with a range of features and functionalities to enhance the rendering capabilities of their projects. Here are some key aspects of the URP package and its usage:

- **Optimized rendering pipeline**: URP offers an optimized rendering pipeline designed to balance performance and visual quality across various platforms and devices. It includes features such as deferred and forward rendering paths, allowing us to choose the rendering technique that best suits their project's requirements.

- **Lightweight rendering**: URP is designed to be lightweight, making it suitable for projects targeting mobile devices, lower-end hardware, and performance-conscious applications. It optimizes rendering processes to achieve smooth performance while maintaining visual fidelity.

- **Shader graph integration**: URP seamlessly integrates with Unity's Shader Graph tool, allowing us to create custom shaders and visual effects without writing code. Shader Graph empowers us to design complex materials, lighting effects, and post-processing effects through a node-based interface.

- **Custom rendering features**: URP provides support for custom rendering features through **Scriptable Render Pipeline** (**SRP**) extensions. We can extend and customize the rendering pipeline by implementing custom render passes, post-processing effects, and shader variants.

- **Enhanced lighting system**: URP includes a flexible lighting system that supports real-time lighting, shadows, and reflections. It offers features such as per-object and per-pixel lighting, dynamic shadows, and light probes for realistic lighting effects.

- **Post-processing effects**: URP includes built-in support for post-processing effects, allowing us to enhance the visual quality of their scenes. It provides a range of post-processing effects such as bloom, depth of field, color grading, and ambient occlusion.

- **Cross-platform compatibility**: URP is designed for cross-platform compatibility, enabling us to create games and applications for various platforms, including mobile devices, consoles, and PCs. It optimizes rendering performance across different hardware configurations and platform specifications.

In summary, the URP package in Unity provides us with a lightweight, flexible, and optimized rendering solution for creating visually stunning and performance-efficient projects. From lighting and shading to post-processing effects and custom rendering features, URP empowers us to bring their creative visions to life while ensuring optimal performance across different platforms and devices.

Next, we'll explore more advanced topics, such as render callbacks and custom render features.

Mastering visual modifications in Unity – advanced techniques with URP and C#

Introducing advanced techniques in URP using C# can greatly modify the visual quality and performance of your Unity projects. Two key features that we can explore and discuss in this section are Custom Render Passes and Render Pipeline Callbacks:

- **Custom Render Passes**:

  - Custom Render Passes allow you to inject custom rendering logic into the render pipeline, enabling you to implement specialized effects or optimizations beyond the built-in features of URP.

  - With Custom Render Passes, you have fine-grained control over the rendering process at various stages, such as before or after opaque rendering, before or after transparent rendering, or even in between specific render queues.

  - You can use Custom Render Passes to implement effects like outline rendering, screen-space effects, custom post-processing, or optimizations such as rendering additional buffers for custom shaders or computations.

- **Render Pipeline Callbacks**:

  - Render Pipeline Callbacks provide a mechanism for hooking into specific events and stages within the render pipeline to execute custom C# code.

  - Using Render Pipeline Callbacks, you can perform tasks such as modifying materials, adjusting rendering settings dynamically, or injecting custom rendering logic at specific points in the rendering process.

  - Render Pipeline Callbacks can be used to implement advanced features such as dynamic material modifications based on game events, procedural generation of textures or geometry, or applying custom shader effects based on runtime conditions.

Next, let's explore an example that demonstrates the application of these advanced techniques within our project.

Illustration of implementing advanced techniques

Here is a step-by-step guide, illustrated with examples, on how to utilize these advanced techniques to create and control the outline effect:

1. Before creating the renderer feature, ensure that your project is configured to use the URP renderer data in your **Quality and Graphics** settings within the **Project Settings**. Right-click in your **Project** tab and navigate to **Create | Rendering | URP Renderer Feature** to generate a new feature script. You can name it `OutlineEffect`:

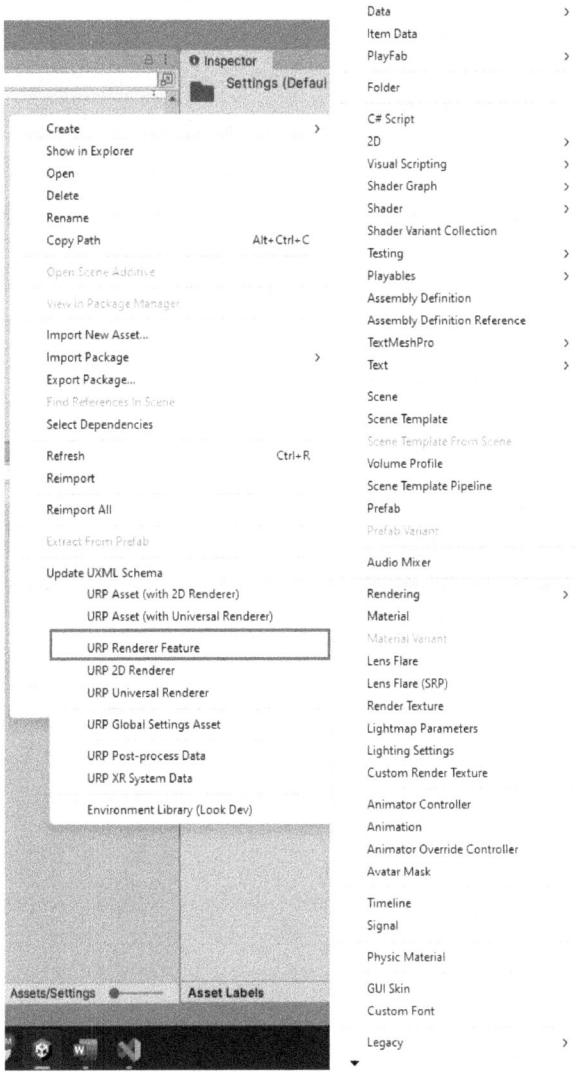

Figure 8.2 – Creating an URP Renderer Feature script

2. Next, we open the `OutlineEffect` script and make modifications as outlined in the following code block:

```
public class OutlineEffect : ScriptableRendererFeature
{
    class OutlineRenderPass : ScriptableRenderPass
    {
        public List<Material> outlineMaterials;

        public OutlineRenderPass(List<Material> materials)
        {
            this.outlineMaterials = materials;
            renderPassEvent = RenderPassEvent.AfterRenderingOpaques;
        }

        // This method is called before executing the render pass..
        public override void OnCameraSetup(CommandBuffer cmd, ref RenderingData renderingData)
        {
        }

        // Here you can implement the rendering logic.
        // Use <c>ScriptableRenderContext</c> to issue drawing commands or execute command buffers
        // https://docs.unity3d.com/ScriptReference/Rendering.ScriptableRenderContext.html
        // You don't have to call ScriptableRenderContext.submit, the render pipeline will call it at specific points in the pipeline.
        public override void Execute(ScriptableRenderContext context, ref RenderingData renderingData)
        {
            CommandBuffer cmd = CommandBufferPool.Get("OutlineRenderPass");

            // Set the render target to the camera's depth buffer
            cmd.SetRenderTarget(renderingData.cameraData.renderer.cameraDepthTargetHandle);

            // Clear the depth buffer to ensure the outline is rendered correctly
            cmd.ClearRenderTarget(false, true, Color.clear);
```

```csharp
            var settings = new DrawingSettings(new
ShaderTagId("UniversalForward"), new
SortingSettings(renderingData.cameraData.camera));
            var filterSettings = new
FilteringSettings(RenderQueueRange.opaque);
            context.DrawRenderers(renderingData.cullResults, ref
settings, ref filterSettings);

            // Draw objects with outline materials
            // Draw objects with outline materials
            foreach (Material material in outlineMaterials)
            {
                var drawSettings = new DrawingSettings(new
ShaderTagId("Outline"), new SortingSettings(renderingData.
cameraData.camera))
                {
                    overrideMaterial = material
                };
                var filterSettingsOutline = new
FilteringSettings(RenderQueueRange.opaque);
                context.DrawRenderers(renderingData.cullResults,
ref drawSettings, ref filterSettingsOutline);
            }

            context.ExecuteCommandBuffer(cmd);
            CommandBufferPool.Release(cmd);
        }

        // Cleanup any allocated resources that were created
during the execution of this render pass.
        public override void OnCameraCleanup(CommandBuffer cmd)
        {
        }
    }

    OutlineRenderPass outlinePass;
    public List<Material> outlineMaterials;

    /// <inheritdoc/>
    public override void Create()
    {
        outlinePass = new OutlineRenderPass(outlineMaterials);
        outlinePass.renderPassEvent = RenderPassEvent.
AfterRenderingOpaques;
    }
```

```
        // Here you can inject one or multiple render passes in the
    renderer.
        // This method is called when setting up the renderer once
    per-camera.
        public override void AddRenderPasses(ScriptableRenderer
    renderer, ref RenderingData renderingData)
        {
            renderer.EnqueuePass(outlinePass);
        }
    }
```

Let's break down the previous code to explain what each part does:

- The `OutlineEffect` class (inherits `ScriptableRendererFeature`):

  - This class represents a custom renderer feature responsible for adding an outline effect to objects in the scene.

  - It inherits from the `ScriptableRendererFeature` class, which allows it to integrate with URP.

- The `OutlineRenderPass` class (inherits `ScriptableRenderPass`):

  - This nested class represents a custom render pass responsible for rendering objects with an outline effect.

  - It inherits from the `ScriptableRenderPass` class, which provides functionality for defining custom rendering logic.

- The `OutlineRenderPass` constructor:

  - The constructor initializes the `OutlineRenderPass` class with a list of materials (`outlineMaterials`) used for rendering the outline effect.

  - It sets `renderPassEvent` to `RenderPassEvent.AfterRenderingOpaques`, indicating that the render pass should execute after rendering opaque objects.

- The `OnCameraSetup` method:

  - This method is called before executing the render pass but doesn't contain any logic in the code.

- The `Execute` method:
  - This method contains the main rendering logic for the outline effect.
  - It retrieves a command buffer (`cmd`) from `CommandBufferPool`.
  - It sets the render target to the camera's depth buffer and clears the depth buffer to ensure the outline is rendered correctly.
  - It defines `DrawingSettings` and `FilteringSettings` for rendering opaque objects without the outline effect.
  - It iterates through the list of `outlineMaterials` and renders objects with the outline effect using the `overrideMaterial` property of `DrawingSettings`.
  - It executes the command buffer and releases it back to the pool.
- The `OnCameraCleanup` method:
  - This method is called after executing the render pass but doesn't contain any logic in the code.
- The `Create` method:
  - This method initializes the `OutlineRenderPass` instance with the provided list of `outlineMaterials`.
  - It sets `renderPassEvent` to `RenderPassEvent.AfterRenderingOpaques`.
- The `AddRenderPasses` method:
  - This method is called when setting up the renderer once per camera.
  - It enqueues the `OutlineRenderPass` instance into the renderer to be executed during the rendering process.

Overall, the `OutlineEffect` class defines a custom renderer feature that adds an outline effect to objects in the scene by utilizing a custom render pass (`OutlineRenderPass`) with a list of outline materials. The `OutlineRenderPass` class implements the rendering logic for applying the outline effect to objects during the rendering process.

3. Next, you can integrate the feature into your URP data scriptable object. You can customize the settings according to your game's requirements. For our demonstration, I've retained the default settings, as depicted in *Figure 8.3*:

220 Implementing External Assets, APIs, and Pre-Built Components with C# in Unity

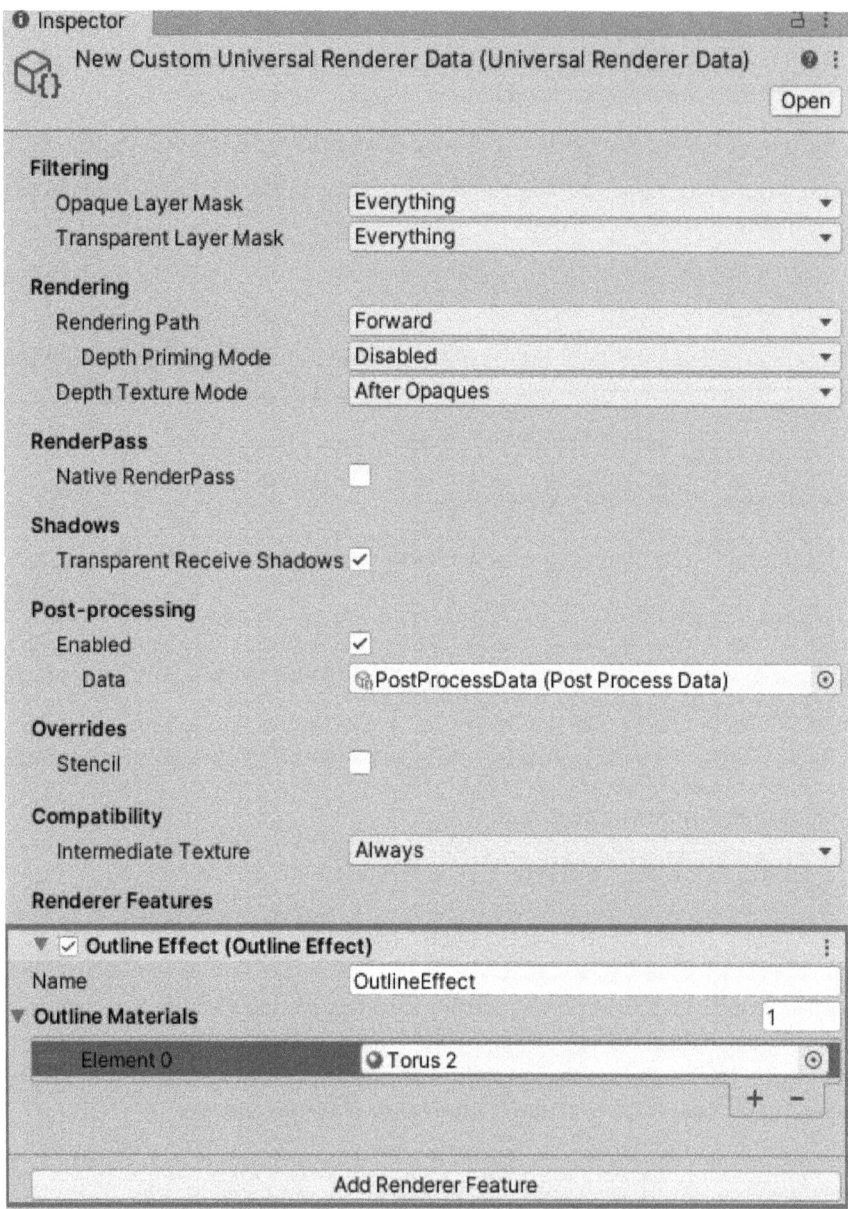

Figure 8.3 – Adding OutlineEffect Feature

You can include additional features to achieve your desired visual effects. Furthermore, you can refer to Unity's official documentation for further details using the following link: https://docs.unity3d.com/Packages/com.unity.render-pipelines.universal@16.0/manual/index.html.

In the following figure, you will observe the disparity before and after applying the feature:

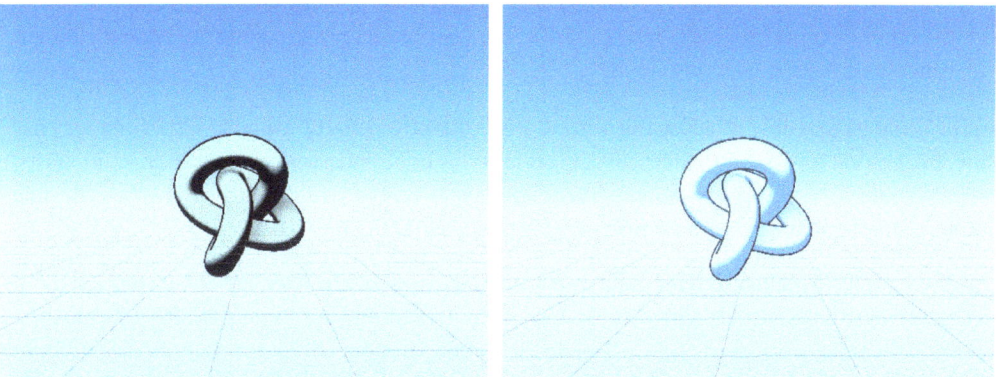

Figure 8.4 –OutlineEffect feature effect

Discover the significant impact and benefits of leveraging the render pass feature for optimizing rendering and enhancing visual effects.

What is the purpose of utilizing the render pass feature?

Using render passes in conjunction with the URP offers several benefits for implementing an outline effect:

- **Modularity and extensibility**: By utilizing render passes, you can modularize your rendering pipeline and separate specific rendering tasks into distinct passes. This makes your rendering pipeline more flexible and easier to maintain. You can add or remove passes as needed without affecting other parts of the pipeline.

- **Performance optimization**: Render passes in URP allow you to control the order in which rendering tasks are executed. This enables you to optimize performance by efficiently batching and sorting objects, reducing overdraw, and minimizing unnecessary render calls. For the outline effect, you can ensure that only the necessary objects are rendered with the outline material, reducing the computational overhead.

- **Integration with URP's rendering pipeline**: URP provides a streamlined rendering pipeline optimized for performance across various platforms. By integrating your custom rendering effects, such as the outline effect, into URP's pipeline using render passes, you ensure compatibility and consistency with URP's rendering features and optimizations.

- **Consistency across platforms**: URP is designed to provide consistent rendering results across different platforms and devices, including desktop, mobile, and consoles. By leveraging URP's features, you can ensure that your outline effect behaves predictably and performs optimally across a wide range of target platforms.

- **Shader graph integration**: URP seamlessly integrates with Unity's Shader Graph tool, allowing you to create custom shaders visually without writing code. You can use Shader Graph to design the outline shader and easily incorporate it into your render pass, making the implementation process more accessible and intuitive.

Overall, while it's possible to apply the outline effect directly without utilizing URP's render pass feature, integrating it with URP offers advantages in terms of performance optimization, modularity, consistency, and compatibility with Unity's rendering pipeline. It provides a more robust and flexible solution for implementing custom rendering effects in your Unity projects.

Game development benefits from pre-built assets and C# scripts, saving time and enhancing creativity. Unity's URP optimizes visuals and performance. Understanding URP versus HDRP aids pipeline selection. URP setup involves package installation and configuration. URP features include lightweight rendering, Shader Graph integration, and advanced techniques such as Custom Render Passes. Render passes in URP offer modularity and performance optimization.

In the upcoming section, we'll explore integrating backend services, understanding their significance in game development, and the reasons for their necessity. Additionally, I'll illustrate their usage through an example featuring one of the available services.

Integrating backend services with C#

In this section, we will understand how the integration of backend APIs with C# provides us with a potent tool to enrich our projects with robust functionalities. Through the utilization of these APIs, we can seamlessly link their Unity projects to external services, facilitating features such as user authentication, data storage, and leaderboards.

Let's explore backend services and understand their significance in games.

Backend services

Backend services refer to the set of functionalities and infrastructure components that support the operation of software applications, including games, from the server-side perspective. In the context of game development, backend services encompass various features and capabilities designed to enhance gameplay experiences, manage player data, and facilitate online interactions. Here are some key aspects of backend services in game development:

- **Data storage**: Provides storage solutions for game-related data, including player profiles, game progress, achievements, inventory, and other persistent game state information. This data is typically stored in databases or cloud storage systems, ensuring reliability, scalability, and accessibility across different platforms and devices.

- **User authentication**: Offers authentication mechanisms to verify the identity of players and ensure secure access to game features and content. Authentication processes typically involve user registration, login, and session management, employing encryption and secure protocols to protect user credentials and prevent unauthorized access.

- **Multiplayer functionality**: Enables the implementation of multiplayer features in games, allowing players to connect, interact, and compete with each other in real time. This includes functionalities such as matchmaking, lobby management, game session orchestration, and synchronization of player actions across networked environments.

- **Real-time communication**: Facilitate real-time communication between game clients and servers, supporting features such as in-game chat, messaging, notifications, and real-time updates. These communication channels enable players to engage with each other, receive important game updates, and participate in collaborative or competitive gameplay experiences.

- **Analytics and insights**: Provides analytics tools and capabilities to track player behavior, monitor game performance, and gain insights into player engagement, retention, and monetization patterns. Analytics data helps us make informed decisions, optimize game mechanics, and tailor experiences to meet player preferences.

- **Live operations and content management**: Supports live operations and content management, allowing us to deploy updates, patches, and new content to games seamlessly. This includes features such as **content delivery networks** (**CDNs**), version control, A/B testing, and live event management, enabling dynamic and evolving gameplay experiences.

In summary, backend services form the foundation of modern game development, providing essential infrastructure and functionalities to support online multiplayer gaming, manage player data, analyze player behavior, and deliver engaging and immersive gameplay experiences across different platforms and devices.

Introduction of backend service providers and their features

Several backend service providers offer comprehensive solutions tailored to the needs of game developers, each with its own set of features and capabilities. Here are some available services, and these are the most commonly used options at the time of writing this book:

- **Firebase**: Developed by Google, Firebase offers a suite of backend services including real-time database, authentication, cloud storage, and hosting. It provides seamless integration with Unity, making it an ideal choice for us seeking a robust and scalable backend solution.

- **PlayFab**: PlayFab offers a comprehensive backend platform specifically designed for game developers. Its features include player authentication, data storage, in-game analytics, virtual currency management, and live operations tools. PlayFab's flexible APIs and SDKs support easy integration with Unity, empowering us to build engaging multiplayer experiences and live service features.

- **Amazon Web Services (AWS)**: AWS provides a wide range of cloud-based services including databases, authentication, content delivery, and analytics. With offerings such as Amazon DynamoDB, Amazon Cognito, and Amazon GameLift, AWS offers scalable solutions for game developers looking to build, deploy, and manage backend infrastructure with flexibility and reliability.

224 Implementing External Assets, APIs, and Pre-Built Components with C# in Unity

We'll use PlayFab in this chapter and in the next section, we will implement it in our project accordingly. Let's begin integrating PlayFab.

Integrating PlayFab

In this guide, I'll walk you through the process of implementing PlayFab and setting it up in your project. Then, we'll create a sample authentication logic to demonstrate its usage.

To begin, you'll need to download the PlayFab Unity package. I've utilized PlayFab SDK 2.188 for this purpose, which you can obtain from the following link: https://github.com/PlayFab/UnitySDK/releases. Once you download it, follow these steps:

1. In *Figure 8.5*, as you can see, we're extracting the PlayFab SDK into our project. Simply click **Import** to initiate the process of importing files and compiling them.

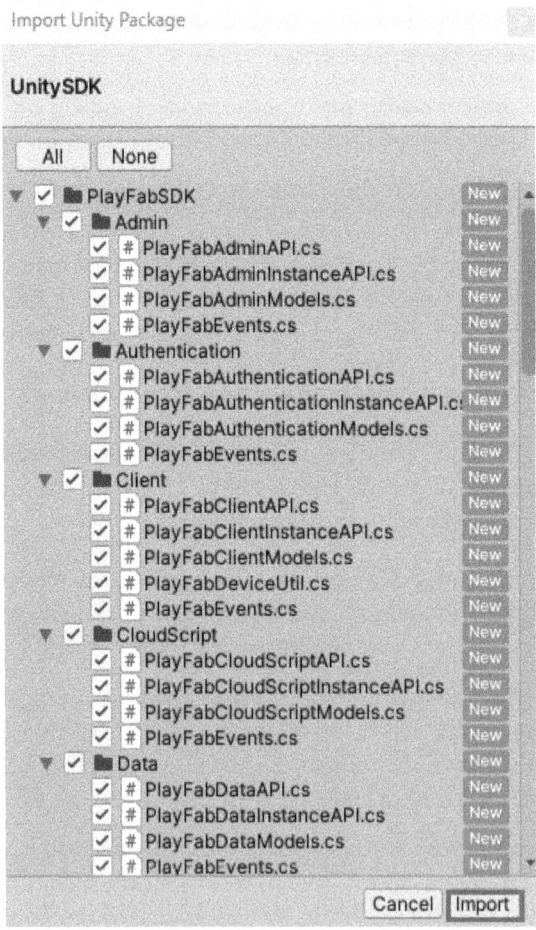

Figure 8.5 – Importing PlayFab SDK

Integrating backend services with C#   225

2. Wait for Unity to finish compiling, then navigate to **Assets | PlayFabSDK | Shared | Public | Resources**. From there, you can select the Scriptable Object **PlayFabSharedSettings** to configure it for your project. In *Figure 8.6*, you can observe the settings of PlayFab that we can configure:

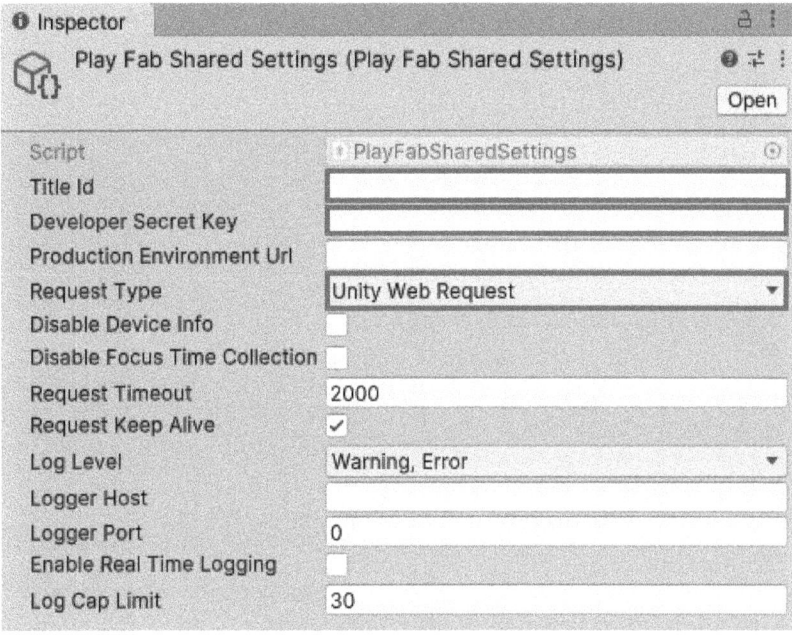

Figure 8.6 – PlayFab Shared Settings

3. For **Request Type**, you can select **Unity Web Request** or choose the option appropriate for your project. However, for our project, I will opt for **Unity Web Request**.

4. We will include the **Title ID** value, which you can obtain from your PlayFab game project dashboard. If you don't have a project yet, you can create one and use its key in your project. *Figure 8.7* shows where you can locate the ID needed for PlayFab settings.

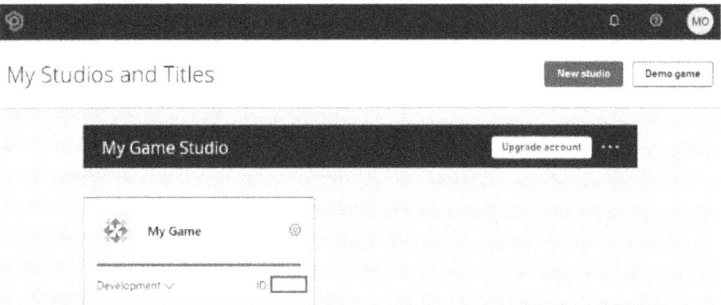

Figure 8.7 – PlayFab title ID

5. Next, access the project to retrieve the secret key; to do that, click on the settings icon and select **Title settings**:

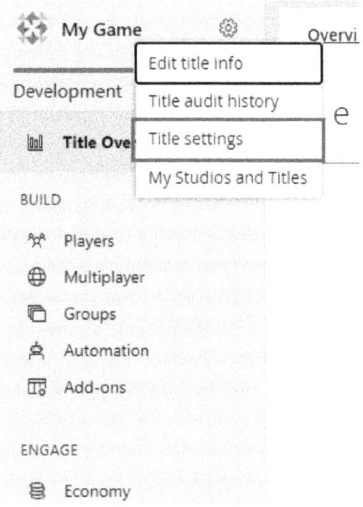

Figure 8.8 – PlayFab Title settings

6. The preceding step will open the settings tabs and from here, we can navigate to the **Secret Keys** tab to retrieve the secret key, as depicted in *Figure 8.9*:

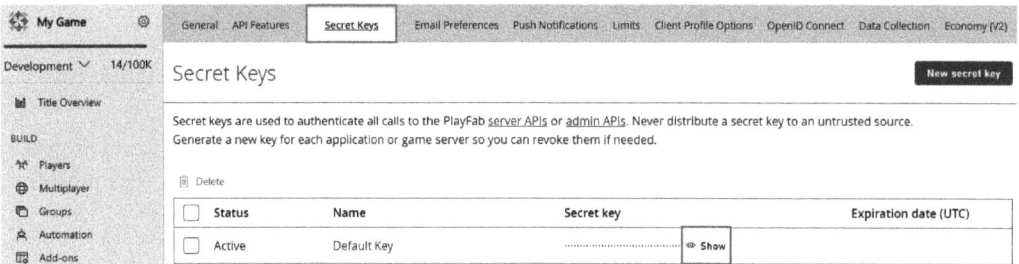

Figure 8.9 – Title secret key

7. Click on **Show** to reveal the secret key. You can then copy it and paste it into the **Developer Secret Key** field in the PlayFab settings in our game.

That's it! You now have the PlayFab SDK integrated into your project. In the next steps, we will begin using it and learn through an example. While this example is just a sample, it will cover the full flow of using this package. There are numerous possibilities for utilizing this package, so feel free to explore their documentation for further insights: https://learn.microsoft.com/en-us/gaming/playfab/.

Developing a sample login system

There are various methods for user login in games, such as using email, guest accounts, and, for mobile platforms, utilizing Play services for Android and Game Center for iOS. PlayFab offers a variety of options to facilitate user login based on the game platform.

For this system, we can establish a well-organized structure by following these steps:

1. We will begin by creating an interface for the login method. In the following code block, you will find a login method along with callbacks for the login state:

   ```
   using PlayFab.ClientModels;
   using PlayFab;

   public interface ILogin
   {
       void Login(System.Action<LoginResult> onSuccess, System.
   Action<PlayFabError> onFailure);
   }
   ```

2. Next, we can create a class for each login method. For guest login, we will utilize the device ID for authentication. In the following code block, we have implemented the `ILogin` interface with the `DeviceLogin` class and incorporated the logic for logging in with the device ID.

   ```
   using PlayFab.ClientModels;
   using PlayFab;


   public class DeviceLogin : ILogin
   {
       private string deviceId;

       public DeviceLogin(string deviceId)
       {
           this.deviceId = deviceId;
       }

       public void Login(System.Action<LoginResult> onSuccess,
   System.Action<PlayFabError> onFailure)
       {
           var request = new LoginWithCustomIDRequest
           {
               CustomId = deviceId,
               CreateAccount = true // Create account if not exists
           };
   ```

```
            PlayFabClientAPI.LoginWithCustomID(request, onSuccess,
onFailure);
    }
}
```

You can follow these steps and create additional login logic, especially if you are targeting mobile platforms, as there will be alternative login methods specific to mobile devices.

3. Then, we can create a `LoginManager` class, which will be responsible for invoking the appropriate login method, as demonstrated in the following code block:

```
using PlayFab.ClientModels;
using PlayFab;
using UnityEngine;

public class LoginManager
{
    private ILogin loginMethod;

    public void SetLoginMethod(ILogin method)
    {
        loginMethod = method;
    }

    public void Login(System.Action<LoginResult> onSuccess,
System.Action<PlayFabError> onFailure)
    {
        if (loginMethod != null)
        {
            loginMethod.Login(onSuccess , onFailure);
        }
        else
        {
            Debug.LogError("No login method set!");
        }
    }
}
```

4. For the next step, we will implement a `PlayfabManager` script to manage the login methods and handle user input, subsequently triggering appropriate actions:

```
using PlayFab.ClientModels;
using PlayFab;
using UnityEngine;

public class PlayFabManager
```

```csharp
{
    private LoginManager loginManager;
    private string savedEmailKey = "SavedEmail";
    private string userEmail;
    private void Start()
    {
        loginManager = new LoginManager();

        // Check if email is saved
        if (PlayerPrefs.HasKey(savedEmailKey))
        {
            string savedEmail = PlayerPrefs.GetString(savedEmailKey);
            // Auto-login with saved email
            EmailLoginButtonClicked(savedEmail, "SavedPassword");
        }
    }

    // Example method for triggering email login
    public void EmailLoginButtonClicked(string email, string password)
    {
        userEmail = email;


        loginManager.SetLoginMethod(new EmailLogin(email, password));
        loginManager.Login(OnLoginSuccess, OnLoginFailure);
    }

    // Example method for triggering device ID login
    public void DeviceIDLoginButtonClicked(string deviceID)
    {
        loginManager.SetLoginMethod(new DeviceLogin(deviceID));
        loginManager.Login(OnLoginSuccess, OnLoginFailure);
    }

    private void OnLoginSuccess(LoginResult result)
    {
        Debug.Log("Login successful!");
        // You can handle success here, such as loading player data

        // Save email for future auto-login
```

```csharp
            if (!string.IsNullOrEmpty(userEmail))
                PlayerPrefs.SetString(savedEmailKey, userEmail);

            // Load player data
            LoadPlayerData(result.PlayFabId);
        }

        private void OnLoginFailure(PlayFabError error)
        {
            Debug.LogError("Login failed: " + error.ErrorMessage);
        }

        private void LoadPlayerData(string playFabId)
        {
            var request = new GetUserDataRequest
            {
                PlayFabId = playFabId
            };

            PlayFabClientAPI.GetUserData(request, OnDataSuccess, OnDataFailure);
        }

        private void OnDataSuccess(GetUserDataResult result)
        {
            // Process player data here
            Debug.Log("Player data loaded successfully");
        }

        private void OnDataFailure(PlayFabError error)
        {
            Debug.LogError("Failed to load player data: " + error.ErrorMessage);
        }
    }
```

In `PlayFabManager`, you'll discover methods to log in using email and device ID, along with callbacks indicating login status. Additionally, I've included an example of how to handle successful user logins by loading their data. This enables us to execute further logic based on the data stored in PlayFab.

That concludes this example, which may seem simple but encompasses the complete process of utilizing PlayFab. This package offers extensive capabilities, including leaderboard management, remote settings configuration, analytics, and matchmaking. As mentioned earlier, explore their documentation for further insights and possibilities: https://learn.microsoft.com/en-us/gaming/playfab/.

In conclusion, we have gained insight into the significance of backend services for our games. We successfully integrated PlayFab into our project and learned to develop a login system through this process.

In the next section, we will delve into analytics APIs, their benefits in games, and the reasons behind their necessity in our game development endeavors.

Integrating analytics APIs with C#

Analytics APIs are software interfaces that enable us to integrate analytics functionality into our applications, including games. These APIs allow us to collect, analyze, and interpret data related to user interactions, behaviors, and performance metrics within our games. Here are some key aspects of analytics APIs:

- **Data collection**: Analytics APIs facilitate the collection of various types of data generated by user interactions within the game. This includes information such as player actions, session durations, in-game purchases, progression milestones, and user demographics.

- **Event tracking**: We can use analytics APIs to track specific events or actions within the game, such as level completions, item acquisitions, quest achievements, and social interactions. By defining and tracking custom events, we can gain insights into how players engage with different aspects of the game.

- **Performance monitoring**: Analytics APIs provide tools for monitoring and analyzing the performance of the game, including metrics related to frame rates, loading times, network latency, and device specifications. This data helps us identify performance bottlenecks, optimize game performance, and ensure smooth gameplay experiences for players.

- **User behavior analysis**: Analytics APIs enable us to analyze user behavior patterns and trends, helping them understand how players navigate the game, which features they engage with the most, and what factors influence their retention and engagement. This information informs game design decisions and helps us tailor the game experience to better meet player expectations.

- **Retention and monetization analysis**: Analytics APIs allow us to track player retention rates over time and analyze factors that contribute to player churn. Additionally, we can analyze monetization metrics, such as revenue per user, conversion rates, and **average revenue per paying user** (**ARPPU**), to optimize monetization strategies and maximize revenue opportunities.

- **Real-time reporting and insights**: Analytics APIs provide real-time reporting and visualization tools that enable us to access actionable insights and make data-driven decisions. Interactive dashboards, charts, and reports allow us to monitor **key performance indicators** (**KPIs**), track progress toward goals, and identify opportunities for improvement.

In summary, analytics APIs empower us to gain valuable insights into player behavior, performance, and monetization, enabling them to optimize game design, enhance player experiences, and drive business success. By integrating analytics functionality into their games, we can make informed decisions and continuously improve the quality and performance of their games.

Integrating GameAnalytics

GameAnalytics is a popular package for Unity game development that provides analytics and insights into player behavior and game performance. It allows us to track various metrics, such as player progression, retention rates, in-game events, and monetization data, to optimize their games and improve player engagement.

Here are some key features and capabilities of the GameAnalytics package for Unity:

- **Event tracking**: GameAnalytics enables us to track custom events within their games, such as level completions, item purchases, achievements unlocked, and tutorial progress. This data helps us understand how players interact with their games and identify areas for improvement.
- **User analytics**: The package provides insights into user behavior and demographics, including active users, session lengths, retention rates, and user segmentation. We can analyze this data to tailor their games to specific player preferences and demographics.
- **Monetization tracking**: GameAnalytics allows us to track in-app purchases, advertising revenue, and other monetization metrics. By analyzing revenue data alongside player behavior, we can optimize their monetization strategies and maximize revenue generation.
- **Real-time dashboards**: The package offers real-time dashboards and reporting tools that visualize game analytics data, making it easy for us to monitor game performance and make data-driven decisions. We can customize dashboards to focus on specific metrics and KPIs.
- **Integration with Unity**: GameAnalytics provides a Unity SDK that seamlessly integrates with Unity projects, allowing for easy implementation and tracking of analytics events and metrics. The SDK supports both Unity Editor and runtime environments, enabling us to test and analyze their games throughout the development lifecycle.
- **Cross-platform support**: GameAnalytics supports multiple platforms, including PC, mobile, console, and web, allowing us to track analytics data across various devices and platforms. This cross-platform support enables us to gain insights into player behavior across different environments.

Overall, GameAnalytics is a valuable tool for gaining insights into player behavior, optimizing game performance, and maximizing revenue through data-driven decisions. Its user-friendly interface, robust feature set, and cross-platform support make it a popular choice among game developers worldwide.

In the subsequent steps, we will integrate GameAnalytics and configure our initial event:

1. We will utilize Version 7.8 of the GameAnalytics Unity SDK, which you can download using the following link: `https://download.gameanalytics.com/unity/7.8.0/GA_SDK_UNITY.unitypackage`.

2. After downloading the package, implement it into your project by clicking on **Import**, as illustrated in *Figure 8.10*.

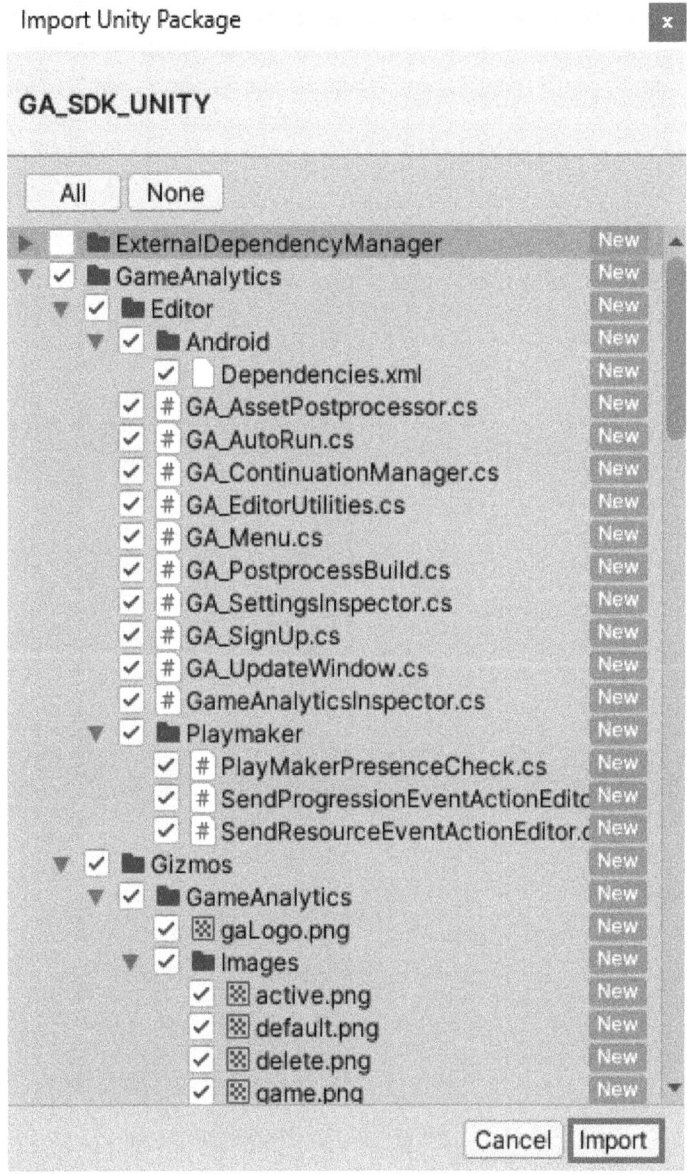

Figure 8.10 – Importing the GameAnalytics package

234   Implementing External Assets, APIs, and Pre-Built Components with C# in Unity

3. After waiting for Unity to compile the files, navigate to **Window | GameAnalytics | Select Settings**, as demonstrated in *Figure 8.11*.

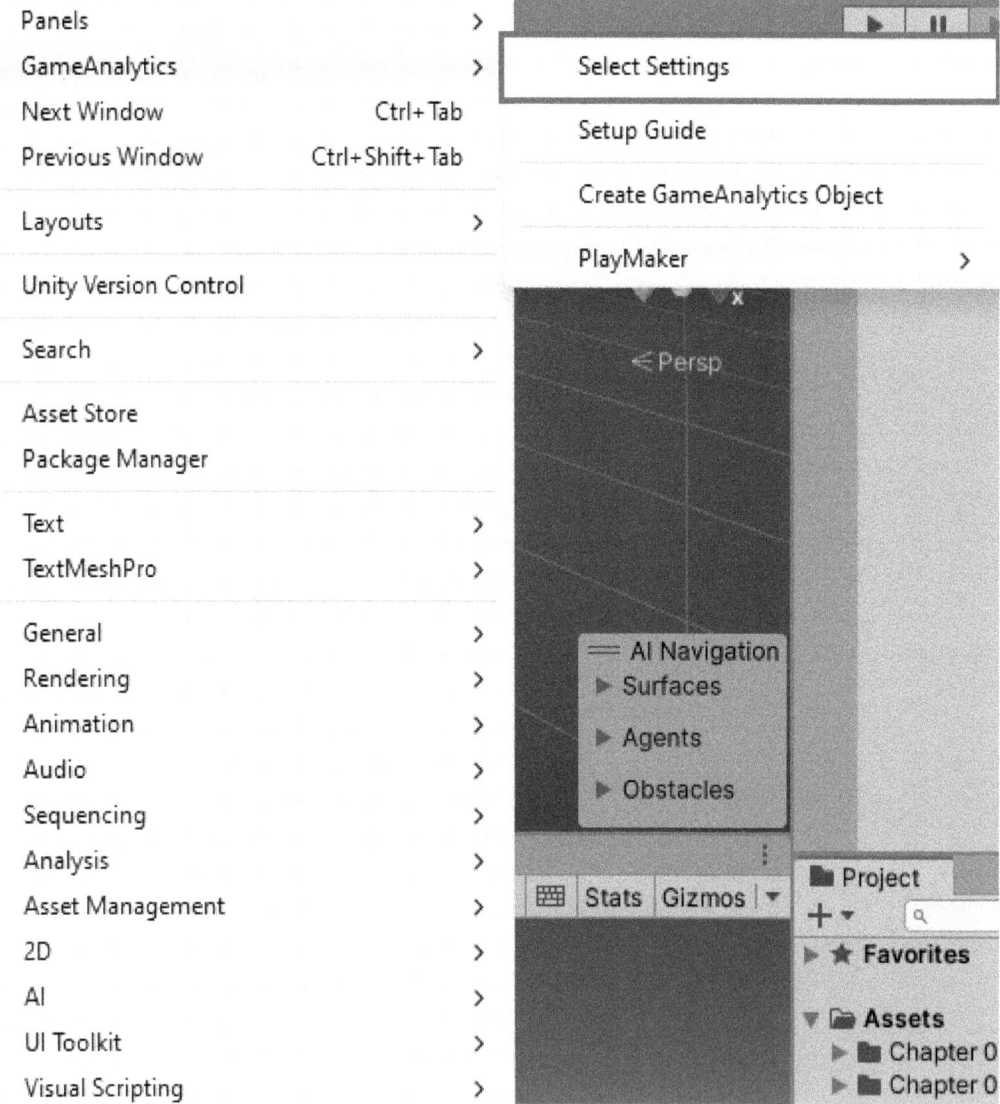

Figure 8.11 – Opening the GameAnalytics settings

4. Following the preceding step will display the GameAnalytics settings. Then, you can log in with your account or sign up and create a project if you haven't already done so, as illustrated in *Figure 8.12*.

Integrating analytics APIs with C#   235

Figure 8.12 – GameAnalytics settings

5. After successfully logging in and having a project in your GameAnalytics dashboard, you'll find the option to link your project and implement it with the appropriate platform, be it Android, iOS, or Windows. For our game, I selected Windows as we are working on a PC game. In *Figure 8.13*, you'll see information related to the project, such as the game and organization, and the important elements, the game key and secret key, which are automatically added upon successful login.

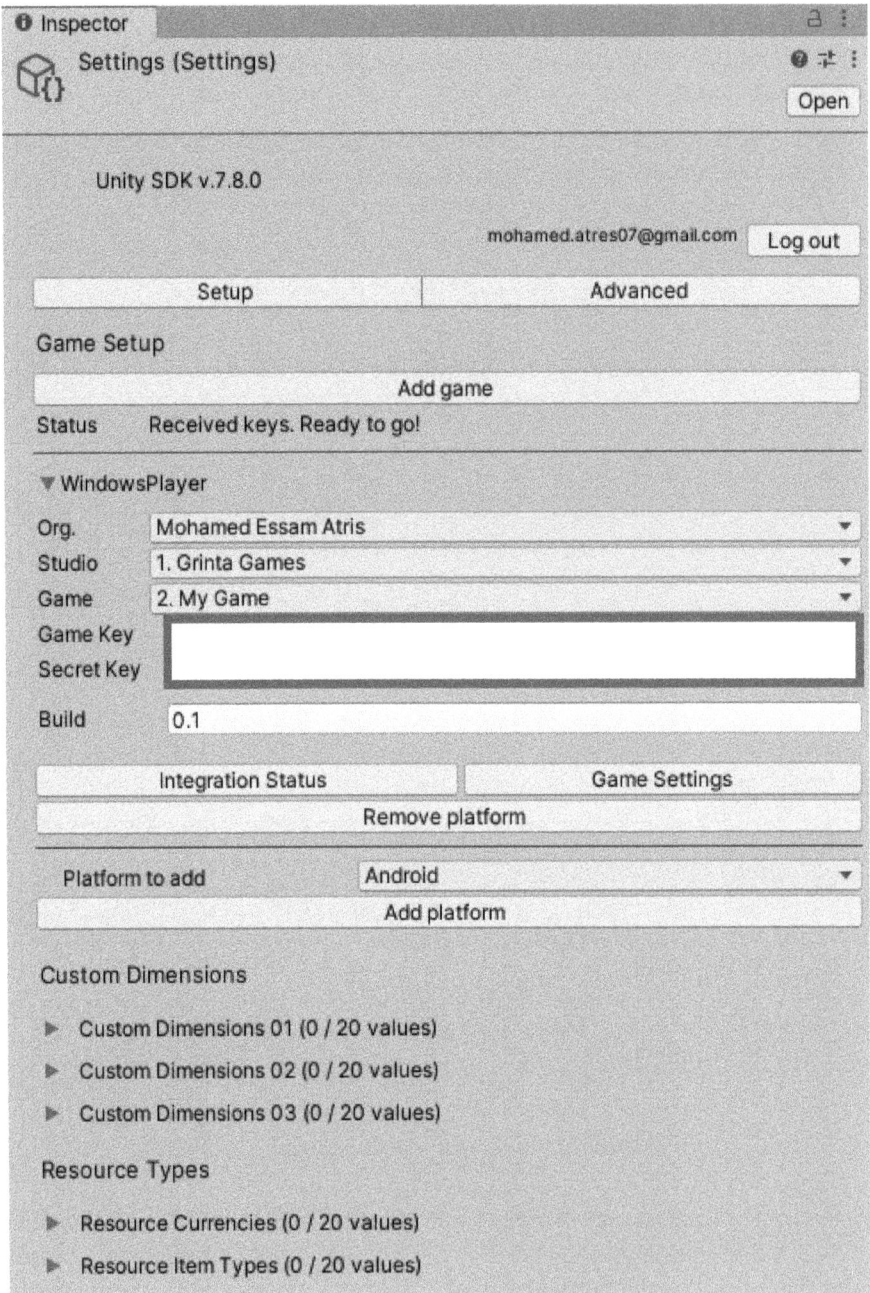

Figure 8.13 – Link our game with GameAnalytics

Then, you need to add the GameAnalytics game object to our scene. Remember, it's a persistent game object, so there's no need to implement it in all scenes. Simply add one game object.

6. You should navigate to **Window | GameAnalytics | Create GameAnalytics Object**, and the game object will be added to your scene, as shown in *Figure 8.14*.

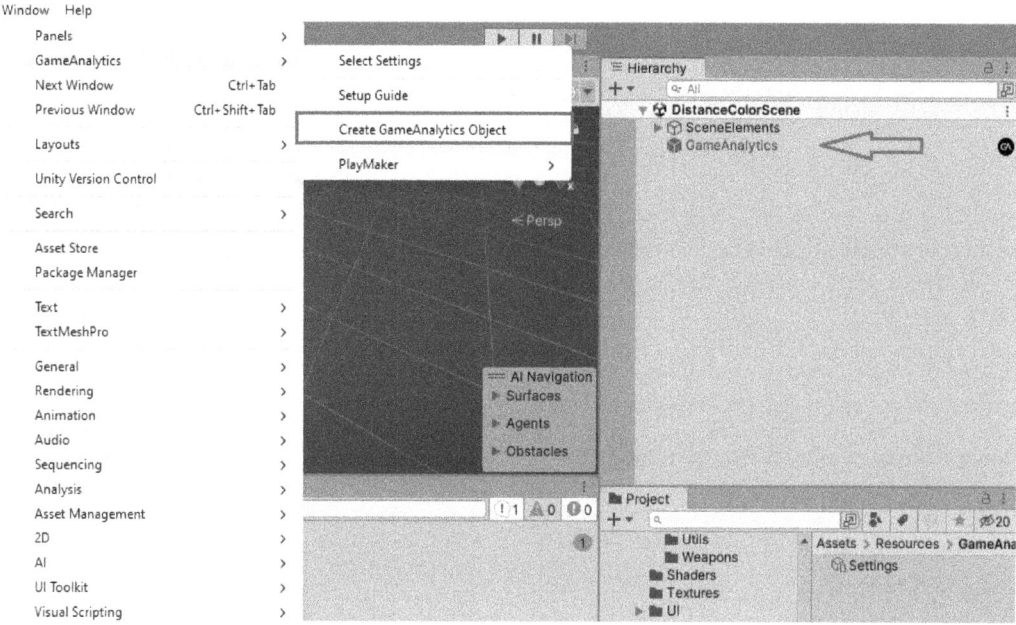

Figure 8.14 – Adding a GameAnalytics object to our scene

Now, we need to begin implementing events into our code, which will depend on what you need to track. Allow me to provide you with an example for clarification.

Example of GameAnalytics usage

You can now initialize GameAnalytics and start using events in your code, as demonstrated in the following code block:

```
private void Start()
{
    GameAnalytics.Initialize();
}
```

We can add this in the `GameManager` script as an example, or if you have a script to handle the initialization of services in your game.

You can utilize it as shown in the following code block. Don't forget to include the `GameAnalyticsSDK` namespace:

```
// Call this method when the player completes a level
public void LevelCompleted(int levelNum)
{
    // Track the event using GameAnalytics
    GameAnalytics.NewDesignEvent("LevelComplete", levelNum);
}
```

And there are various types of events available for better data collection. For more detailed information, you can refer to the GameAnalytics documentation: https://docs.gameanalytics.com/event-types.

You need to build the scene containing the GameAnalytics game object first to start sending events. It may take a few minutes before results start appearing on the website.

You can visit your game on the GameAnalytics website and then navigate to the real-time section to view the data, as depicted in *Figure 8.15*.

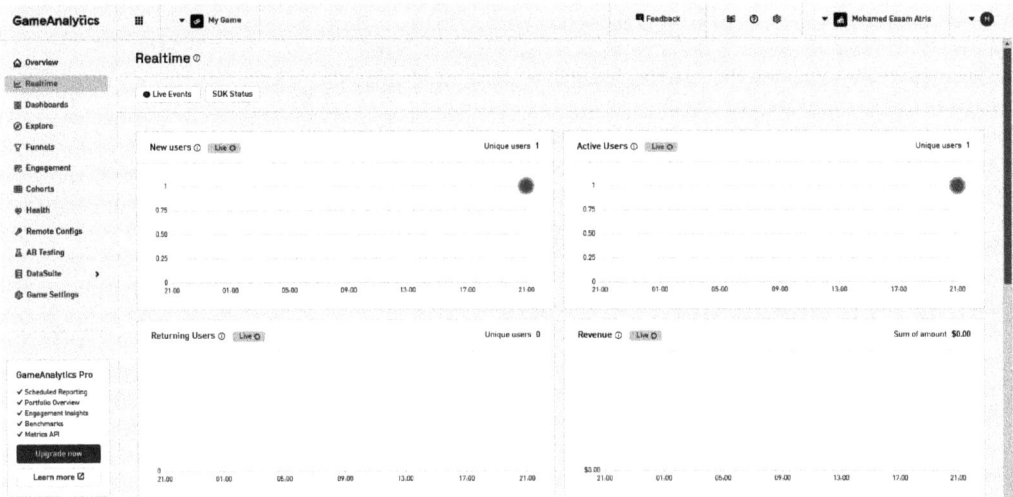

Figure 8.15 – Real-time data from our game

Now that we've integrated an analytics API, specifically GameAnalytics, into our project, we've successfully incorporated it and put it to use.

> **Note**
>
> If you've integrated any package, don't spend too much time on its possibilities initially. Simply integrate it, check for errors, create a sample, and then explore its full potential gradually. Don't complicate things unnecessarily at the outset.

Incorporating third-party assets is a valuable skill for any developer. Many successful games rely on external resources to save time and ensure top-notch quality that might be challenging to achieve independently.

Summary

In this chapter, we delved into the integration of pre-built assets and APIs using C# in Unity, a pivotal aspect of game development. We began by exploring the utilization of pre-built assets to enhance game visuals and optimize performance, followed by the integration of rendering pipelines to achieve better visual fidelity. The discussion then shifted to the importance of backend services, highlighting the significance of authentication logic as an example of their utility in game development. Additionally, we explored analytics APIs and their role in understanding player behavior and optimizing game performance, demonstrating how to implement them effectively into our game projects.

Looking ahead to *Chapter 9*, we will focus on optimizing game performance using Unity's profiling tools. You'll learn to leverage tools like the Profiler, Frame Debugger, and Memory Profiler to identify and address performance bottlenecks, optimize rendering, and manage memory usage. Through hands-on exercises and practical insights, you'll gain mastery over optimization techniques to ensure your game runs smoothly and efficiently. Get ready to elevate your game's performance in the upcoming chapter!

9
Optimizing the Game Using Unity's Profiler, Frame Debugger, and Memory Profiler

Welcome to *Chapter 9* of your Unity game development journey, where we will explore optimizing game performance using Unity's Profiler, Frame Debugger, and Memory Profiler. In this chapter, we will learn how to identify and address performance bottlenecks, optimize rendering, and manage memory efficiently. We'll cover Unity's profiling tools, dive into performance optimization techniques such as physics, audio, AI, and scripting optimizations, and delve into memory management and optimization, including Memory Profiler usage and asset importing optimizations. Mastering these skills will ensure smooth gameplay and an immersive player experience.

In this chapter, we're going to cover the following main topics:

- Introducing Unity profiling tools
- Performance optimization techniques
- Memory management and optimization

Technical requirements

You will need to install the following to follow along with me in this chapter:

- **Primary IDE – Visual Studio 2022**: The tutorials and code samples have been crafted using Visual Studio 2022. Ensure it's installed so that you can follow along seamlessly. Feel free to explore Rider or other IDEs if you prefer, though the instructions are tailored for Visual Studio.
- **Unity version 2022.3.13**: Download and install Unity, choosing version 2022.3.13 for optimal compatibility with the provided content.

The code files of this chapter can be found at: `https://github.com/PacktPublishing/Mastering-Unity-Game-Development-with-C-Sharp/tree/main/Assets/Chapter%2009`.

Introducing Unity profiling tools

Welcome to Unity's profiling tools! These tools are essential for understanding and improving the performance of our games. They provide valuable insights into how our games are running and help us optimize them for a smoother experience across different devices and platforms.

So, why do we need to utilize profiling tools? Profiling tools are invaluable assets in the quest for optimization, which is the process of fine-tuning our games to run as efficiently as possible. These tools act as our detective companions in the world of game development, helping us investigate and identify areas where our game might be slowing down or using too much memory. By using these tools, we can make targeted improvements to our game's performance, ensuring that players have a seamless and enjoyable gaming experience.

So, what does optimization mean in game development? Optimization is the process of making our games run as efficiently as possible, involving finding ways to reduce unnecessary computations, minimize memory usage, and improve rendering performance. Just like a well-organized city ensures smooth traffic flow and efficient resource management, optimization ensures that our game's code and graphics work together harmoniously to deliver a captivating experience to players. This optimization is crucial because it directly impacts the player's experience. No one wants to play a game that lags, stutters, or crashes unexpectedly. By optimizing our games, we can ensure that they run smoothly on a variety of hardware configurations, providing players with a consistent and enjoyable gaming experience across different platforms.

Exploring Unity's profiling tools in depth

Unity's profiling tools offer a comprehensive suite of features to help us understand and improve our game's performance. The Profiler allows us to analyze CPU and GPU usage in real time, giving us valuable insights into where optimizations are needed. The Frame Debugger, on the other hand, helps us visualize how our game's graphics are rendered.

In the upcoming sections, we'll take a closer look at each of these profiling tools and learn how to use them effectively to optimize our games. So, let's get ready to dive into the world of Unity profiling!

The Profiler

The Profiler in Unity is like a helpful detective for your game. It checks how the game is doing – for example, how much the computer is thinking (CPU), how the graphics are doing (GPU), and how much memory is used. It's like a tool to catch issues and make your game work better.

To open the Profiler, go to **Window** | **Analysis** | **Profiler**. A new window will appear, as shown in *Figure 9.1*:

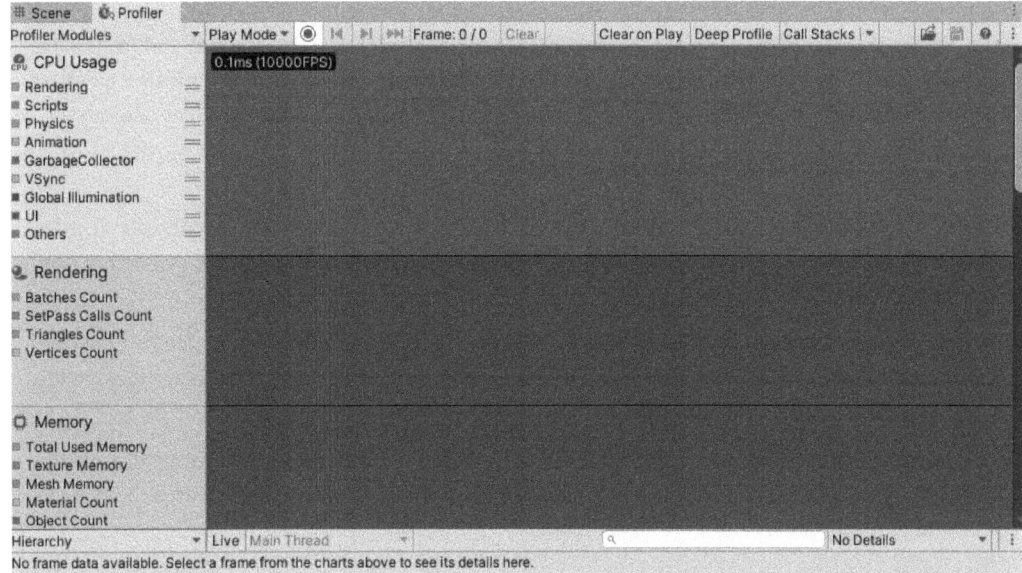

Figure 9.1 – The Profiler

Now that we've opened the Profiler, let's dive into how it works.

Understanding the functionality of Unity's Profiler

The Profiler in Unity works by continuously monitoring different aspects of your game's performance while it's running. It collects data on CPU usage, GPU usage, memory allocation, rendering performance, and more, allowing us to gain insights into how our game is utilizing system resources.

When you open the Profiler in Unity, it displays a variety of graphs and charts that visualize this data in real time. These graphs show metrics such as CPU usage over time, memory usage by different components of the game, and the time it takes to render each frame.

The Profiler gathers this data by instrumenting your game code with profiling markers. These markers track the time it takes for specific functions and operations to execute, allowing us to identify performance bottlenecks and areas for optimization.

For example, if the Profiler shows a spike in CPU usage during gameplay, we can use the Profiler's **Call Stacks** view to pinpoint which functions are consuming the most CPU time. It can then analyze the code within those functions to identify inefficiencies or areas for optimization.

Similarly, if the Profiler detects excessive memory usage, we can use the memory allocation view to identify where memory is being allocated and deallocated in the code. This can help identify memory leaks or inefficient memory usage patterns that may be impacting performance.

Overall, the Profiler in Unity provides us with valuable insights into our game's performance, allowing us to identify and address issues that could impact the player experience. By using the Profiler effectively, we can optimize our games to run smoothly and efficiently on a variety of platforms and devices.

In Unity, optimizing the performance of your game is crucial for delivering a smooth and immersive player experience. The Unity Profiler is a powerful tool that offers insights into various aspects of your game's performance through its diverse modules, each focusing on different areas of analysis.

The main modules of the Unity Profiler are as follows:

- **CPU Profiler**: This module monitors the CPU usage of your game during runtime. It helps identify performance bottlenecks related to scripting, physics calculations, rendering, and other CPU-intensive tasks.
- **GPU Profiler**: The GPU Profiler focuses on monitoring the GPU usage of your game. It provides information about rendering performance, including the time spent on drawing calls, shaders, and graphics-related computations.
- **Memory Profiler**: This module tracks memory usage in your game, including allocations, deallocations, and memory leaks. It helps identify areas where memory is being used inefficiently or where resources are not managed properly.
- **Audio Profiler**: The Audio Profiler monitors the performance of audio-related operations in your game, such as playing audio clips, mixing audio channels, and processing audio effects. It helps optimize audio performance and troubleshoot any issues related to audio playback.
- **Physics Profiler**: This module focuses on analyzing the performance of physics calculations in your game. It provides insights into the time spent on physics simulations, collisions, rigid body dynamics, and other physics-related computations.
- **UI Profiler**: The UI Profiler is specifically designed to analyze the performance of **user interface** (**UI**) elements in your game. It helps identify UI-related bottlenecks, such as layout calculations, rendering overhead, and event handling.
- **Network Profiler**: The Network Profiler monitors network activity in your game, including data transmission, latency, and network-related events. It helps optimize network performance and troubleshoot issues related to multiplayer networking or online gameplay.
- **Rendering Profiler**: This module focuses on analyzing rendering performance in your game. It provides insights into rendering overhead, draw calls, batching, and other graphics-related optimizations.

Collectively, these modules provide a comprehensive view of your game's performance, allowing you to identify and address performance issues effectively. By using the Unity Profiler's various modules, we can optimize our games for better performance, smoother gameplay, and enhanced player experiences.

In this chapter, we will focus on the CPU Profiler and learn how to use it to identify performance related to the CPU.

The CPU Profiler module

The CPU Profiler module is an essential tool in Unity for analyzing the performance of your game. It provides a detailed breakdown of where your game spends its time during runtime, including areas such as rendering, scripting, and animation. This section delves into various aspects of the CPU Profiler module, covering chart categories, the module details pane, live settings, and more.

Chart categories

The **CPU Usage** Profiler module's chart categorizes the time spent on the game's main thread into nine categories. These categories are **Rendering**, **Scripts**, **Physics**, **Animation**, **GarbageCollector**, **VSync**, **Global Illumination**, **UI**, and **Others**. By understanding the distribution of time across these categories, we can pinpoint areas of improvement and optimize our game's performance accordingly.

By understanding each part and its role or impact, we can easily pinpoint the problem areas in scripts or animations. This allows us to focus our work on addressing these specific issues. You can refer to *Figure 9.2* for the charts and their defined colors:

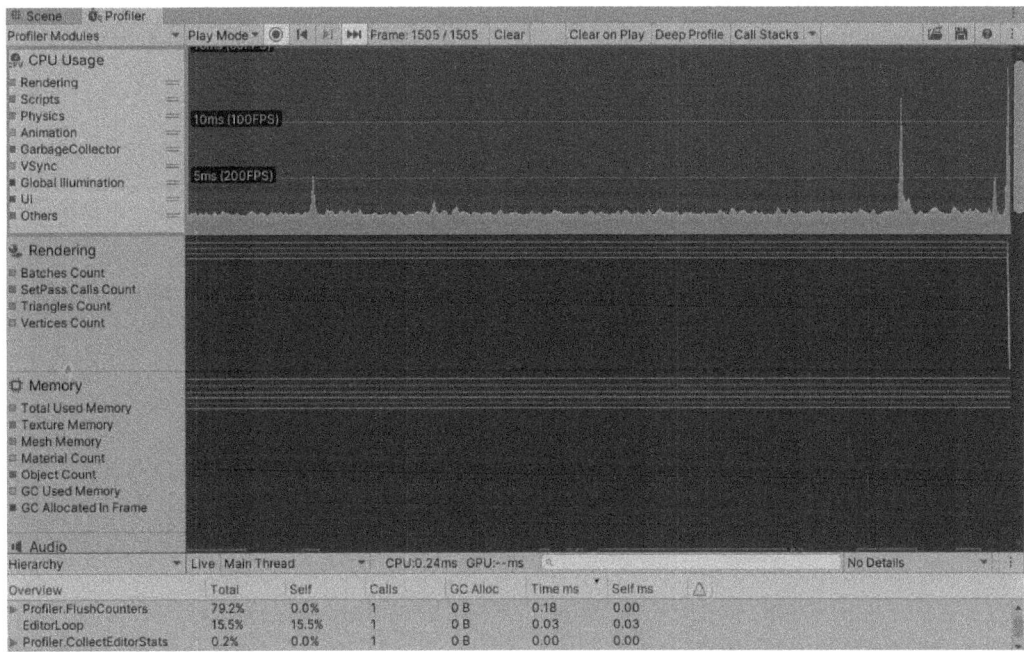

Figure 9.2 – CPU module

In the following table, I have listed each category, along with common activities that may occur within it, indicating the time spent or the impact on performance:

Category	Activities Performed in Real Time
Rendering	Processing data for the GPU and waiting for GPU operations. It includes tasks such as rendering meshes, handling shaders, managing textures, and other graphics-related computations.
Scripts	`MonoBehaviour` update methods and coroutine executions. It involves executing script code, handling game logic, and managing interactions between game objects.
Physics	Executing physics simulations and related processes. including collision detection, rigid body interactions, joint handling, and other physics-related calculations.
Animation	Animation system processing and performance considerations, including processing keyframes, blend trees, animation state transitions, and other animation-related tasks.
GarbageCollector	Garbage collection and memory allocation activities, which include memory allocation, deallocating unused memory, managing object life cycles, and optimizing memory usage.
VSync	Waiting for vertical synchronization activities. This includes syncing the frame rate of the game with the refresh rate of the display, ensuring smooth and tear-free rendering.
Global Illumination	Global illumination includes calculations related to lighting in scenes, such as lightmap baking, real-time GI computations, light probes, and reflection probes.
UI	UI activities involve rendering and interactive elements, such as canvases, text elements, buttons, panels, and other UI components.
Others	These are additional CPU activities that are not part of the other categories. This can include various engine tasks, editor-related activities, audio processing, networking tasks, and other miscellaneous computations that occur during runtime but don't fit into the defined categories.

Understanding the activities within each category allows us to target specific areas based on our optimization requirements for the project.

Module details pane

You have the option to display the selected frame in three different views, allowing you to discern how to switch between them, as shown in *Figure 9.3*:

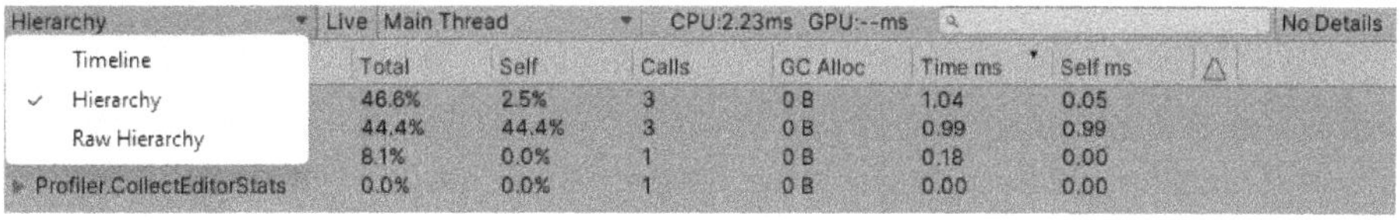

Introducing Unity profiling tools   247

Figure 9.3 – Views dropdown

Let's understand how these views work:

- **Timeline**: This view provides an overview of time distribution across different threads on a single time axis, aiding visualization of parallel execution
- **Hierarchy**: This view groups timing data by internal hierarchical structure, offering detailed insights into function calls and memory allocations
- **Raw Hierarchy**: This is similar to the **Hierarchy** view but provides additional details about performance warnings and thread groupings

Now that we're aware of the available views in the Profiler, we can switch between them to gain a better understanding of how the frame operates.

Using Live settings while profiling

The "Live" setting in the Unity CPU Profiler provides a dynamic and immediate view of performance metrics as we interact with our game, enabling efficient on-the-fly analysis and optimization.

Let's enable Live settings and see how it works:

- Enable the Live setting in the CPU Profiler module before you start recording.
- As we interact with our game and trigger different events, the Profiler immediately displays real-time information about the current frame in the details pane.
- We can see how each action affects CPU usage, memory allocation, and other performance metrics instantly.
- This real-time feedback allows us to identify performance bottlenecks quickly, make adjustments on the fly, and see the impact of optimizations immediately.

We can also enable the **Show Full Scripting Method Names** option to display the full method names. This can be particularly useful when you're dealing with complex scripts or when you need precise visibility into the functions being executed. You can enable this option through the settings, as shown in *Figure 9.4*:

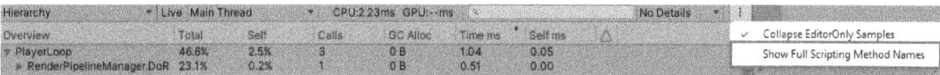

Figure 9.4 – Show Full Scripting Method Names

Before diving into the practical part, it's essential to understand common Profiler markers.

Common markers

Unity's code is instrumented with various Profiler markers, offering insights into performance-critical tasks and areas of optimization. By leveraging these markers, we can identify bottlenecks and streamline performance-critical operations, enhancing the overall efficiency and responsiveness of our games.

Unity's code is marked with numerous Profiler indicators that offer insights into the performance of your game. These markers are invaluable for identifying bottlenecks and optimizing your code. Let's delve into the main categories of Profiler markers and their functions:

- **Main thread base markers**:

    The main thread base markers serve to differentiate between time spent on your game and time devoted to Editor and Profiler tasks. These markers are crucial for understanding the timing of frames on the main thread. Here are some examples:

    - `PlayerLoop`: Contains samples originating from your game's main loop. When targeting the Editor while the Player is active, `PlayerLoop` samples the nest under `EditorLoop`.
    - `EditorLoop` (Editor-only marker): Contains samples from the Editor's main loop when profiling a player in the Editor. `EditorLoop` samples indicate time spent rendering and running the Editor alongside the Player.
    - `Profiler.CollectEditorStats` (Editor-only marker): Includes samples related to collecting statistics for active Profiler modules. These samples provide insight into the overhead that's incurred by the Player when collecting module statistics.

- **Editor-only markers**:

    Certain markers exclusively appear when profiling in Unity Editor, offering insights into Editor-specific activities such as security checks and Prefab-related tasks. Here is an example:

    - `GetComponentNullErrorWrapper`: A marker exclusive to the Unity Editor, aiding in identifying null component usage

- **Script update markers**:

    Unless you're utilizing the Job System, most scripting code falls under these markers. They cover various `MonoBehaviour` update methods and coroutine executions. Here is an example:

    - `BehaviourUpdate`: Contains all samples of `MonoBehaviour.Update` methods

- **Rendering and VSync markers**:

    These markers reveal CPU activities related to processing data for the GPU and waiting for GPU operations to complete. Here is an example:

    - `WaitForTargetFPS`: Indicates the time spent waiting for the targeted FPS specified by `Application.targetFrameRate`

- **Backend scripting markers**:

    These markers highlight scripting backend activities, aiding in troubleshooting issues related to garbage collection and memory allocation. Here is an example:

    - `GC.Alloc`: Represents an allocation in the managed heap, subject to automatic garbage collection

- **Multithreading markers**:

    These markers focus on thread synchronization and the Job System, offering information about parallel processing and sync points. Here is an example:

    - `Idle`: Contains samples indicating the length of time a Worker Thread remains inactive

- **Physics markers**:

    Physics markers provide insights into the execution of physics simulations and related processes such as collision detection and joint handling. Here is an example:

    - `Physics.FetchResults`: Contains samples that collect the results of the physics simulation from the physics engine

- **Animation markers**:

    These markers pertain to the Animation system, offering details on animation processing stages and performance considerations. Here is an example:

    - `Director.PrepareFrame`: Schedules and awaits `Director.PrepareFrameJob` jobs, evaluating the state machines for active Animator components

- **Performance warnings**:

    The CPU Profiler identifies common performance issues and displays warnings to alert developers, helping them optimize their code effectively. Here is an example:

    - `Animation.DestroyAnimationClip`: Indicates a performance issue with calls related to destroying `AnimationClips`, triggering resource-intensive operations

With a thorough understanding of these Profiler markers, we can pinpoint performance bottlenecks and optimize our Unity games for enhanced efficiency and responsiveness.

You can learn more about common markers in the official Unity documentation: `https://docs.unity3d.com/Manual/profiler-markers.html`.

By becoming familiar with the common markers, we've seen that they prove to be invaluable tools in our optimization journey. They allow us to concentrate on specific areas efficiently, ensuring that our efforts are both effective and precise.

Understanding the profiling process

Let's discuss general tips for the profiling process, including how to identify bottlenecks and gain a better understanding of the entire process.

Profiling is most effective when it's used at three specific times:

- Establish a baseline by profiling before implementing major changes
- Track changes during development and ensure they do not negatively impact performance or exceed resource budgets
- After development, profile again to confirm that the changes that have been made have achieved the desired improvements in performance

Avoid profiling until you identify issues in your game. Additionally, refrain from excessive profiling; determine the required frame rate for your game. Each frame should adhere to a time budget aligned with your target **frames per second** (**FPS**). For instance, a game aiming for 30 FPS should consume less than 33.33 ms per frame (1,000 ms divided by 30 FPS). Similarly, targeting 60 FPS allows for 16.66 ms per frame.

> **Note**
> Achieving the most precise profiling outcomes necessitates running and profiling builds directly on the intended target devices.Top of Form

Identifying bottlenecks

You should determine whether your game is CPU- or GPU-bound so that you can focus your optimization efforts correctly. For instance, note that while VSync is optional on all platforms, it's typically enabled on mobile devices and may contribute to CPU time waiting.

VSync, short for **Vertical Synchronization**, is a graphics technology that synchronizes the frame rate of a game with the refresh rate of the monitor or display device. This synchronization prevents issues such as screen tearing, where parts of different frames appear on the screen simultaneously, leading to a visually jarring experience. VSync ensures that each frame is displayed in full before the next frame is rendered, creating a smoother and more visually pleasing experience for the player.

The performance of a project is determined by the chip or thread that requires the most time to process. This area is where optimization efforts should be concentrated. For instance, consider a game with a target frame time budget of 16.66 ms with VSync enabled:

- If the CPU frame time (excluding VSync) is 10 ms and the GPU time is 12 ms, there's no issue as both are within budget.
- If the CPU frame time is 20 ms and the GPU time is 12 ms, the CPU performance needs to be optimized as the GPU won't benefit from optimization. Consider transferring some CPU tasks to the GPU.

- If the CPU frame time is 8 ms and the GPU time is 20 ms, focus on optimizing the GPU workload as it is GPU-bound.
- If both the CPU and GPU times are at 20 ms, you're bound by both and need to optimize them below 16.66 ms to achieve a frame rate of 60 FPS.

We'll learn more about CPU- and GPU-bound issues in the following subsections.

CPU-bound issues

It's considered a CPU-bound issue when the CPU time exceeds the allocated time budget. Let's walk through an example to illustrate how to identify and resolve such issues using the Profiler. Utilizing the **Timeline** and **Hierarchy** views in the Profiler helps us gain a clearer understanding of the specific issue. Refer to *Figure 9.5* for detailed information on a spike frame:

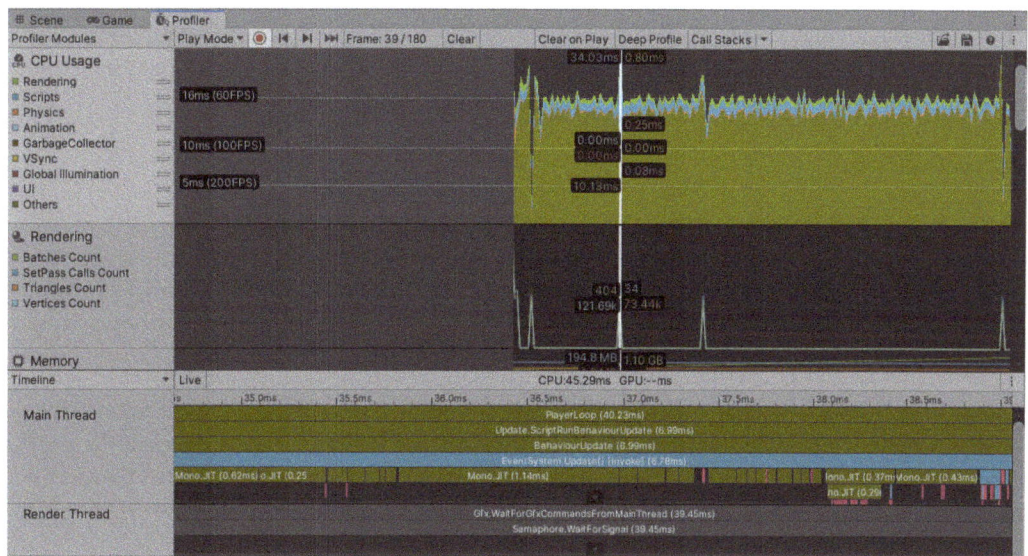

Figure 9.5 – A spike frame

The gfx.waitForCommandsFromMainThread marker indicates a potential bottleneck on the main thread that affects overall performance. This occurs when the render thread waits for commands from the main thread, suggesting that tasks or commands that are being processed on the CPU are taking longer. Consequently, the game experiences a CPU-bound issue, causing delays in rendering. Addressing these bottlenecks and optimizing CPU-bound issues can significantly enhance game performance and responsiveness.

Identify the CPU bottleneck by analyzing which thread is the most active. Profiling helps pinpoint bottlenecks accurately for focused optimization. Guesswork can lead to ineffective optimizations or even worsen performance.

The primary threads for identifying performance issues typically include the following:

- **The main thread**: This thread handles game logic and script execution, including tasks related to physics, animation, UI, and rendering. It accounts for a significant portion of the processing time.
- **The render thread**: This thread is responsible for processing scene elements during rendering, such as camera culling, depth sorting, and draw call batching. It converts Unity's scene representation into specific graphics API calls for GPU rendering.
- **The job worker threads**: These threads utilize the C# Job System to offload specific tasks onto separate Worker Threads, reducing the main thread's workload. Various Unity systems, such as physics, animation, and rendering, also leverage the Job System for improved performance.

You need to identify any loops in your code where spikes occur, determine what is causing the high CPU usage or prolonged processing time, and investigate if it corresponds to a common marker in the Profiler. Understanding the meaning of these markers helps you address the issue effectively. Optimize your code based on your findings, monitor the Profiler again after applying fixes, and continue this iterative process until you achieve your target frame rate.

GPU-bound issues

If your game experiences prolonged activity in Profiler markers such as `Gfx WaitForPresentOnGfxThread`, indicating idle time for the render thread, and simultaneously shows markers such as `Gfx PresentFrame` or `<GraphicsAPIName> WaitForLastPresent`, it suggests a GPU-bound scenario. In this context, GPU-boundness is characterized by heavy GPU utilization and potential delays in frame rendering and presentation.

If your game appears to be heavily using the GPU, you can use the Frame Debugger to quickly examine the batches of draw calls that are sent to the GPU. I'll discuss this tool in more detail in the next section. However, it's essential to note that while the Frame Debugger provides insights into scene construction, it doesn't offer specific GPU timing details. So, you can switch between the Profiler and the Frame Debugger to fix any issues related to GPU.

Let's explore the factors that can lead to GPU performance issues in our projects. The following are some common issues:

- Complex particle systems with a high number of particles or intricate behaviors can impact GPU performance
- Real-time reflections or refractions, particularly in scenes with many reflective surfaces, can be GPU-intensive

- Shader permutations or shader variants for different materials or effects can increase GPU workload, especially if they're not managed efficiently
- Dynamic weather or environmental effects, such as rain, fog, or dynamic skies, can add GPU overhead if they're not optimized
- Dynamic Occlusion culling and visibility calculations can affect GPU performance, especially in scenes with complex geometry or many moving objects
- High screen resolutions, especially 4K displays or retina displays on mobile devices, can put a heavy load on the GPU

Here are some useful tips while using the Profiler:

- Turn off the **VSync** and **Others** categories in the **CPU Usage** Profiler module. The **VSync** marker indicates periods of inactivity in the CPU's main thread, and hiding these markers can enhance the clarity of your profiling analysis.
- Disable **VSync** in your project build to gain a clear understanding of the interactions between the main thread, render thread, and GPU. Profiling a build with **VSync** disabled can simplify the interpretation of profiler data.
- Be mindful of when to conduct profiling in either Play mode or Editor mode. Utilize Play mode for profiling game performance and Editor mode for monitoring Unity Editor processes. Profiling the Editor can aid in identifying performance bottlenecks and improving productivity.
- Opt for profiling in the Editor when you need to quickly iterate on resolving performance issues. After identifying problems, use Play mode profiling to efficiently iterate on changes and validate solutions.

Optimizing graphics performance and identifying rendering bottlenecks in Unity becomes streamlined and efficient with the powerful capabilities of the Frame Debugger tool. We'll dive deeper into this in the next section.

The Frame Debugger

The Frame Debugger is a powerful tool that's used for analyzing and debugging the rendering process of a frame in your game. It allows you to inspect each step involved in rendering, such as draw calls, batching, textures, and materials. This tool is crucial for optimizing graphics performance and identifying rendering bottlenecks.

You can open the **Frame Debugger** tool from the **Window | Analysis | Frame Debugger** menu:

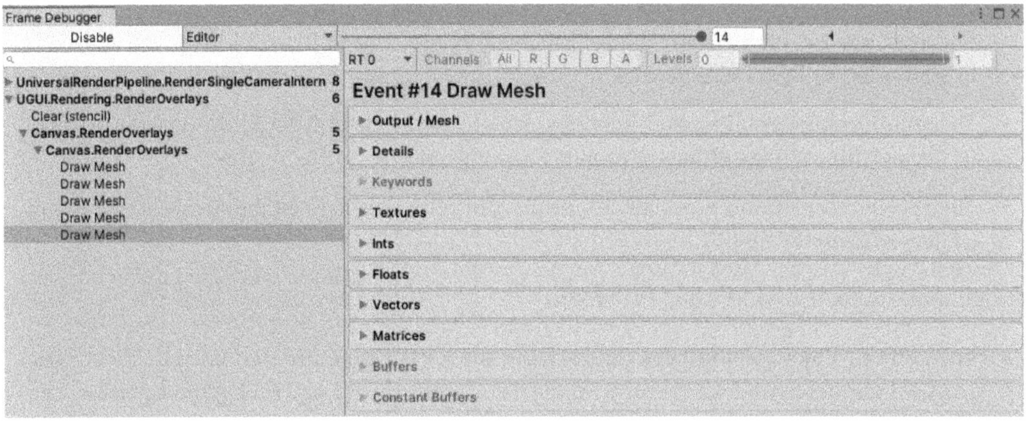

Figure 9.6 – Frame Debugger

Now that we've learned how to open the Frame Debugger, let's explore how it works and what it does.

Understanding how the Frame Debugger operates

The Frame Debugger works by intercepting and analyzing the rendering commands that are sent to the graphics API (for example, DirectX or OpenGL). It captures information about each draw call, including the shaders, textures, materials, and meshes involved. This captured data is then presented in a visual interface, allowing developers to inspect and understand the rendering pipeline of a frame.

The Frame Debugger operates in real time, meaning you can pause the game in Play mode, analyze the current frame's rendering, and make optimizations on the fly.

Exploring the key functions of the Frame Debugger

The primary functions of the Frame Debugger are as follows:

- Capturing and displaying each draw call that's made during the rendering process
- Showing how objects are batched together for optimized rendering performance
- Providing details about the shaders, textures, materials, and meshes that are used in rendering
- Identifying render targets and offscreen render textures

Let's explore the Frame Debugger. This is what the **Frame Debugger** window looks like:

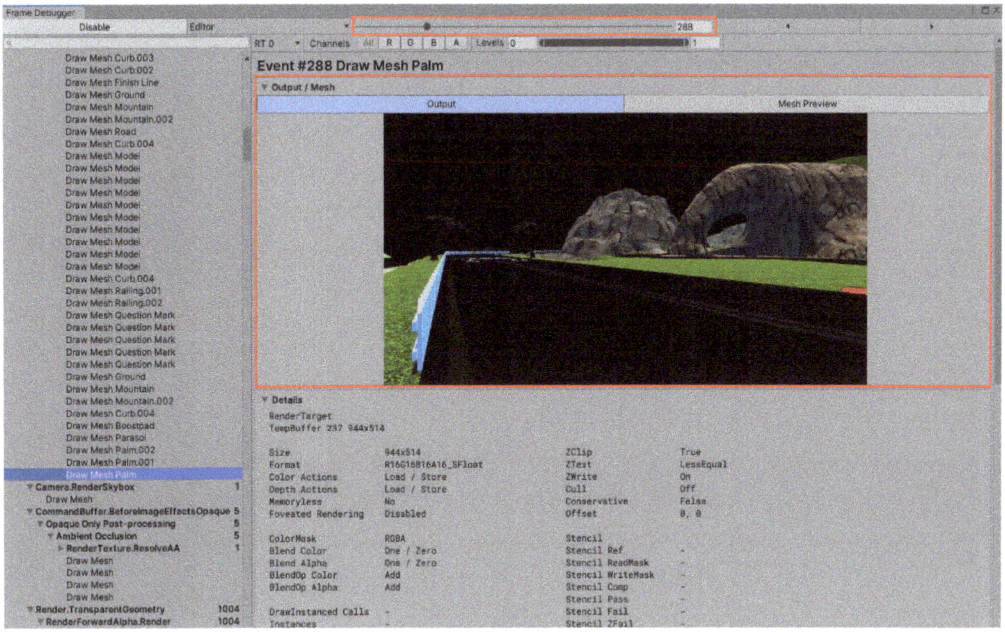

Figure 9.7 – The Frame Debugger window has been enabled

After enabling the Frame Debugger, the game will pause, and you'll be able to view all graphics-related details for that frame. This includes every draw call from the initial black screen to the current scene. In Unity 2022, which is the version we're using, the Frame Debugger features an **Output / Mesh** section with two tabs: one displaying the full output or current state of the graphics/scene, and the other showing the drawn mesh, such as the example of a palm tree in this instance. You can see this mesh in *Figure 9.8*:

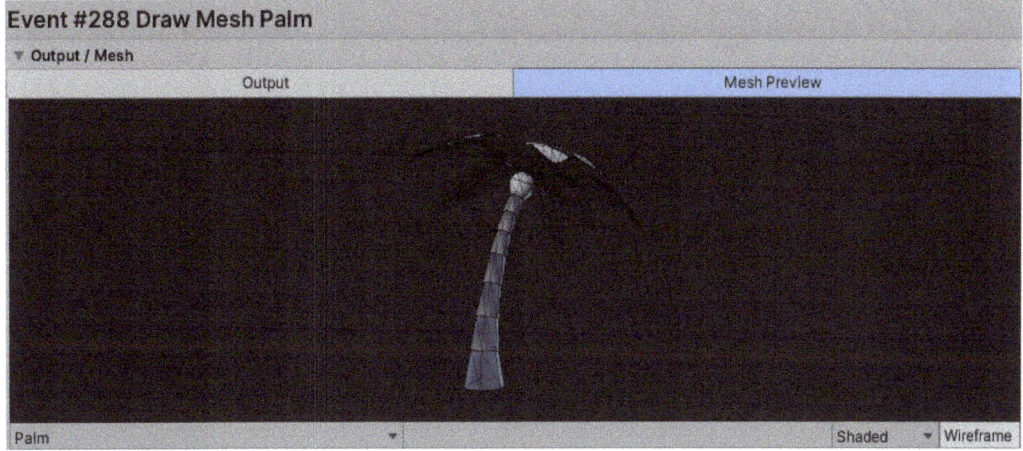

Figure 9.8 – Mesh Preview

The details about each draw call will be presented in a separate section that contains important information such as **RenderTarget**, **Vertices**, **Indices**, and **Used Shader**:

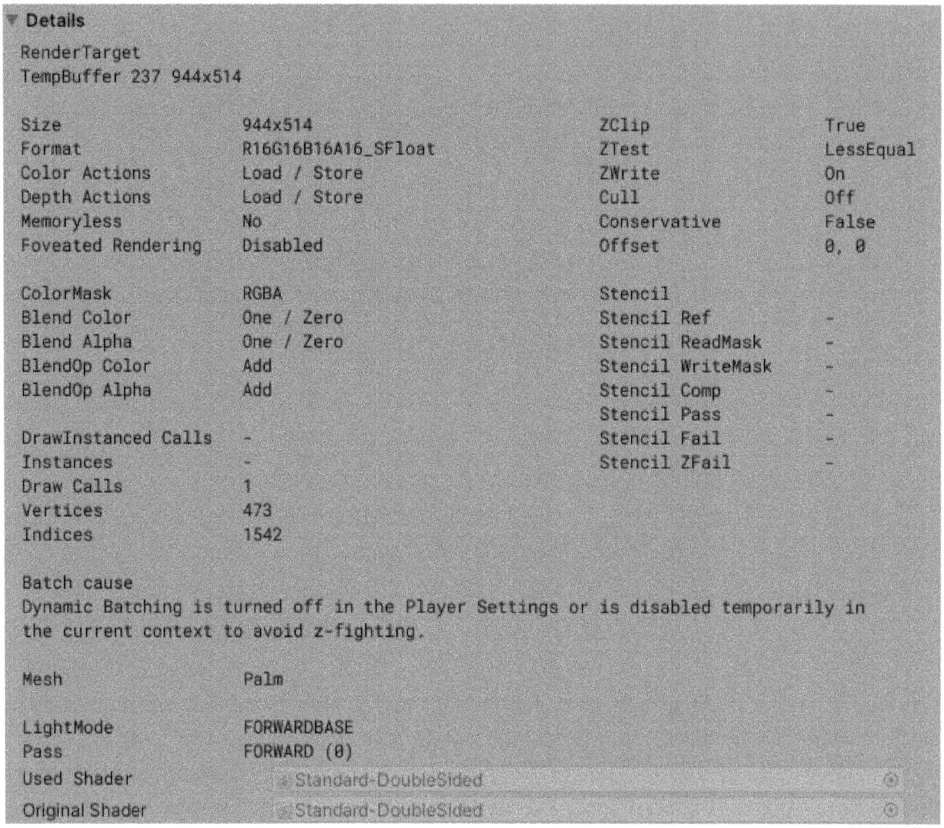

```
▼ Details
 RenderTarget
 TempBuffer 237 944x514

 Size                    944x514                  ZClip              True
 Format                  R16G16B16A16_SFloat      ZTest              LessEqual
 Color Actions           Load / Store             ZWrite             On
 Depth Actions           Load / Store             Cull               Off
 Memoryless              No                       Conservative       False
 Foveated Rendering      Disabled                 Offset             0, 0

 ColorMask               RGBA                     Stencil
 Blend Color             One / Zero               Stencil Ref        -
 Blend Alpha             One / Zero               Stencil ReadMask   -
 BlendOp Color           Add                      Stencil WriteMask  -
 BlendOp Alpha           Add                      Stencil Comp       -
                                                  Stencil Pass       -
 DrawInstanced Calls     -                        Stencil Fail       -
 Instances               -                        Stencil ZFail      -
 Draw Calls              1
 Vertices                473
 Indices                 1542

 Batch cause
 Dynamic Batching is turned off in the Player Settings or is disabled temporarily in
 the current context to avoid z-fighting.

 Mesh                    Palm

 LightMode               FORWARDBASE
 Pass                    FORWARD (0)
 Used Shader             Standard-DoubleSided
 Original Shader         Standard-DoubleSided
```

Figure 9.9 – The Details section

Additionally, the Frame Debugger includes sections for the used **Textures**, **Vectors**, **Floats**, and other sections, as shown in *Figure 9.10*:

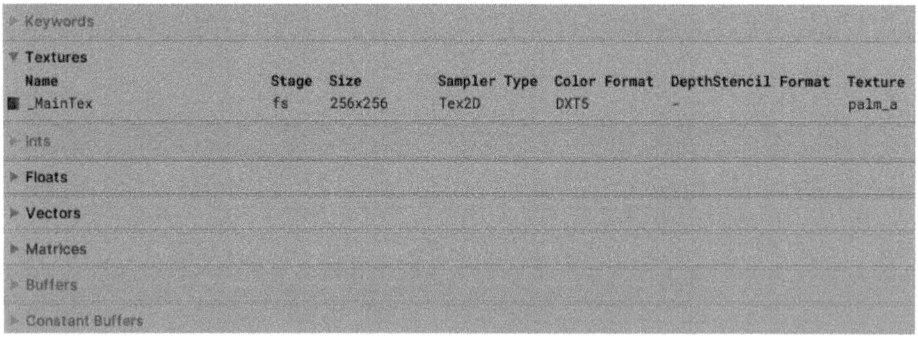

```
▶ Keywords
▼ Textures
  Name              Stage    Size      Sampler Type   Color Format   DepthStencil Format   Texture
  ■ _MainTex        fs       256x256   Tex2D          DXT5           -                     palm_a
▶ Ints
▶ Floats
▶ Vectors
▶ Matrices
▶ Buffers
▶ Constant Buffers
```

Figure 9.10 – The other sections in the Frame Debugger

Once you have identified the contents of the frame, the optimization process depends on employing specific strategies and techniques tailored to the unique aspects of each game. Addressing issues requires thorough research to pinpoint areas for optimization, and this process often involves iterative steps to achieve optimal performance. One of the most important ways to reduce draw calls is to use batching. Let's take a closer look.

Draw call batching

Draw call batching refers to a technique that's used for optimizing draw calls by merging meshes, allowing Unity to render them in fewer draw calls. Unity offers two default draw call batching methods:

- **Static batching**:

  In this process, Unity combines and renders static GameObjects together.

  Static batching in Unity refers to the process of optimizing draw calls by combining meshes either at build time or during runtime. When using static batching, it's essential to ensure that certain criteria are met for GameObjects to be eligible for static batching:

  - The GameObject must be active
  - It should have a **Mesh Filter** component that is enabled and references a mesh with a vertex count greater than 0
  - The GameObject should also have a **Mesh Renderer** component that is enabled and uses a material without a shader that disables batching
  - Meshes that are to be batched together must share the same vertex attributes

  When utilizing static batching, Unity allows the entire batch of meshes to be transformed collectively, such as moving, rotating, or scaling them as a single entity. However, transformations cannot be applied to individual meshes within the batch.

  It's worth noting that enabling read/write access for the mesh is necessary to use runtime static batching effectively. Overall, static batching is a useful technique for optimizing draw calls and improving performance in Unity projects.

- **Dynamic batching**:

  Dynamic batching is a process where Unity combines small meshes by transforming their vertices on the CPU and grouping similar vertices, ultimately rendering them in a single draw call.

  To enable dynamic batching for meshes in Unity, follow these steps:

  I. Navigate to **Edit | Project Settings | Player**.
  II. In the **Other Settings** section, activate the **Dynamic Batching** option.

Unity will automatically group moving meshes into a single draw call if they meet the specified criteria.

Dynamic batching in Unity doesn't work on GameObjects with mirrored transformations in their **Transform** components. For instance, if one GameObject has a scale of 1 and another has a scale of -1, Unity cannot batch them together.Top of Form

In general, Unity combines draw calls for GameObjects using identical materials, so it's crucial to maximize batching efficiency by sharing materials among multiple GameObjects. If you have two material assets that are almost identical except for their textures, consider merging the textures into a single, larger texture within the same atlas. This allows you to use a single material asset instead of two. When accessing shared material properties from a C# script, ensure that you use `Renderer.sharedMaterial` instead of `Renderer.material`. Using `Renderer.material` creates a duplicate of the material, preventing Unity from batching draw calls for that renderer.

The following are the additional methods you can utilize to decrease the number of draw call batches:

- Use Occlusion culling to eliminate objects that are hidden behind foreground elements and minimize overdraw. Keep in mind that this may increase CPU processing, so use the Profiler to evaluate the impact of transferring the workload from GPU to CPU.

- Employ GPU instancing to reduce batches, particularly for numerous objects that share the same mesh and material. Limiting the number of models in your scene can enhance performance, and with careful implementation, you can create a complex scene without repetitiveness.

- Leverage the SRP Batcher to decrease GPU setup between draw calls by grouping **Bind** and **Draw** GPU commands. To maximize SRP batching benefits, utilize multiple Materials but restrict them to a few compatible shader variants, such as the **Lit** and **Unlit** shaders in the **Universal Render Pipeline (URP)** and **High Definition Render Pipeline (HDRP)**, minimizing variations between keyword combinations.

Utilizing these techniques can significantly enhance rendering performance and streamline the development process in Unity games.

Now, let's explore the optimization techniques for various categories in any game to improve performance.

Performance optimization techniques

In this section, we will delve into the crucial aspects of performance optimization techniques in Unity. Performance optimization plays a pivotal role in ensuring that your game runs smoothly, utilizes system resources efficiently, and delivers a seamless experience to players. By implementing optimization techniques, analyzing performance data, and adopting efficient scripting practices, developers can significantly enhance their game's performance and overall quality. Let's explore these skills in detail to understand how they contribute to creating high-performance games in Unity.

The following subsections cover key areas for optimization techniques.

Physics and collisions

To boost the performance and efficiency of physics and collisions in Unity, strategic optimization techniques play a crucial role. Here, we'll explore two such techniques and detail their respective problems, solutions, examples, and outcomes:

- **Collision layer masking**:

    - **Problem**: There are unnecessary collision checks between objects that don't interact with each other, leading to wasted computational resources.

    - **Solution**: Use collision layer masking to specify which layers should interact with each other, avoiding unnecessary collision checks.

    - **How it works**: Assign different layers to objects based on their interaction requirements. Configure the physics settings to only enable collisions between specific layers that need to interact.

    - **Example**: Let's consider a 2D platformer game where the player character interacts with enemies, collectibles, and environmental obstacles. By assigning different layers to these objects (for example, Player, Enemy, Collectible, and Obstacle), you can configure the physics settings to enable collisions only between specific layers. Here's an example:

        - The Player layer interacts with the Enemy and Obstacle layers but not with the Collectible layer
        - The Enemy layer interacts with the Player and Obstacle layers but not with the Collectible layer
        - The Collectible layer does not interact with the Player, Enemy, or Obstacle layers:

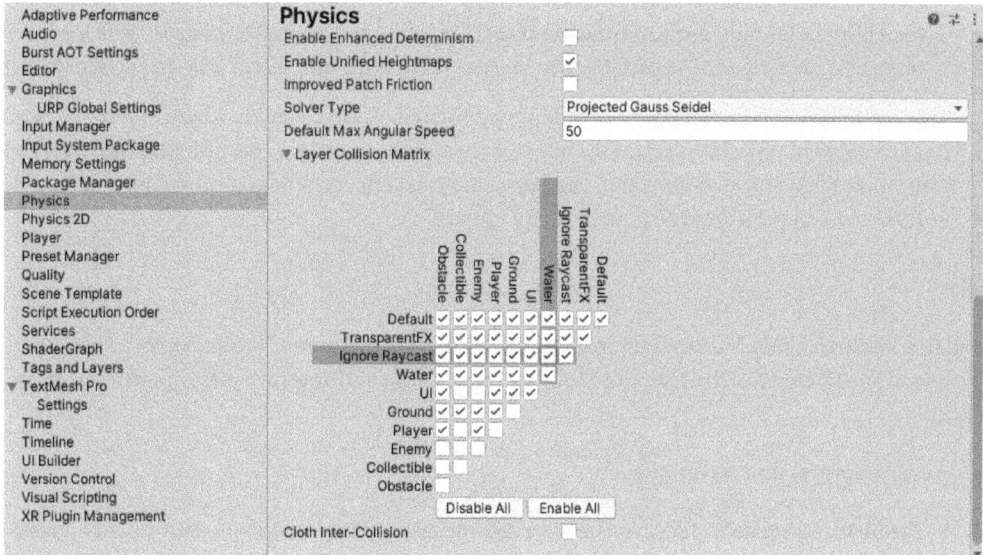

Figure 9.11 – Physics settings

In your scripts, when performing collision checks using raycasts or collider triggers, you can apply layer masks to filter out unnecessary collisions. For instance, when you're checking for enemy collisions, you can specify a layer mask that includes only the Enemy layer, ignoring collisions with collectibles or obstacles.

- **Result**: A reduced number of collision checks and improved performance by eliminating unnecessary physics calculations.

In Unity, optimizing physics and collisions through collision layer masking involves strategically assigning layers, configuring physics settings, and applying layer masks to streamline collision checks and enhance performance.

- **Simplified collision detection**:

    - **Problem**: Full physics calculations for collision detection on objects that don't require realistic physical interactions can be resource-intensive.
    - **Solution**: Use triggers as simplified collision detection for non-essential objects.
    - **How it works**: Triggers in Unity are collider components that detect when another collider enters or exits their volume without physically colliding with them. They are ideal for scenarios where you need to detect interactions without simulating physical forces.
    - **Example**: In a game where collectible coins are scattered around the level, instead of using rigid body-based collisions for the coins, you can attach trigger colliders to them. When the player's character overlaps with a coin's trigger collider, you can handle the collection logic without the need for full physics calculations.
    - **Result**: Using triggers reduces the computational overhead associated with physics calculations for objects that only require collision detection without physical responses. This leads to improved performance, especially in scenarios with a large number of non-essential objects.

    This technique is beneficial for optimizing performance in scenarios where objects do not require detailed physics interactions but still need basic collision detection functionality. By using simplified collision detection methods, you can conserve computational resources and improve overall performance in your Unity project.

Audio

Optimizing audio in Unity is crucial for maintaining a smooth and immersive gameplay experience. Let's explore an advanced technique to reduce memory usage and improve audio performance in your game:

- **Audio compression technique**:

    - **Problem**: Large audio files can consume significant memory, leading to performance issues.

- **Solution**: Compress audio files using formats such as Ogg Vorbis or MP3 to reduce memory usage without compromising quality. You can learn more about Unity's importing settings by referring to the official Unity documentation at https://docs.unity3d.com/Manual/class-AudioClip.html#:~:text=Whenever%20importing%20a%20file%2C%20Unity,to%20the%20original%20as%20possible:

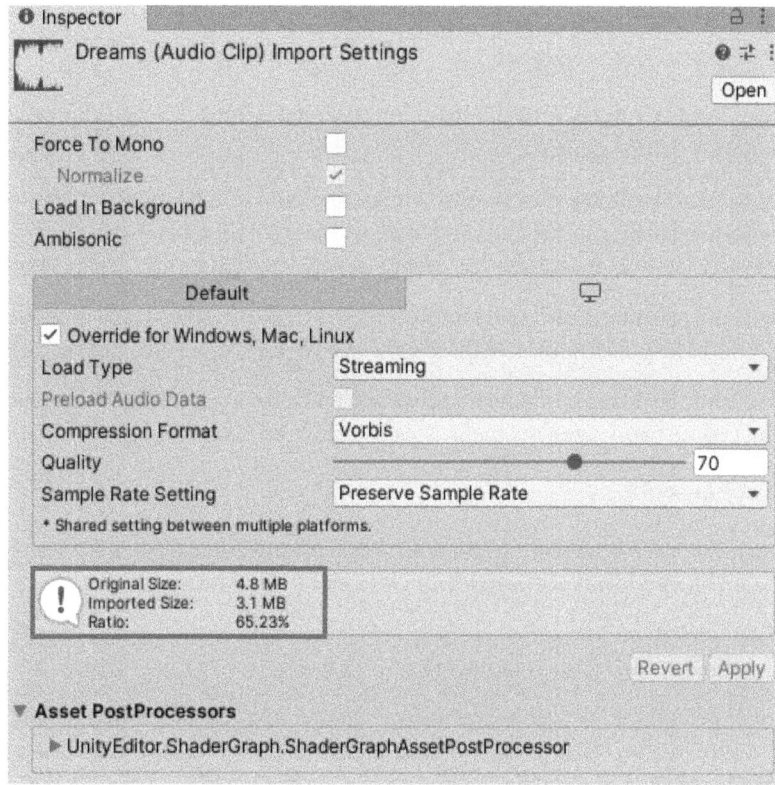

Figure 9.12 – Imported audio settings

- **Example**: Compressing background music and sound effects in a game.
- **Result**: Reduced memory footprint, faster loading times, and smoother gameplay.

By employing advanced audio optimization techniques such as compression and streaming, you can significantly enhance your game's performance while maintaining high-quality audio output.

UI

I covered this topic in detail in *Chapter 5, Designing Optimized User Interfaces with C# for Unity Games*. You can check it out for more details. Optimizing UI is a crucial part of performance, especially in mobile games, as it directly impacts user experience and device resource utilization.

Networking and multiplayer

Optimizing networking and multiplayer functionality in Unity games is crucial for ensuring smooth gameplay experiences across various devices and player interactions. Here, we'll explore key techniques and strategies for enhancing networking performance and implementing effective multiplayer mechanics in Unity games:

- **Latency compensation techniques**:

    - **Problem**: Latency can cause delays in multiplayer games, leading to synchronization issues and gameplay inconsistencies.

    - **Solution**: Implement latency compensation techniques to mitigate the effects of network latency on gameplay. This depends on the networking solution you have implemented. You can refer to their documentation for specific networking solutions, such as Photon.

    - **Example**: Use techniques such as client-side prediction, interpolation, and lag compensation to predict and smooth out the movement of networked objects based on input and network data.

    - **Results**: Improved responsiveness and synchronization in multiplayer games, reducing the impact of network latency on player experience and enhancing gameplay smoothness.

- **Network object pooling**:

    - **Problem**: Excessive instantiation and destruction of networked objects can lead to network congestion and performance issues.

    - **Solution**: Implement network object pooling to reuse existing networked objects instead of creating and destroying them frequently.

    - **Example**: In a multiplayer game, instead of instantiating and destroying bullets each time they are fired, use an object pool to recycle bullets. When a bullet is no longer needed, it is returned to the pool and can be reused later.

    - **Results**: Reduced network overhead and improved performance due to fewer object instantiations and destructions, leading to smoother gameplay experiences.

These techniques are instrumental in optimizing networking within Unity games as they effectively minimize network overhead, enhance data transmission efficiency, and contribute to a more satisfying multiplayer experience for players. The effectiveness of these optimizations, however, is contingent upon the specific networking solution that's implemented within the game.

AI and pathfinding

Effective AI and pathfinding techniques are pivotal for creating immersive and engaging gameplay experiences in Unity games. We'll explore two key solutions: A* (A-star) pathfinding and hierarchical pathfinding, along with behavior trees and state machines, to optimize AI navigation and behaviors:

- **Using behavior trees**:

  - **Problem**: Inefficient pathfinding algorithms can lead to high computational overhead and slow performance, especially in complex game environments with dynamic obstacles.
  - **Example**: Implementing the A* algorithm in Unity using the NavMesh system.
  - **How it works**: A* is a popular pathfinding algorithm that efficiently finds the shortest path between two points on a graph or grid. In Unity, the NavMesh system utilizes A* for AI navigation, allowing agents to navigate dynamic environments while avoiding obstacles.
  - **Result**: Improved AI navigation performance, reduced computational cost, and smoother movement of AI agents in complex game scenes.

- **Using state machines for AI behavior**:

  - **Problem**: AI behaviors lacking realism and diversity can result in predictable and monotonous gameplay experiences.
  - **Example**: Implementing state machines for AI character behaviors.
  - **How it works**: State machines model AI behaviors as a set of states, transitions, and actions. Each state represents a specific behavior or condition, and transitions define how AI agents switch between states based on environmental stimuli or internal variables.

  Here's a simplified structure of a state machine for AI behavior:

  State interface/class:

  - `Enter`: The method that's called when entering the state
  - `Update`: The method that's called during each update cycle while in the state
  - `Exit`: The method that's called when exiting the state

  Concrete states:

  - `Idle State`: This represents the AI being idle, with its own `Enter`, `Update`, and `Exit` methods specific to idle behavior.
  - `Attack State`: Represents the AI attacking, with its own `Enter`, `Update`, and `Exit` methods specific to attack behavior
  - Other states as needed, each with their own behavior methods

State machine manager:

- `Current State`: Keeps track of the AI's current state
- `Change State`: This method transitions the AI from one state to another by updating the `Current State` variable
- `Update`: The method to be called in each update cycle, which, in turn, calls the `Update` method of the current state

Usage:

- Initialize the AI with an initial state (for example, `Idle State`)
- During each update cycle, call the `Update` method of the state machine manager to execute the behavior of the current state
- When conditions change (for example, the AI detects an enemy), use the `Change State` method to switch to the appropriate state (for example, `Attack State`)

This structure outlines the components and their relationships in a state machine for AI behavior. You can implement this structure in any programming language by creating classes/interfaces for states, implementing a manager to handle state transitions, and integrating them into your AI system.

- **Result**: Modular and organized AI behavior design, easier debugging and maintenance of AI logic, and improved adaptability to changing game conditions.

Build size

Efficient build size is crucial for delivering optimized and polished Unity games to players. Let's explore a technique known as build size reduction through asset compression to enhance build efficiency:

- **Build size reduction**:

  - **Problem**: Large build sizes can lead to longer download times and increased storage requirements for players.
  - **Solution**: Implement asset compression techniques such as texture compression, audio compression, and code stripping to reduce the overall size of the build. For texture compression, it's recommended to use dimensions that are powers of two, such as 64x64. This approach is beneficial for compression, resulting in reduced memory usage and a smaller final build size.
  - **Example**: Use texture compression formats such as ETC2 for Android builds and ASTC for iOS builds to significantly reduce the size of texture assets without compromising quality. The size of the texture is shown in the following figures:

Performance optimization techniques 265

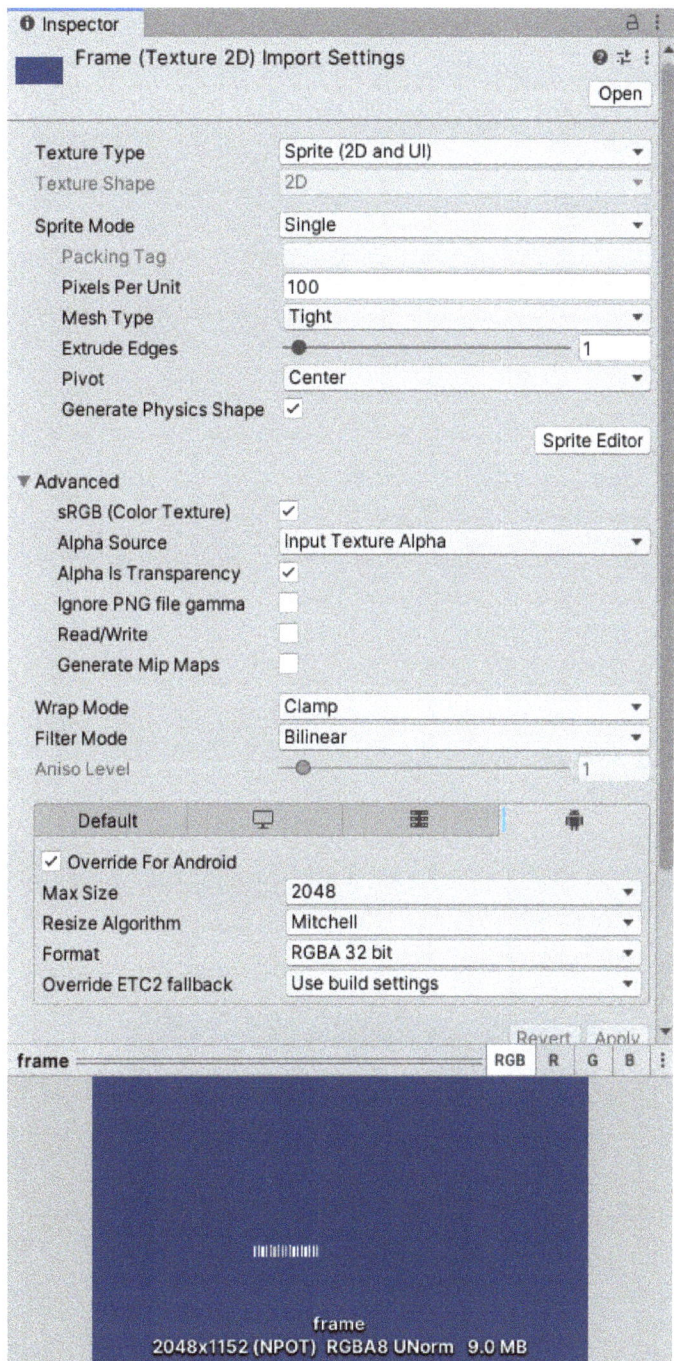

Figure 9.13 – Before using the compression format

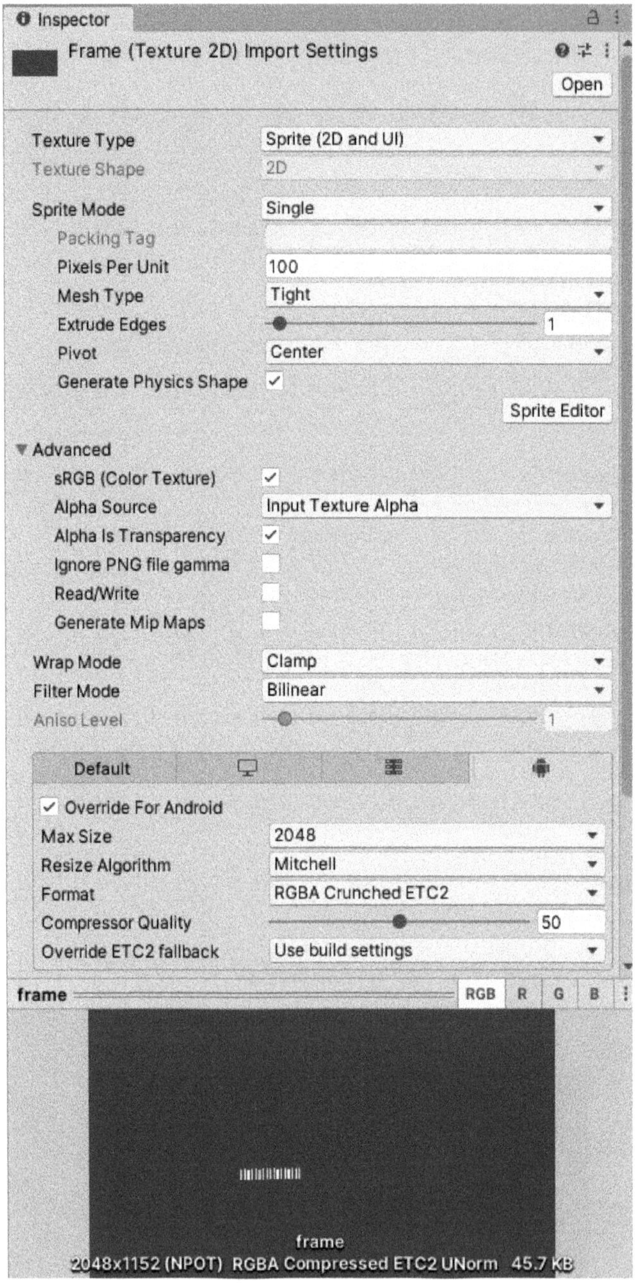

Figure 9.14 – After using a compression format

- **Result**: Reduced build size, faster download times, and improved performance on devices with limited storage.

Rendering

Optimizing rendering is essential for delivering visually stunning games while maintaining optimal performance. Let's explore two powerful techniques: a **level of detail** (**LOD**) system for efficient mesh rendering and Occlusion Culling to minimize unnecessary rendering, resulting in enhanced performance and visual quality:

- **LOD system**:

  - **Problem**: High-poly models and complex scenes can lead to performance issues, especially on lower-end devices.

  - **Solution**: Implement a LOD system where objects have multiple versions with varying levels of detail. The system switches to lower-detail versions as objects move farther from the camera, reducing the rendering workload.

  - **Example**: Use Unity's **LOD Group** component to create LOD levels for meshes, ensuring smooth transitions between LOD levels based on camera distance. Ensure that you have the necessary meshes ready by either requesting them from artists, utilizing assets from the asset store, or creating them manually if you possess the skills. It's important to create low-poly meshes from the original ones to optimize performance:

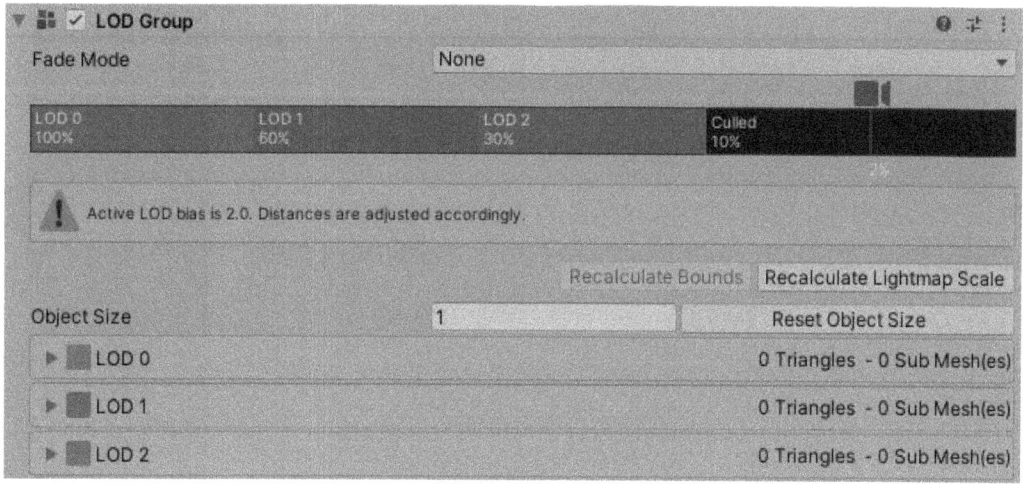

Figure 9.15 – The LOD Group component

  - **Result**: Improved performance by reducing the number of polygons that are rendered without compromising visual quality.

- **Occlusion culling**:

    - **Problem**: Rendering off-screen objects consumes resources and affects performance, even though they are not visible to the player.
    - **Solution**: Use Occlusion culling to prevent objects that are occluded by other objects or not within the player's view frustum from being rendered.
    - **Example**: Configure Occlusion culling volumes in Unity to define areas where Occlusion culling should be applied, optimizing rendering by skipping occluded objects:

Figure 9.16 – The camera before the starting line

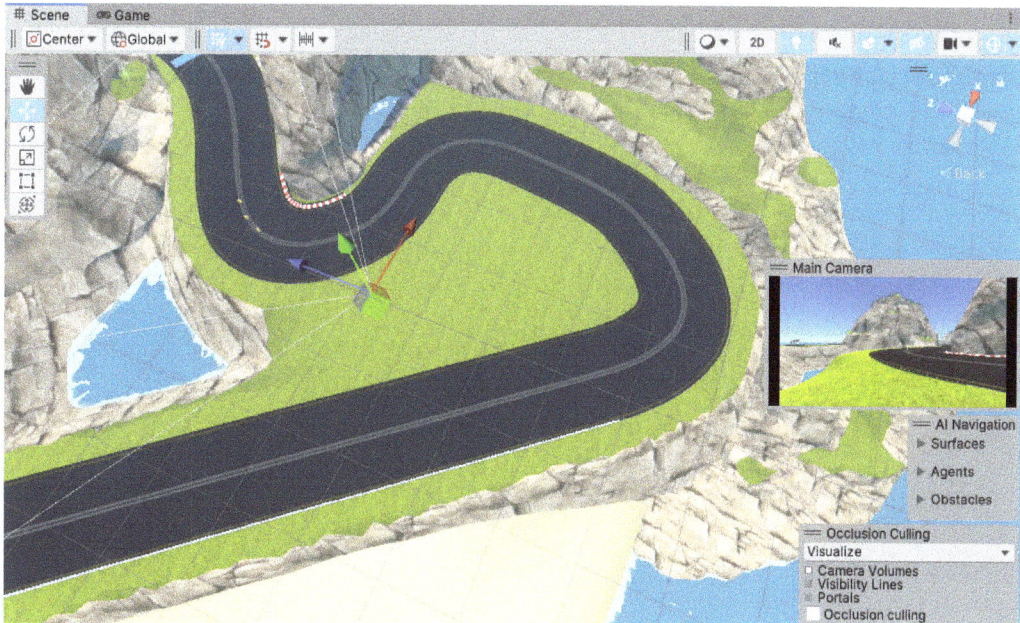

Figure 9.17 – The camera after the starting line

- **Result**: Reduced rendering workload, improved frame rates, and enhanced overall performance, especially in complex scenes.

Scripting

Efficient scripting practices are crucial for optimizing game performance and ensuring smooth gameplay experiences. Let's explore two powerful techniques: object pooling for efficient object management and coroutine optimization to enhance coroutine performance, resulting in improved overall game performance and responsiveness.

Object pooling

Let's consider a solution for object pooling:

- **Problem**: Instantiating and destroying objects frequently during gameplay can lead to performance overhead due to memory allocation and garbage collection.
- **Solution**: Implement object pooling, where a set of pre-allocated objects is reused instead of you having to instantiate and destroy them repeatedly.
- **Example**: Create an object pool manager script in Unity that manages pools of objects, such as bullets, enemies, or particles. Activate and deactivate objects from the pool as needed instead of creating new instances.

Let's explore an example of how to utilize `ObjectPoolManager` and understand its functionality.

In the following code block, the `ObjectPoolManager` class is responsible for handling all operations related to the pooled objects. To make it accessible from other scripts, we will implement it as a singleton:

```csharp
public class ObjectPoolManager : MonoBehaviour
{
    // Static instance of the ObjectPoolManager
    private static ObjectPoolManager instance;

    // Property to access the ObjectPoolManager instance
    public static ObjectPoolManager Instance
    {
        get
        {
            if (instance == null)
            {
                instance = FindObjectOfType<ObjectPoolManager>();
                // If not found, create a new GameObject and add the ObjectPoolManager script to it
                if (instance == null)
                {
                    GameObject obj = new GameObject("ObjectPoolManager");
                    instance = obj.AddComponent<ObjectPoolManager>();
                }
            }
            return instance;
        }
    }
    private void Awake()
    {
        if (instance != null && instance != this)
        {
            Destroy(gameObject);
        }
        else
        {
            instance = this;
            DontDestroyOnLoad(gameObject);
        }
    }
```

This script uses a static `Instance` property to implement the singleton pattern for `ObjectPoolManager`. It also includes an `Awake` method to ensure that only one instance of `ObjectPoolManager` exists in the scene and persists between scene changes if needed.

In the following code block, I will continue implementing the logic related to the object pooling by `GetPooledObject` and `ReturnToPool` functions of the objects:

```
    // Define a dictionary to store object pools
    private Dictionary<string, Queue<GameObject>> 
objectPools = new Dictionary<string, Queue<GameObject>>();

    // Create or retrieve an object from the pool based on 
the name of it
    public GameObject GetPooledObject(string objectName)
    {
        if (objectPools.ContainsKey(objectName))
        {
            if (objectPools[objectName].Count > 0)
            {
                GameObject obj = objectPools[objectName].
Dequeue();
                obj.SetActive(true);
                return obj;
            }
        }
        Debug.LogWarning("No available object in the pool 
with name: " + objectName);
        return null;
    }

    // Return an object to the pool
    public void ReturnToPool(string objectName, GameObject 
obj)
    {
        obj.SetActive(false);
        objectPools[objectName].Enqueue(obj);
    }
```

Here's an explanation for each part:

- `private Dictionary<string, Queue<GameObject>> objectPools = new Dictionary<string, Queue<GameObject>>();`: This line declares a private dictionary named `objectPools` that stores object pools based on their names. Each name corresponds to a queue of GameObjects.

- `public GameObject GetPooledObject(string objectName)`: This method retrieves an object from the object pool based on its name. It checks if an object pool with the given name exists and if there are available objects in the pool. If available, it dequeues an object, activates it, and returns it. If no object is available, it logs a warning and returns null.
- `public void ReturnToPool(string objectName, GameObject obj)`: This method returns an object to the object pool based on its name. It deactivates the object and enqueues it back into the corresponding object pool queue.

Lastly, I'll create a function to instantiate pooled objects from other scripts, as demonstrated in the following code block:

```
// Create an object pool for a specific prefab so I can
dynamically add object to the pool in runtime
    public void CreateObjectPool(GameObject prefab, int poolSize,
string objectName)
    {
        if (!objectPools.ContainsKey(objectName))
        {
            objectPools[objectName] = new Queue<GameObject>();

            for (int i = 0; i < poolSize; i++)
            {
                GameObject obj = Instantiate(prefab);
                obj.SetActive(false);
                objectPools[objectName].Enqueue(obj);
            }
        }
        else
        {
            Debug.LogWarning("Object pool with name " + objectName
 + " already exists.");
        }
    }
```

Here's an explanation of the `CreateObjectPool` method:

- `public void CreateObjectPool(GameObject prefab, int poolSize, string objectName)`: This method creates an object pool for a specific prefab with a given pool size and object name. It checks if an object pool with the same name already exists. If not, it creates a new queue in the dictionary and instantiates objects based on the prefab to populate the pool.

Here's an example of how to use this manager:

```
public class ExampleUsage : MonoBehaviour
  {
      public GameObject prefabToPool;
      public int poolSize = 10;
      public string objectName = "MyTag";

      void Start()
      {
          // Create an object pool with the specified prefab,
pool size, and tag
          ObjectPoolManager.Instance.
CreateObjectPool(prefabToPool, poolSize, objectName);

          // Get an object from the pool
          GameObject obj = ObjectPoolManager.Instance.
GetPooledObject(objectName);

          if (obj != null)
          {
              // Use the object
              obj.transform.position = Vector3.zero;
          }

          // Return the object to the pool
          ObjectPoolManager.Instance.ReturnToPool(objectName,
  obj);
      }
  }
```

- **Result**: Reduced memory overhead, improved performance, and smoother gameplay experience, especially in scenarios with frequent object creation and destruction.

Coroutine optimization

Now, let's consider a solution for coroutine optimization:

- **Problem**: Using coroutines extensively without optimization can lead to performance issues, especially when you're dealing with long-running or frequent coroutines.

- **Solution**: Optimize coroutines by employing techniques such as using `WaitForSeconds` instead of `WaitForSecondsRealtime`, minimizing `WaitForSeconds` calls, and avoiding nested coroutines where possible. Additionally, consider defining or caching `WaitForSeconds` instances to avoid creating new instances each time the coroutine is executed, which can improve memory efficiency. The following code block shows an example of how to define `WaitForSeconds`:

  ```
  // Define WaitForSeconds as a variable
      private WaitForSeconds waitShort = new WaitForSeconds(2f);
  ```

- **Example**: Refactor coroutine-heavy scripts to reduce the number of coroutine instances, optimize yield instructions, and use alternatives such as `InvokeRepeating` for repetitive tasks.
- **Result**: Improved performance by reducing coroutine overhead, smoother gameplay, and better frame rates, especially in complex scenes with many coroutines running simultaneously.

We now know about some common issues and their appropriate solutions. In the next section, we'll move on and learn how to optimize memory.

Memory management and optimization

Memory profiling in Unity involves utilizing tools such as the Memory Profiler module and package to analyze and optimize memory usage, allowing us to identify areas for improvement and enhance overall performance. You'll learn more about the Memory Profiler package in this section.

You can analyze memory usage in your Unity application through two methods. First, the Memory Profiler module provides essential insights into memory usage, highlighting areas where your application consumes memory. Second, by integrating the Memory Profiler package into your project, you gain access to an enhanced **Memory Profiler** window within Unity Editor. This advanced tool allows for more detailed analysis, including storing and comparing snapshots to identify memory leaks and examining memory layouts to detect fragmentation issues.

The Memory Profiler

The Memory Profiler in Unity is a tool that's used for analyzing and optimizing memory usage in Unity projects. It helps us understand how our game uses memory and identify areas where memory can be optimized.

You need to install this package into your project. Go to the **Package Manager** window and select **Memory Profiler**, as shown in *Figure 9.18*:

Memory management and optimization   275

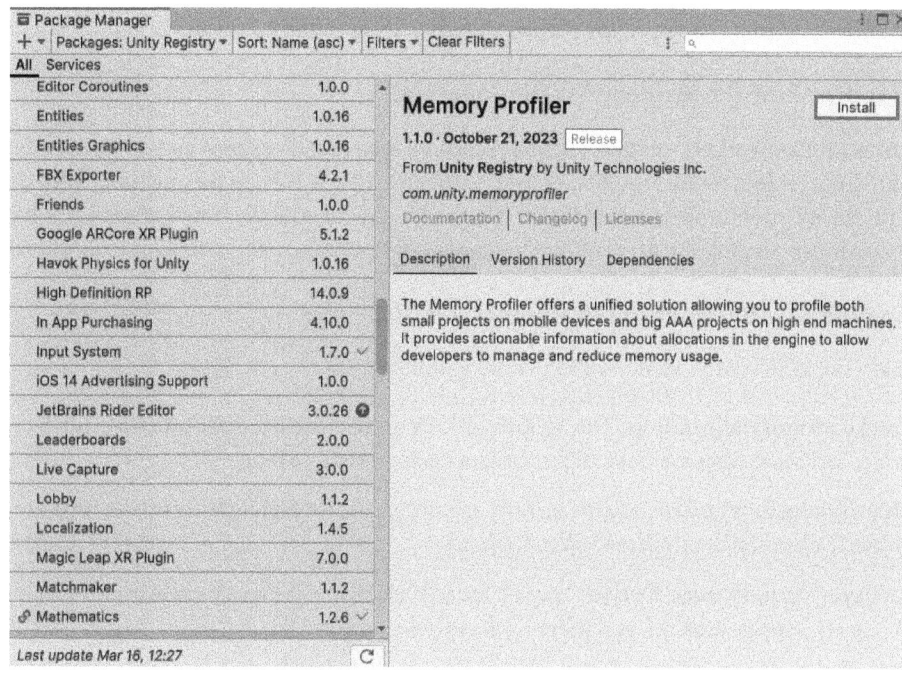

Figure 9.18 – Installing the Memory Profiler package

Wait for Unity to finish installing the Memory Profiler package, then open it from the **Window | Analysis | Memory Profiler** menu. If this is your first time using it in your project, an empty window will open, as shown in *Figure 9.19*:

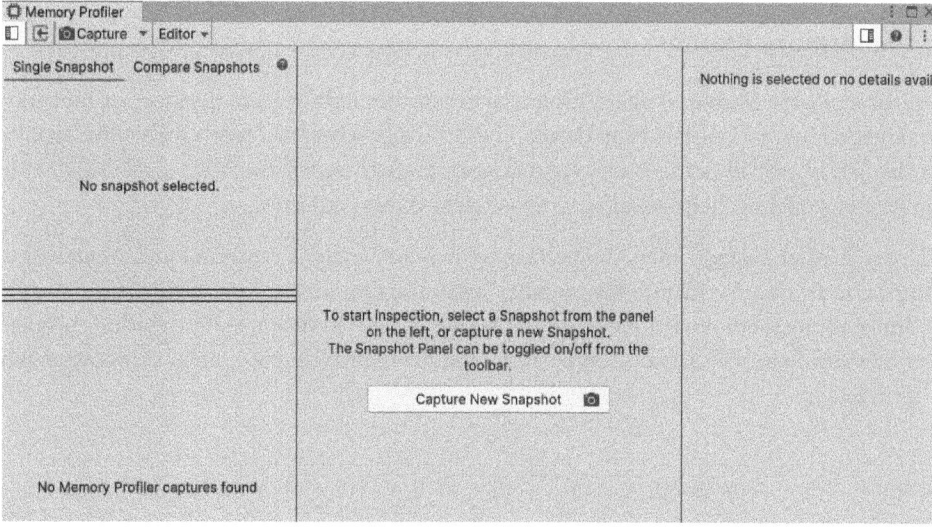

Figure 9.19 – The Memory Profiler panel

Now that we've learned how to open the Memory Profiler, let's explore how it works and what it does.

Understanding how the Memory Profiler operates

The Memory Profiler works by monitoring and recording memory allocations and usage in real time while your Unity project is running. It tracks various metrics, such as heap size, memory allocations by type, instance counts, and memory leaks. It provides a detailed breakdown of memory usage, allowing developers to pinpoint areas of high memory consumption and potential memory leaks.

Exploring the key functions of the Memory Profiler

The primary functions of the Memory Profiler are as follows:

- **Tracks memory allocations**: The Memory Profiler tracks memory allocations made by your game, including heap memory, object instances, and resource usage
- **Identifies memory leaks**: It helps identify memory leaks by highlighting objects that are not properly disposed of or released from memory
- **Analyzes memory usage by type**: You can see a breakdown of memory usage by different types of objects, scripts, textures, and other assets in your project
- **Provides instance counts**: The Memory Profiler shows how many instances of each object type are currently in memory, helping you understand memory consumption patterns
- **Offers insights into resource usage**: It provides insights into how resources such as textures, audio clips, and other assets contribute to memory usage

Now, let's learn how to use the Memory Profiler.

Using the Memory Profiler

Before we dive into the Memory Profiler, it's crucial to consider and adhere to the memory limitations of your target devices in multiplatform development. Design scenes and levels within the specified memory budget for each device to ensure optimal performance based on hardware capabilities. Setting clear limits and guidelines helps maintain compatibility across platforms.

The Memory Profiler package offers comprehensive memory analysis capabilities. Utilize it to store and compare snapshots for identifying memory leaks and optimizing your application's memory layout. Unlike the Memory Profiler module, this package extends its functionality to include managed memory analysis, snapshot saving, comparison, and detailed memory content exploration with visual breakdowns:

Memory management and optimization   277

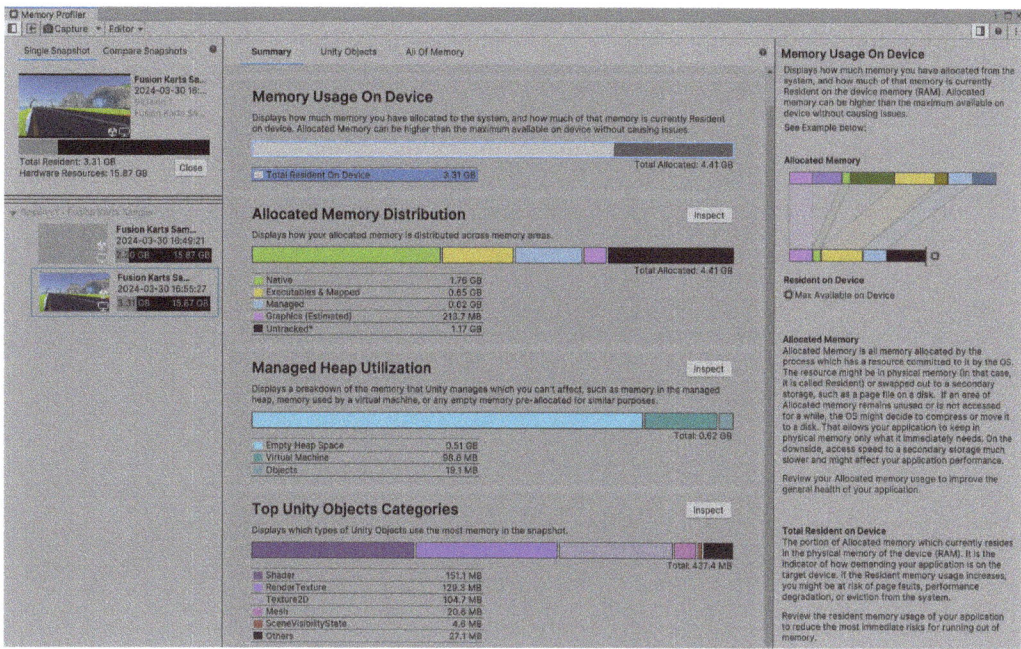

Figure 9.20 – The Summary tab in the Memory Profiler

The **Summary** tab provides an overview of the memory status in the chosen snapshot(s).

Once you click on any area of the summary, further details about it will appear in the right-hand panel.

Another tab we should consider is **Unity Objects**, which showcases Unity objects that are utilizing memory, along with their respective allocations in native and managed memory, and the combined total. You can utilize this data to spot duplicate memory entries or pinpoint objects with significant memory usage. You can also utilize the search bar to filter entries in the table based on your specified text. This can be seen in *Figure 9.21*:

278   Optimizing the Game Using Unity's Profiler, Frame Debugger, and Memory Profiler

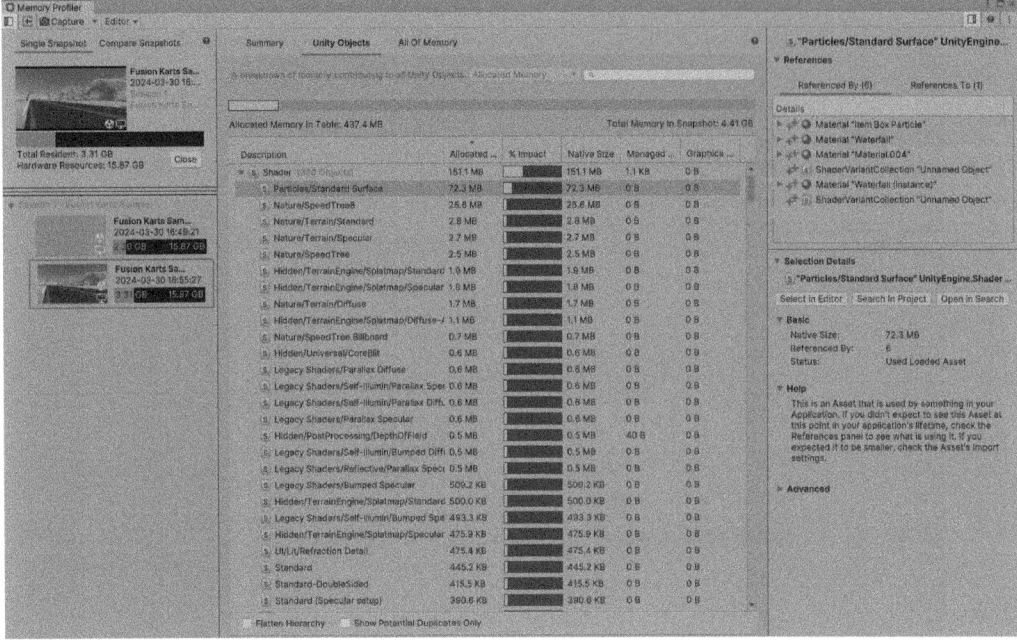

Figure 9.21 – The Unity Objects tab in the Memory Profiler

Lastly, The **All Of Memory** tab is exclusive to **Single Snapshot** mode, providing a comprehensive breakdown of all tracked memory in the snapshot. It visualizes memory usage, showcasing sizable portions managed either by Unity or the platform. This tab is instrumental in discerning non-Unity-related memory consumption and uncovering potential memory issues not evident in the **Unity Objects** tab:

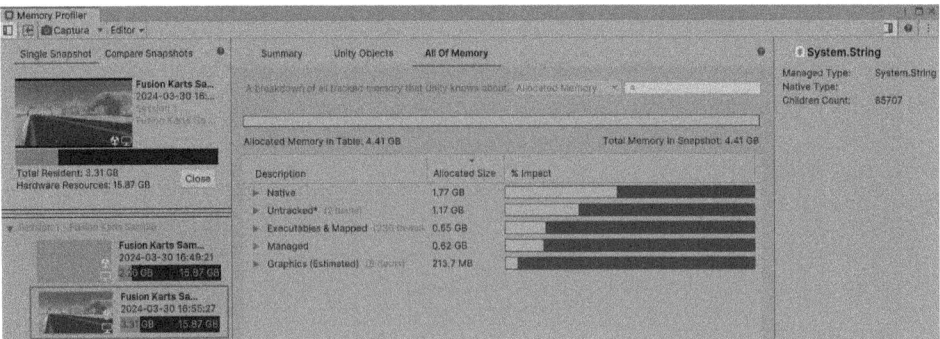

Figure 9.22 – The All Of Memory tab in the Memory Profiler

You can identify optimization candidates by following these steps:

1. Open a snapshot by referring to the instructions for opening snapshots.
2. Access the **Unity Objects** tab.

3. Ensure the table is sorted in descending order, which is the default setting in the **Memory Profiler** window. If the sort order has been changed, select the **Total Size** column header to revert to descending order for this process. This arrangement highlights objects with the highest memory usage at the top of the table.

You can search through the results in one of two ways:

- Expand groups to view individual objects within each group
- Consider enabling the **Flatten hierarchy** property to exclusively display individual objects in the table

If you're uncertain about which objects might use excessive memory, leave the **Flatten hierarchy** property disabled and inspect the groups to identify the largest objects. Enable this property if most assets are understood but there's a suspicion of a few outliers consuming too much memory.

Additionally, enable the **Show Potential Duplicates Only** property to identify objects flagged by the Memory Profiler as potential duplicates. Utilize the **References** component and **Selection Details** component for detailed insights into these objects. This information helps differentiate expected duplicates, such as multiple instances of a Prefab in a scene, from problematic duplicates, such as unintentionally created objects or instances not disposed of correctly by Unity.

Here are some considerations when it comes to memory profiling:

- Use different memory usage based on settings such as quality levels, graphics tiers, and AssetBundle variants, especially on more powerful devices.
- **Quality Level** and **Graphics** settings can impact the size of RenderTextures that are used for shadow maps.
- Resolution scaling affects screen buffers, RenderTextures, and post-processing effects.
- Texture quality settings influence the size of all textures.
- Maximum LOD can impact models and other elements.
- AssetBundle variants such as HD and SD versions can result in different asset sizes based on the device's specifications.
- The target device's screen resolution affects the dimensions of RenderTextures that are utilized for post-processing effects.
- The supported Graphics API can affect shader sizes based on API-specific variants.
- Content generated dynamically during gameplay, such as procedural levels, can significantly impact memory usage. Monitor the memory footprint of dynamically generated assets to ensure efficient memory management.
- Conduct thorough testing on target devices with varying specifications, screen resolutions, and hardware configurations to identify and address memory issues specific to each platform.

By considering these aspects and conducting comprehensive memory profiling, you can optimize memory usage across different platforms, ensuring optimal performance and resource utilization in your Unity projects.

One effective method to improve memory optimization in Unity is by optimizing the import settings for assets.

Importing models

Importing models is a critical aspect of 3D game development, and optimizing this process can significantly enhance memory usage and overall performance. In this section, we'll explore key settings, as shown in *Figure 9.23*, that can be adjusted to achieve these optimizations effectively:

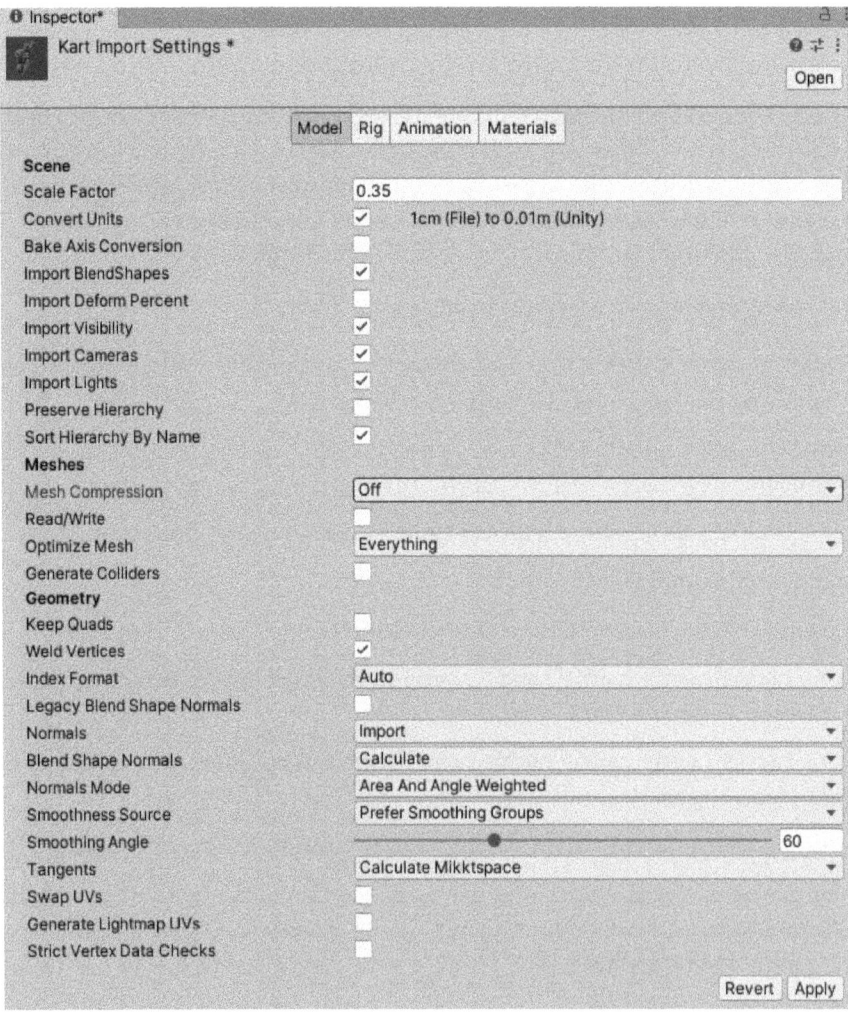

Figure 9.23 – The model's settings

Mesh Compression is a setting that determines the level of compression that's applied to imported mesh data. It affects the file size of the mesh asset and can impact both memory usage and rendering performance:

- **Options**: Unity provides three options for **Mesh Compression**:

  - **Off**: No compression is applied, resulting in larger file sizes but potentially better rendering performance.

  - **Low**: Applies a basic compression algorithm to reduce file size while still maintaining visual quality. This is suitable for many cases as it doesn't have a significant impact on rendering performance.

  - **Medium/High**: Utilizes more advanced compression techniques to further reduce file size. However, higher compression levels may lead to slightly lower rendering performance due to additional decompression overhead.

- **Best practices**: Use **Mesh Compression** judiciously based on the specific requirements of your game. For complex models or those with intricate details, consider using **Low** compression to balance file size reduction with rendering performance. Test different compression levels to find the optimal balance for your project.

The **Read/Write Enabled** setting determines whether the mesh data can be accessed and modified at runtime. Enabling this setting allows scripts to read and modify mesh properties during gameplay:

- **Impact on performance and memory**: Enabling Read/Write for a mesh increases memory usage because the mesh data needs to be stored in a format that allows runtime modifications. However, it can also provide flexibility for dynamic mesh operations, such as deformation or procedural mesh generation.

- **Best practices**: Only enable Read/Write for meshes that require runtime modifications. For static meshes that do not change during gameplay, leave this setting disabled to reduce memory overhead.

The **Optimize Mesh** setting determines whether Unity applies additional optimizations to the imported mesh data to improve rendering performance:

- **Effect on performance and memory**: Enabling **Optimize Mesh** allows Unity to perform optimizations such as vertex welding, which reduces the number of vertices in the mesh without significantly affecting visual quality. This can lead to improved rendering performance by reducing the workload on the GPU.

- **Best practices**: Enable **Optimize Mesh** for meshes that can benefit from vertex reduction without compromising visual fidelity. This is particularly useful for models with redundant or overlapping vertices as it can significantly reduce memory usage and enhance rendering performance.

Setting the **Animation Type** option to **None** for a static game object in the **Rig** tab can have a positive impact on both performance and memory usage. When you choose **None**, Unity skips any processing related to animation rigging and does not allocate resources for animation-related calculations during runtime. This can be seen in *Figure 9.24*:

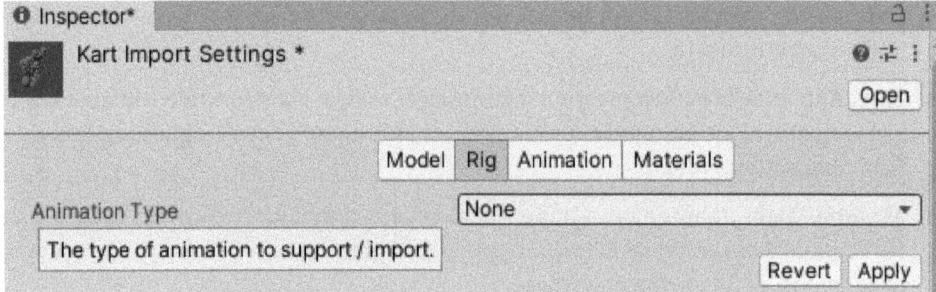

Figure 9.24 – The Rig tab in the model settings

Let's look at how setting **Animation Type** to **None** can affect performance and memory.

Performance impact:

- By setting **Animation Type** to **None**, Unity avoids processing animation data and calculations for the game object. This reduces the workload on the CPU and GPU, especially during the rendering and animation playback phases.

- Since there are no animation updates to perform, Unity can optimize the rendering pipeline by skipping unnecessary computations related to bone transformations, blend shapes, or animation state updates.

- This optimization can lead to smoother frame rates and improved overall performance, particularly for static objects that do not require any animation functionality.

Memory impact:

- Setting **Animation Type** to **None** also has a memory-saving benefit. Unity does not allocate memory for storing animation clips, rigging data, or animation-related components (for example, Animator or Animation Controller) for game objects with this setting applied.

- This reduction in memory usage can be significant, especially for scenes with multiple static objects or large models that do not need animation features.

- By minimizing memory allocation for animation-related resources, you free up more memory for other game assets and reduce the overall memory footprint of your Unity project.

Best practices:

- Set **Animation Type** to **None** for static game objects or models that do not require animation functionality. This is particularly effective for environment props, static scenery elements, or architectural models.

- For dynamic objects that require animation, such as characters or interactive elements, choose the appropriate **Animation Type** based on their animation requirements (for example, **Generic**, **Humanoid**, **Legacy**, and so on).

- Regularly review and optimize animation settings for each game object to ensure efficient use of resources and improved performance.

In summary, setting **Animation Type** to **None** for static game objects can be a beneficial optimization strategy as it reduces both CPU/GPU workload and memory usage in your Unity project.

Lastly, when considering the **Anim. Compression** option in the **Animation** tab of model settings in Unity, choosing between **Optimal Compression** or **Keyframe Reduction** can indeed have an impact on both performance and memory usage. This can be seen in *Figure 9.25*:

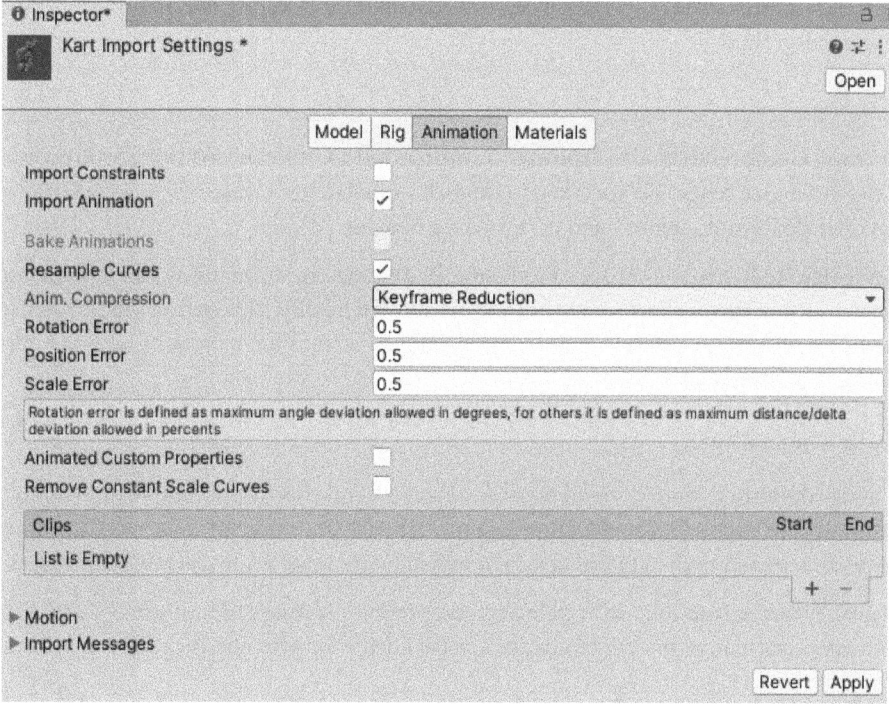

Figure 9.25 – The Animation tab in the model settings

Let's look at how each option affects your project.

Optimal Compression:

- **Performance impact**: **Optimal Compression** aims to reduce the size of animation clips while preserving visual quality. This can result in improved performance during runtime, especially for devices with limited processing power or memory bandwidth.

- **Memory impact**: By compressing animation data efficiently, **Optimal Compression** reduces the memory footprint of animation clips. This can be beneficial for projects with many animations or large animation files, leading to lower memory usage and better resource management.

Keyframe Reduction:

- **Performance impact**: **Keyframe Reduction** focuses on minimizing the number of keyframes in animation clips while maintaining smooth motion. This can lead to improved performance by reducing the computational overhead of interpolating between keyframes during animation playback.

- **Memory impact**: While **Keyframe Reduction** can help save memory by reducing the data needed for animation playback, it may not be as efficient in terms of memory optimization as **Optimal Compression**. However, it can still contribute to lowering the overall memory usage of animation clips.

Best practices:

- **Optimal Compression**: Use **Optimal Compression** for animations that require a balance between file size reduction and visual quality. It's suitable for a wide range of animations and can offer significant memory and performance benefits.

- **Keyframe Reduction**: Consider **Keyframe Reduction** for animations where reducing the number of keyframes won't significantly impact visual fidelity. This option can be particularly useful for repetitive or simple animations, helping to streamline memory usage and improve playback performance.

Choosing the right option:

- Evaluate the animation requirements of your project and choose the compression option that best suits your needs. **Optimal Compression** is generally recommended for most scenarios due to its balanced approach to reducing file size and memory usage while maintaining visual quality.

- Regularly test animations with different compression settings to find the optimal balance between performance, memory usage, and visual fidelity for your specific project requirements.

In conclusion, both **Optimal Compression** and **Keyframe Reduction** in the **Anim. Compression** option can impact performance and memory in Unity. Choose the compression setting that aligns with your project's animation complexity, visual quality standards, and target platform capabilities to achieve the best results.

To automate this process, we can create an asset `PostProcessor` script, which is an editor script that allows us to set default settings for importing assets. The following is an example code block demonstrating a `CustomMeshPostProcessor` class that achieves the desired default settings when importing meshes. Simply create this script and place it in the `Editor` folder of your project. Once implemented, the script will automatically apply these settings when importing new models. Feel free to customize it and add more settings as needed for your game:

```
using UnityEditor;
using UnityEngine;

public class CustomMeshPostprocessor : AssetPostprocessor
{
    void OnPreprocessModel()
    {
        ModelImporter importer = assetImporter as ModelImporter;
        importer.isReadable = false; // Set Read/Write option to disabled
        importer.meshCompression = ModelImporterMeshCompression.Medium; // Set Mesh Compression to Medium
    }
}
```

Overall, optimizing the import settings for models in Unity is crucial for achieving efficient memory usage and overall performance in your game. By carefully configuring these settings and following best practices, you can significantly enhance the user experience while maintaining optimal resource utilization.

Importing textures

The topic of importing textures is highly impactful in optimizing both game and memory performance, with notable effects extending to UI performance as well. The available settings are shown in *Figure 9.26*:

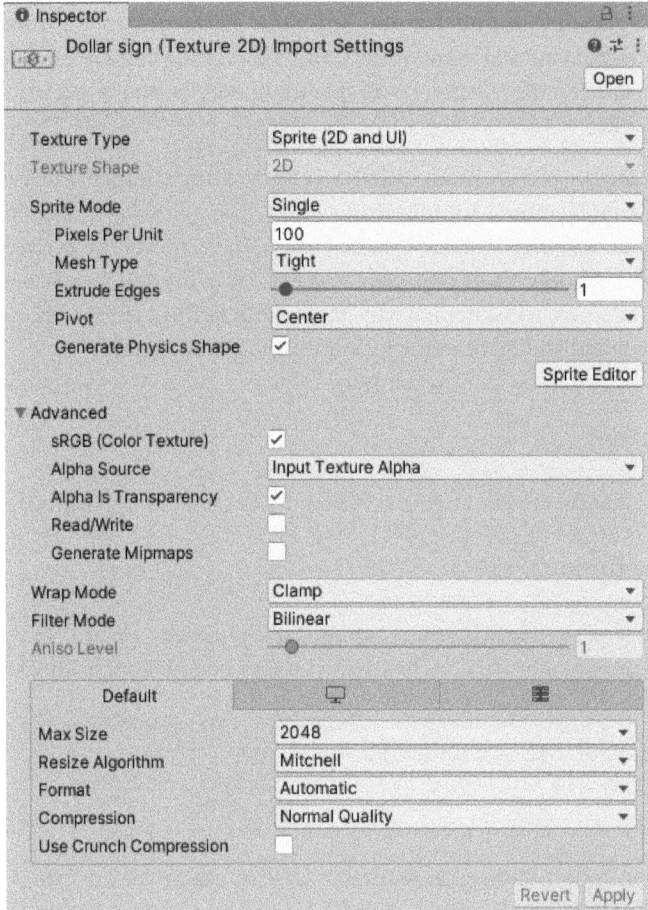

Figure 9.26 – Texture settings

When importing textures into Unity, two key settings that can impact performance and memory usage are **Read/Write** and **GenerateMipMaps**. Let's delve into each setting and understand their effects.

Read/Write:

- **Performance impact**: Enabling **Read/Write** allows scripts to access and modify texture data at runtime. While this flexibility can be beneficial for certain features, such as dynamic texture updates or procedural generation, it comes with a performance cost. Each texture marked as **Read/Write** consumes additional memory and may require more processing power during runtime.

- **Memory impact**: Textures with **Read/Write** enabled occupy more memory compared to those without this option. This is because Unity allocates space for both the texture data and an additional copy that can be modified at runtime. As a result, enabling **Read/Write** for multiple textures can lead to increased memory usage, especially on resource-constrained platforms.

GenerateMipMaps:

- **Performance impact**: Generating MipMaps creates a series of pre-calculated texture levels (MipMaps) that improve rendering quality and performance. However, this process requires additional computational resources during texture import or runtime generation, impacting loading times and initial performance.

- **Memory impact**: Including MipMaps increases the memory footprint of textures since each MipMap level adds to the total texture size. While MipMaps enhance rendering performance by providing optimized texture sampling at different distances, they also consume more memory, especially for large textures with numerous MipMap levels.

Best practices:

- **Read/Write**: Only enable **Read/Write** for textures that require runtime modification or dynamic updates. For static textures used as sprites, backgrounds, or UI elements, disable **Read/Write** to conserve memory and improve performance.

- **GenerateMipMaps**: Use **GenerateMipMaps** for textures that will benefit from improved rendering quality and performance, such as textures used for 3D models or distant terrain. Consider the trade-off between enhanced visual fidelity and increased memory usage when deciding whether to include MipMaps.

Choosing the right settings:

- Evaluate the specific requirements of each texture in your project. Enable **Read/Write** and **GenerateMipMaps** judiciously based on whether the texture needs runtime modification and whether MipMaps are necessary for optimized rendering.

- Regularly monitor the memory usage and performance impact of textures with different settings to optimize resource utilization and maintain efficient runtime behavior.

In conclusion, managing **Read/Write** and **GenerateMipMaps** settings when you're importing textures into Unity is crucial for balancing performance, memory usage, and visual quality. Selecting the appropriate settings based on the intended usage of each texture helps optimize resource allocation and enhances overall application performance.

Another aspect to consider is compression settings, which vary based on the target platform, each with its unique configurations. While specific platform settings are extensive and platform-dependent, there are some general tips for optimizing compression.

Maximum size:

- Adjusting the maximum size of textures determines their dimensions upon import. Higher resolutions offer better visual quality but consume more memory. Consider the device's capabilities and the texture's intended use to strike a balance between quality and performance.
- **Best practice**: Set the maximum size based on the target platform and the texture's role in the game. Use lower resolutions for background elements or distant objects to conserve memory.

Resize algorithm:

- The resize algorithm dictates how textures are scaled when their dimensions exceed the maximum size. Different algorithms may impact image quality and memory usage.
- **Best practice**: Choose an algorithm that suits the texture type. Use sharper algorithms for detailed textures and smoother ones for gradients or patterns to preserve quality.

Format:

- Texture format determines how the image data is stored, impacting compression, memory usage, and visual fidelity. Common formats include PNG, JPG, and TGA, each with its compression levels and quality trade-offs.
- **Best practice**: Select a format based on the texture's content and usage. Use PNG for lossless quality, JPG for photographic textures with compression, and TGA for high-quality images with transparency.

Compression:

- Compression methods reduce texture size and memory footprint. Unity offers options such as **Normal Quality**, **High Quality**, and **Low Quality** for compression, each affecting image quality and memory usage differently.
- **Best practice**: Choose compression settings based on performance requirements and visual standards. Use higher-quality compression for critical textures and lower quality for background or non-critical elements.

Crunch compression:

- Crunch compression is an additional method to further reduce texture file sizes while maintaining acceptable quality. It's beneficial for optimizing memory usage, especially on resource-constrained platforms.
- **Best practice**: Enable crunch compression for textures where file size reduction is crucial, such as UI elements or frequently used textures. Balance the compression level to preserve visual quality while minimizing memory impact.

Memory management and optimization   289

Remember, these settings may vary in impact based on the platform, so testing and iteration are key. Regularly monitor memory usage and performance metrics to fine-tune texture settings for optimal results on each target platform.

By carefully configuring importing settings, you can reduce memory usage and improve overall performance in your Unity project.

Another crucial technique for memory optimization in Unity is utilizing sprite atlases.

Sprite Atlases

Sprite Atlases in Unity are essential tools for optimizing memory and performance, especially for UI elements. They allow you to combine multiple sprites into a single image, reducing draw calls and texture memory usage. Let's learn how to use Sprite Atlases effectively while considering their best practices and impact on memory and performance.

Creating a Sprite Atlas

> **Note**
> Make sure you have the **2D Sprite** package installed in your project via **Package Manager**.

In your **Project** tab, right-click and select **Create | 2D | Sprite Atlas**, as shown in *Figure 9.27*:

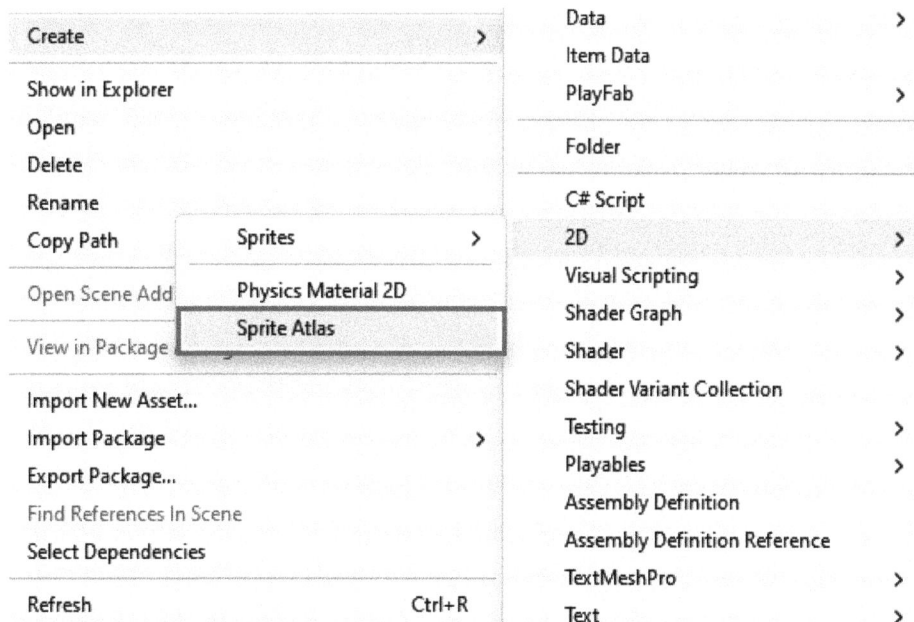

Figure 9.27 – Sprite Atlas

> **Note**
>
> Make sure you've enabled the **Sprite Packer** option in **Edit | Project Settings | Editor** so that you can start using this package.

Enable **Sprite Packer**, as shown in *Figure 9.28*:

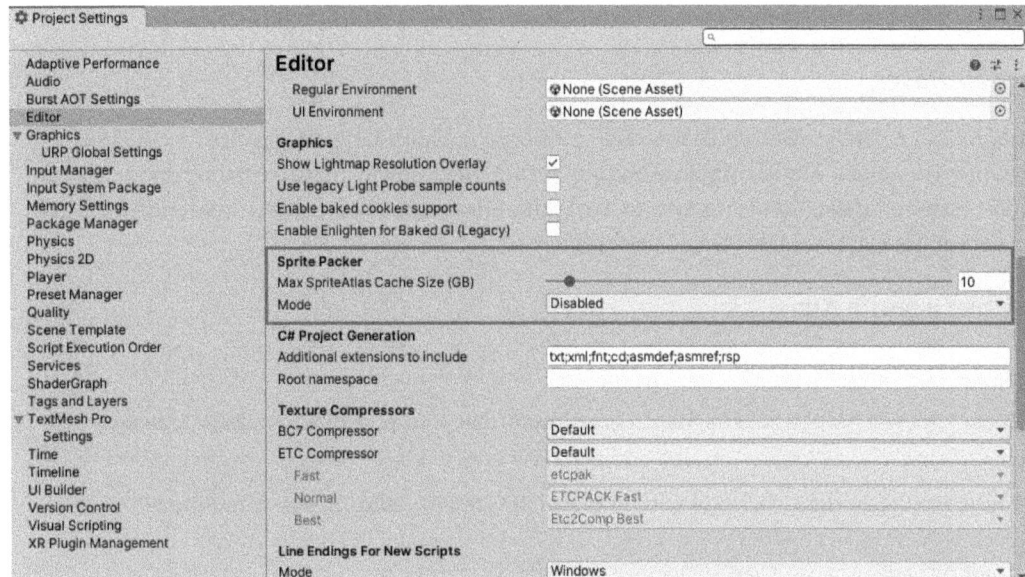

Figure 9.28 – Enabling Sprite Packer in Project Settings

After creating the sprite atlas, navigate to it to begin adding textures. Click on the + sign to select individual textures or a folder containing textures. Then, click on **Pack Preview** to combine them into an atlas file, as shown in *Figure 9.29*:

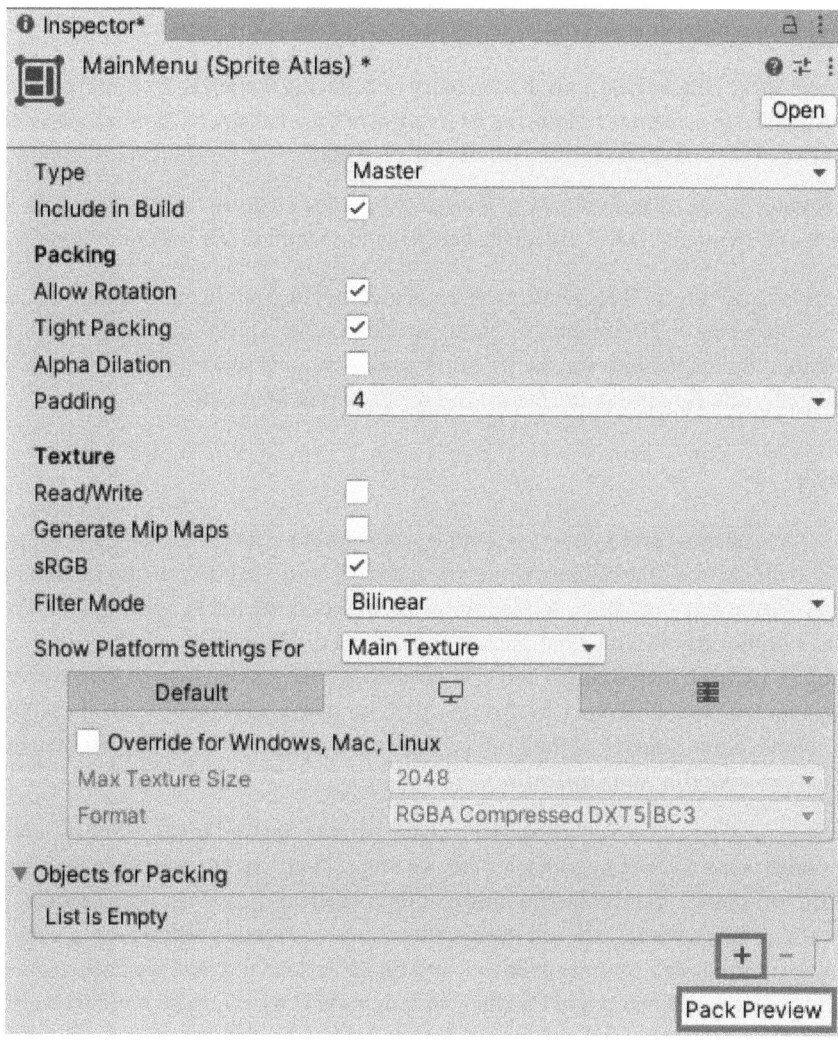

Figure 9.29 – Sprite Atlas settings

Here are some best practices you should consider:

- Merge frequently used sprites into a single Sprite Atlas to minimize draw calls and enhance performance
- Use the packing options in the **Sprite Packer** window to optimize how sprites are packed within the atlas, minimizing wasted space
- Avoid including excessively large sprites or unnecessary sprites in the atlas to keep the atlas' size manageable

Sprite Atlases have an impact on memory and performance. Let's take a closer look:

- **Memory**: Sprite Atlases help conserve memory by reducing the number of individual textures that are loaded into memory. However, be mindful of the total size of the Sprite Atlas as it still occupies memory based on its dimensions and content.
- **Performance**: Sprite Atlases improve performance by reducing the number of draw calls required to render UI elements. This is especially beneficial for complex UIs with numerous sprites.

Sprite Atlases primarily affect UI elements in terms of memory and performance. They are designed to optimize the rendering of 2D graphics, so their impact on other aspects of your game, such as 3D models or audio, is minimal. However, for UI-heavy games or applications, properly utilizing Sprite Atlases can significantly enhance performance and memory management.

Summary

In this chapter, we embarked on a journey to optimize our game's performance using Unity's powerful profiling tools. Building upon the skills we've already acquired, we delved into an introduction to Unity profiling tools, reinforcing our ability to identify performance bottlenecks and apply optimization techniques to significantly enhance our game's performance. This chapter further deepened our understanding of memory management and optimization, guiding us on how to effectively manage memory usage and optimize memory performance in our game. Through practical exercises and insights, we solidified our mastery of the Profiler, Frame Debugger, and Memory Profiler, ensuring that our game runs smoothly and efficiently.

Looking ahead to *Chapter 10*, we will discover a treasure trove of tips and tricks to enhance our Unity development skills using C#. The next chapter focuses on productivity-boosting shortcuts, advanced techniques and workflows, and troubleshooting common challenges in Unity development. We will learn how to utilize shortcuts for efficient development, apply advanced techniques to enhance our game development processes, and troubleshoot and find solutions to common challenges we may encounter. This chapter will equip us with valuable insights that we can implement to improve our workflow, overcome challenges, and unlock new possibilities in Unity game development using C#.

10
Tips and Tricks in Unity

Welcome to the concluding chapter of our journey through game development using C#! In this chapter, we'll delve into advanced techniques and workflows that are designed to boost productivity and enhance your game development skills. We'll start by exploring essential Unity Editor shortcuts, followed by time-saving code editor shortcuts for C# scripting. Next, we'll dive into optimizing your prefab workflow and mastering the use of prefabs effectively. Moving on to advanced techniques, we'll uncover the power of Scriptable Objects for data-driven development and delve into creating custom editors to enhance your workflow and user experience. Lastly, we'll tackle troubleshooting and common challenges, mastering debugging tools and addressing platform-specific challenges such as mobile optimization and cross-platform development. Get ready to level up your game development skills as we navigate these productivity-boosting strategies and advanced techniques!Top of Form

In this chapter, we're going to cover the following main topics:

- Productivity-boosting shortcuts with C#
- Advanced techniques and workflows with C#
- Troubleshooting and common challenges

Technical requirements

All the code files required for this chapter can be found at: `https://github.com/PacktPublishing/Mastering-Unity-Game-Development-with-C-Sharp/tree/main/Assets/Chapter%2010`.

Productivity-boosting shortcuts with C#

In this section, we'll delve into a variety of essential shortcuts and tricks that can significantly enhance your Unity development workflow. We'll start by exploring Unity Editor shortcuts, which are vital for quickly and efficiently navigating Unity Editor. Next, we'll focus on code editor shortcuts, where you'll learn time-saving keyboard shortcuts specifically tailored for C# scripting in your preferred code editor. Following that, we'll discuss prefab workflow optimization, offering tips on effectively using prefabs and shortcuts for efficient prefab management. Each of these topics will help streamline your development process and make working with Unity more efficient and productive.

Shortcuts are incredibly productive tools that help us save valuable time, which is crucial in our workflow.

Unity Editor shortcuts

In this subsection, we will unlock the power of Unity Editor shortcuts for efficient navigation and management, saving us valuable time and enhancing productivity in Unity development.

Hierarchy navigation shortcuts

First, let's start exploring Unity's hierarchy navigation shortcuts for organized and efficient editing of GameObjects in complex scenes. Let's dive into these helpful shortcuts:

- *Ctrl/Cmd + Left Arrow*: Collapses the selected GameObject's hierarchy in the **Hierarchy** view, as shown in the following figure:

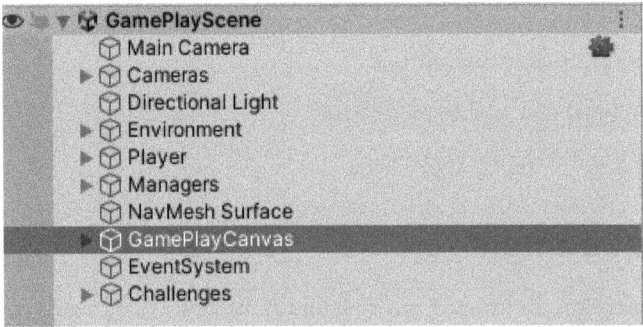

Figure 10.1 – Collapsing the selected GameObjects

- *Ctrl/Cmd + Right Arrow*: Expands the selected GameObject's hierarchy in the **Hierarchy** view, as shown in the following figure:

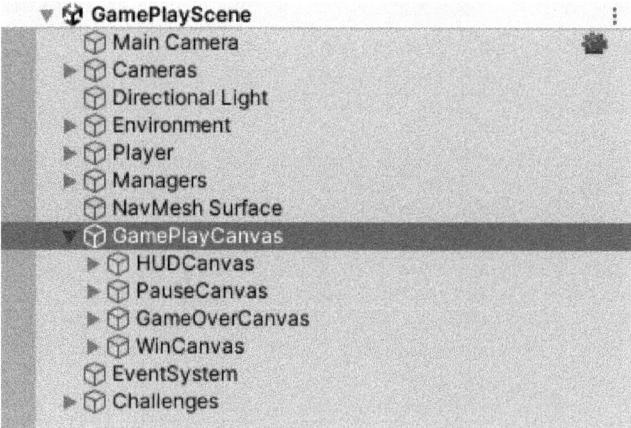

Figure 10.2 – Expanding the selected GameObjects

Next, we'll explore another category of shortcuts, this time focusing on GameObjects.

GameObject creation and management shortcuts

Here, we will explore Unity's GameObject creation and management shortcuts for efficient creation, component addition, parenting, and hierarchy maintenance in scenes. Let's dive into these productivity-enhancing shortcuts:

- *Ctrl/Cmd + Shift + N*: Creates an empty GameObject:

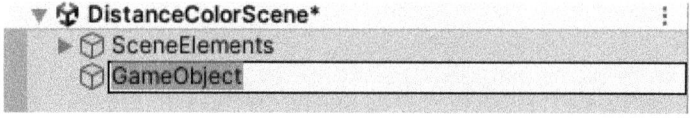

Figure 10.3 – Creating an empty GameObject

- *Ctrl/Cmd + Shift + A*: Adds a component to the selected GameObject:

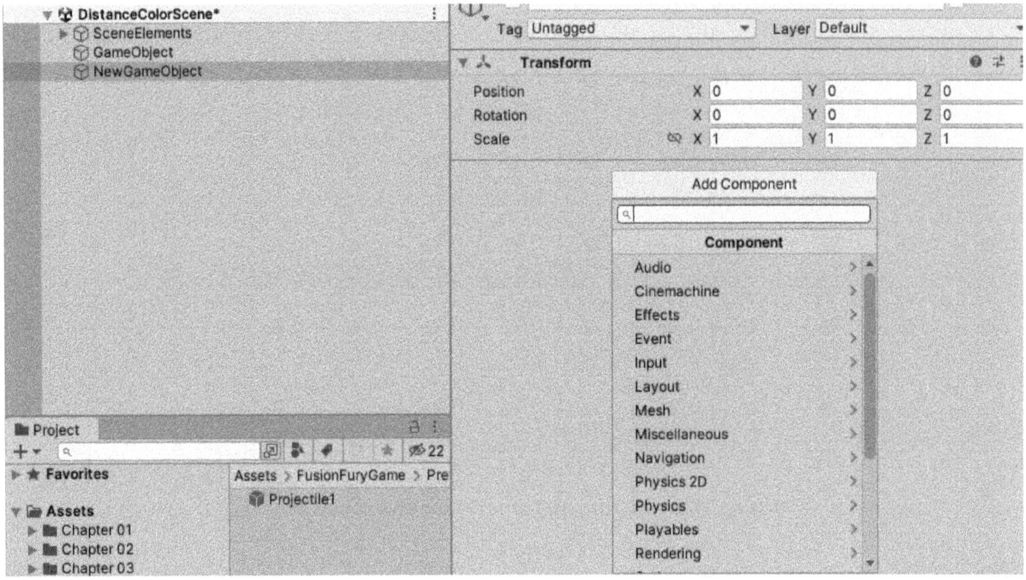

Figure 10.4 – Adding a component to the selected GameObject

- *Ctrl/Cmd + Shift + V*: Pastes the GameObject as a child of another GameObject:

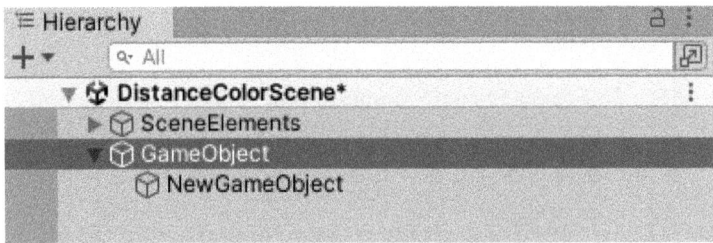

Figure 10.5 – Pasting the GameObject as a child of another GameObject

- *Ctrl/Cmd + Shift + G*: Creates an empty parent for the selected GameObject:

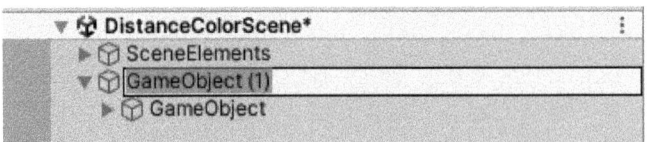

Figure 10.6 – Creating an empty parent for a GameObject

The preceding shortcuts are just simple examples of shortcuts that can enhance your productivity. You can learn more shortcuts by navigating to **Shortcuts** (**Edit** | **Shortcuts**).

After navigating to **Shortcuts**, you'll see the panel shown in *Figure 10.7*. Notice the options to create profiles, categorize shortcuts in the left list, and modify existing shortcuts. You can also assign shortcuts for empty slots:

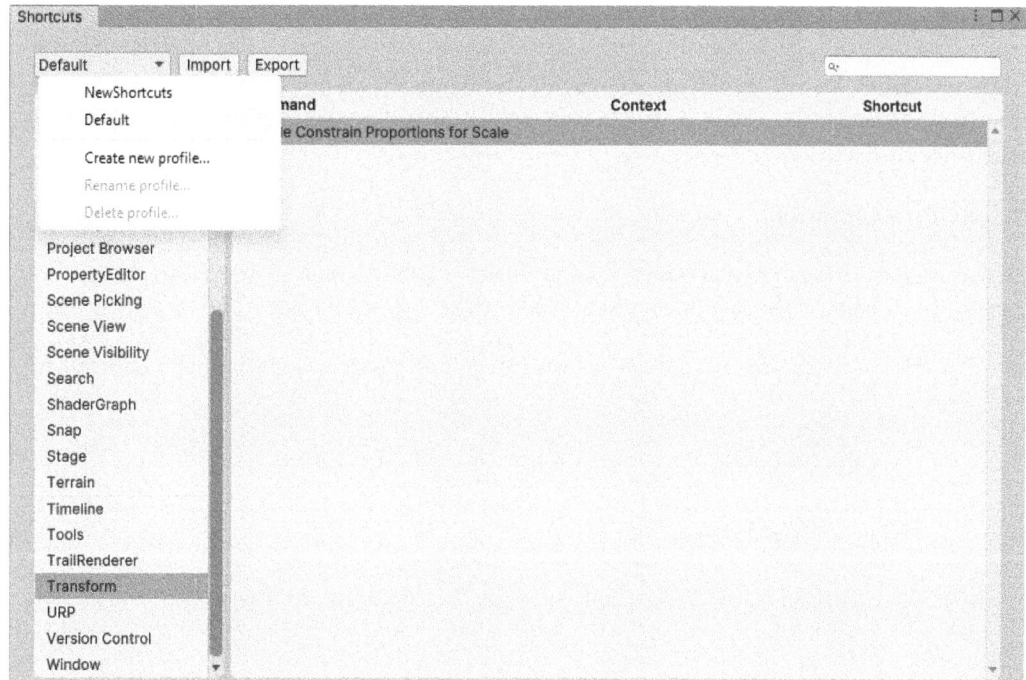

Figure 10.7 – The Shortcuts panel

If you need to create a specific profile for your work, simply click on the **Create new profile..** option. This will bring up the following panel, where you can assign the name of the new profile:

Figure 10.8 – The Create profile panel

298   Tips and Tricks in Unity

After creating a new profile, you can modify the default shortcuts within it.

Utilizing these Unity Editor shortcuts leads to increased productivity by reducing development time, allowing for more efficient use of time on essential tasks.

Now, let's explore the time-saving Visual Studio shortcuts that can enhance your productivity.

Visual Studio shortcuts

In this subsection, we will explore the efficiency-boosting Visual Studio shortcuts, which are categorized into navigation, refactoring, and code generation, to streamline your coding experience and enhance productivity.

Navigation shortcuts

We'll start by discovering a range of powerful navigation shortcuts in Visual Studio that are designed to streamline your coding experience and boost productivity. Let's delve into these time-saving shortcuts:

- *Ctrl + T*: Opens a search window so that you can quickly navigate to any file, type, or member:

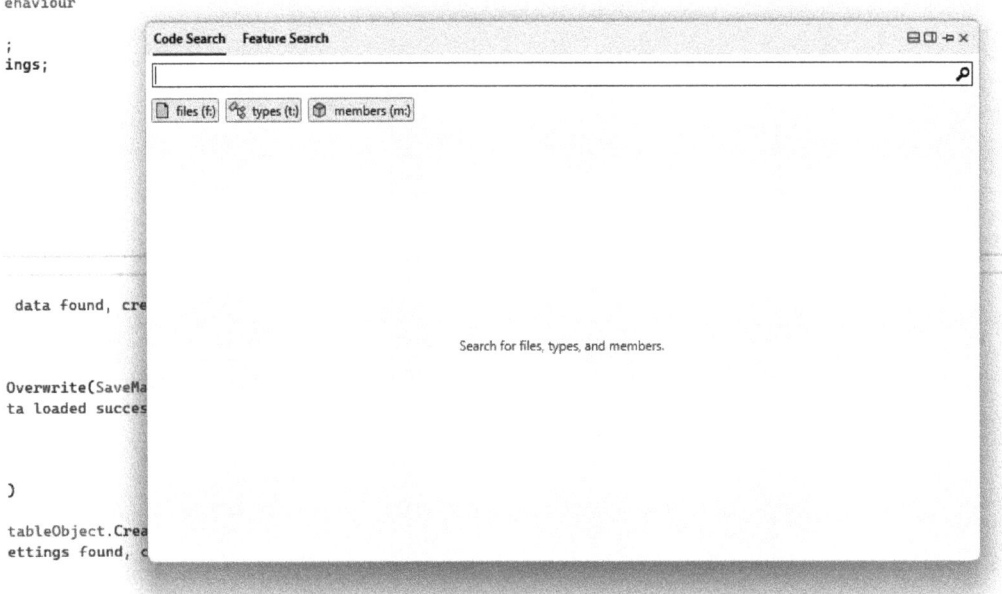

Figure 10.9 – The Search panel

- *Ctrl + Shift + V*: Allows you to view the clipboard history so that you can paste previously copied items:

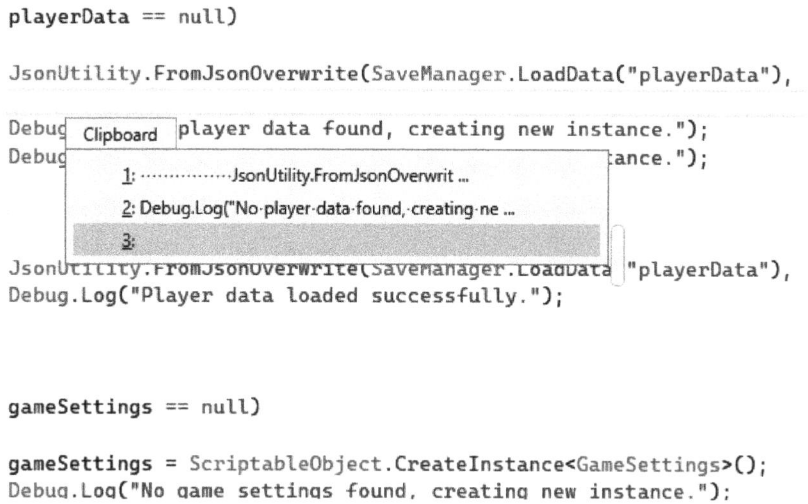

```
playerData == null)

JsonUtility.FromJsonOverwrite(SaveManager.LoadData("playerData"),

Debug   Clipboard    player data found, creating new instance.");
Debug                                                 ance.");
          1: ············ JsonUtility.FromJsonOverwrit ...
          2: Debug.Log("No·player·data·found,·creating·ne ...
          3:

JsonUtility.FromJsonOverwrite(SaveManager.LoadData "playerData"),
Debug.Log("Player data loaded successfully.");



gameSettings == null)

gameSettings = ScriptableObject.CreateInstance<GameSettings>();
Debug.Log("No game settings found, creating new instance.");
```

Figure 10.10 – Editor's clipboard

Next, let's explore another category of shortcuts, this time focusing on refactoring.

Refactoring shortcuts

Let's discover how Visual Studio's refactoring shortcuts can help you improve code readability, maintainability, and overall code quality with ease. Let's dive into these efficient refactoring tools!

- *Ctrl + R, R*: Renames a symbol across your code base:

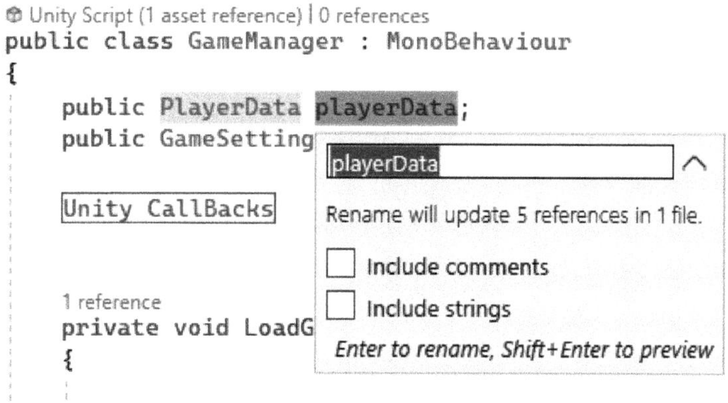

```
🔹 Unity Script (1 asset reference) | 0 references
public class GameManager : MonoBehaviour
{
    public PlayerData playerData;
    public GameSetting
                        playerData                          ∧
                        Rename will update 5 references in 1 file.
    Unity CallBacks
                        ☐ Include comments
                        ☐ Include strings
    1 reference
    private void LoadG  Enter to rename, Shift+Enter to preview
    {
```

Figure 10.11 – Renaming a symbol

- *Ctrl + R, M*: Extracts method to refactor code into a separate method:

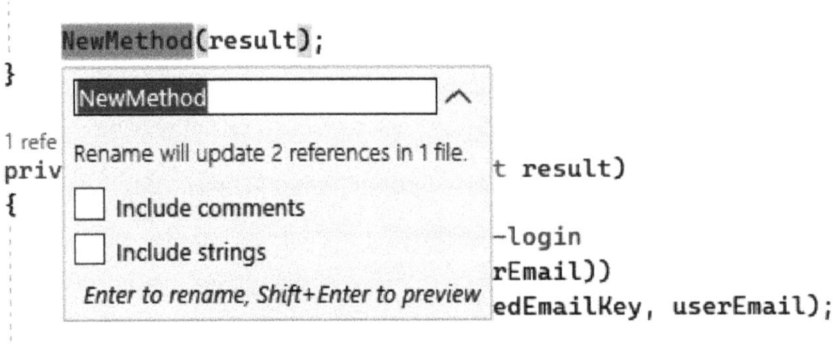

Figure 10.12 – Extracting a method

Next, let's explore another category of shortcuts, this time focusing on code generation.

Code generation shortcuts

Here, we will explore Visual Studio's code generation shortcuts, powerful tools that are designed to streamline coding tasks, automate repetitive actions, and enhance code consistency and readability. Let's dive into these time-saving shortcuts:

- *Ctrl + K, S*: Surrounds selected code with a code snippet (such as `try-catch` or `if-else`):

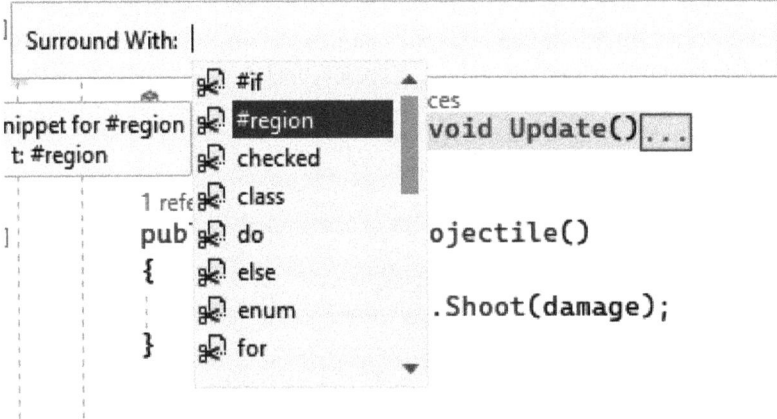

Figure 10.13 – Surrounding selected code

- *Ctrl + Space*: Shows IntelliSense to help autocomplete code or display suggestions for code completion:

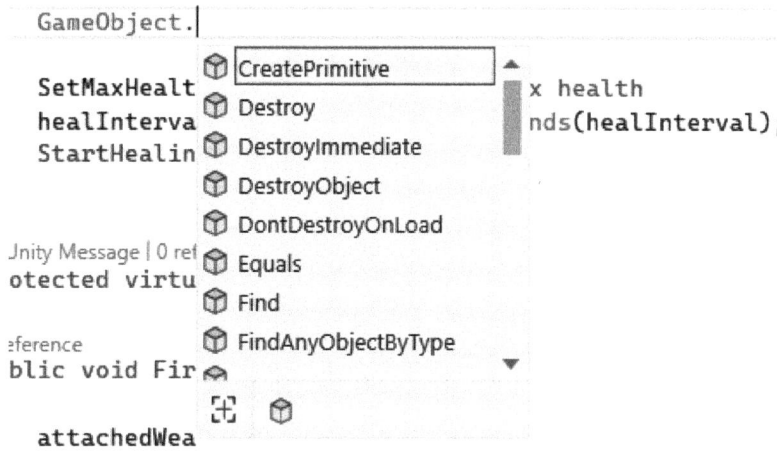

Figure 10.14 – Autocompleting code

You can access and modify Visual Studio shortcuts by navigating to **Tools | Options | Environment | Keyboard**.

> **Note**
> These shortcuts are specifically designed for Visual Studio. To learn more about shortcuts for your editor, you can navigate to its **Shortcuts** panel.

In conclusion, mastering Visual Studio's powerful shortcuts for navigation, refactoring, and code generation is key to optimizing your coding workflow and achieving greater efficiency in your development projects. By exploring and utilizing these time-saving tools, you can enhance code readability, streamline coding tasks, and ultimately boost productivity in your programming endeavors.

Optimizing your prefab workflow is essential for efficient Unity development, allowing you to streamline asset management, enhance modularity, and increase productivity throughout your project.

Prefab workflow optimization

Prefab workflow optimization encompasses various techniques and strategies to effectively manage prefabs, improve reusability, and maintain consistency across your Unity project. The following are some techniques you can implement to improve your workflow:

- **Prefab variants**: Use prefab variants to create variations of a base prefab with overridden properties or components. This allows you to maintain consistency while customizing specific instances of prefabs.

To create a prefab variant, first, select the base prefab you want to derive from. Then, right-click on it in the **Project** window and choose **Create | Prefab Variant**. This will create a new variant of the base prefab. You can customize the properties, components, and hierarchy of the variant while maintaining a connection to the base prefab. This allows you to make changes that are specific to the variant without them affecting other instances of the base prefab.

- **Nested prefabs**: Utilize Unity's nested prefab feature to create modular and reusable components with nested hierarchies. This allows for better organization and easier updating of complex prefab structures.

  To create a nested prefab, simply drag one prefab onto another in the Unity hierarchy. This will make the dragged prefab a child of the other prefab, creating a nested relationship. Nested prefabs allow you to encapsulate reusable components or objects within a parent prefab, making it easier to manage and update complex prefab structures. Changes that are made to nested prefabs are automatically reflected in all instances of the parent prefab.

- **ScriptableObjects with prefabs**: Combine ScriptableObjects with prefabs to create data-driven prefabs. Store configuration data, parameters, or references to other assets in ScriptableObjects and apply them to prefabs dynamically at runtime or in the editor.

  To use ScriptableObjects with prefabs, you can create a `ScriptableObject` asset that holds configuration data, parameters, or references to other assets. Then, you can apply these `ScriptableObject` assets to prefabs by assigning them as properties or parameters in scripts attached to the prefab instances. This allows for data-driven prefab customization and flexibility.

- **Prefab PrefabUtility events**: Utilize `PrefabUtility` events such as `Prefab InstanceUpdatedCallback` or `PrefabInstanceRemovedCallback` to perform custom actions or validations when prefabs are modified or removed in the editor. This allows for custom workflow automation and validation checks.

  You can utilize `PrefabUtility` events such as `PrefabInstanceUpdatedCallback` or `PrefabInstanceRemovedCallback` to perform custom actions or validations when prefabs are modified or removed in the editor. By subscribing to these events in your editor scripts, you can trigger custom logic or workflows based on prefab modifications, allowing for automated validation checks or workflow optimizations.

Let's explore a practical example demonstrating the implementation of one of these techniques.

Updating component properties across prefab instances

Let's consider a scenario where you have a large number of prefabs in your Unity project, and you need to update a specific component or property across all instances of a particular prefab in the scene. Manually updating each instance can be time-consuming and error-prone. However, with the use of C# scripting and Unity's `PrefabUtility` API, you can automate this process efficiently.

Problem: You have a game with hundreds of enemy prefabs scattered throughout your scenes. Due to a gameplay change, you need to update the movement speed property of the `EnemyMovement` component in all enemy prefabs.

Solution: You can create a C# script to iterate through all instances of the enemy prefab in the scenes and update the movement speed property of the `EnemyMovement` component programmatically, like so:

```
using UnityEngine;
using UnityEditor;

public class EnemyPrefabUpdater : MonoBehaviour
{
    public float newMovementSpeed = 10f; // New movement speed value

    [MenuItem("Tools/Update Enemy Prefabs")]
    static void UpdateEnemyPrefabs()
    {
        GameObject[] enemyPrefabs = Resources.LoadAll<GameObject>("Prefabs/Enemies"); // Load all enemy prefabs from Resources folder

        foreach (GameObject prefab in enemyPrefabs)
        {
            // Instantiate prefab to apply changes
            GameObject instance = PrefabUtility.InstantiatePrefab(prefab) as GameObject;

            // Update movement speed property of EnemyMovement component
            EnemyMovement enemyMovement = instance.GetComponent<EnemyMovement>();
            if (enemyMovement != null)
            {
                enemyMovement.movementSpeed = newMovementSpeed;
            }

            // Save changes to prefab
            PrefabUtility.ApplyPrefabInstance(instance, InteractionMode.UserAction);

            // Destroy temporary instance
            DestroyImmediate(instance);
        }

        Debug.Log("Enemy prefabs updated successfully.");
    }
}
```

Let's take a closer look at the `UpdateEnemyPrefabs` method.

This method is marked as static and is decorated with the `[MenuItem]` attribute, making it a custom menu item that can be accessed from Unity Editor's **Tools** menu:

- `static void UpdateEnemyPrefabs()`: This `static` method iterates through all enemy prefabs located in the `Prefabs/Enemies` folder within the Unity project's `Resources` directory
- `GameObject[] enemyPrefabs = Resources.LoadAll<GameObject>("Prefabs/Enemies");`: This line loads all GameObject prefabs from the `Prefabs/Enemies` folder using the `Resources.LoadAll()` method
- `foreach (GameObject prefab in enemyPrefabs) { ... }`: This `foreach` loop iterates through each enemy prefab that's loaded from the `Resources` folder

Follow these steps to utilize this component effectively and achieve the desired solution:

1. Attach the `EnemyPrefabUpdater` script to any GameObject in your scene.
2. Set the `newMovementSpeed` variable to the desired value for the movement speed property.
3. In the Editor, go to **Tools | Update Enemy Prefabs** to execute the script.

    The script will iterate through all enemy prefabs in the specified folder, update the movement speed property of the `EnemyMovement` component, and save the changes back to the prefabs.

Overall, this script provides a convenient way to update the properties of multiple enemy prefabs in Unity Editor with a single menu command, enhancing workflow efficiency and productivity.

By implementing these prefab workflow optimization techniques, you can simplify asset management, accelerate development iterations, and ensure a more organized and scalable project structure in Unity.

Let's dive deeper into the world of Unity game development as we explore advanced techniques and workflows that specifically involve using C#.

Advanced techniques and workflows with C#

In this section, we'll delve into the details of advanced C# techniques and workflows within Unity, offering insights into how these strategies can enhance your game development process. We'll cover several key topics, including ScriptableObjects and custom editors.

ScriptableObjects

ScriptableObjects are dynamic assets in Unity that allow you to store and manage data separately from GameObject instances. They're perfect for implementing data-driven systems and facilitating communication between different parts of your game. Let's look at the different ways you can leverage ScriptableObjects:

- **Data-driven development**:

    Use ScriptableObjects to store data such as game settings, character stats, item attributes, and more. This allows for easy modification and iteration without the need to modify code. You learned more about data-driven development in *Chapter 6, Effective Game Data Handling and Management with C#*.

- **Event systems**:

    Event-driven architectures are a powerful way to facilitate communication between different game elements in a decoupled manner. By using ScriptableObjects as events, we will create a flexible and robust system for handling interactions and triggering actions within our game.

The following are the benefits of event systems with ScriptableObjects:

- **Decoupled communication**: Event systems based on ScriptableObjects enable decoupled communication between different components in your game. This means that components can interact with each other without needing direct references, leading to cleaner and more modular code.

- **Flexibility and extensibility**: ScriptableObjects provide a flexible and extensible way to define custom events and data structures. This allows you to create event types tailored to specific interactions or game mechanics, empowering you to design complex systems with ease.

- **Centralized event management**: By centralizing event management in ScriptableObjects, you can maintain a clear and organized structure for handling game events. This makes it easier to debug, modify, and extend your event system as your project evolves.

- **Loose coupling**: Using ScriptableObjects for event communication promotes loose coupling between game elements. This means that changes to one part of your code base are less likely to have unintended consequences on other parts, leading to more robust and maintainable code.

Let's learn by considering a real scenario in a game and how we can use ScriptableObjects for event-driven architecture.

Imagine a tower defense game where towers need to react to enemy spawns, player upgrades, and environmental effects. We'll implement an event system using ScriptableObjects to handle these interactions:

1. First, let's define custom events using ScriptableObjects for enemy spawns, player upgrades, and environmental effects:

    ```
    using UnityEngine;
    using UnityEngine.Events;

    // Scriptable Object representing an enemy spawn event
    [CreateAssetMenu(fileName = "EnemySpawnEvent", menuName = "Events/Enemy Spawn")]
    public class EnemySpawnEvent : ScriptableObject
    {
        public UnityAction<Vector3> onEnemySpawn;

        public void RaiseEvent(Vector3 spawnPosition)
        {
            onEnemySpawn?.Invoke(spawnPosition);
        }
    }

    // Scriptable Object representing a player upgrade event
    [CreateAssetMenu(fileName = "PlayerUpgradeEvent", menuName = "Events/Player Upgrade")]
    public class PlayerUpgradeEvent : ScriptableObject
    {
        public UnityAction<int> onPlayerUpgrade;

        public void RaiseEvent(int upgradeLevel)
        {
            onPlayerUpgrade?.Invoke(upgradeLevel);
        }
    }

    // Scriptable Object representing an environmental change event
    [CreateAssetMenu(fileName = "EnvironmentChangeEvent", menuName = "Events/Environment Change")]
    public class EnvironmentChangeEvent : ScriptableObject
    {
        public UnityAction<Color> onEnvironmentChange;

        public void RaiseEvent(Color newColor)
        {
    ```

```
            onEnvironmentChange?.Invoke(newColor);
        }
    }
```

2. Next, we'll subscribe to these events within the `Tower` class and implement the logic to react when these events are raised:

```
using UnityEngine;

public class Tower : MonoBehaviour
{
    public EnemySpawnEvent enemySpawnEvent;
    public PlayerUpgradeEvent playerUpgradeEvent;
    public EnvironmentChangeEvent environmentChangeEvent;

    private void OnEnable()
    {
        enemySpawnEvent.onEnemySpawn += ReactToEnemySpawn;
        playerUpgradeEvent.onPlayerUpgrade +=
ReactToPlayerUpgrade;
        environmentChangeEvent.onEnvironmentChange +=
ReactToEnvironmentChange;
    }

    private void OnDisable()
    {
        enemySpawnEvent.onEnemySpawn -= ReactToEnemySpawn;
        playerUpgradeEvent.onPlayerUpgrade -=
ReactToPlayerUpgrade;
        environmentChangeEvent.onEnvironmentChange -=
ReactToEnvironmentChange;
    }

    private void ReactToEnemySpawn(Vector3 spawnPosition)
    {
        // Logic to react to enemy spawn
        Debug.Log("Tower reacting to enemy spawn at position: "
+ spawnPosition);
    }

    private void ReactToPlayerUpgrade(int upgradeLevel)
    {
        // Logic to react to player upgrade
        Debug.Log("Tower reacting to player upgrade, level: " +
upgradeLevel);
```

```
    }

    private void ReactToEnvironmentChange(Color newColor)
    {
        // Logic to react to environment change
        Debug.Log("Tower reacting to environment change, new
color: " + newColor);
    }
}
```

3. Next, we'll raise events from related components. The EnemySpawner, PlayerManager, and EnvironmentManager classes are responsible for invoking the respective events:

```
using UnityEngine;

public class EnemySpawner : MonoBehaviour
{
    public EnemySpawnEvent enemySpawnEvent;

    public void SpawnEnemy(Vector3 spawnPosition)
    {
        // Logic to spawn enemy
        // ...

        // Raise enemy spawn event
        enemySpawnEvent.RaiseEvent(spawnPosition);
    }
}

public class PlayerManager : MonoBehaviour
{
    public PlayerUpgradeEvent playerUpgradeEvent;

    public void UpgradePlayer(int upgradeLevel)
    {
        // Logic to upgrade player
        // ...

        // Raise player upgrade event
        playerUpgradeEvent.RaiseEvent(upgradeLevel);
    }
}
```

```
public class EnvironmentManager : MonoBehaviour
{
    public EnvironmentChangeEvent environmentChangeEvent;

    public void ChangeEnvironmentColor(Color newColor)
    {
        // Logic to change environment color
        // ...

        // Raise environment change event
        environmentChangeEvent.RaiseEvent(newColor);
    }
}
```

In this example, we've created three custom events using ScriptableObjects: `EnemySpawnEvent`, `PlayerUpgradeEvent`, and `EnvironmentChangeEvent`. Each event encapsulates a specific game event and provides a mechanism to raise the event with relevant data.

The `Tower` class subscribes to these events and implements event handlers to react to enemy spawns, player upgrades, and environmental changes. Other components, such as `EnemySpawner`, `PlayerManager`, and `EnvironmentManager`, raise these events when relevant actions occur in the game.

This implementation demonstrates the power of using ScriptableObjects for decoupled communication between game elements, enabling flexible and modular event-driven architectures in Unity.

Unlocking the full potential of Unity's editor goes beyond the default **Inspector** view. With custom editors, we can tailor interfaces to their exact specifications, enhancing productivity and user experience.

Custom editors

Custom editors are essential for extending Unity's editor functionality beyond the default **Inspector** view. They allow you to create specialized interfaces tailored to your specific needs, providing more efficient workflows and enhancing user experience. The following are advanced techniques in custom editor development:

- Customizing property drawing
- Using scene gizmos

We will go over each of these advanced techniques in the following subsections.

Customizing property drawing

We can customize how properties are displayed in the **Inspector** view by using attributes such as [Header], [Space], [Range], [TextArea], and others. You can also create custom property drawers to completely control the UI for specific data types or classes.

In custom inspectors and editors, the ability to tailor how properties are displayed is crucial. Unity provides a variety of attributes, allowing us to create visually appealing and organized UIs within the **Inspector** window. I will mention some of these attributes and their usage here:

- [ContextMenu("Menu Item Name")]: This attribute is used to create custom context menu items that appear when right-clicking on a component or asset in Unity Editor. *Figures 10.15* and *10.16* demonstrate the use of this attribute in the editor:

```
[ContextMenu("Add Component Item")]
0 references
void AddComponentItem()
{
    gameObject.AddComponent<Rigidbody>();
}
```

Figure 10.15 – The ContextMenu attribute

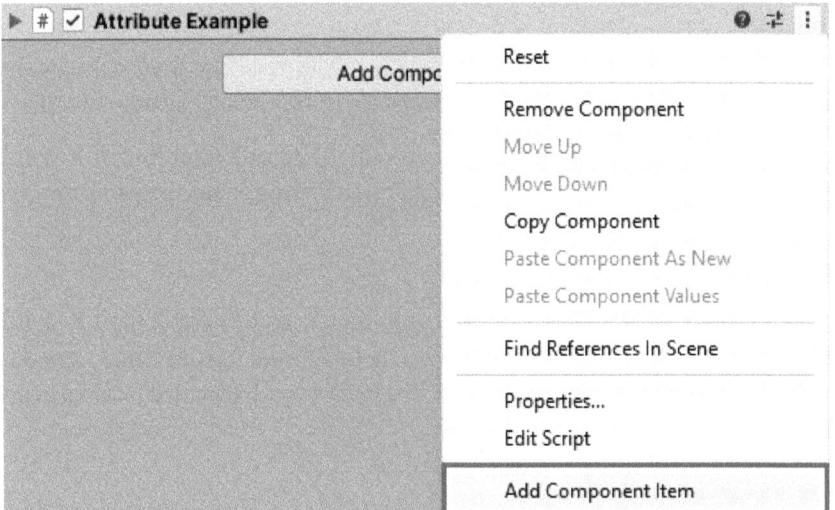

Figure 10.16 – ContextMenu usage

- `[AddComponentMenu("MenuName/SubmenuName/ComponentName")]`: This attribute adds the component to a specific menu hierarchy in the **Add Component** menu. *Figures 10.17* and *10.18* demonstrate the use of this attribute in the editor:

```
[AddComponentMenu("Custom/Attribute Example")]
public class AttributeExample : MonoBehaviour
{
```

Figure 10.17 – The AddMenuComponent attribute

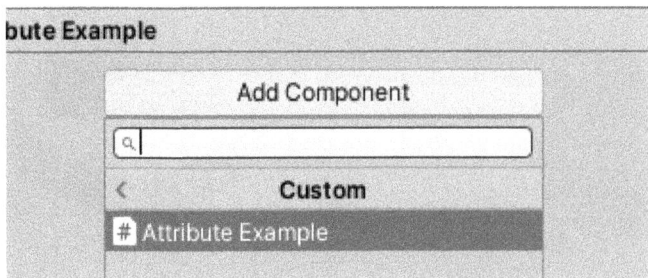

Figure 10.18 – AddMenuComponent usage

- `[ColorUsage(bool showAlpha, bool hdr)]`: This attribute provides color picker options for the **Color** and **Gradient** fields in the **Inspector** view, allowing you to specify whether to display the alpha channel and use **high dynamic range** (**HDR**) colors. *Figures 10.19* and *10.20* demonstrate the use of this attribute in the editor:

```
[ColorUsage(true, true)]
public Color colorUsage;
```

Figure 10.19 – The ColorUsage attribute

Figure 10.20 – ColorUsage usage

While I won't cover every attribute exhaustively, I'll mention others for your awareness and encourage you to explore and utilize them as needed in your code:

- [RequireComponent(typeof(ComponentType))]: Automatically adds the specified component to the GameObject when the script is attached, ensuring that the required component is always present.

- [Range(min, max)]: Restricts a float or int property to a specified range of values, displayed as a slider in the **Inspector** view for easy value selection.

- `[HideInInspector]`: Completely hides the property from the **Inspector** view, ensuring that it is not visible or editable by the user.
- `[TextArea(minLines, maxLines)]`: Renders a multi-line text field in the **Inspector** view for string properties, with adjustable minimum and maximum lines for better text editing.
- `[Tooltip("Tooltip Text")]`: Adds a tooltip to the property in the **Inspector** view, providing helpful information when hovering over the property with the mouse cursor.
- `[ReadOnly]`: Renders the property as read-only in the **Inspector** view, preventing users from modifying its value but still displaying it for reference.
- `[Space(height)]`: Inserts vertical space of the specified height (in pixels) between properties in the **Inspector** view, aiding in visual separation and readability.
- `[Header("Section Name")]`: Creates a labeled header for grouping related properties in the **Inspector** view, enhancing organization and readability.
- `[SerializeField]`: Forces Unity to serialize a private field, making it visible and editable in the **Inspector** view despite its access level.
- `[ExecuteInEditMode]`: Executes the script's code in **Edit** mode, allowing you to perform actions or updates in the editor without entering **Play** mode.
- `[Multiline(int lines)]`: Specifies that a string property should be displayed as a multi-line text area in the **Inspector** view, with the specified number of lines for text input.
- `[System.Flags]`: Converts an enum into a bitmask field in the **Inspector** view, allowing you to select multiple enum values simultaneously using checkboxes. This is handy for defining multiple options at once.
- `[Delayed]`: Delays updating the property value until the user has finished editing in the **Inspector** view. This is useful for performance optimization.
- `[DisallowMultipleComponent]`: Restricts the GameObject to have only one instance of the component, preventing duplicates.
- `[SelectionBase]`: Highlights the GameObject in the **Hierarchy** view when selecting a child object, making it easier to identify in complex scenes.
- `[ExecuteAlways]`: Forces the script to execute its methods even in **Edit** mode, allowing for immediate feedback during development.
- `[SerializeReference]`: Serializes a reference-type property, supporting polymorphism and inheritance in serialized objects.
- `[FormerlySerializedAs("OldName")]`: Renames a serialized field without losing its serialized data.
- `[HelpURL("URL")]`: Links to online documentation or resources related to the property or component.

- [CanEditMultipleObjects]: Allows you to edit multiple objects with the same component simultaneously in the **Inspector** view.

- [RuntimeInitializeOnLoadMethod]: Marks a method to be executed when the game starts or the editor is loaded.

- [ExecuteInEditMode, HelpURL("URL")]: Combines ExecuteInEditMode with a help URL for easy access to documentation.

By mastering attribute customization, we can design intuitive and efficient inspector interfaces that enhance the editing experience and streamline workflow in Unity.

Scene gizmos

Scene gizmos in Unity are powerful tools for visually representing game elements, debugging information, and other critical data directly within the **Scene** view. By adding custom scene gizmos, we can enhance our workflow, improve visualization, and streamline the debugging process. Here are some important details to consider:

- **Visual representation**: Gizmos allow us to visually represent game elements, such as vectors, rays, spheres, cubes, lines, and more, directly in the **Scene** view. This visual representation helps you understand the positioning, orientation, and behavior of objects during runtime and in the editor.

- **Debugging aid**: Gizmos are powerful debugging tools that help us identify issues, visualize data, and debug complex systems more effectively. For example, we can use gizmos to display paths, boundaries, collision zones, trigger areas, and other critical information that aids in debugging and testing.

- **Enhanced workflow**: By adding custom gizmos, we can enhance our workflow by improving visualization, simplifying debugging tasks, and providing valuable insights into the game's mechanics and interactions. This streamlined workflow can save time and effort during the development and testing phases.

- **Interactive feedback**: Gizmos can provide interactive feedback during gameplay and editor mode, allowing us to dynamically adjust parameters, visualize changes, and fine-tune game elements directly in the **Scene** view. This interactive feedback loop fosters rapid iteration and prototyping, leading to better design decisions and optimized gameplay experiences.

Let's showcase one of the applications of gizmos in Unity.

In the following code block, the `DisplayForwardDirection` class showcases a method to visually represent the forward direction of a GameObject through a drawn ray:

```
using UnityEngine;

public class DisplayForwardDirection : MonoBehaviour
{
    [SerializeField]
    private Color gizmoColor = Color.blue; // Color for the arrow gizmo

    [SerializeField]
    private float gizmoSize = 1f; // Size of the arrow gizmo
    #if UNITY_EDITOR
    private void OnDrawGizmos()
    {
        // Set the gizmo color
        Gizmos.color = gizmoColor;

        // Calculate the forward direction in world space
        Vector3 forwardDirection = transform.TransformDirection(Vector3.forward) * gizmoSize;

        // Draw the arrow gizmo
        Gizmos.DrawRay(transform.position, forwardDirection);
    }
    #endif
}
```

Now, attach the `DisplayForwardDirection` script to your desired GameObject. Afterward, you can customize the color or size of the ray. Refer to *Figure 20.21* for an illustration of the attached component:

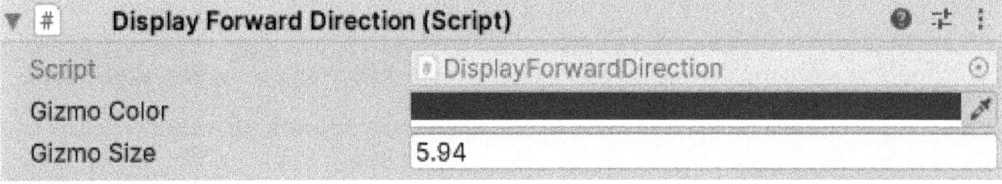

Figure 10.21 – The DisplayForwardDirection script

Figure 20.22 shows the ray extending in the forward direction from the displayed cylinder:

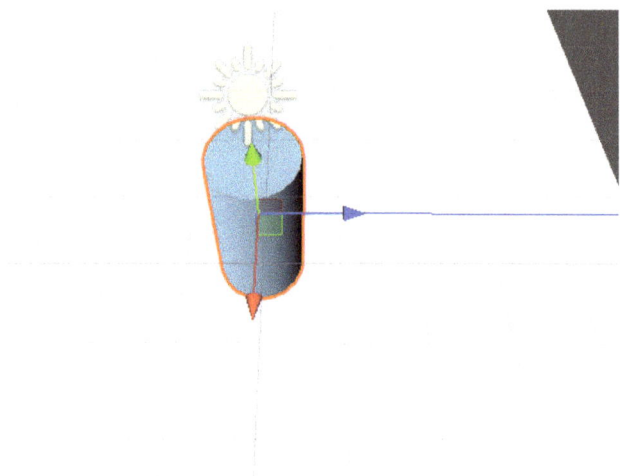

Figure 10.22 – The ray extending forward

In summary, leveraging custom scene gizmos in Unity significantly enhances the development workflow, improves debugging capabilities, optimizes game performance, and fosters better communication and collaboration among team members. Integrating scene gizmos effectively can lead to more efficient development cycles and higher-quality games.

By integrating these advanced techniques and workflows into your Unity projects, you'll not only expand your skills but also unlock new possibilities for creating engaging and immersive gaming experiences.

Navigating the complexities of game development often involves encountering troubleshooting and common challenges that require adept problem-solving skills. We'll consider this in the following section.

Troubleshooting and common challenges

In this section, we'll delve into essential debugging techniques and strategies to help you identify and resolve errors effectively. Additionally, we'll explore platform-specific challenges, focusing on mobile optimization, cross-platform development, and the intricacies of targeting diverse gaming platforms.

Let's start with debugging, which is an essential skill in game development, allowing developers to identify and fix errors in their code effectively.

Debugging techniques

In this subsection, we'll delve into mastering debugging tools and techniques in Unity, equipping you with the skills to troubleshoot and resolve code issues efficiently.

Let's begin by exploring the different types of debugging messages. Utilizing debugging messages effectively is a valuable skill that can greatly benefit us in troubleshooting and improving our code.

The following code block contains the four main types of debugging messages that you can use and customize in Unity:

```
Debug.Log("Info Message", gameObject); // Info level log
    Debug.LogWarning("Warning Message", gameObject); // Warning level log
    Debug.LogError("Error Message", gameObject); // Error level log
    Debug.LogException(new System.Exception("Custom Exception"), gameObject); // Exception level log
```

You can format the debug messages so that they include additional information within the text. This is shown in the following code block:

```
Debug.LogFormat("[Scoreboard] Player score: {0:N0}", playerScore); // Custom log message with formatting for numbers
    Debug.LogFormat("[{0}] Game started at {1}", gameObject.name, System.DateTime.Now.ToString("HH:mm:ss")); // Custom log message with time stamp
```

You can also style the debug messages with colors, as shown in the following code block:

```
    Debug.Log("<color=green>[GameManager]</color> Game initialized successfully."); // Custom log message with color formatting
```

Next, we will discover how to utilize the Code Editor Debugger in Unity to navigate breakpoints, empowering you to efficiently debug and resolve bugs in your projects.

Code Editor Debugger

Let's walk through the steps of using the Code Editor Debugger so that you can apply the following techniques to your code wherever debugging is needed:

1. Place breakpoints on the left-hand side of your code panel, as demonstrated in *Figure 10.23*:

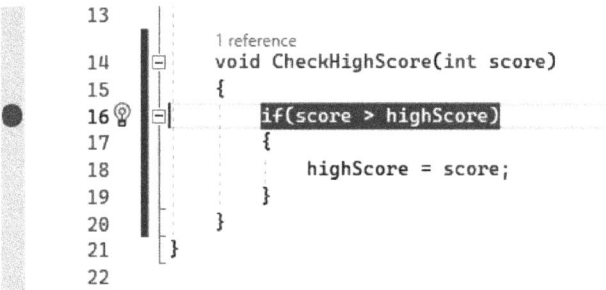

Figure 10.23 – Adding a breakpoint

2. Afterward, click on **Attach to Unity**, as shown in *Figure 10.24*. The build will begin, waiting to sync with Unity:

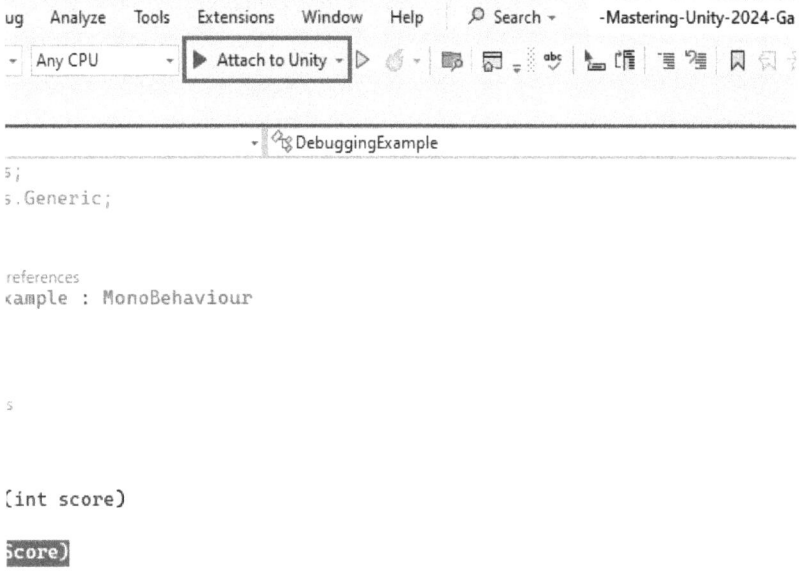

Figure 10.24 – The Attach to Unity button

If it's your first time using the debugger, you'll see the message shown in *Figure 10.25*. You can click on **Enable debugging for this session** for this project only, or **Enable debugging for all projects** to enable it across all projects:

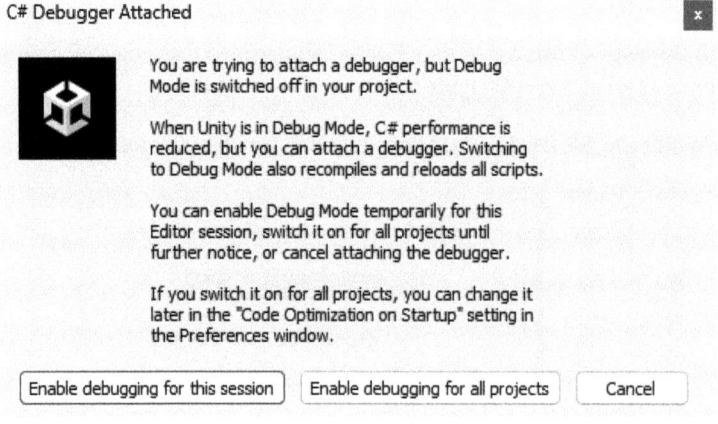

Figure 10.25 – Attaching the C# debugger

3. Play the game in the editor and wait for the code to reach the breakpoint. The game will pause, and the editor will open at the breakpoint's location. Hover your mouse over the line to view variable information and conditions, as shown in *Figure 10.26*:

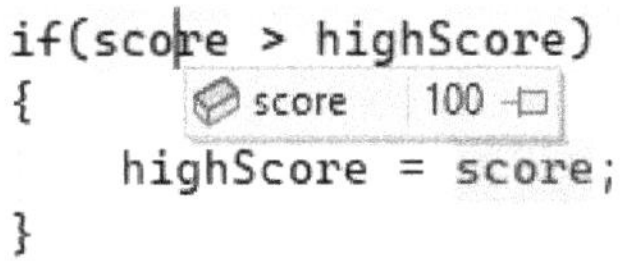

```
if(score > highScore)
{         score   100
    highScore = score;
}
```

Figure 10.26 – Data displayed on hovering

4. After reviewing the data, you can resume your session by pressing the **Continue** button, as shown in *Figure 10.27*. If no breakpoints have been set, the game will proceed as usual; however, any breakpoints that are present will be executed again when they're encountered:

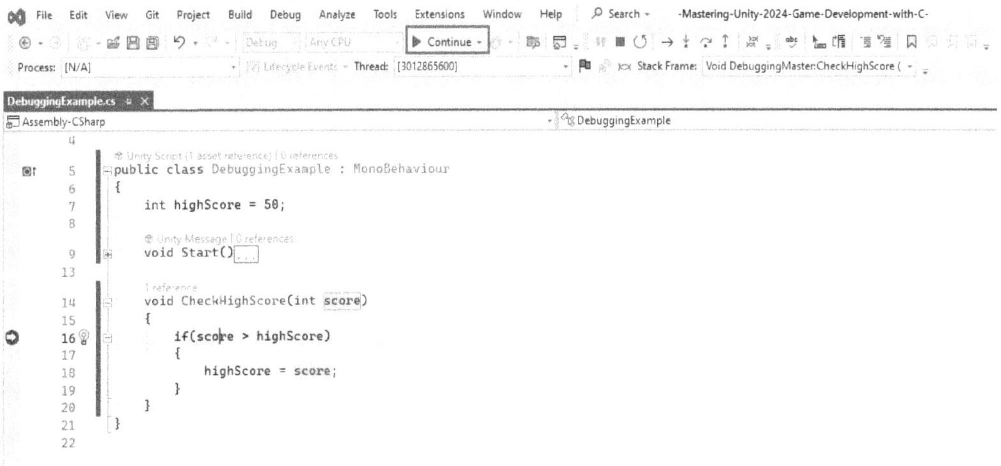

Figure 10.27 – The Continue button

You can follow these steps to start debugging by using breakpoints in your games. This method is highly useful for displaying comprehensive information about custom classes and conditions, as well as showing all data in the breakpoint line. Additionally, you can use **Step Into** or **Step Over** at certain points to gain a full understanding of what a particular chunk of code does.

Exception handling and error logging

Exception handling involves managing unexpected errors or exceptions that occur during runtime, preventing crashes, and ensuring the stability of your application. Unity provides various mechanisms to handle exceptions gracefully, such as `try-catch` blocks, custom error logging, and handling specific exception types.

The following are the benefits of exception handling and error logging:

- **Preventing crashes**: By implementing robust exception handling, you can catch and manage errors before they cause your application to crash, providing a smoother and more reliable user experience
- **Graceful error handling**: Proper exception handling allows you to respond to errors gracefully, providing meaningful error messages to users and logging detailed information for debugging purposes
- **Debugging and troubleshooting**: Error logging plays a crucial role in debugging and troubleshooting issues in your code base as it provides a record of errors, along with relevant contextual information

Let's demonstrate this with three examples:

- *Example 1 – basic exception handling*

    In the following code block, I've implemented a basic `try-catch` block to handle errors in a numbers array. I can then debug the error to understand its nature and resolution:

    ```
    try
    {
        int[] numbers = { 1, 2, 3 };
        Debug.Log(numbers[5]); // Trying to access an out-of-bounds index
    }
    catch (Exception ex)
    {
        Debug.LogError("An error occurred: " + ex.Message); // Log the error message
    }
    ```

- *Example 2 – custom error logging*

    In the following code block, I've implemented a custom try-catch logging method:

    ```
    public class GameManager : MonoBehaviour
    {
        void Start()
        {
            try
            {
                // Code that may throw an exception
            }
            catch (Exception ex)
            {
    ```

```
            LogErrorToFile("GameManager", ex.Message); // Custom 
method to log errors to a file
        }
    }

    void LogErrorToFile(string context, string errorMessage)
    {
        // Code to log errors to a file or external logging 
system
        Debug.LogErrorFormat("[{0}] Error: {1}", context, 
errorMessage);
    }
}
```

Inside the catch block, there's a call to a custom method called `LogErrorToFile`. This method is responsible for logging the error message to a file or an external logging system. In this example, it uses Unity's `Debug.LogErrorFormat` method to log an error message in the console with a specified format.

- *Example 3 – handling specific exceptions*

In the following code block, I've implemented a specific exception:

```
void Start()
{
    try
    {
        int result = DivideNumbers(10, 0); // Dividing by zero 
will throw a DivideByZeroException
        Debug.Log("Result: " + result);
    }
    catch (DivideByZeroException ex)
    {
        Debug.LogError("Division by zero error: " + ex.Message);
    }
}

int DivideNumbers(int a, int b)
{
    if (b == 0)
    {
        throw new DivideByZeroException("Cannot divide by 
zero.");
    }
    return a / b;
}
```

By implementing robust exception handling and error logging practices such as these, you can enhance the stability and reliability of your Unity applications, ensuring smoother gameplay experiences for users and simplifying the debugging process for developers.

Platform-specific challenges are a crucial aspect of game development that requires expertise and strategic considerations to optimize performance across different devices and platforms.

Platform-specific challenges

As experienced Unity developers, we understand the intricate challenges posed by platform-specific optimizations, especially in mobile environments and cross-platform development scenarios.

The following are some tips and tricks regarding mobile optimization:

- Utilize **level of detail** (**LOD**) techniques to manage complex scenes and improve performance on mobile devices
- Implement dynamic batching and static batching to reduce draw calls and optimize rendering for mobile platforms
- Optimize shader complexity and use mobile-friendly shaders to ensure smooth performance across various mobile hardware
- Implement performance optimizations such as object pooling and texture compression
- Utilize Unity's Profiler and performance tools for in-depth analysis and optimization
- Utilize GPU instancing and dynamic batching for efficient rendering on mobile devices
- Implement asynchronous loading and asset streaming to manage resource-intensive scenes seamlessly
- Leverage Unity's Addressable Asset System for optimized asset management and dynamic content loading
- Optimize UI elements for mobile devices by using canvas scaling modes such as **Constant Pixel Size** or **Scale with Screen Size** to ensure UI elements are displayed correctly across different screen resolutions
- Implement occlusion culling to optimize rendering by only rendering objects that are within the camera's view, improving performance in complex scenes
- Minimize the use of dynamic lights and use baked lighting whenever possible to reduce GPU overhead and improve performance on mobile platforms
- Implement efficient audio management by using audio pooling, streaming audio clips, and reducing the number of simultaneous audio sources to conserve resources on mobile devices
- Use texture atlases and sprite packing to reduce the number of draw calls and optimize memory usage by combining multiple textures into a single texture atlas

- Perform regular profiling and performance testing on target mobile devices to identify bottlenecks, optimize critical areas, and ensure smooth and efficient gameplay on various devices

The following are some cross-platform development strategies you should consider:

- Employ platform-specific compilation directives to customize behavior across different platforms
- Design modular architectures and feature flags to accommodate platform variations without compromising code base integrity
- Utilize Unity Cloud Build and automated testing frameworks for streamlined deployment and compatibility testing
- Use platform-specific compilation directives (`#if UNITY_IOS`, `#if UNITY_ANDROID`, and so on) to customize code behavior for different platforms
- Implement responsive UI design principles to create adaptive user interfaces that work seamlessly on different screen resolutions and aspect ratios
- Implement advanced approaches for developing games that run seamlessly on multiple platforms, such as PCs, consoles, and mobile devices, with a focus on code architecture and platform-specific optimizations
- Utilize Unity's Addressable Asset System to manage and load assets efficiently across different platforms, allowing for dynamic content updates without the need to recompile the entire project
- Use remote configuration services to dynamically adjust game settings, features, and content based on platform-specific requirements or user preferences
- Leverage cloud-based analytics and monitoring tools to gather real-time performance data and user feedback across different platforms, enabling data-driven optimizations and updates
- Implement localization and internationalization features to support multiple languages and cultural preferences across various platforms, enhancing global accessibility and user engagement
- Implement platform-specific input mapping and control customization options, allowing players to adjust control schemes based on their preferred devices and platforms
- Utilize Unity's Build Report Tool and performance analysis features to monitor build sizes, memory usage, frame rates, and other performance metrics across different platforms, enabling data-driven optimizations
- Implement platform-specific testing and QA processes, including beta testing programs, device compatibility testing, and platform-specific bug tracking, to identify and address platform-specific issues and ensure high-quality releases on all platforms

By mastering these platform-specific challenges and implementing advanced optimization techniques, we can deliver high-quality games that perform optimally across a wide range of devices and platforms, showcasing our expertise as Unity developers.

In summary, mastering these troubleshooting techniques and grasping platform-specific considerations will equip you with the skills needed to overcome common challenges and provide players with seamless and optimized gameplay experiences on different platforms.

Summary

In this concluding chapter, we explored advanced game development techniques and productivity-enhancing strategies using C#. We started by covering essential Unity Editor shortcuts and time-saving keyboard shortcuts in code editors. We also delved into prefab workflow optimization, ScriptableObjects for data-driven development, and creating custom editors to improve user experience. Additionally, we mastered debugging tools, tackled platform-specific challenges such as mobile optimization, and provided insights for effective cross-platform development.

As we conclude this book, I want to express my heartfelt gratitude to you, the reader, for embarking on this learning journey with us. Remember, the essence of this book lies not in memorizing specific techniques but in understanding the underlying concepts and principles. May this knowledge empower you to unleash your creativity and innovate in your game development endeavors. Keep pushing the boundaries, exploring new possibilities, and creating captivating experiences for players around the world. Thank you for being a part of this journey, and I wish you continued success and fulfilment in your game development endeavors.

Index

Symbols

2D Camera (CinemachineVirtualCamera) 72

A

Action Maps 61
adaptive difficulty scaling 121
AES encryption methods 177
AI logic 88
  coding 89
  exploring 99-120
  implementing, with C# 88, 89
Amazon Web Services (AWS) 223
analytics APIs 231
  GameAnalytics 232
  integrating, with C# 231
  key aspects 231
arrays 158
audio compression technique 260, 261
Audio Profiler 244
average revenue per paying user (ARPPU) 231

B

backend services
  Amazon Web Services (AWS) 223
  analytics and insights 223
  data storage 222
  Firebase 223
  integrating, with C# 222
  live operations and content management 223
  multiplayer functionality 223
  PlayFab 223
  PlayFab, integrating 224-226
  providers 223
  real-time communication 223
  sample login system, developing 227-230
  user authentication 222
BaseView class 149, 150
  UITween component 151
  utilizing 151-153
behavioral patterns 38
  Flyweight design pattern 41-44
  Observer design pattern 38, 44-48
  Singleton design pattern 38-41
  State 38
  Strategy 38

behavior trees
  using 263
binary
  deserialization 163, 164
  serialization 163
bottlenecks identification, profiling process 250
  CPU-bound issues 251, 252
  GPU-bound issues 252, 253
  job worker threads 252
  main thread 252
  render thread 252
build size reduction 264

C

C#
  advanced techniques and workflows 304
  using, for productivity-boosting shortcuts 294
camelCase 48
centralized VCS (CVCS) 190
  structure 190
  working 190, 191
challenge logic
  implementing 122-128
challenges 120
  C# implementation 121
  difficulty levels, balancing for broad appeal 121
  versus missions/quests 120
Cinemachine 58, 69
  benefits 70
  dynamic cinematic experiences 78-82
  gameplay dynamics, enhancing 75-78
  using, in game 70-74

clean code 24
  principles of writing 25
  writing 24
C# naming conventions 48
code conflict management
  code conflict origins, exploring 194
  conflict resolution, navigating in Unity projects 194, 195
  conflict resolution, navigating with CLI 198-201
  mastering 194
  practical conflict resolution 195-197
Code Editor Debugger 317-319
code formatting 48
  comments 49
  indentation 48
  spacing 48
coding conventions
  additional best practices 49
  best practices 48
  classes 48
  code formatting 48
  error handling and exception management 49
  meaningful and descriptive names 48
  method and class length 49
  methods 48
  namespaces 48
  variables 48
collaboration
  best practices 192
  branching, mastering 193
  strategies, merging 193
collision layer masking 259, 260
content delivery networks (CDNs) 223
coroutine optimization 273, 274

Index

CPU Profiler module 244, 245
  chart categories 245, 246
  details pane 246
  Live settings 247
creational patterns 37
  factory method 37
  object pool 37
  singleton 37
custom data structures 159
custom editors 309
  property drawing, customizing 310-314
Custom Save System 170
  advantages 181
  features 170-173
  SaveManager script 173-180

D

data-driven gameplay, with C# 181
  challenge system 183-185
  data, creating for stats 181-183
data organization and serialization 158
data structures 158
  arrays 158
  custom data structures 159
  dictionaries 159
  lists 158
debugging techniques and strategies 316, 317
  Code Editor Debugger 317-319
  error logging 319, 320
  exception handling 319-322
  platform-specific challenges 322, 323
Dependency Injection (DI) 37, 40
  benefits 40
Dependency Inversion Principle (DIP) 34-36

depth of field (DOF) 71
design patterns 37
  behavioral patterns 38
  creational patterns 37
  structural patterns 37
dictionaries 159
distributed VCS (DVCS) 188
  structure 189
  working 189
draw call batching methods
  static batching 257
DRY principle 53
dynamic batching 257

E

event systems, with ScriptableObjects
  benefits 305
existing code bases 202
  practical exploration 202-205
eXtensible Markup Language (XML) 158

F

field-of-view (FOV) adjustments 70
Firebase 223
Flyweight design pattern 41-43
  cons 44
  pros 44
Frame Debugger 253
  draw call batching 257
  dynamic batching 257, 258
  key functions 254-256
  working 254
Freelook Camera (CinemachineFreeLook) 71

G

GameAnalytics 232
   capabilities 232
   features 232
   integrating 232-237
   usage example 237, 238
Game Design Document (GDD) 4
   elements 5-7
game mechanics 86
   balance 86
   essential principles 86
   feedback 86
   player agency 87
   relationship, with code 87
game performance
   enhancing, with proper data structure selection 159, 160
Git commands 191
GPU Profiler 244
graphical user interface (GUI) tools 192

H

HacknPlan Management tool 19
   agile methodology support 19
   example 20, 21
   game design documentation 20
   integration with, VCS 19
   Kanban boards 19
   roadmap planning 20
   task management 19
   team collaboration 19
   time tracking 19
Heal method 92
HealOverTime method 92
health management 88

High-Definition Render Pipeline (HDRP) 210
high dynamic range (HDR) 311

I

IDamage interface 93
   writing 89-92
IHealth interface 93
   integrating, into player 90
   writing 89
import settings
   Animation Type to None setting 282, 283
   Keyframe Reduction 284
   Mesh Compression 281
   Optimal Compression 283
   Optimize Mesh setting 281
   Read/Write Enabled setting 281
initialization vectors (IVs) 178
Interface Segregation Principle (ISP) 33, 34

J

JavaScript Object Notation (JSON) 158, 161
   deserialization 161
   serialization 161

K

key performance indicators (KPIs) 231
KISS principle 53

L

latency compensation techniques 262
level of detail (LOD) system 267

Liskov Substitution Principle (LSP) 31, 32
 versus Open-Closed Principle (OCP) 32
lists 158

M

memory optimization 274, 278, 280
 models importing 280-285
 textures importing 285-289
Memory Profiler 244, 274
 installing 275, 276
 key functions 276
 using 276-279
 working 276
memory profiling 274
 considerations 279, 280
Model-View-Controller (MVC) 140
 structure 141
Model-View-ViewModel (MVVM) 140, 142
 implementing 153, 154
 right path selection, for Unity UI 143, 144
 structure 142, 143
 UI development enhancement suggestions 144, 145

N

network object pooling 262
Network Profiler 244
new Input System 58-61
 advanced techniques 68, 69
 implementing 61-68
 interactions 68
 processors 69
NewtonSoft 172

O

object-oriented programming (OOP) 25
object pooling 269, 270
ObjectPoolManager
 utilizing 270-273
Observer design pattern 44-47
 cons 47
 pros 47
occlusion culling 268, 269
Open-Closed Principle (OCP) 28-30
 versus Liskov Substitution Principle (LSP) 32

P

PascalCase 48
performance optimization techniques 258
 AI and pathfinding 263
 audio 260, 261
 build size 264
 networking and multiplayer functionality 262
 physics and collisions 259, 260
 rendering 267-269
 scripting 269, 270
 UI 261
Physics Profiler 244
pitch 4, 5
player behavior design 88
 coding 89
 implementing, with C# 88, 89
player experience 7
 key components 7, 8
PlayerPrefs 166
 alternatives 169
 limitations 169
 usage tips 167-169

Index

PlayFab 223
  integrating 224-226
pre-built assets
  leveraging, with C# 210
prefab workflow optimization
  component properties, updating across prefab instances 302-304
  nested prefab 302
  prefab PrefabUtility events 302
  prefab variants 301
  ScriptableObjects with prefabs 302
productivity-boosting shortcuts, with C# 294
  prefab workflow optimization 301, 302
  Unity Editor shortcuts 294
  Visual Studio shortcuts 298
Profiler 242
  Audio Profiler 244
  CPU Profiler 244
  functionality 243
  GPU Profiler 244
  Memory Profiler 244
  Network Profiler 244
  Physics Profiler 244
  Rendering Profiler 244
  UI Profiler 244
Profiler markers
  animation markers 249
  backend scripting markers 249
  editor-only markers 248
  main thread base markers 248
  multithreading markers 249
  performance warnings 249
  physics markers 249
  rendering and VSync markers 248
  script update markers 248

profiling process 250
  bottlenecks, identifying 250
  Frame Debugger 253
project organization
  project structure 9
project structure, for efficient development
  HacknPlan Management tool 19-21
  mastering 9
  naming standards 16
  Unity project, organizing 10
  version control system, using 9
  workflow optimization 16

R

refactoring techniques 49
  duplicated code 52, 53
  long and complex method 50, 51
Rendering Profiler 244
reward systems 121
  C# implementation 121
  exploring 121
  implementing 128-132

S

save and load systems 166
SaveManager script 173
scene gizmos 314-316
ScoreManager class 131
ScriptableObjects 164, 305-309
  serialization 164-166
Scriptable Render Pipeline (SRP) extensions 213
serialization 160, 161
SetMaxHealth method 92

Index

shooting mechanics 88
shoot system
  implementing 94-99
simplified collision detection 260
Single Responsibility Principle (SRP) 25-28
Singleton design pattern 38
  cons 40
  pros 40
  structure 38, 39
SOLID principles 25
  Dependency Inversion Principle
    (DIP) 34-36
  Interface Segregation Principle (ISP) 33, 34
  Liskov Substitution Principle (LSP) 31, 32
  Open-Closed Principle (OCP) 28-30
  Single Responsibility Principle (SRP) 25-28
source of truth (SoT) 191
Sprite Atlases 289
  creating 289-292
StartHealingOverTime method 92
state machines, for AI behavior
  concrete states 263
  state interface/class 263
  state machine manager 264
  using 263
static batching 257
structural patterns 37
  decorator 37
  flyweight 37
Subversion (SVN) 191

T

TakeDamage method 92
texture settings
  compression 288
  crunch compression 288
  GenerateMipMaps 287
  maximum size 288
  Read/Write 286
  resize algorithm 288

U

UI best practices
  Canvases, splitting up 135-137
  Canvas, hiding 139
  fullscreen UIs, effective handling 139
  Graphic Raycaster, avoiding 137
  Raycast Target, turning off 137, 138
  UI element animations, implementing 139
  UI object pools, managing 138
UI design, games 134
UIManager class 146-148
  utilizing 148, 149
UI Profiler 244
UI system
  BaseView class 149
  creating 145
  UIManager class 146-148
UITween component 151
Unity Editor shortcuts 294
  GameObject creation and management
    shortcuts 295-298
  hierarchy navigation shortcuts 294, 295
Unity plugins 58
  best practices 82, 83
  Cinemachine 69
  integrating 59
  new Input System 59-61
  optional upgrades 58
Unity profiling tools 242
  common markers 248
  CPU Profiler module 245

exploring 242
Profiler 242
Unity project
folder structure 11-16
organizing 10
Universal Render Pipeline (URP) 210
advanced techniques, implementing 214, 215-220
features 213
functionality 213
installing, into project 212, 213
render pass feature 221
versus HDRP 210, 211
user interface (UI) 192

V

version control system, game project 9
best practices 10
working 10
version control systems (VCSs) 187, 188
centralized VCS 190, 191
distributed VCS 188, 189

Virtual Camera (CinemachineVirtualCamera) 71
Visual Studio shortcuts 298
code generation shortcuts 300, 301
navigation shortcuts 298, 299
refactoring shortcuts 299, 300
VSync (Vertical Synchronization) 250

W

workflow optimization, game project 16
assets, separating 19
presets, using 17
settings, applying from preset 17, 18

X

XML 162
deserialization 162, 163
serialization 162

packtpub.com

Subscribe to our online digital library for full access to over 7,000 books and videos, as well as industry leading tools to help you plan your personal development and advance your career. For more information, please visit our website.

Why subscribe?

- Spend less time learning and more time coding with practical eBooks and Videos from over 4,000 industry professionals
- Improve your learning with Skill Plans built especially for you
- Get a free eBook or video every month
- Fully searchable for easy access to vital information
- Copy and paste, print, and bookmark content

Did you know that Packt offers eBook versions of every book published, with PDF and ePub files available? You can upgrade to the eBook version at packtpub.com and as a print book customer, you are entitled to a discount on the eBook copy. Get in touch with us at customercare@packtpub.com for more details.

At www.packtpub.com, you can also read a collection of free technical articles, sign up for a range of free newsletters, and receive exclusive discounts and offers on Packt books and eBooks.

Other Books You May Enjoy

If you enjoyed this book, you may be interested in these other books by Packt:

Learning Design Patterns with Unity

Harrison Ferrone

ISBN: 978-1-80512-028-5

- Implement a persistent game manager using the Singleton pattern
- Spawn projectiles with object pooling to optimize performance and memory usage
- Build a flexible crafting system using the Factory Method pattern
- Design an undo/redo system for player movement using the Command pattern
- Implement a state machine to control a two-person battle system
- Modify existing character objects with special abilities

Learning C# by Developing Games with Unity

Harrison Ferrone

ISBN: 978-1-83763-687-7

- Understanding programming fundamentals by breaking them down into their basic parts
- Comprehensive explanations with sample codes of object-oriented programming and how it applies to C#
- Follow simple steps and examples to create and implement C# scripts in Unity
- Divide your code into pluggable building blocks using interfaces, abstract classes, and class extensions
- Grasp the basics of a game design document and then move on to blocking out your level geometry, adding lighting and a simple object animation
- Create basic game mechanics such as player controllers and shooting projectiles using C#
- Become familiar with stacks, queues, exceptions, error handling, and other core C# concepts
- Learn how to handle text, XML, and JSON data to save and load your game data

Packt is searching for authors like you

If you're interested in becoming an author for Packt, please visit `authors.packtpub.com` and apply today. We have worked with thousands of developers and tech professionals, just like you, to help them share their insight with the global tech community. You can make a general application, apply for a specific hot topic that we are recruiting an author for, or submit your own idea.

Share your thoughts

Now you've finished *Mastering Unity Game Development with C#*, we'd love to hear your thoughts! Scan the QR code below to go straight to the Amazon review page for this book and share your feedback or leave a review on the site that you purchased it from.

`https://packt.link/r/1835466362`

Your review is important to us and the tech community and will help us make sure we're delivering excellent quality content.

Download a free PDF copy of this book

Thanks for purchasing this book!

Do you like to read on the go but are unable to carry your print books everywhere?

Is your eBook purchase not compatible with the device of your choice?

Don't worry, now with every Packt book you get a DRM-free PDF version of that book at no cost.

Read anywhere, any place, on any device. Search, copy, and paste code from your favorite technical books directly into your application.

The perks don't stop there, you can get exclusive access to discounts, newsletters, and great free content in your inbox daily

Follow these simple steps to get the benefits:

1. Scan the QR code or visit the link below

```
https://packt.link/free-ebook/9781835466360
```

2. Submit your proof of purchase
3. That's it! We'll send your free PDF and other benefits to your email directly